Contents

The publisher would like to thank the following for their kind permission to reproduce their photographs:

(Key: b-bottom; c-centre; l-left; r-right; t-top)

Alamy Images: Bob Ebbesen 179cr, David Grossman 90cl, Jacky Chapman / Janine Wiedel Photolibrary 321tr, Picture Partners 48tl, Roger Bamber 193b, Sally & Richard Greenhill 122tl, Superstock. Ingram Publishing 272cr, Zak Waters 317cl; **Bananastock:** 146br, 237, 240tr; **Corbis:** Mika 311tl, Radius Images 336tl; **Crown Copyright Courtesy of the Department of Health in association with the Welsh Government, the Scottish Government and the Food Standards Agency in Northern Ireland.:** Crown Copyright 2012 151b; **DK Images:** Dave King 136tr, Vanessa Davies 204br; **Education Photos:** Linda Westmore 339tr; **Fotolia.com:** AndersenRise 261t; **Getty Images:** Altrendo Images / Stockbyte 49tr, Bill Sykes / Cultura 201tl, Kidstock / Blend Images 244bl, Realistic Reflections 226br, Superstock 71tl, Tim Platt 29c; **Imagemore Co., Ltd:** 168tl; **Imagestate Media:** Phovoir 216bl; **iStockphoto:** C E Futcher 279, 282tr; **Pearson Education Ltd:** Studio 8 8cr, 17tl, 56bl, 66bl, 77, 80tr, 83bl, 89cl, 108bl, 176t, 182tr, 225tl, Trevor Clifford 138/2, Gareth Boden 189, 192, 202bl, 235tr, 236bl, Rob Judges 104/2, 149, Lord and Leverett 242cr, 252, 313cl, MindStudio 111b, Roddy Paine 163, 166tr, 173b, 187tr, jules Selmes 19tr, 33tr, 54t, 58, 61, 64tr, 68br, 79b, 109, 109/2, 112, 135b, 170tl, 172tr, 195br, 217, 220tr, 247br, 257, 260tr, 264t, 267tr, 286cr, 289tr, 303br, 305tr, 307, 309bl, 310, 333cl, 335bl, 337br, Sozaijiten 138, StillVision 156tl, Ian Wedgewood 63c, 298tr; **Penny Tassoni:** 162bl; **PhotoDisc:** Kevin Peterson 306bl; **Science Photo Library Ltd:** Astier 149tl, BSIP Beranger 115b, Joti 46br; **Shutterstock.com:** Aliaksei Lasevich 340bl, Andre Blais 107tr, Andrey Stratilatov 315cr, Anniwalz 4tl, ansar80 161tr, 164tl, Apollofoto 110tl, Auremar 324bl, Beata Becla 325, 328tr, Blend 60bl, Elena Elisseeva 76bl, Flashon Studio 308tl, Gabriela Insuratelu 256bl, Gina Smith 277tr, Golden Pixels LLC 37, 40tr, Goodluz 131tr, Jaimie Duplass 215tr, Kzenon 124br, Laurin Rinder 59tr, Leungchopan 36bl, lithian 190tl, Mangostock 35tr, Matka-Wariatka 147cr, michaeljung 218tl, 238tl, Minerva Studio 62tl, mrfiza 38tl, Nadezhda1906 133, Narunza 278bl, 280tl, Ngarare 75tr, Oliveromg 3, 6tr, 320tl, Piotr Marcinski 188bl, Rido 2bl, Rui Vale de Sousa 258tl, SnowWhiteimages 326tl, Thomas M Perkins 207tr, Tyler Olsen 343tr, Warren Goldswain 323tr, Wavebreakmedia Ltd 154br, Wong Yu Liang 255tr, Yuri Arcurs 78tl, 132bl, 134tr; **Veer/Corbis:** Terra 144bl

Cover images: *Front:* **Masterfile UK Ltd:** Marc Vaughn

All other images © Pearson Education

Picture Research by: Susie Prescott

In some instances we have been unable to trace the owners of copyright material, and we would appreciate any information that would enable us to do so.

The author and publisher would like to thank the following individuals and organisations for permission to reproduce their materials:

pp. 42, 205 Articles from the Convention on the Rights of the Child, copyright 1989 United Nations. Reprinted with the permission of the United Nations.

pp. 51–52, 220, 233, 246, 292 Department of Education. © Crown copyright

p. 151 © Crown copyright 2011, Department of Health in association with the Welsh Assembly Government, the Scottish Government and the Food Standards Agency in Northern Ireland.

p. 171 Scientific Advisory Committee on Nutrition (2011) 'Dietary Reference Values for Energy', London: Scientific Advisory Committee on nutrition. © Crown copyright 2012.

p. 226 © World of Inclusion (www.worldofinclusion.com) and Richard Rieser.

Every effort has been made to contact copyright holders of material reproduced in this book. Any omissions will be rectified in subsequent printings if notice is given to the publishers.

Louise Burnham would like to thank parents and staff of Breaside school in Bromley for the use of their children's writing samples.

BTEC NATIONAL
edexcel

::BTEC

Student Book 2

CHILDREN'S PLAY, LEARNING & DEVELOPMENT

ALWAYS LEARNING

PEARSON

Published by Pearson Education Limited, Edinburgh Gate, Harlow, Essex, CM20 2JE.

www.pearsonschoolsandfecolleges.co.uk

Text © Penny Tassoni, Louise Burnham, Brenda Baker, Karen Hucker and the NCMA (National Childminding Association) 2013
Typeset by Phoenix Photosetting, Chatham, Kent, UK
Original illustrations © Pearson Education Limited and Katie Mac/NB Illustration Ltd 2013
Cover design by Pearson Education Limited and Andrew Magee Design
Picture research by Susie Prescott
Front cover photo: Masterfile UK Ltd: Marc Vaughn
Indexing by Wendy Simpson.

The rights of Penny Tassoni, Louise Burnham, Brenda Baker, Karen Hucker and the NCMA to be identified as authors of this work have been asserted by them in accordance with the Copyright, Designs and Patents Act 1988.

First published 2013

17 16 15 14 13
10 9 8 7 6 5 4 3 2 1

British Library Cataloguing in Publication Data
A catalogue record for this book is available from the British Library

ISBN 978 1 446 90269 1

Printed in Spain by Grafos SA

Websites
There are links to relevant websites in this book. In order to ensure that the links are up to date, that the links work, and that the sites aren't inadvertently links to sites that could be considered offensive, we have made the links available on our website at www.pearsonhotlinks.co.uk. Search for the title, BTEC National Children's Play, Learning and Development Student Book 2 or ISBN 978 1 446 90269 1.

Copies of official specifications for all Edexcel qualifications may be found on the Edexcel website: www.edexcel.com.

A note from the publisher
In order to ensure that this resource offers high-quality support for the associated BTEC qualification, it has been through a review process by the awarding organisation to confirm that it fully covers the teaching and learning content of the specification or part of a specification at which it is aimed, and demonstrates an appropriate balance between the development of subject skills, knowledge and understanding, in addition to preparation for assessment.

While the publishers have made every attempt to ensure that advice on the qualification and its assessment is accurate, the official specification and associated assessment guidance materials are the only authoritative source of information and should always be referred to for definitive guidance.

BTEC examiners have not contributed to any sections in this resource relevant to examination papers for which they have responsibility.

No material from an endorsed book will be used verbatim in any assessment set by BTEC.

Endorsement of a book does not mean that the book is required to achieve this BTEC qualification, nor does it mean that it is the only suitable material available to support the qualification, and any resource lists produced by the awarding organisation shall include this and other appropriate resources.

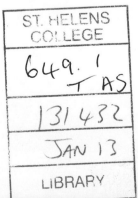

About this book

This book is designed to help you through your BTEC National Children's Play, Learning and Development course, and includes 14 units: core units 9 to 11, mandatory specialist units 12 to 14, and eight optional specialist units. This book builds on core units 1 to 8, which are covered in Pearson's BTEC National Children's Play, Learning and Development Student Book 1.

About your BTEC National in Children's Play, Learning and Development

Choosing to study for a BTEC National Children's Play, Learning and Development qualification is a great decision to make for lots of reasons. In recent years, there has been a growing understanding that children's earliest experiences shape their life chances and it is vital that children receive the best possible early education and care. As a future early years professional, you can play a significant part in making sure that the provision children receive is of the highest quality.

Your BTEC National Children's Play, Learning and Development qualification is a vocational or work-related qualification. This means that it will give you the opportunity to gain specific knowledge, understanding and skills that are relevant to your chosen subject or area of work. This new BTEC course is a great foundation to build your skills for employment or further study.

What will you be doing?

The BTEC Nationals in Children's Play, Learning and Development are structured into **core units**, **mandatory specialist units** and **optional specialist units**. How many units you do and which ones you cover depend on the type of qualification you are working towards. The following table shows you how the units in this book fit into the Certificate or Diploma qualifications.

Core units	
Unit 9 Observation, Assessment and Planning for Play and Development	Certificate Diploma
Unit 10 Diversity, Equality and Inclusion in the Early Years	Certificate Diploma
Unit 11 Reflecting on Own Early Years Practice	Certificate Diploma
Mandatory specialist units	
Unit 12 Research Skills	Diploma
Unit 13 Health, Education and Social Services for Children and Their Families	Diploma
Unit 14 Food and Mealtimes in the Early Years	Diploma

Optional specialist units	
Unit 15 Working With Children Under Three Years	Diploma
Unit 16 Working With Children in Home-based Care	Diploma
Unit 18 Working With Children With Additional Needs	Diploma
Unit 19 Promoting Mathematical Development in Children Aged From Four up to Eight Years	Diploma
Unit 20 Promoting Literacy in Children Aged From Four up to Eight Years	Diploma
Unit 22 Implementing the Early Years Foundation Stage in England	Diploma
Unit 24 Supporting Children's Imaginative Play	Diploma
Unit 28 Promoting Children's Development Outdoors	Diploma

Student Book 1, covering core units 1 to 8, is also available. You can find details about this from your teacher/tutor or at www.pearsonschoolsandfecolleges.co.uk

About the authors

Best-selling author **Penny Tassoni** trained as an early years and primary teacher. Now working as an education consultant and trainer, she specialises in the whole spectrum of learning and play. Penny has written 30 books about early years and frequently writes articles for national early years magazines. In addition to this, Penny is a well-known speaker both in the UK and internationally. She has in-depth knowledge of the BTEC Nationals in Children's Play, Learning and Development, and uses her accessible and friendly style of writing to bring the information to life for learners on this course.

Louise Burnham has worked as an early years and primary teacher and SENCO. She also led teaching assistant training and worked on childcare and teaching courses at a London FE college for a number of years. Louise has written 12 books for early years and teaching assistant qualifications, and continues to work with early years and teaching assistant students.

Brenda Baker has worked in early years settings and as a primary teacher. She then taught childcare and education in an FE college and, for a number of years, managed its Health and Social Care Department. In recent years she has contributed to textbooks and support materials for learners and teachers/tutors of early years and teaching assistant qualifications. She has extensive experience of BTEC qualifications.

Karen Hucker has worked in both secondary schools and FE, teaching childcare and education and health and social care. She is currently Principal of a sixth form college, but earlier in her career she managed its Health and Social Care Department. She has been an author for a number of years, contributing to numerous textbooks and support materials. She has extensive experience of both the vocational and academic curriculum post-16.

The **NCMA** (National Childminding Association) is a professional membership association. Since 1977 they have worked with registered childminders and nannies as well as other individuals and organisations such as local and national government, to ensure families in every community in England and Wales have access to high-quality home-based childcare, play, learning and family support. We are very grateful to the NCMA for their contribution (Unit 16 in this book).

How to use this book

This book contains many features that will help you apply your skills and knowledge to work-related situations and assist you in getting the most from your course.

These introductions give you a snapshot of what to expect from each unit – and what you should be aiming for by the time you finish it.

How the unit is assessed.

Learning aims describe what you will be doing in the unit.

A learner or early years professional shares their experiences related to the content of the unit.

Features of this book

There are lots of features in this book to help you learn about what's included in each unit and to enable you to reflect on, or consider, key concepts. These pages show some of the features that you will come across when using the book.

Get started with a short activity or discussion about the subject of the unit.

Activities will help you learn about key points.

Key terms boxes give definitions of important words and phrases that you will come across.

A thought-provoking 'Reflect' feature will challenge your own attitudes and beliefs, and encourage you to reflect on best practice.

Case study

Hearing problems?

Nilaya has recently started in your nursery. She does not seem to be listening when adults are talking and often seems to be in her own world. Her records do not show that she has any kind of impairment.

1 Should you have any concerns?

2 If so, what should you do?

Examples from real settings that focus on situations you could find yourself in when working in early years. These examples will make you consider how you might act in those situations and help you to improve your practice.

Assessment practice 18.7   3C.P9 | 3C.D2

Write a report about how settings should work in partnership with parents to support children who have additional needs. Give examples of the kinds of formal and informal opportunities that may arise for adults in the setting to speak with parents about their children, and evaluate the impact of positive relationships between the setting and the family.

Activities that relate to the unit's assessment criteria. These activities will help you prepare for your assignments. They may include suggestions for tasks that help build towards your assignment, as well as helping you to develop your knowledge, skills and understanding.

Portfolio building activity   CYPW

SHC 33, Assessment criterion 1.1; CYP 3.7, Assessment criteria 4.1 and 4.2; EYMP 4, Assessment criterion 3.1

1 Explain how equality, diversity, inclusion and participation lead to positive outcomes for children and young people.

2 Use examples from your own placement to support your understanding.

For students taking the BTEC National Certificate or Diploma and wishing to gain occupational competence, you will also need to pass the Level 3 Diploma for the Children and Young People's Workforce. This feature provides opportunities for you to create some of the additional evidence for your portfolio.

In addition, some areas of text are shaded in pink. This indicates that the information relates to additional knowledge that is required for the Children and Young People's Workforce qualification.

(See p.xi for more information about the Level 3 Diploma for the Children and Young People's Workforce.)

Theory into practice

Ask if you can have access to copies of any IEPs that have been devised for children in your setting. Are all of the staff aware of the needs of these children?

Useful features that help you to understand how the theories and topics you are learning about relate to work with children.

Research

Find out a bit more about the CAF by visiting the Department for Education website and downloading the 'Common Assessment Framework for children and young people' guide for practitioners. You can access this guide by going to www.pearsonhotlinks.co.uk and searching for this title.

Suggestions for ideas or sources of additional information that you can research in order to broaden your understanding of a topic.

Ready for work?

Trish Jones Nursery assistant

I am a nursery assistant at Sunshine Nursery and have been here for just over two years. At the moment I am working on my early years qualification and have decided to complete my own maths GCSE in order to do this, as I did not get a good grade when I was at school. It has been very interesting, as I have had my own issues with mathematics and I have had to develop my own confidence while working with the children. Although I found maths difficult at school, it has been really good for me to look at it again and to find out about some of the fun aspects that can be transferred to my work with the children. I am now full of enthusiasm for it and as a result have asked the setting manager if we can run an information evening for parents, which I am getting involved in. This will in turn be good for the children. It has even been good for me at home as I have been able to have more understanding of what my own teenage children are doing for their homework! My line manager says that it has been great to watch me develop my confidence in this area and I am so pleased that I have.

Someone who works in early years explains how this unit of their BTEC helped them to develop as an effective practitioner. This feature gives you a chance to think more about the role that the person does, and whether you would want to follow in their footsteps once you have completed your BTEC.

Skills for practice

Support learning
- Make sure that you support mathematics in different situations, for example, indoor and outdoor, and formal and informal.
- Use as many opportunities as you can to develop children's counting skills and assess their learning.
- Remember that activities such as counting songs and nursery rhymes, puzzles, measuring and talking about shapes are all forms of mathematics.
- Use ICT with children to reinforce mathematical concepts.
- Use mathematics with children in other areas of learning, for example, recording how much they score in basketball or writing numbers outside during hopscotch.
- Use other activities to consolidate mathematical concepts, for example, cooking, which uses measuring and counting.
- Look for mathematics in the environment, for example, patterns in tiles and shapes.
- Devise activities and trips for children that will encourage them to think about numbers in the environment, for example, maths walks in the local area.

Tips and guidance about the practical skills that you need to develop in order to work with children. In some units these tips link to the **Skills for Practice log** that you will need to complete while on placement if you are taking the BTEC National Certificate or Diploma in Children's Play, Learning and Development.

255

▮ BTEC Assessment Zone

You will be assessed in two different ways for your BTEC National Children's Play, Learning and Development qualification. For most units, your teacher/tutor will set assignments for you to complete. These assignments may take the form of projects where you research, plan, prepare, make and evaluate a piece of work or activity, case study or presentation. (For Units 11 and 12 these assignments are written and set by Edexcel.) For Unit 1 of your BTEC (which was covered in Student Book 1), you are assessed by a paper-based exam.

The table in this BTEC Assessment Zone explains what you must do in order to achieve each of the assessment criteria.

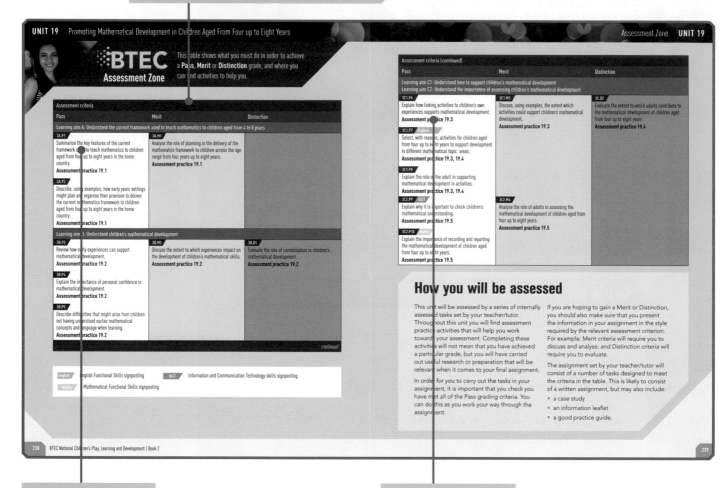

You will be assessed against the different assessment criteria shown in this table.

Assessment practice activities in this book will help you to prepare for your assignments and to cover the criteria.

The Level 3 Diploma for the Children and Young People's Workforce

If you are taking the Level 3 Diploma for the Children and Young People's Workforce alongside your BTEC National Certificate or Diploma, units in the Children and Young People's Workforce qualification are referred to in this book within the **Portfolio building activities**. The unit reference numbers given in these features are the generic numbers used by the sector, but the table below shows the equivalent unit numbers in the Edexcel Level 3 Diploma for the Children and Young People's Workforce that may be referred to in this book. We hope this will be a helpful 'translation' if you are following the Edexcel specification.

Separate documentation is available for teachers/tutors on the Edexcel website, which provides detailed information about how to deliver and assess the Children and Young People's Workforce Diploma alongside the BTEC. These co-delivery materials can be downloaded by teachers/tutors free of charge from the Edexcel website: www.edexcel.com/quals/btec-nat-cpld/Pages/co-delivery.aspx

If you are unsure about any of the information relating to the Children and Young People's Workforce qualification, please speak to your teacher/tutor.

Unit title	Sector unit no.	Edexcel unit no.
Promote communication in health, social care or children's and young people's settings	SHC 31	8
Engage in personal development in health, social care or children's and young people's settings	SHC 32	9
Promote equality and inclusion in health, social care or children's and young people's settings	SHC 33	10
Principles for implementing duty of care in health, social care or children's and young people's settings	SHC 34	11
Understand child and young person development	CYP 3.1	1
Promote child and young person development	CYP 3.2	2
Understand how to safeguard the wellbeing of children and young people	CYP 3.3	3
Support children and young people's health and safety	CYP 3.4	4
Develop positive relationships with children, young people and others involved in their care	CYP 3.5	5
Working together for the benefit of children and young people	CYP 3.6	6
Understand how to support positive outcomes for children and young people	CYP 3.7	7
Context and principles for early years provision	EYMP 1	12
Promote learning and development in the early years	EYMP 2	13
Promote children's welfare and well being in the early years	EYMP 3	14
Professional practice in early years settings	EYMP 4	15
Support children's speech, language and communication	EYMP 5	16
Promote the well being and resilience of children and young people	SCMP2	18

Introduction

As a professional working with children you will need to observe, assess and plan for their development, interests and strengths. Observing children is quite a skill but, once mastered, it is fascinating and rewarding. By making observations you can begin to understand a child and start to think and plan for their needs and interests. This requires knowledge of child development and play. It also requires an understanding of the curriculum framework that is being used in your setting.

In this unit you will look at the importance of this process and how to observe and plan for children, based on the conclusions of your observations.

Assessment: You will be assessed by a series of assignments set by your teacher/tutor.

Learning aims

In this unit you will:

A   understand the importance of observation and assessment in work with children

B   be able to present records of observations of children

C1   be able to draw valid conclusions from observations of children

C2   understand the importance of planning to support children's play and development

D   be able to create, implement and review activity plans for children.

> Learning how to observe children has helped me become more aware of their needs and able to plan more effective activities.
>
> Jay, *a student on an early years course*

Observation, Assessment and Planning for Play and Development

9

BTEC Assessment Zone

This table shows what you must do in order to achieve a **Pass**, **Merit** or **Distinction** grade, and where you can find activities to help you.

Assessment criteria		
Pass	**Merit**	**Distinction**
Learning aim A: Understand the importance of observation and assessment in work with children		
3A.P1 Explain the importance of observing and assessing children in early years settings. **Assessment practice 9.1**	**3A.M1** Analyse issues to be considered when observing and assessing children in early years settings. **Assessment practice 9.1**	
Learning aim B: Be able to present records of observations of children		
3B.P2 Justify the selection of a set of observational methods to observe the development of a child in an early years setting, giving valid reasons for your choice. **Assessment practice 9.2** **3B.P3** Present full and effective records to show that valid observation of a child's play and development has taken place. **Assessment practice 9.2**	**3B.M2** Analyse the appropriateness of selected observational methods for assessing the play and development of a child in an early years setting. **Assessment practice 9.2**	**3B.D1** Evaluate the validity of the selected observational methods used, making recommendations to address potential weaknesses. **Assessment practice 9.2**
Learning aim C: 1 Be able to draw valid conclusions from observations of children 2 Understand the importance of planning to support children's play and development		
3C1.P4 Describe how observations of the child's stages of development and interests can be used to contribute to planning to meet play and development needs. **Assessment practice 9.2** **3C1.P5** Describe the observed behaviour making use of relevant theories of development. **Assessment practice 9.2** **3C1.P6** Select, giving valid reasons, different play activities and strategies which could enable the observed child to progress further. **Assessment practice 9.2** **3C2.P7** Explain the role of planning in early years settings to support children's play and development. **Assessment practice 9.2**	**3C.M3** Analyse how observation and assessment have contributed to planning to meet a child's play and development needs. **Assessment practice 9.2** **3C.M4** Discuss the relevance of theories of development to what has been observed about a child's progress. **Assessment practice 9.2** **3C.M5** Assess different play activities and strategies which could enable the observed child to progress further. **Assessment practice 9.2**	**3C.D2** Evaluate how observation, assessment and planning have contributed to the observed child's progress in relation to theories of development. **Assessment practice 9.2**

continued

Assessment criteria (*continued*)

Pass	Merit	Distinction
Learning aim D: Be able to create, implement and review activity plans for children		
3D.P8 I&CT English Present appropriate activity plans for an observed child to support their play and development linked to the relevant curriculum. **Assessment practice 9.2**	**3D.M6** Analyse the extent to which the plans and implemented activities supported the child's play and development. **Assessment practice 9.2**	**3D.D3** Evaluate own practice in the planning, creation and implementation of activities in terms of how it supported the child's play and development. **Assessment practice 9.2**
3D.P9 Review the effectiveness of the planning methods, plans and implemented activities in supporting the child's play and development. **Assessment practice 9.2**		

English English Functional Skills signposting   I&CT Information and Communication Technology skills signposting

How you will be assessed

This unit will be assessed by a series of internally assessed tasks set by your teacher/tutor. Throughout this unit you will find assessment practice activities that will help you work towards your assessment. Completing these activities will not mean that you have achieved a particular grade, but you will have carried out useful research or preparation that will be relevant when it comes to your final assignment.

In order for you to carry out the tasks in your assignment, it is important that you check you have met all of the Pass grading criteria. You can do this as you work your way through the assignment.

If you are hoping to gain a Merit or Distinction, you should also make sure that you present the information in your assignment in the style that is required by the relevant assessment criteria. For example, Merit criteria will require you to discuss, assess and analyse, and Distinction criteria will require you to evaluate.

The assignment set by your teacher/tutor will consist of a number of tasks designed to meet the criteria in the table. This is likely to consist of a written assignment, but may also include activities such as:

- observations of young children
- a report drawing conclusions from observations
- a presentation to your peers and teacher/tutor
- an assignment.

Getting started

Do you know how many different types of observation methods there are and why they might be used? List the methods that you know about already. By the end of this unit, see if you can add to your list.

A Understand the importance of observation and assessment in work with children

Observing and assessing children is key to effective professional working. In this section, we will look at the many reasons why early years professionals and others observe and assess children.

Observing and assessing children

There are many reasons for observing and carrying out assessments on children, shown in Figure 9.1.

Assessments are particularly important as a tool to:

- learn more about children's needs and interests
- consider children's progress in relation to normative development
- check the child's progress in relation to curriculum outcomes
- share information with parents about their child.

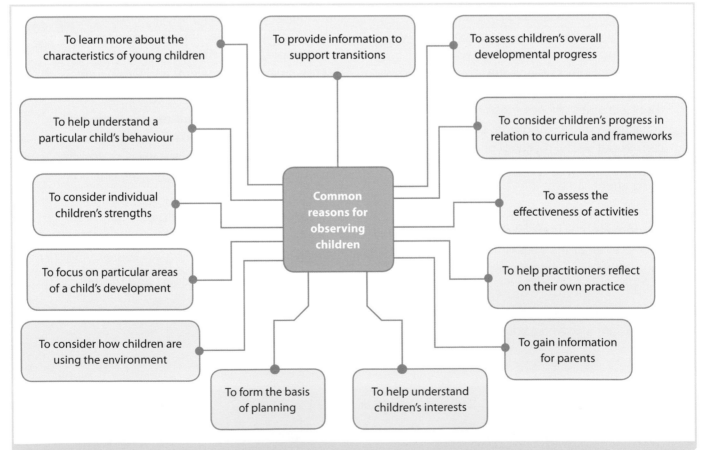

Figure 9.1 The common reasons for observing children

Children's needs and interests

Observing children helps you learn more about them and so should, in theory, help you work more effectively. You might spot a 4-year-old who is left-handed and so remember to put out left-handed scissors or, when observing another child, you might notice a movement they make that shows when they need the toilet. These are examples of small day-to-day needs, but observing a child might also reveal that they require more significant support, such as speech and language therapy. Identifying a need for this kind of support should happen as early as possible in the child's life, as this has been shown to result in more positive outcomes.

It is useful not to fall into the trap of only observing children when there is a problem or concern. Observations also tell you about children's strengths and interests, and this information can be used to help plan play and other activities for them.

Sharing information with parents

Working closely with parents is essential in early years practice. Parents have a right to know how their child is progressing and what they have spent time doing. As we will see later in this section, wherever possible, parents should contribute to the observation and planning process as they will also have knowledge and ideas about their child.

Link

Go to Unit 5 in Student Book 1 to find more information about how important it is to work closely with parents.

Providing information to support transition

Observations and assessments may also be shared, with parental consent, with other practitioners and professionals to support transition. You may provide information about how best to help the child settle or ideas for resources and activities that the child enjoys. You may also pass on records about the child's progress in relation to a curriculum framework where appropriate.

Reflecting on practice

As well as focusing on children, observations should also be used to focus on your practice with children.

The term 'reflective practitioner' is often used here. This means thinking about the impact that you have on children's enjoyment, learning and behaviour. By observing children's responses during sessions and activities, you can reflect on how effective you are, and consider ways in which you might become more effective.

Link

Go to Unit 11: Section B to find more information about reflecting on your performance.

Using observations and assessments to inform planning

As you can see in Figure 9.1, observations and assessments are used to help plan activities, resources and play opportunities for groups and individual children. Observations and assessments are also needed to ensure that children are making progress within the curriculum frameworks of their country. For example, a child aged 3 living in England is likely to attend a setting that is using the Early Years Foundation Stage (EYFS), while a child of the same age living in Wales is likely to be in a setting using the Foundation Phase.

Types of assessment

It is good practice for settings to observe children during play and adult-directed activities, and to use the information gained to support the planning process. Two types of assessment are generally used in settings: **formative assessment** and **summative assessment**.

Key terms

Formative assessment – assessment that takes place during the learning process on an ongoing basis, or 'assessment for learning'.

Summative assessment – assessment of what a child knows and can do at the end of a period of learning, or 'assessment of learning'.

Formative assessment

Formative assessment is where a child's progress is tracked on an ongoing basis. Most settings will do some observations and use these immediately to consider what the child's next steps might be in particular areas of the curriculum or their development. Formative assessment supports short-term planning.

Summative assessment

Most settings will periodically review a child's progress in all areas of the curriculum. This often takes the form of an overall report. Summative assessment allows for an overview of the child's progress, interests and development. Summative assessments are helpful in long-term planning. They are also likely to be shared with other settings when the child is due to move, but this can only take place with parental consent. In England, settings following the EYFS are required to produce two summative assessments: one when the child is 2 years old and another when the child has finished their reception year.

Early Years Foundation Stage Profile (England only)

This is a type of summative assessment that is carried out by teachers towards the end of the reception year. The Early Years Foundation Stage Profile requires teachers to make judgements about children's progress in relation to the early learning goals. These are targets that have been set by the English government and it is hoped most children will be able to meet them by the end of this stage. From 2013, teachers will record whether children are working towards, have met or have exceeded the early learning goals. The judgements that teachers make must be based on observations that have taken place throughout the year.

The importance of parental involvement

It is recognised that parents are partners with us in the care and education of their children, and so you should involve them in every area of your work. Parents are key to helping you fully understand children's interests, needs and overall development. They should, if they wish, be involved in the ongoing observation and assessment of their children. It is good practice to find out about what children do when they are at home and what parents have noticed about their children's interests and development. This is important because children often behave differently at home than they do in the setting. At home, children may be more relaxed and also have different opportunities. For instance, they are likely to interact with siblings or other family members. They are also likely to do a range of different activities such as helping in the garden, going shopping or going to the park. Some children may also speak a language at home that is different to that used in the setting.

It is important to involve parents in the care of their children.

The involvement of parents may take different forms according to the age of the child, the type of setting and the parents' wishes. All settings should provide written summaries of the child's progress as well as parents' meetings, but it is good practice to do far more than this. There are many ways in which settings work alongside parents in the observation and assessment process. Table 9.1 shows some of these.

Issues when observing and assessing children

There are many issues to consider when observing children. It is important to understand these before you begin observing and assessing children. Figure 9.2 outlines the issues.

Table 9.1 How settings can work alongside parents

Ways settings work alongside parents	How they are helpful
Sharing photographs, film clips and sound recordings	As children do different things at home, some settings invite parents to share photographs, film clips and sound recordings with them.
Observations in the home	Some parents may be interested in observing their child and looking out for particular milestones when their child is at home.
Sharing observations with parents	It is good practice for settings to show and talk about observations on or near the day that they have been carried out.
Observations in the setting	Some settings invite parents to observe their child in the setting. They may give parents some points to look out for.
Summative assessment	Some settings create summative assessments using parental input. Others create specific sections in which parents can make their comments about their child.

Gaining permission

The starting point of any observation is to gain permission. As observation is integral to working effectively with children, settings usually have an agreement with parents that observations and assessments can take place. Digital observation methods such as photography and film are increasingly being used, and parents may sometimes opt out of allowing these methods or may impose strict conditions on how they can be used.

If you are on placement, you should ask your supervisor for permission to carry out an observation. In order that permission can be given, it is helpful for parents or supervisors to know:

- the purpose of the observation
- the method of observation
- how the information gained will be used
- who will have access to the observation.

Confidentiality

Information recorded during observations must be treated as confidential. It is also worth noting that it comes under the scope of the Data Protection Act 1998.

Figure 9.2 Issues to consider when observing and assessing children

> **Research**
>
> Find out more about the Data Protection Act 1998 and what it means for you and your setting on the Directgov website. You can access this website by going to www.pearsonhotlinks.co.uk and searching for this title.

It is usual for settings to have policies in place that say who can look at children's records and assessments. This may include the **key person**, the manager and of course the parents. Most settings operate a **need-to-know policy**.

If you submit observations as part of an assignment, it is important to change the names of children and settings. This avoids a child being identified by others who have no direct reason to know about the child. The need for confidentiality is one reason why digital methods such as photography or film clips are not likely to be appropriate for observations submitted as part of an assignment.

Participant bias

When you carry out an observation, it can be very hard to remain objective. This is called **participant bias**. There are many possible reasons for participant bias.

- **Relationship with a child**

When an observer has a relationship with a child, they are likely to have subconsciously made judgements about the child based on what they already know. This means they may miss things that do not 'fit' this existing picture. Participant bias is also seen in assessments of children, as someone who knows a child may mark that child favourably or sometimes be more critical in their assessment.

- **Values and beliefs**

Observers may have certain beliefs about groups of children, which make it hard to observe them objectively or make accurate assessments. An example of this is gender. If an observer subconsciously believes that girls are more cooperative than boys, the interpretation of a girl answering back to an adult may be different than it would be for a boy.

- **Information from other adults**

You have seen that parents and others are important in the assessment process, but observers who have already been given information about a child can find it hard to observe objectively. They may pay more attention to information that concurs with what they have been told than to things that contradict this.

- **Developmental knowledge**

Having a good knowledge of development is important, as without it observers may not pick up on behaviours that are atypical or of interest. On the other hand, if an observer has a particular interest in certain areas of behaviour, they may focus on these to the exclusion of others.

- **Method of recording**

Some methods of recording are 'open', and allow the observer to decide what is of interest and which behaviours to note down. This makes it easier for participant bias to be shown.

Avoiding participant bias

It is difficult to avoid participant bias, but being aware that it may occur is the first step. In addition, it can be useful to choose a variety of recording methods for a clearer overall picture. It is also important to listen carefully to alternative points of view about a child and to consider these when next observing the child.

Assessment practice 9.1   3A.P1 | 3A.M1

You have been asked to write a guide for an early years learner magazine about observing and assessing children. Write an article that includes:

- the importance of observations and assessments
- different methods that can be used
- how to select the appropriate methods according to the information that needs to be collected
- issues to be considered when observing and assessing children.

B Be able to present records of observations of children

There are many different methods of observing and assessing children. In this section, we will look at several different methods, the reasons why they might be used and their benefits and drawbacks.

Observational methods

Each observation technique has advantages and limitations, so it is useful to learn to use several. While there are different techniques for doing it, remember that observing children is always about collecting information. Knowing what you need to learn about the child is therefore important when choosing a technique. There are two broad methods of data collection: closed data methods and open data methods.

• Closed data methods

Closed data methods focus our attention very narrowly. A good example of a closed data method is a checklist, which usually consists of groups of statements. The observer reads the statements and then considers whether or not this is what they are seeing while they observe the child. Closed data methods are considered to be less subjective than open data methods. Their major drawback is that they can focus your attention so narrowly that data might be missed – for example, whether children smile as they skip. Closed data methods tend to be good for assessing children's skills and achievements.

• Open data methods

Open data methods allow us significantly more freedom, as the observation format is not as narrow. The observer is able to focus on whatever takes their attention. This increases the likelihood of subjectivity, but does mean you might gain more information about children. Snapshot observations are examples of open data recording. In this type of observation, the observer jots down what is perceived as interesting when watching a child.

Figure 9.3 shows commonly used methods of observation.

Figure 9.3 Popular methods of observation

Checklists/tick charts

Checklists, or tick charts, are a popular closed method of observing children, because they are easy to use and understand – they are used in many settings by a range of professionals. A sheet is prepared with a list of statements. In some settings these statements relate to the curriculum framework, or they may be compiled to include developmental milestones.

When to use this method

Checklists or tick charts can be used when you need to look at a child's skills or knowledge. This is also a good method to see how much progress a child has made, as the same tick chart can be used a few weeks later. For example, in the classroom a checklist may be used to see how many letter sounds a child knows. Checklists are often used to compare a particular child's development or knowledge with children of a similar age.

How to use this method

You need to read carefully through the listed tasks or skills before beginning the observation. When you observe the child, note whether or not a child is able to do each with a tick or remark. This is an observation technique that can be done unobtrusively, by simply watching the child and hoping that they will show the skills to be recorded, or you can ask the child a specific question or to show you skills such as writing their name.

Figure 9.4 shows an example of a checklist.

Advantages of checklists

- This is an easy method to use and you can draw up your own list of skills or knowledge that you want to observe.
- Parents can be involved in looking out for skills at home.

Disadvantages of checklists

- Observers who have been working with children may want to show progress and so find it hard to complete these tests accurately.
- Some statements may not relate exactly to what a child is observed doing, so the observer may have to estimate whether or not the child can perform a task.
- Space for comments may be restricted, so observers may not be able to record whether the child showed a skill or knowledge easily or needed prompting, for example.
- Checklists and tick charts do not help us to understand children's interests or why they have gained skills or knowledge.

Child ....

Child's age ....   Observer ....

Date of observation ....   Time ....

Activity	Yes	No	Comments
Puts together three-piece puzzle			
Snips with scissors			
Paints in circular movements			
Holds crayons with fingers, not fist			
Can thread four large beads			
Turns pages in a book one by one			
Can put on and take off coat			

Figure 9.4 An example of a checklist

Time samples

Time samples are interesting and versatile. They provide information about a child's activity at regular intervals (e.g. what a child is doing during a session at 10-minute intervals). Time samples can be structured and written in code form, or they may be freer, with observers simply using a running commentary style as the sample is taken.

When to use this method

This is a useful method to use to look at a child's activity overall or as part of a session. It is less intensive than the target child or the written narrative methods and leaves the observer free to look at other children between samples. It is a good method for observing children's all-round development in a range of contexts. For example, you may observe social interaction while the child is playing indoors with the sand, followed by outdoor play using a range of equipment. Time samples can also be used to observe children's interests and concentration span.

How to use this method

The starting point for this method is to decide how structured the time sample needs to be. A structured recording will mean that you need to draw a sheet in advance and familiarise yourself with codes. You will also need to decide how often you will sample the child's activity – this may depend on the length of time you intend to observe them for. For example, you may use five-minute intervals for observations that last for less than an hour, or 15-minute intervals for all-day observations. It is unlikely that sample times greater than 15 minutes will be very informative.

Once you have determined the range of the time sample, the next step is simply to record what you see when it is time to observe. While it can be interesting to observe the child in the meantime, it is important only to record at the sample times.

Figure 9.5 shows an example of a time sample recording sheet.

Advantages of time samples

- They provide information about children's activity over a relatively long period.
- They can be used to provide information about children's overall development.
- They can give an indication of children's interests and levels of concentration.

Disadvantages of time samples

- They do not record information about what a child is doing outside the sample time.

Written narrative/running record

This method is probably one of the most straightforward. It requires the observer to put into writing what is being seen. There is a surprising amount of skill required, though, as it can be hard to find descriptive language and be able to write it down quickly enough to keep up. The speed at which the observer must write means that only a small amount of information can be recorded and its selection is likely to be very subjective. The language that is used to record is also subjective. Observers will not have the time to consider vocabulary carefully and will probably put down the first word that comes to them that they feel fits the situation. For instance, they may use 'snatches', which is more emotive than 'takes quickly'. Most observers using this method find it helpful to pause from time to time to finish off sentences. Afterwards, notes will need to be rewritten so they are legible.

When to use this method

This is a versatile method that is often used as a starting point for future observations. You can choose to record any area of development, or look at a child more holistically and note down things of interest as they occur.

How to use this method

You will need a reliable pen and notepad.

Begin by noting the start time of the observation as well as the context. Then, as you watch the child, write down what you are seeing. This method is sometimes referred to as 'running commentary'. Most observers find that they need to stop after a few minutes, as they are unable to write quickly enough to record everything a child is doing or saying. It is good practice to note the time of each stop and start so that anyone reading it later does not assume that the commentary is continuous. It is also usual for the

Name of child Bryony Matthews				Date of birth	20-08-08
Date of observation	14-9-2012	Start time	10.00 am	End time	11.00 am
Purpose of observation Plays + interaction with other child?					
10.00		Book corner. Alone taking books out of shelves and making piles			③
10.05		Book corner, with adult. Tidying books. Rolling on floor			②
10.10		Book corner. Adult reading story. 2 x other children with BM. BM moves away slightly			⑤
10.15		Book corner. Adult + BM talking. Pointing out pictures. Pushes other child away			⑤
10.20		Sand tray. Standing watching 3 x children at play. Eye contact			②
10.25		Water tray. 2 x other children (ST + TM) Hitting water with hands. Smiling at ST			③
10.30		ST passes BM a funnel. ST smiles, uses funnel, laughs (water tray)			④
10.35		Book corner. Alone. Rolling on floor lifting rug around her			②
10.40		Book corner. Alone. Tapping books on shelves one by one			②
10.45		Snack table. Waiting for turn. Watching 2 x others pour drinks			③

Figure 9.5 A time sample recording sheet: this observer is using a code number to record the intensity of the child's engagement as well as recording what the child is doing every five minutes.

writing to be in the present continuous tense, for example, 'he is going towards the door' rather than 'he went towards the door'.

Advantages of written narrative

- This is quite an open method of recording, so it can provide quite a lot of information.
- No preparation is required.
- This method provides a 'portrait' of a child and so is popular with parents.

Disadvantages of written narrative

- This way of recording can be quite subjective, as it is impossible to record everything a child does and says while observing them.

- It can be hard to write quickly and to choose words well, so this technique requires practice.

Snapshot observations

This method is a variation on written narrative, and has been used widely by early years settings. The idea is that the child is observed very briefly, for perhaps a minute or so, because the adult has seen something of interest that the child is doing or has decided in advance that the child needs to be seen in a particular area of play or showing a particular skill. This short observation is often written on a sticky note. Snapshot observations are also used as the starting point of the 'learning journey' method of assessment and planning.

Key term

Learning journey – a way of assessing and planning for children's development using a narrative approach that can easily be shared and constructed with parents and children.

Link

Go to Section C2 in this unit to find more information about the 'learning journey' method of assessment and planning.

Advantages of snapshot observations

- They do not take long to write.
- Parents like to see what their child has been doing and these provide accessible information.
- They allow for spontaneous observation and recording.

Disadvantages of snapshot observations

- They are very short and may not provide sufficient information.
- They may be subjective, as this is an open method of observation.

Target child observations

Target child observations note the actions and responses of a particular child over a continuous period of time. Target child observations require the observer to be very focused and to work intensively. The observer uses codes to ensure that they can record what the child is doing minute by minute.

When to use this method

This method is often used to learn about individual children and, while it can be used to provide a holistic observation, it is often used to focus on children's social and language interaction.

How to use this method

This is an observation method that does need to be planned ahead. It requires the observer to focus on only one child and means that the observer is not able to work with other children at the same time.

1 Start by deciding which child is to be observed.
2 Prepare or photocopy a record sheet (see Figure 9.6 for an example).
3 Read through and check that you can remember the codes to use.
4 Write the start time on the sheet and use a stopwatch or clock to keep time.
5 For each minute, record what the child is doing. Use codes to ensure that you can keep up.

Advantages of target child observation

- It provides detailed information about a child's activity over a continuous period.
- Codes are used to enable the observer to write more efficiently. These can be made up by the observer to suit the observation.

Disadvantages of target child observation

- The observer needs to be familiar with the coding system and practise using it.
- It can be difficult for others to understand the notes if non-standard codes are used.

Digital recordings

As technology has become increasingly cheap and easy to use, many settings are now using digital methods to record children. There are many advantages to using these methods. However, as with all methods of recording, it is vital to gain parental consent and ensure that all recordings are kept secure.

Good organisation is also required for these methods, as it can be easy to forget when recordings were made. Settings using this method often create a digital folder for each child so that recordings are not lost and can be kept in date order.

Using a camera

Using a camera either to photograph or film children and young people is becoming increasingly popular as an observation technique. Either photography or filming can help you notice details that you might otherwise miss.

When to use this method

This method can be used to film groups of children as well as individual children. If you wish to film

Individual child-tracking observation

Name of child   Hamza   Observer   Steph   Date   22/10/12

Age of child   3 yrs   2 months   No. of adults present   2   No. of children present   6

Free play/structured play/directed activity

Time	Description of activity	Language	Grouping	Level of involvement
10.00 am	TC scooping sand using left hand repeated movements	TC →	P	4
10.02	TC burying r. hand, scooping with other	→ TC ←	I	4
10.03	TC nods head. Other child copies TC, TC smiles	C → TC	P	3

Key

Grouping	Language		Level of involvement
WG = Whole group	TC → A	Balanced interaction between adult and child	1 = No activity
SG = Small group			2 = Frequently distracted
P = Pair	TC → C	Balanced interaction between target child and another child	3 = Fairly continuous activity
I = Individual			4 = Absorbed in activity
	A → C	Adult interacts with more than one child	
	C → TC	Another child interacts with target child	
	→ TC ←	Target child talks to himself/herself	
	TC →	No interaction	

Figure 9.6 An example of a target child observation record sheet

children with sound, it is important to choose situations in which there is not too much ambient noise. It is also important to be aware of any children who may wander into view whose parents have not given permission for them to be recorded in this way.

set the camera so that it does this automatically. It is also important to get children used to being filmed first, otherwise they may be more interested in what you are doing than carrying on with their play or activity.

How to use this method

This is a straightforward method, as you need only decide what to film and then get started. It is worth practising first to ensure you can use the equipment easily. Remember to check that the camera has sufficient battery power. It is important to write down the time and date of the observation or to

Advantages of using a camera

- It is easy to review what children are doing and notice details.
- This method is popular with parents, as they can see what their children have been doing.
- Older children can use this as a medium to show us what is important in their lives.

Using a camera is a popular observation technique.

Disadvantages of using a camera

- Confidentiality can be an issue. Children can only be filmed with parental consent, and this includes children who are not the focus of the observation but who may stray into the shot.
- Recordings have to be kept secure.
- Background noise may prevent you from hearing what children are saying.
- Photographs only give limited information. It is not possible to know what the child did or said in the moments leading up to the photograph or film, or immediately afterwards.

Sound recordings

It is now easy to record children's speech onto a variety of devices including mobile phones, MP3 players and other gadgets.

When to use this method

Sound recordings work well for recording children's speech. It is particularly useful to make several recordings of the same child over time as a way of checking that children's speech is progressing.

How to use this method

Choose a quiet place and note the name of the child and the date, either on a piece of paper or into the recording device. Talk to the child naturally to encourage them to respond as usual. If a child's speech is unclear, either because of their age or stage of development, make sure that you recast what has been said. This is good practice – it is essential so

that anyone else listening to the recording afterwards can understand what the child was trying to say. For instance, 'We go guirrel?' may be recast as, 'Yes, we are going to see the squirrels later.'

Play back the recording to check that it is sufficiently clear, then transfer it into the child's digital folder.

Advantages of sound recordings

- Recordings can be done while you are with the child, which makes this a time-efficient way of recording.
- Parents can hear their child's speech develop if several recordings are made over time.
- Parents can make recordings of their child's speech at home. This can be useful if the child speaks a language different from that used in the setting.
- Where there are suspected speech and language difficulties, recordings can be played to other professionals as part of the referral process.

Disadvantages of sound recordings

- It can be difficult to hear what children are saying in noisy environments.
- It is not possible to see the child's body language or facial expression or to see the context in which speech is taking place.
- If recordings do not specify the time, date and name of the child, it may not be clear later when they were made or who was speaking.

Information from other sources

Strictly speaking, the term 'observation' relates only to what you have actually seen and recorded at a particular time. Having said this, in practice, the term is used more widely and covers information gained in retrospect or from indirect sources; for example, it might include something a parent tells you. Information gained that is not actually seen and recorded at the time is described as **non-contemporaneous**.

Key term

Non-contemporaneous – in the context of observing children, this refers to events that are recorded or reported after they have occurred.

Advantages of non-contemporaneous information

Information from others can help you build a holistic picture of a child in a range of situations and over a period of time. This is important, as you cannot be with the child in every situation or for every hour of the day. Other people can also provide additional viewpoints and so potentially counter participant bias.

Disadvantages of non-contemporaneous information

The biggest disadvantage of non-contemporaneous information is because no direct recording is available, you cannot be sure that it is accurate or reliable. For example, a child may tell you what has happened but may not include details that you would have wanted to focus on. You may not be given a full picture of what has happened, or an event might be exaggerated. In addition, parents and others may have different expectations of children and this may colour their reporting. For instance, parents may say that their child has shown very difficult behaviour when, actually, the behaviour is quite typical for the age range.

Event samples

Event samples are sometimes referred to as 'frequency counts'. The aim of these observations is to find out how often a specific type of behaviour or response takes place and also the context in which it occurs. They are often used when a child is showing unwanted behaviour, but may also be used more broadly. They can help a practitioner to work out the reasons for certain responses, and also provide evidence to show whether responses or incidents are increasing or decreasing. Event samples are non-contemporaneous, as recording takes place after the event or incident has occurred.

When to use this method

Event samples focus narrowly on the particular response of a child. For example, you might decide to investigate how often a child has a tantrum and the context in which this occurs, or you might look at how often a child interacts with other children.

How to use this method

A sheet that directs the user to the type of information to be collected has to be drawn up. There are no standard formats, as the recording columns need to reflect the observer's information requirements. Commonly collected information includes the date and time as well as the context. Figure 9.7 shows an event sample focusing on the number of times a child interacts with other children in a setting. In this situation, it will be important to see whom the child talks to and for how long. It will also be useful to find out whether the child initiates the contact or if the other children do.

Once the record sheet is drawn up, it is only filled in when the specific behaviour or response is noted. In settings where several adults might work with a child, the person who was working with the child at the time could fill in the record sheet.

Event	Time	Activity of child	Social group	Language used	Comments
1	11.07	Playing in the water tray	Sam, Katie, Mustafa, Ben	'Look, look! Water fell.'	Sam leaned over and said this to Mustafa and Ben
2	11.16	Playing with two beakers in the water tray, trying to transfer water between the two	Sam, Mustafa, Ben	'Water splash, splash, splash.'	Sam was showing Mustafa, while splashing Ben

Figure 9.7 Part of an event sample showing how often Sam interacts with other children

Advantages of event samples

- They can help us understand the frequency and patterns of a child's behaviour or responses.
- They can be a way of monitoring the success of strategies by providing a baseline.
- They produce detailed information on the behaviour being observed, can indicate events that may trigger the behaviour and confirm if there is the need for concern.

Disadvantages of event samples

- Others may need to fill in the record sheet if the observer is absent.
- They require the observer to concentrate on one child for a long period of time.
- It is possible that the child being observed will know they are being observed and that this could affect the outcome.

Sociograms

Sociograms are used with children from around 4 years old to look at patterns of friendships within groups. By asking children about their friendship preferences, a chart is created that shows which children are frequently named, whether friendships are reciprocated and whether certain children find it difficult to name friends or are not named themselves.

> ### Key term
>
> **Sociogram** – a recording method whereby children indicate their friendship preferences.

When to use this method

Talk to children one at a time when no other children are with them. Ask them to name their friends and, if necessary, use a prompt question such as, 'Who do you like playing with?' Remember to give children enough time to respond, and record the names that are given by each child. Then create the sociogram chart.

This practitioner is talking individually to a child in order to create a sociogram.

How to use this method

It can be interesting to use sociograms as a starting point for further observations. Consider following up with those children who are not named by other children or who had difficulty in naming any friends. It is also important to follow this up with information from parents and colleagues who may have seen children play with each other or who may have heard children talk about other children.

Advantages of using sociograms

- They can provide an indication that some children need more support in making friends.

Disadvantages of using sociograms

- This can be a very unreliable method to use with 4-year-olds, who will often base their answers on whom they have just played with.
- It can be more reliable with older children, but there is a danger that older children will mention names simply to please the questioner.

Information from parents and others

Parents and colleagues see children in different situations and so may have different views of a particular child's development. Information from parents can be gained from questionnaires, structured face-to-face interviews or informal chats. Some practitioners also encourage parents to observe their children at home using a recording method such as filming.

Advantages of using information from parents and others

- Parents and other professionals will see children in different situations and so may provide information that would otherwise be difficult to collect.
- In the case of other professionals, we may not have the expertise to collect it ourselves while they do.

Disadvantages of using information from parents and others

- Parents may show participant bias as they want to present their child in the best light or try to second-guess what the setting wants. It may be hard to verify the accuracy of observations or to understand the context in which they have taken place.

Selecting appropriate observation methods

It is important to choose the right method of observation, so begin by thinking about what type of information you are trying to collect. For example, if you are focusing on a child's speech and language, you might decide to carry out a sound recording as well as a time sample. This will give information about how the child talks in relation to their age and stage of development as well as whom the child communicates with and how often over the course of a session.

Questions to consider

- What information do I need to collect?
- How focused does the recording need to be?
- How much time do I have to spend recording?
- How reliable must the recording method be?
- Do I need a combination of recording methods?
- Do I want open or closed methods of recording?
- How skilled am I at using the recording method?

Presenting records of observation

As observations will be used to support planning and assessment, it is important that they are presented in ways that are easy to understand and refer back to. The following should be considered when presenting records of any observations that you carry out.

Legibility

It is important that records of observations are neat and legible, so that other people can understand them. Observations may be read by parents, key persons and other professionals such as inspectors. As part of your course, you may also have to present observations as part of an assignment. These must also be neat and legible.

Accuracy and detail

It is important that we record information accurately and, wherever possible, in detail. This can take practice, but it is essential as otherwise there is a danger that inaccurate conclusions will be drawn about a child's interests, needs or development.

Non-judgemental tone

It may be hard, but you should aim only to record what you see or hear – without elaboration and without using words that imply a judgement. You should not state what did not happen, such as 'he did not say thank you', as this was not observed.

Date of observation

It is important to write down the date the observation was carried out. This helps observations to be put in order and allows us to see the progress that children are making. It also helps the observation to be seen as valid.

Age of child

It is usual to note the child's age at the beginning of the observation. This is usually recorded in years and months (for example, 4 years, 3 months). This helps anyone reading the observation to see how what has been observed relates to the typical development.

Contextual information

It is usual to note down information that helps the reader understand the full picture of what was happening at the time. This will include the number of children and adults around the child at the time of the observation. This is important, because children's behaviour changes according to the group size and whom they are with. You should also note down what the child was doing or what was happening when the observation began. For instance, 'four children were around the sand tray and an adult had just added some more sand'.

Purpose of the observation

It can be helpful to write out the reason for carrying out the observation, as this helps anyone reading it to see what the focus of the observation was meant to be. For example, 'the observation was carried out to determine whether child X talked more when alone with an adult or in a small group'.

Did you know?

Many qualifications require that learners present observations and assessments of children. The reason for this is that it shows whether learners have a good underpinning knowledge of child development. So, what makes a good observation?

- Clear aims and relevant method – the more focused you are as an observer, the more accurate and detailed your observation record will be.

- Open methods of recording – to show your skills, the best methods of recording tend to be open ones. This is because you can collect a wide pool of information about a child. Closed methods such as a checklist provide less insight into a child's responses.

- Detail – the more detailed your information, the easier it is to support your conclusions with evidence.

C1 Be able to draw valid conclusions from observations of children

Observing children is just one step of the process of assessing children and making plans for their play and development. Once you have observed children, you need to interpret what you have recorded. This is an important step, as the conclusions that you draw should influence the short-term planning for the child. Your conclusions will also be used to help parents and others understand the child's developmental progress. This section looks at ways in which you might draw these conclusions.

Identifying stage of development from observations

One of the key reasons for observing children is to check that they are making developmental progress.

Looking at the normative development may help you realise that a child's development is completely typical for their age group. On the other hand, looking at the normative development may help you realise that the child needs further support.

Normative development is looked at especially in children's earliest years. This is because the early identification of needs often makes a significant difference to later outcomes. One of the reasons why early identification is so important is that different areas of development are interlinked. For example, a child with atypical speech and language development may find it hard to control their behaviour and so may not be invited to play with other children.

Checking normative development is especially important when we look at young children's behaviour. A child with a peer group whose behaviour is in advance of expected development may appear to be 'difficult and uncooperative' when, in reality, their behaviour is within the expected range for their age.

Looking at normative development can also help us to be aware of what the child needs to go on and do. This might help us in planning equipment and activities and also checking that we are providing sufficient challenges.

How to relate normative development to an observation

A good starting point is to look at the developmental milestones given for the child's age in reference books, and see how they relate to the skills and knowledge that the child showed in the observation. For instance, if the child was busy pouring sand from one container to another, how do these fine motor skills relate to the expected developmental norms or milestones?

Once you have established how the child's fine motor skills relate to the developmental norms, you can then write a conclusion that shows the correlation. This has the advantage of showing the reader how the conclusion was reached. One way of doing this is to start by stating what you have observed and then quoting directly or indirectly what is stated in a reference book or on a trusted website. See an example in Figure 9.8, where a learner has made an indirect reference in support of her observation to the author Carolyn Meggitt's work.

> Janie, aged 3 years, repeatedly poured sand from one container to another. She often did this without spilling any. According to Carolyn Meggitt, this is typical of this age group.

Figure 9.8 An example of an indirect reference

Did you know?

Did you know that there are different ways of referencing? To access a helpful website for the Harvard system, go to www.pearsonhotlinks.co.uk and search for this title.

Children's interests and preferences

Observations can and should also be used to look at children's interests and preferences. This will help when planning for the provision of toys, resources and activities. Open recording styles of observation such as filming, written record or target child are particularly useful. When looking at an observation, think about the following:

- With what or whom did the child spend the most time?

This may indicate a friendship preference or a play interest.

- What level of engagement did the child show?

High levels of concentration and perseverance, especially during child-initiated play, are often indicators of interests and play preferences.

- Facial expression

Children may smile, laugh or look intensely interested in things. This may indicate an interest or play preference.

How to identify interests and preferences

As with development, you should try to show the link between the interests and preferences that you have observed and your conclusions. In some cases you may realise that although you have seen the child smile or laugh, you have not recorded it. This is not good practice because, in theory, you are drawing conclusions about something for which you have no evidence. (This is one reason why it is important when starting out to keep practising observation. The more you do it, the more skilled you will become.) Read the following observation in Figure 9.9 by Akbar, an early years practitioner, to see a good example of an observation record.

> During the observation I saw Michael spend most of the hour playing with a toy shark, which he used in both the sand and the water trays. He also asked if he could take it to the snack table with him.
>
> *Akbar, an early years practitioner*

Figure 9.9 An example of an observation note

Planning activities and experiences

As well as providing developmental information, observations also have to be used to help us plan activities and experiences that will support the child further. This is often in relation to the curriculum framework that is being used in the setting. Many settings design observation sheets that include a section titled 'Next steps'. This is where ideas for what could be planned next to support a child's progress or interests may be written.

Relating observations to planning activities and experiences

A good starting point is to look at the information from the observation and then pick out which parts relate to the curriculum framework that is being used. You may, for example, have observed a child playing a board game. From this observation, there could be several links to the curriculum framework. You might consider their social skills, as the game required them to take turns, and also whether the child understood the concept behind the game.

Once you have identified possible areas to consider, you will then need to look in detail at the curriculum framework and consider what to provide next for the child. It may be that the child would benefit from playing the game again, as they enjoyed it, but would also benefit from further practice in recognising numbers.

Suggestions for next steps

After nearly every observation, you should think about what the observation has told you about the child and what else could be planned to support the child further. You should consider the child's interests when doing this, as well as suggestions contained in the curriculum framework. It can also be helpful to look at the developmental milestones, which may suggest what the child is likely to be working towards. Information and ideas from parents are also important, based on what they know about their children.

Suggestions for activities, resources and play opportunities do not have to be very detailed, but should be sufficient to be followed up in the planning process. It is also good practice to make links to the observation so that it is clear what the next steps have been based on. Read the example in Figure 9.10 written by Steven, an early years practitioner.

> Lorna showed that she enjoyed dropping things and having the attention of an adult. This game could be repeated, but extended by providing other objects for Lorna to drop. The adult could also name the object each time they returned it to Lorna, as this might help her to learn a new word.
>
> *Steven, an early years practitioner*

Figure 9.10 An example of how to use information to support a child's future learning

Relating theories of play and development to observations

Through observations, you can also think about how a child's play and interests link to theories of play and development. By looking at the information gained from the observations and thinking about the theories, you are more likely to understand the reasons behind the behaviours that children have shown.

This can help you to be more strategic in guiding behaviour. It can also help you see what the child needs from you in terms of planning and further experiences. Earlier in the course, you looked at some key theories of development, and you are likely to be able to see these in action when you watch babies and children.

Link

Go to Unit 2 in Student Book 1 to find more information about theories that link to play schemas.

The importance of relating theories to what you observe children doing is one reason why you are asked to record this as part of the observations you submit during training.

Theory into practice

Find out whether your setting observes children at play and relates these observations to play schemas.

How to relate theories to observations

As with relating normative development to records of observations, the key is first of all to read through the observation carefully. You should then look in reference books for theories of play or child development and consider whether you can see any links. Record these links by explaining what you saw, which theory of play or development it may link to and why you have made this association. Read the example in Figure 9.11 written by Sarah, an early years practitioner.

Hasan repeatedly dropped his spoon on the ground and each time giggled when an adult picked it up for him. I think that the attention he gained from the adult acted as a positive reinforcement and so prompted him to repeat this behaviour.

Sarah, an early years practitioner

Figure 9.11 An example of an observation note

More than one theory at work!

In most observations, you should see that there is more than one theory at work. The case study is a good example of this. Children may be using objects to symbolise other objects, such as using a cupful of sand to stand for a cup of tea. They may also be looking for adult support, attention or praise. In addition, the way that they are playing may be giving them particular cognitive benefits.

▌Atypical development

From time to time, you may work with children whose development does not seem to link to the usual patterns associated with their age group. If you are a learner, you should first raise this with the child's key person. It may be that differences in the child's developmental pattern have already been identified. If, on the other hand, you are working as the child's key person, you should carry out a further observation, perhaps at a different point in the day or where the child is engaged in a slightly different activity. Double-checking that you are not jumping to conclusions is very important, and making sure that you have some evidence to support your concerns is also helpful. This evidence, usually in the form of observations, can be used to support other professionals if a referral is needed.

Working with parents

If, after observing the child further, you still feel that there may be potential concerns, you should talk to the child's parents. It may be that they too have a similar concern or that the child behaves differently at home. As there are many factors that can affect children, the next step may be to carry out a series of observations over a couple of weeks, or the decision might be taken with parents to start a referral process. If a referral is made, it will be important to work closely with the parents so that information can continue to be shared.

Case study

Analysing observations

Meghan is 18 months old. She has been given a washing-up bowl full of coloured dried rice. She has been dropping toy animals into the rice and covering them over. She has then taken great pleasure in uncovering them and showing them to her key person. She has spent 15 minutes repeating this play.

After looking again at Units 1 and 2 in Student Book 1, see if you can relate theory to practice by answering the following questions:

1 Why does Meghan repeat these actions?
2 What play schema does this relate to?
3 Why does she keep showing the animals to her key person?
4 What skills is she learning and practising through this hiding and finding?

Referring children

If there are concerns about a child's development, the parents must give consent before any referrals can take place. The route to referral will depend very much on the type of concern that is raised and also how referrals work in your local area. For many referrals, parents will need to go to their family doctor or health visitor, who will in turn arrange an appointment with the relevant service, although in some areas there are drop-in clinics, for speech and language therapy, for example.

Working with other professionals

When a referral has taken place, you may share observations and assessments with other professionals, with the parents' consent. You may also be asked to observe the child in order to monitor the effectiveness of strategies and the child's developmental progress. In some cases, this may mean using a format given to you by another professional. It is important to remember that information cannot be shared in this way unless parents have given consent.

C2 Understand the importance of planning to support children's play and development

All settings working with children will have a range of planning techniques. These will depend on the number of children in the setting, the curriculum framework that is being used and also the beliefs of the setting itself. In this section, we look at the importance of planning and the range of methods used in settings.

The importance of planning

Children can learn a lot from simply playing and being with adults but it can also be helpful for activities and play opportunities to be planned for them that impart a variety of different skills and knowledge. To ensure this happens, professionals working with children carry out planning based on children's needs and interests. Where a curriculum is being followed, planning will also ensure that activities meet its requirements.

As well as ensuring that children's needs are met, planning also has other advantages. In group settings, it helps staff to be organised and prevents situations in which children's needs may be overlooked. Planning can also give everyone, including children, a focus and this creates a more stimulating environment that aids children's overall development.

Requirements of the curriculum framework

You will need to find out about how the curriculum framework in your country influences the planning process. Most inspectorates that look at how settings implement a curriculum framework will look at the planning in the setting. They are likely to check that all parts of the curriculum are being delivered and that these are appropriately tailored to meet individual children's needs. To show that this is happening, your setting may have a tracking system in place to help staff plan activities in a balanced way, to include a balance of those that are adult-directed and child-initiated. You may also find that plans for individual children are drawn up that show how, over a period of time, the setting will support their progress.

Research

Find out about the requirements for planning that relate to the curriculum being used in your setting.

Factors that influence planning

There are many factors that influence what we plan in the long and the short term with the children we work with. In some ways, planning is a little bit like a jigsaw puzzle, as there are many pieces to consider. Getting all the pieces in the right order means that children's developmental needs can be met alongside their interests, while ensuring that they make good progress. Figure 9.12 shows the information required in the planning process.

Observations of children

There is little point in planning any activities or play opportunities unless you are sure that they are suitable for children and that they will enjoy them. By carrying out observations, as you have seen earlier in this unit, you can work out what developmental needs children have and what their next steps might be. You can also observe their interests and think about what they enjoy doing.

Evaluations of previous activities

As well as carrying out observations on children, you can also use your evaluations of activities that they have been involved with to help you with your planning. For instance, a small group of children who enjoyed playing a particular card game may enjoy playing a similar game.

The curriculum framework

In settings that follow a curriculum framework, planning will be heavily influenced by it. In England, for example, settings using the EYFS will need to plan activities that cover all of the seven areas of learning with the aim of helping children reach the early learning goals. In schools, children may be working towards literacy and numeracy goals, depending on the curriculum that is being followed.

Figure 9.12 Information that supports the planning process

Research

Find out more about the early years curriculum in your country. You can access the relevant website by going to www.pearsonhotlinks.co.uk and searching for this title.

Information from parents

Parents can often help you in your planning. They may have long-term goals for their child and wherever possible you should be trying to support them. In addition, parents may give you information about what they see their child doing at home and have ideas about how to build on these interests and strengths.

Information from children

You should be involving children in planning as much as you can. You may listen to children's ideas about the equipment, resources and activities that they would like to use and do. You can also learn about children's interests and preferences from observations as well.

Information from other professionals

Where children are receiving support from other professionals such as speech and language therapists or physiotherapists, it is good practice wherever possible for settings to use information about activities or support that the child needs when preparing plans.

Plans for children with additional needs

Children with identified additional needs may have individual education plans (IEPs) drawn up with the aim of focusing activities and adult support on specific developmental needs. IEPs should be looked at by settings when they are drawing up their plans.

Link

Go to Unit 18 to find more information about additional needs.

The ethos of the setting

Some settings have their own very distinct ethos and this is reflected in the curriculum. A Forest School setting might plan to take children out into the woods to support their acquisition of outdoor skills. Similarly, a Montessori setting would follow the methods outlined by Maria Montessori, and their planning would be tailored accordingly.

Planning methods

There are a number of ways in which settings carry out planning. As planning processes and formats change from setting to setting, it is worth finding out each of your placements' processes.

Long-term planning – groups

Most settings will have some type of long-term planning. Some settings' long-term planning is done every three or four months, although others may plan for a year at a time. Long-term planning helps settings to schedule in specific activities or topics, outings and festivals. Where a curriculum is being followed, such as those in schools, long-term planning will also be linked to curriculum expectations for the year group. Long-term planning for most settings centres around the whole group rather than individual children, as it is only of a very general nature.

Short-term planning

Most settings will also have some form of short-term planning. This is likely to show what groups and individual children will be doing over a relatively short period of time – a week or a day, for instance. Short-term planning is likely to show links to curricula frameworks and also to children's developmental needs and interests. Short-term planning often consists of more than one type of plan.

Weekly plans

Many settings will have weekly plans. These show the activities, play and outings that are planned for the week. They may also include specific activities for individual children as well as for groups of children.

Daily plans

Some settings also produce daily plans. These show the activities, play opportunities and the routine for the day in more detail. They may also be used to indicate which adults will be working with which groups of children, and where.

Activity plans

These show single activities or groups of activities and are drawn up to support individual children's developmental needs, or to help groups of children make progress within a curriculum area.

Continuous provision sheets

Most settings offering early years provision will provide a play-based curriculum. The term 'continuous provision' is used to describe the way that resources and activities for play are provided continually both indoors and out. This allows children to choose what to play with and is one way in which settings can provide both adult-directed and child-initiated play simultaneously. As most settings have plenty of toys and resources that cannot all be made available all the time, many will plan what to put out on either a daily or a weekly basis. Resources and activities are likely to be chosen to give children access to several types of play. Settings may also link their provision to the curriculum framework in the planning. Where resources or activities are put out with specific children in mind, this might be indicated on the sheet. An example of a continuous provision sheet is shown in Figure 9.13.

Plans for individual children

Alongside plans that show what has been planned for groups of children, most settings will also have individual plans for children that will feed into the group plans. Planning for individual children is usually done in the medium and short term. This is because children's interests and needs can change quite rapidly.

Individual education plans

For children with additional needs, most settings will use medium-term plans. These are often called individual education plans (IEPs) and they will be

Activity	Monday	Tuesday	Wednesday	Thursday	Friday
Small-world play	Cars + sawdust	Cars (ML+ST)	Dinosaurs Turf ← →		
Role play 1	In the living room ——————————————————→				
Role play 2	← At the hairdressers'	Develop through week ——→			
Board games and jigsaws	2 x 4 pieces (ST)				
Sensory materials	Gloop ←——→		Soap flakes?		
Mark-making area	At the printers' ←	Develop through week ——————————→			
Water	Clockwork toys				
Dough	Cake cases + buttons (LT)				
Sand	Buttons				
Construction	Wooden blocks				
Exploration and investigation	Digi microscope (collect things on walk)				
Creative area	Collage + Junk modelling (ST) ——————→			Visit to scraps	
ICT	Beebots (BT)	Digi microscope ——————————————→			Beebots
Other	Sewing kits ←——→		Marble run		

Figure 9.13 A continuous provision sheet: many settings only partially fill in the sheet at the start of the week. The sheet is added to and changed based on children's observed interests. These interests can be marked with children's initials.

compiled with the input of a Special Educational Needs Coordinator (SENCO) and the child's parents. The plan will show some particular developmental areas that will be the focus of activities, usually over a four- to six-week period. Children's IEPs will help support the setting's short-term plans, so it is important that suggested activities from the IEP are also included in the group planning.

Link

Go to Unit 10: Section C to find more information about planning for activities from the IEP.

Learning journeys

Many settings have combined observation, assessment and planning for individual children by using 'learning journeys'. The idea behind these is to build up a portfolio of children's progress and interests, which can be shared with parents, but also with the children themselves. Most settings that use learning journeys find that they are a great way of bringing together observations and planning. Figure 9.14 shows how a snapshot observation accompanied by a photograph is used to record an area of learning. These can form the basis of an assessment, along with some ideas about activities that can be planned as a result of the observation.

Observations are carried out fortnightly by each child's key person to review the different areas of development. Every six weeks, a summative record is produced to show the child's progress in each of the seven areas of learning based on these observation sheets. At planning meetings, key persons talk about what activities, needs or interests their key children have. These are then incorporated into the weekly plans.

Reviewing plans

As with other areas of work with children, it is important for settings to review the effectiveness of their planning systems. This is because when planning systems are working well, children's individual needs are met and activities are sufficiently challenging, and this in turn means that children are likely to be making good progress. Settings need to consider whether their planning reflects the needs and interests of the children and also the requirements of the curriculum framework that they are using. It is also important that children's individual needs are reflected within group planning. This can be demanding, as there is often a tension between creating a manageable system where staff are not spending too long on paperwork while ensuring that planning is sufficiently detailed and robust. This is one reason why settings will often continually review and try to improve their planning systems.

Observation	Ayse found her shoes when I said that it was time to go outdoors. It took her a moment, but she was able to work out which shoe went on the correct foot. She managed to fasten the buckles without any support. She was very pleased with herself.
What does the observation mean?	Ayse can now put on most of her clothes and shoes herself.
What next?	• Give Ayse time so that she can get dressed herself. • Show her how to use a zip and find dressing-up clothes that have zips. • Look out for role-play clothes that will help her to practise using buttons, zips and buckles.
Links to the EYFS	PSE Self-care (30–50 months) PD Using equipment and materials (30–50 months)
Notes for the next observation	CLL Look out for examples of mark making and also record speech.

Figure 9.14 An example of a learning journey format

Here are some questions to help you review plans and planning systems:

- Are each child's interests and strengths reflected in the planning?
- Do plans reflect the education requirements of the curriculum being used?
- Are plans used and referred to by adults working with children?
- How do plans show what will be happening in the setting on a day-to-day basis?
- How are plans shared with and contributed to by parents?

D Be able to create, implement and review activity plans for children

Activity plans are used in many settings to help promote acquisition of specific skills and knowledge. Learning how to create, implement and review an activity plan provides us with a valuable thought process that will be useful on an almost daily basis. In this section, we look at how you might create, implement and review plans.

Creating appropriate plans for play, development and learning

A good activity plan is really a way of organising your thoughts about providing for children. Figure 9.15 lists the things to think about when creating an activity plan.

Formats for planning activities

There is no single format for creating an activity plan. In some settings, paperwork for activity plans is kept to a minimum, while in others, more emphasis is placed on this. Whatever format is used in your setting, the process of planning an effective activity remains the same. It is likely that your training provider will give you a sample format to help you get used to the process of creating plans. As you have already seen, you will have a number of things to think about, such as resources, the role of the adult, the links to the curriculum and the reason behind the activity. Figure 9.16 is an outline of a sample activity plan that you can use or adapt. If you decide to create your own format, make sure you allow sufficient space for detailed planning.

Research

Find out about the way that your setting plans activities for children.

How to implement activity plans

If you have written a good activity plan or gone through a strong thought process, most of the work of setting up and organising the activity should be straightforward. You should already know what you need in terms of resources, where you might go and, importantly, what benefits the activity is likely to offer the child. All that remains is to implement the plan, which is a skill in itself and depends on a few basic principles.

Involving children

Good activities involve the children fully. Young children find it hard to sit and watch and be passive, so be ready to get children involved early on. This might include them helping to set up an activity or being encouraged to make suggestions. It also means the design of the activity should allow for choice, suggestions and plenty of participation.

Talking and listening

Children benefit from talking as they are learning. Simply listening to an adult is not likely to help their learning process. If you have planned an adult-directed activity, you will need to make sure that children have plenty of opportunities to talk spontaneously and freely, such as chatting while they are cooking with you.

Activity
Think about what you will call the activity. For example, this could be something like 'bubble painting'. Is an explanation of the activity required?

Purpose
What is the reason behind the activity?
This could be to develop a specific skill that would support a child's development, extending a child's or a group of children's interest in a particular area, or to develop a skill or knowledge detailed within a curriculum framework.

Rationale
Give an explanation about why you have chosen this particular activity. We know that children learn best when an activity is interesting and they can be fully involved in it, so you should focus here on why the activity will appeal to children. (At this point, you may realise that your activity is not exciting or interesting enough, and if this is the case you will need to think about planning another activity.)

Maximum group size
Is the activity going to be carried out by more than one child? If so, are there a maximum number of children that can participate?

Benefits
What are the overall benefits of the activity for the child or children? Think about developmental benefits and try to make your points as detailed as possible.

Links to the curriculum
If you are in a setting that follows a curriculum framework, you should state the links between the activity and areas of the curriculum.

Resources and location
Think about what resources you will need. Resources may include things such as aprons. Think also about whether the activity needs to take place in a specific place.

Time required for preparation and clearing away
Think about how much time you will need to prepare for the activity and also clear it away.

Health and safety risk management
Think about whether the resources you need or the activity itself may have health and safety implications. If this is the case, explain how you will manage the risks.

The role of the adult
Outline what the adult will be doing during the activity. They may take on an active role, showing children how to carry out the activity or guiding them through it, or they could take on a facilitating role where the adult reacts to, and is guided by, the child's interests and play during the activity. If you are working with a child who has an additional need, you should also explain how you will meet this need. For example, if you are working with a child who has a hearing loss you should make sure that you locate the activity in a quiet area.

Vocabulary
In some settings, you may be asked to write a list of vocabulary that you will need to attempt to use with the child/children during the activity, so bear this in mind when planning your activity.

Figure 9.15 Things to think about when creating an activity plan

Activity	
Aim and rationale	
Links to curriculum	
Resources	
Location	
Health and safety	
Individual needs	
The role of the adult	
Additional comments	

Figure 9.16 A sample activity plan

Learning should be fun

We know that children are most likely to learn, concentrate and persevere when an activity is fun. This means that you should constantly monitor their reactions and reflect on whether they are engaged in the activity. This might also mean you have to adapt the activity or even, in some cases, abandon it.

Allowing for spontaneity

Most experienced early years practitioners will tell you that children are very creative and will often find inspiration and have ideas that we had not thought of. It is good practice to be flexible, and not to worry if children learn or discover something other than what you planned. In addition to children changing the activity, unexpected events such as the arrival of snow, a rainbow or a hamster on the loose may

mean that carrying on with the planned activity may no longer be appropriate. Being ready to adapt and change your plans is therefore important.

Review plans and planning methods

Reviewing plans and activities is important, as it enables us to improve our planning, and also to think about children's needs and possible next steps. After you have carried out an activity, you will probably have plenty to reflect on, but it is worth spending time thinking about the following:

- **How engaged were the children during the activity?**

This is quite a good starting point. Children who were very engaged and who participated well are likely to have benefited. If this was the case, it may be that you could build on this activity again for a particular child or group of children. On the other hand, you may have found that a child or some children lost interest. This might mean that a different approach is needed with those children in future.

As we know that language is connected with learning, you might also like to reflect on how much speech individual children used and to whom they spoke, or, in the case of babies, vocalised.

- **Did the activity meet its original aim?**

Look back at the plan's original purpose and consider whether you feel that this was achieved. If not, think about why this was and whether other types of activities might have been more suited to the child or children.

- **How did the activity link to the curriculum framework?**

If you made links to the curriculum framework, think about whether these links were correct. It may be that more was covered than you expected. Most settings keep track in some way of the parts of the curriculum that have been covered.

- **Which aspects of the activity and the plan were successful, and why?**

It is important to understand why activities with children work well. This gives us useful insights for future planning. Factors that affect the success of an activity include the type of resources used, the level of challenge or novelty, the way in which the adult was involved and to what extent the activity built on children's interests.

Why is this adult-directed activity working well?

- **What aspects of the activity could have been improved, and why?**

While some activities go to plan, others do not. There are a huge number of reasons for this. It might be that the timing or the location was not good. It could be that the number of children was too great or that your style was too controlling. Some activities may not have been sufficiently appealing or challenging for children, or there may not have been enough variety or interest in the resources.

We also know that young children are affected by whom they are with. It may be that your relationship with the child or children is not sufficiently developed for them to feel totally at ease. This is particularly important to reflect on when you are working with children under 3 years old.

Next steps for the children

After each activity, you should think about children's next steps. It could be that a child really enjoyed the activity and it would be worth repeating it, or perhaps a child struggled with a concept or skill and so adapting the activity or thinking of a new approach might be important. If you spotted that children were keen to use the resources differently, you might think about how to organise this.

Next steps for you

You should spend time thinking about what you have learned from the activity. Perhaps you have learned about the importance of preparation or about children's interests at certain ages. It may be that you have learned what to do if an activity is not enjoyable for children. It can be helpful spending time talking to an experienced practitioner about what happened during the activity, as their thoughts might help you gain more insights.

Writing up a review of an activity

It is easy to make statements such as 'all the children enjoyed this activity', but it is good practice to provide a reason for your statement and to make it as detailed as possible. See Figure 9.17 for an example.

> Zoe and Thomas were engrossed in the activity and were disappointed when it was lunchtime. I think that this indicates that this activity worked well for them. Damian, on the other hand, lost interest within five minutes or so and I feel that this activity may not have been sufficiently challenging for him.
>
> *Grace, an early years practitioner*

Figure 9.17 An example of an observation note

Further reading and resources

Barber, J. and Paul-Smith, S. (2010) *Early Years Observation and Planning in Practice*, London: Practical Pre-School Books.

Walker, M., Hobart, C. and Frankel, J. (2009) *A Practical Guide to Child Observation and Assessment* (4th ed.), Cheltenham: Nelson Thornes.

Tassoni, P. (2012) *Penny Tassoni's Practical EYFS Handbook* (2nd ed.), Oxford: Heinemann.

Assessment practice 9.2   3B.P2 | 3B.P3 | 3B.M2 | 3B.D1 | 3C1.P4 | 3C1.P5 | 3C1.P6 | 3C2.P7 | 3C.M3 | 3C.M4 | 3C.M5 | 3C.D2 | 3D.P8 | 3D.P9 | 3D.M6 | 3D.D3

1 You have been shortlisted for a prestigious job in a children's centre. As part of the interview process, you are required to show detailed knowledge of the observation, assessment and planning process. On the day of the interview, you will be expected to carry out observation, assessment and planning, and afterwards you will be asked in-depth questions to assess your underpinning knowledge and your ability to self-evaluate. In preparation for this, you have decided to practise this process and also have a mock interview with your current placement supervisor.

2 Carry out five observations on one child using a variety of observational methods.

3 Present these observations.

4 Explain why you used these observation methods.

5 Use the observations to analyse the child's play and development using theories of development, play and developmental milestones.

6 Using your analysis of the child's stage of development, interests and play, make suggestions for a range of activities, then produce and implement two activity plans.

7 Evaluate your own practice in observing, assessing, planning and implementing activities.

8 Consider the importance of observing, assessing and planning for children in early years settings.

Ready for work?

Kristie Hannagin   Preschool staff member

We are very proud of our observation and planning process. It has taken some time for us to feel that it is working well, but I feel that we now have a pretty robust system that adults new to the setting and, importantly, parents can understand. This is important because we try to share and involve parents in every aspect of our work and, thanks to the easy-to-use system, parents are able to contribute their own observations and ideas. This is normally done with the child's key person.

As a manager who used to work in the National Health Service, I am very keen for staff to be aware of children who are not making the usual developmental progress. I always advise my staff to have a quick look at the developmental milestones before they begin to observe a child, especially if they are new to working with the age group or they have not been with them for a while.

We also try to make sure that information gained from observations is not just put in a child's folder and then forgotten. Each week, when staff are dong their short-term planning, children's key persons will contribute ideas for activities, toys and resources based on what they know their key children need. We also show this on the planning sheet by adding the child's initials in the appropriate place.

Skills for practice

What can I do to stop a child from coming up to me when I am observing other children?
This is quite a common problem. You can try telling children that you are busy but will talk to them or play with them later on. If this does not work, try using closed body language and avoid making eye contact with them.

I have tried to use target child observation, but I keep forgetting the codes.
You can devise your own codes if this makes it easier. Then you can either rewrite the observation substituting conventional codes or you can retain your own, but put a clear key at the bottom. This means that someone else can read what you have written.

I observed that a child who is now 4 years old does not have hand preference. I am not sure what activities I should plan. Help!
Hand preference can be strengthened with activities that require both hands, but where one hand stabilises an object and the other is active.

Unscrewing a bottle or peeling a banana are examples of this type of two-handed activity.

When should you share observations with parents?
It is good practice to share observations with parents as soon as you have carried them out. While some parents may be interested in reading or seeing them, others may prefer you to explain to them what you have seen.

My setting does not write up observations with theories and links to milestones. Why does my teacher/tutor ask me to do this?
Learner observations and conclusions are often more detailed than those used in settings. This is because learner observations train you in the process of observing and thinking about children. The idea is that later on you will have these skills and use them to think about children, even if you do not write down everything you know.

Introduction

You will have heard the terms diversity, equality and inclusion, but do you know what they mean? In this unit you will explore the importance of valuing diversity and the effects that prejudice and discrimination can have on young children's lives. As you gain a better understanding of these concepts you will be able to recognise inclusive practice. You will also know the strategies that can be used to ensure that every child is valued irrespective of their background, culture, additional needs, disability or gender.

Assessment: You will be assessed by a series of assignments set by your teacher/tutor.

Learning aims

In this unit you will:

A   understand the importance of valuing diversity and countering discrimination in early years practice

B   understand inclusive practice in early years settings

C   understand how children with additional needs may be supported in early years practice.

I came to this country when I was 5 years old. I couldn't speak English very well so I felt really left out when I first went to school. What I really enjoyed was story time, when one of the teachers told me and two other children stories and rhymes in our home language. I'm really looking forward to studying this unit. I think I will understand how to support children because of my experience.

Devaki, *a student on an early years course*

Diversity, Equality and Inclusion in the Early Years

10

BTEC Assessment Zone

This table shows what you must do in order to achieve a **Pass**, **Merit** or **Distinction** grade, and where you can find activities to help you.

Assessment criteria		
Pass	**Merit**	**Distinction**
Learning aim A: Understand the importance of valuing diversity and countering discrimination in early years practice		
3A.P1 Outline the role of legislation and regulatory frameworks to counter discrimination and ensure equality in early years practice. **Assessment practice 10.1**	**3A.M1** Discuss the potential barriers to implementing equality in an early years setting. **Assessment practice 10.1**	
3A.P2 I&CT Explain why diversity should be valued in early years settings. **Assessment practice 10.1**		
3A.P3 I&CT English Explain why discriminatory behaviour and attitudes should be challenged in early years settings. **Assessment practice 10.1**		
Learning aim B: Understand inclusive practice in early years settings		
3B.P4 I&CT Explain the benefits of inclusive practice in early years settings for children and families. **Assessment practice 10.2**	**3B.M2** Analyse the extent to which different strategies contribute to effective inclusive practice in early years settings. **Assessment practice 10.2**	**3B.D1** Evaluate the extent to which reflection on own attitudes and practice might contribute to the promotion of diversity, equality and inclusion in early years practice. **Assessment practice 10.2**
3B.P5 I&CT Examine different strategies an early years setting can use to demonstrate inclusive practice. **Assessment practice 10.2**	**3B.M3** Analyse the extent to which inclusive practice used by adults in early years settings could impact on outcomes for children. **Assessment practice 10.2**	
3B.P6 Explain how adults in an early years setting can help children to value and respect others. **Assessment practice 10.2**		

continued

Assessment criteria (*continued*)

Pass	Merit	Distinction
Learning aim C: Understand how children with additional needs may be supported in early years practice		
3C.P7 Outline the framework and requirements to provide support for children with additional needs in early years settings. **Assessment practice 10.3**	**3C.M4** Discuss ways in which children with additional needs can be supported in early years settings. **Assessment practice 10.3**	**3C.D2** Evaluate the role of adults in effective planning to support children with additional needs in early years settings. **Assessment practice 10.3**
3C.P8 Describe the influence of models of disability on early years practice. **Assessment practice 10.3**		
3C.P9 Explain the role of the appointed special educational needs coordinator in an early years setting. **Assessment practice 10.3**		

English English Functional Skills signposting

I&CT Information and Communication Technology skills signposting

How you will be assessed

This unit will be assessed by a series of internally assessed tasks set by your teacher/tutor. Throughout this unit you will find assessment practice activities that will help you work towards your assessment. Completing these activities will not mean that you have achieved a particular grade, but you will have carried out useful research or preparation that will be relevant when it comes to your final assignment.

In order for you to carry out the tasks in your assignment, it is important that you check you have met all the Pass grading criteria. You can do this as you work your way through the assignment.

If you are hoping to gain a Merit or Distinction, you should also make sure that you present the information in your assignment in the style that is required by the relevant assessment criterion. For example, Merit criteria require you to discuss and analyse, and Distinction criteria require you to evaluate.

The assignment set by your teacher/tutor will consist of a number of tasks designed to meet the criteria in the table. This is likely to consist of a written assignment but may also include activities such as:

- a policy document
- a case study
- an information pack
- examples from an early years setting.

Getting started

Carry out an audit on your setting, to see ways in which it reflects the diversity of the children, their families and the staff. You could look at the:
- book corner
- wall displays
- celebrations
- resources; for example, in the home corner.

A Understand the importance of valuing diversity and countering discrimination in early years practice

Before embarking on this unit it is important to gain an understanding of the positive and negative terminology that you will come across.

Terminology

As you start to explore the following terms you will begin to see relationships between them. For instance, equality and diversity are interdependent concepts, because when diversity is recognised and celebrated it is also likely that equality is being practised in the setting. In contrast, where there is discrimination, this means that equality is not in place.

You will often come across each of the following terms in early years settings, so it is important that you understand the meaning of each one.

Positive terminology

Positive terminology includes the following:

- **Diversity** – differences between individuals, for example, family background, culture, experience and gender.
- **Equality** – children having the same opportunities to enjoy life and achieve their potential.
- **Inclusion** – breaking down barriers to ensure that children and young people, whatever their background or situation, are able to access the same services and participate fully.

Negative terminology

Negative terminology includes the following:

- **Stereotyping** – making assumptions about an individual because of their background, experience or individual needs – for example, a child who has a physical disability may be assumed to have learning difficulties.
- **Prejudice** – using inappropriate language or responding differently because a child belongs to a particular group.
- **Discrimination** – not giving equality of opportunity to groups or individuals because they belong to a particular group. Discrimination may be institutional (policies and procedures are discriminatory) or individual (the practice of practitioners or others).

Discrimination may be direct or indirect. Direct discrimination happens when children and young people are not allowed to access services or activities because of their particular situation – their race, gender or disability, for instance. Indirect discrimination is more difficult to spot and may be more common. It may not even be intended. It happens when practice or procedures do not take account of the individual. For example, a child who is vegetarian because of their religion is unable to join in a celebration tea because the food does not include vegetarian options.

Activity

Write the six positive and negative terms on a piece of A4 paper, spacing them out. Draw a line between terms where you feel there is a relationship, and write that relationship on the joining line. For instance, you might join the term 'prejudice' with 'discrimination', stating that 'prejudice can often lead to discrimination'.

Theory into practice

The Early Years Foundation Stage Framework (EYFS) highlights the importance of recognising the individuality of children. Read more about the guiding principle 'The Unique Child' in the framework. You can access the framework and find out more about the EYFS by going to www.pearsonhotlinks.co.uk and searching for this title.

Give an example of practice where you have taken into account the concept of 'The Unique Child'.

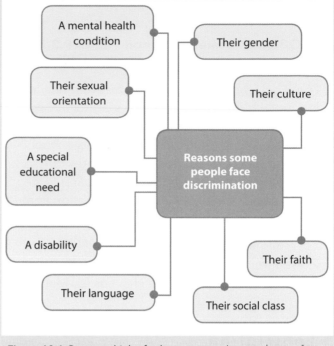

Figure 10.1 Can you think of other reasons why people may face discrimination?

Groups that may face prejudice and discrimination

Have you ever experienced discrimination? There are times when everyone feels that they are being treated differently from their peers. Figure 10.1 shows why some people may face particular problems of prejudice and discrimination.

Effects of prejudice and discrimination on children's life chances

All prejudice and discrimination has a negative effect on children's lives. Prejudice can lead to discrimination. When discrimination is at work children are being denied the care and education to which they are entitled.

Children with a disability often face discrimination. Discrimination happens because children with a disability face more barriers to participation due to their mobility, learning or communication difficulties. If children do not participate fully this quickly leads

to isolation. Have you ever made assumptions about someone's abilities because of their disability? It is important that we focus on children's abilities and interests to ensure that they are not excluded from the curriculum, either directly or indirectly.

Discrimination is also a barrier to learning because our attitudes affect the expectations we have of children. This may result in an 'attainment gap' starting in the early years, which widens as the child progresses through school. Eventually it affects their life and work opportunities. Research has highlighted that particular groups do less well at school. Of particular concern are children who are vulnerable because of their economic circumstances.

Discrimination for any reason can seriously affect children's social and emotional development. Even very young children can pick up on the attitudes and actions of adults or in some cases of other children. This can make children feel as if they do not belong, which can have a long-term effect on their ability to build friendships. Children who are excluded or feel that an activity is 'not for them' will easily lose confidence in their own ability. It will affect how they view themselves, leading to low self-esteem.

SHC 33, Assessment criterion 1.2; CYP 3.7 Assessment criterion 3.1

Marik is 11 years old. He has had severe hearing loss since birth. Although Marik's disability has caused communication difficulties, he has made good academic progress at his primary school because he is well supported. He is now due to transfer to secondary school but his parents are concerned that he may face discrimination from staff or other children.

1 How might discrimination affect Marik?

2 What might the impact of discrimination be on the outcomes and life chances for Marik?

Legislation

There are a number of laws that aim to counter discrimination and promote good relations and inclusion. Where discrimination exists individuals can call on these laws to protect their right to equal treatment. Some laws deal with the rights of particular groups, such as those with disabilities. Others, such as the Children Act, are in place to promote the specific rights of children and young people. Key legislation is outlined in Table 10.1.

The United Nations Convention on the Rights of the Child (UNCRC) 1989

This is not legislation as such, but an agreement. It sets out the rights of children and young people whatever their background or need. Children's Rights are set out in 54 Articles. Article 2 states the rights of children not to be discriminated against 'irrespective of the child's or his or her parent's or legal guardian's race, colour, sex, language, religion, political or other opinion, national, ethnic or social origin, property, disability, birth or other status'.

By signing the agreement in 1991 the UK government was required to put into place laws that protect and promote these rights.

Table 10.1 Key legislation relating to discrimination

Legislation	Purpose
Children Act 1989	States that the child's needs are paramount. When planning for and delivering support, early years services must take into account the child's background and experience including their race, culture and language. Services must also promote well-being and racial identity.
Children Act 2004	Introduces additional obligations for childcare services but the principles of equality set out in the 1989 Act remain.
Disability Discrimination Act 2005	Places a duty on schools to produce a Disability Equality Scheme (DES) and an Access Plan. Schools must encourage participation in all aspects of school life and eliminate harassment and unlawful discrimination.
Race Relations (Amendment) Act 2000	Outlines the duty of all organisations to promote good relationships between people from different races.
Human Rights Act 1998	Sets out the rights of all individuals and allows them to take action against authorities when their rights have been affected.
Equality Act 2010	Combines nine equality laws. It sets out the legal responsibilities of public bodies, including early years services and schools, to provide equality of opportunity for all. It states that everyone, whatever their background, race, culture, age, gender, faith or additional needs, must be treated fairly.

Link

Go to Unit 13: Section A to find more information about the UNCRC.

Potential barriers to implementing equality in early years

There are a number of barriers that may prevent legislation from being effective. Figure 10.2 outlines some of these barriers.

In some circumstances, professionals may not even be aware of their responsibilities in countering discrimination. Laws can be quite complex, making it difficult for early years professionals to know how they apply to themselves and their own particular service or setting. Even when they are understood, legislation and guidance are frequently updated. This may lead to ambiguous or out-of-date policies. The result may be that staff are unsure of the aims of the setting and procedures they must follow.

Legislation will be less effective where there is no commitment to inclusion. Provision of information and training opportunities for all staff are essential. The manager plays a crucial role in ensuring good practice but all staff must feel that they are able to question practice or even to **whistle blow** when they have concerns.

Adhering to legislation is not always straightforward. In some cases there may even be conflicting policies.

You may have read about instances in schools where there has been conflict between the health and safety policy and a child's rights to wear specific items of clothing or jewellery as part of their religion.

You must also be mindful of indirect discrimination. This can happen when practitioners, other adults or children lack understanding about individual children and their families. It may result in practitioners inadvertently discriminating against children by not providing appropriate activities, information or resources. Do you know, for example, the dietary requirements of all of the children in your care, or the language that they speak at home?

Lack of understanding of ways to acknowledge and encompass cultural identity in planning and delivery of services can lead to **tokenism**. This happens when 'lip service' is paid to diversity. For example, minority cultures might only be reflected in posters on the wall or at particular times of the year when festivals are celebrated. This may give an appearance of inclusivity even though inclusive practice is not evident in day-to-day activities.

Key terms

Tokenism – giving the appearance of an inclusive environment.

Whistle blowing – an employee who raises concerns about the wrongdoing of another person or group of people in the workplace.

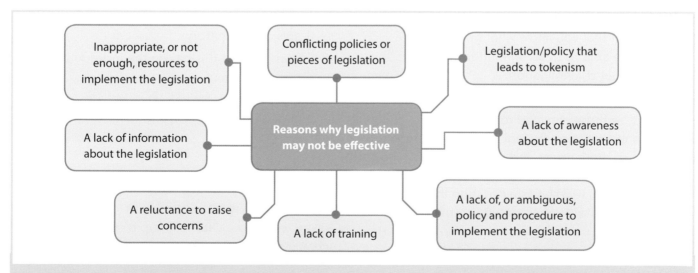

Figure 10.2 Barriers to implementing equality in early years

Challenging discriminatory behaviour and promoting respect

All childcare workers have a duty not only to protect children from discrimination but also to actively promote respect for others. Discrimination may be institutional or individual. It may be practised by adults working in a setting or by others such as parents or people from outside organisations. We have already covered the effects that discrimination can have on children. By challenging discriminatory behaviour and promoting respect you are dealing with the immediate effects on children and improving their long-term outcomes.

Discrimination should always be challenged. If you ignore it, it could be assumed that you condone discriminatory language or behaviour. Consider how a child or their family might feel if they experience discrimination that is then ignored. They may feel that you share the view of the perpetrator or believe that the discriminatory treatment is normal practice. Even young children can be made to feel that they are in some way inferior. At the very least they will feel let down, but it is more likely that you will lose the respect of the child and their family.

It can be difficult to challenge discrimination, particularly if it is institutional. In this case you will need to raise it (or whistle blow) with a senior manager or Ofsted, the official body for inspecting and regulating settings. To be able to challenge discrimination it is essential for you to have a good understanding of legislation and the policy, procedures and practice in your own setting. If you feel confident that you know what good practice is, you will be able to deal more effectively with concerns about discrimination.

We must also be prepared to challenge our own prejudices, as these can lead to **labelling** or even to discriminatory practice. Prejudice can be overcome by becoming more aware and undertaking training to develop a greater understanding of diverse groups in society. Figure 10.3 shows a situation that you may well have to deal with. How would you respond?

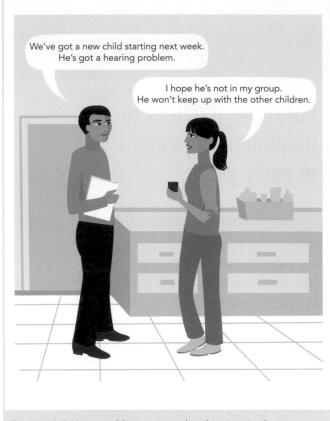

Figure 10.3 How would you respond in this situation?

Activity

It is important to develop assertiveness strategies, as they will give you the confidence to challenge discrimination.

Working in a small group, plan and act out discriminatory scenarios. In your group, take it in turns to practise your response using the three-part message below:

1 Say what has happened or what has been said that is discriminatory.

2 Say what effect this has on the individual, the group and others.

3 Suggest an alternative way to behave, or an anti-discriminatory strategy.

Key term

Labelling – a label or description (often negative) given to an individual or group because of a characteristic. It is often the result of prejudice.

Assessment practice 10.1

Claire works in a nursery class with children aged 3 to 4 years. She enjoys the work but has been concerned by the attitudes of another member of staff, Paula. Claire has noticed that Paula tends to have favourites – all girls. Paula often excludes boys from her activities, saying that they soon lose concentration or are too messy.

Yesterday, when Claire was in the staff room she overheard the manager telling Paula that a new child, from a traveller family, was about to start at the nursery. Later, Claire heard Paula say that the child was bound to have behaviour problems, adding that she didn't want to be the child's key worker as she was bound to be trouble.

1 Produce a leaflet that could be circulated among early years practitioners that includes:
   - an outline of current legislation that aims to counter discrimination and ensure equality
   - reasons why diversity should be valued in the setting.

2 Give reasons why Claire must challenge Paula's attitude towards groups and individual children in the setting.

3 In a small group, discuss and record your ideas about the reasons why equality is not being implemented in the setting. Share your ideas with the whole group.

B Understand inclusive practice in early years settings

What is inclusive practice?

Inclusive practice is about breaking down barriers that prevent participation. When discussing inclusive practice, practitioners sometimes think only of ways to include children with a disability or a special educational need. Removing the barriers for these children is essential, but you should think wider than that. Practitioners must recognise that each child is unique and place them at the centre of planning and delivering services. Children may feel excluded for many different reasons. It might be because of a disability but it could just as easily be because of their physical appearance, culture or social background.

Inclusive practice gives a setting a positive ethos. This is difficult to define, but you can recognise when children are playing purposefully and mixing happily with other children and adults. Every child feels valued and has a sense of belonging. There is recognition, acceptance and celebration of both differences and similarities. The resources, ranging from displays on the walls to the kitchen equipment in the home corner, will reflect the background and experience of a diverse community.

Inclusion is not about treating each child the same, but is about providing them with the same opportunities and access to high-quality care and education. Children may need additional support, adapted resources or activities to achieve their goals, but they should all have the same opportunity to enjoy life and achieve their potential.

In an inclusive setting, staff will share a common understanding of the values and principles of inclusion. Inclusive practice is also about ensuring the participation of everyone involved in the setting: staff, children and parents. There will be an atmosphere in which staff feel able to challenge practice and contribute to the development of policy. The views of children and parents will be listened to, and there will be a real opportunity for them to contribute to the development of services.

SHC 33, Assessment criterion 1.1; CYP 3.7, Assessment criteria 4.1 and 4.2; EYMP 4, Assessment criterion 3.1

1 Explain how equality, diversity, inclusion and participation lead to positive outcomes for children and young people.

2 Use examples from your own placement to support your understanding.

Research

Obtain the policies and procedures from your own setting that relate to inclusive practice and equal opportunity.

- Consider how these work for the benefit of children.
- Identify two ways in which you can improve your own practice.

The benefits of inclusive practice

Inclusive practice promotes a sense of belonging. Children who have a sense of self-worth have more confidence and feel more able to make choices. They develop a 'can do' attitude, are more motivated and are more likely to achieve their full potential.

Developing self-esteem and sense of identity

Research shows that a child's resilience and ability to cope with **transition** is greatly improved when they have good self-esteem.

Key term

Transitions – the changes that happen in all children's lives, such as starting school or personal changes such as family break-up.

Improving relationships between individuals and groups

Inclusive practice gives a positive message and develops an atmosphere of mutual respect between children, and between adults and children. Children will feel valued for who they are regardless of their background, culture, faith or individual needs. It gives them a feeling of well-being, which can impact on all areas of their development. Good social and emotional development is essential for mental health.

Improving outcomes

Putting the child at the centre of planning and delivery promotes positive attitudes to learning and cognitive development. This can have a long-term effect on a child's attainment and life chances. Children are more likely to develop and learn when practitioners focus on what they can do rather than their difficulties. Activities and resources that reflect children's backgrounds and experiences make learning more relevant and fun.

Integrated services

Inclusion is about breaking down barriers to learning and development. When services work closely together this is more likely to be achieved. Integrated services benefit children and their families as these lead to the early identification of their holistic needs. This enables targeted support to be put into place from different professionals or specialists.

Link

Go to Unit 13: Section C to find more information about multi-agency work.

Strategies for inclusive practice

The law requires all early years settings to have policies and procedures in place to provide a framework for inclusive practice. This must permeate all aspects of early years practice. Read the strategies below. Which have you noticed being used in your own setting?

Best practice checklist

Remember the following guidelines for best practice:

- Recognise and remove any barriers to accessing services or taking part in activities.
- Be a good role model – do not just pay 'lip service' to anti-discriminatory practice, but demonstrate it in everything you do.
- Know and understand the backgrounds, experience and individual needs of all children in your care.
- Appreciate, celebrate and promote the diversity and individuality of children and their families.
- Listen to and involve children and their families in the delivery of services, and respond to their concerns.
- Provide resources that reflect the diversity of children and families.
- Take time to reflect on your own attitudes and practice, and participate in relevant training.

Case study

Inclusive practice

Asma has just qualified as a childcare practitioner and started her new job in a nursery class attached to a primary school. Her manager, Steve, asked her to carry out an art and craft activity on her first morning that had already been planned for a group of six children aged 3 to 4 years. As it was Asma's first day she did not know the children well but did know that one of the children had recently moved to England from Poland and that her English was poor. The other children in the group were of either British or Pakistani origin. At lunchtime, Asma noticed that another child, Jack, had mobility problems, which affected his walking and fine motor control. When she asked Steve about this he said not to worry, as Jack could play with the construction blocks if he couldn't manage the activity.

1 What should Asma say to Steve?
2 What effect might it have on Jack if he cannot join in with the activity?
3 How can Asma ensure that all the children are included?
4 Asma will need to plan her own art and craft activity in future. What should she take into account to ensure that the activity is inclusive?

How do you support children to build and maintain friendships?

Supporting children to develop positive attitudes

Adults have an important role to play in developing positive attitudes and mutual respect between children, and between children and adults. Positive attitudes can be promoted informally through everyday contact with children or formally through curriculum activities. Your own attitudes and actions will provide a model for children, so it is important that you demonstrate consideration and fairness in all your interactions. Even ordinary activities such as the way you greet children and families will affect their attitudes towards others.

The way you greet children and families will send an important message.

The Early Years Foundation Stage Framework (EYFS) and National Curriculum include aspects that actively promote positive attitudes. Personal, social and emotional development is one of the three prime areas of learning in the EYFS. The goals that children aged 0 to 5 years work towards in this area of learning are:

- developing self-confidence and awareness
- managing their feelings and behaviour
- making relationships.

Supporting children to achieve these goals will have an impact on their self-image. It will also help them to develop respect for other children and adults. From the age of 5 years Personal, Social and Health Education (PSHE) forms part of the National Curriculum. This programme has a particular focus on rights and responsibilities and helps to prepare children for living in a diverse society. More information on curriculum content can be found at the Department for Education website. You can access this website by going to www.pearsonhotlinks.co.uk

Positive attitudes through everyday activities

Helping children to form positive images of others is an important part of the adults' role. There are many fun ways to do this:

- **Books, stories and story telling** – providing books that reflect diversity in society, and include stories featuring children who are disabled or from minority cultural groups as the main characters; books showing women and men in 'non-stereotypical' roles; stories from around the world and stories in the children's home language.
- **Music and movement** – introducing a wide range of songs, music and musical instruments from around the world (see Figure 10.4).

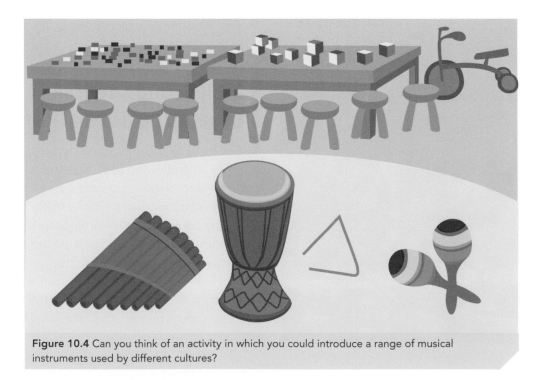

Figure 10.4 Can you think of an activity in which you could introduce a range of musical instruments used by different cultures?

- **Play/home corners** – ensuring that the diverse cultural groups are reflected in the resources provided – for example, packaging from a wide range of foods, cooking and serving utensils, dressing-up clothes and fabrics.
- **Cooking** – introducing recipes from a range of cultures – for example, making different types of bread or using a variety of fruit and vegetables.
- **Circle time** – sharing information and experiences, and discussing differences and similarities in a positive way.

Developing positive attitudes towards other children

Children must have their rights protected, but should also learn about their responsibilities towards others. From time to time children use inappropriate terminology, treat others differently or even shun them because they see them as 'different'. It is important to respond when this happens. Even young children understand when their actions are wrong,

particularly if you encourage them to empathise with the child who is affected. For example, 'You've made Cameron unhappy by saying he can't play with you', or 'We don't use that word in our nursery – it's unkind.'

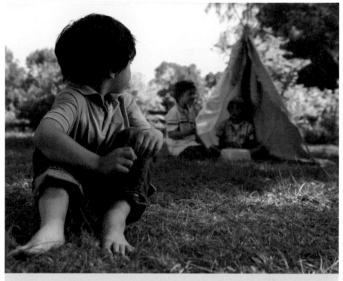

Why might children feel left out?

Assessment practice 10.2
3B.P4 | 3B.P5 | 3B.P6 | 3B.M2 | 3B.M3 | 3B.D1

You are planning to open a new private nursery, which will provide care and education for babies and young children.

Before you can gain accreditation you are required to show that the nursery will demonstrate inclusive practice.

Produce a report showing that you understand what is meant by inclusive practice and how it will be demonstrated in all aspects of nursery life. You should include:

- an introduction explaining the benefits of inclusive practice for children and families

- strategies you intend to use
- ways in which you and your staff will help children to value and respect others
- how you will ensure that practice is reviewed and the importance of this
- how the strategies you have identified will contribute to inclusive practice
- a statement that reflects on your own attitudes and practice and how this will contribute to the overall promotion of diversity, equality and inclusion in the nursery.

C Understand how children with additional needs may be supported in early years practice

In law, children with 'special educational needs' (SEN) are those with 'learning difficulties or disabilities that make it harder for them to learn or access education than most children of the same age'. There are many reasons why a child may have additional needs; for instance, a learning difficulty, physical disability, sensory impairment or behavioural difficulties. Legislation places a duty on early years settings and schools to provide for children with additional needs to enable them to reach their full potential. Frameworks give detailed guidance on how this should be achieved.

Legislation

Table 10.2 outlines legislation that is relevant to children with additional needs.

> **Link**
>
> Go to Unit 18 to find more information about additional needs.

Table 10.2 Legislation relevant to children with additional needs

Legislation	Purpose
Children Act 2004	Places a duty on children's services to work closely. It also introduces the five outcomes that all children's services must work towards. It provides a framework for information sharing and the early identification of children's needs.
Education Act 1996	Places a duty on local authorities to produce a policy to identify children with additional needs and to show how these needs will be met. The Act gives all children the right to access the National Curriculum and attend mainstream schools. It requires every local authority to carry out a formal assessment of children's holistic needs.
Special Educational Needs and Disability Act (SENDA) 2001	Strengthened the rights of children to be educated in mainstream schools. It makes it unlawful for educational providers to discriminate against learners with a special educational need or a disability. Reasonable adjustment must be made to the provision to ensure that children are not disadvantaged. Guidance in relation to the Act is provided by the SEN Code of Practice (see below).

> **Reflect**
>
> Remind yourself of the legislation covered earlier in this unit, because it also protects the rights of children with additional needs.

The SEN Code of Practice 2001

The SEN Code of Practice applies to all early years education settings and schools that receive government funding, social services departments and health services. It provides statutory guidance on meeting the requirements of legislation. The Code covers:

- children's rights to have their needs met
- the requirement that children's additional needs should, wherever possible, be met in mainstream early years settings or schools
- the need for early identification of additional needs
- procedures to put in place for assessment, support and review
- the requirement to appoint a Special Educational Needs Coordinator (SENCO)
- the principle that that the child must be placed at the centre of planning and review
- the rights of parents to participation
- the need for additional needs to be met through an integrated approach.

Link

Go to Unit 13: Section C to find more information about different models of multi-agency working.

Educational frameworks

Early years settings and schools must adopt a staged approach to providing support. When additional needs are identified, the setting will intervene, depending on the child's age, through Early Years Action or School Action.

Early Years Action/School Action

When an additional need has been identified, the setting will put support into place to meet the specific need of the child. An assessment will be made and support and resources will be provided by the setting. Targets will be identified and progress will be monitored and reviewed regularly.

Early Years Action Plus/School Action Plus

Children move to this stage of support when their needs cannot be fully met by the early years setting or school. At this stage, professionals from outside agencies will become involved.

Where children do not make satisfactory progress, a statutory assessment will be recommended, which

may lead to a Statement of Educational Needs. For children with complex needs, an assessment may happen even though they have not progressed through the stages.

Statutory assessment

A statutory assessment will be carried out where there is concern about a child's well-being, learning or development. It will take into account the whole child – their social, emotional, cognitive and physical needs. This will require a multi-agency approach and may involve, for instance, a speech and language therapist, health visitor or behavioural specialist. It will also involve the child and their parent(s). Following the review, intervention strategies will be put in place to support the child to meet their targets. The assessment may result in a Statement of Special Educational Needs.

Monitoring and review

At each stage a child's progress is monitored and a review meeting will be held that is attended by all those involved: the child, parents, practitioners and specialists. Following the review a decision will be made. If the child has met or even exceeded their targets they may remain on that stage or revert back to the previous stage. Where the child's progress is not satisfactory they will move to the next stage of the process.

Statement of Special Educational Needs

This is a formal statement, which identifies the child's educational and other needs. It states what their needs are and the support that must be put into place to meet those needs. It is reviewed annually. A statement does not always follow a statutory assessment. It is only put into place when the early years setting or school is not able to provide for the child's needs.

EYFS and Key Stage 1 curriculum

The EYFS and the National Curriculum give clear guidance on an inclusive approach to learning and assessment.

The EYFS framework advises that early years settings must meet the needs of all children in relation to equality, stating that 'providers must have and implement a policy, and procedures, to promote equality of opportunity for children in their care, including support for children with special educational needs or disabilities'.

The National Curriculum Inclusion Statement outlines the duty of schools to implement a whole-school approach to both the national and wider curriculum by:

- providing a curriculum that ensures active participation and achievement of all learners
- recognising learners' entitlement to high-quality learning experiences
- meeting the needs and interests of all learners
- recognising and overcoming potential barriers to learning and assessment.

Medical and social models of disability

Medical model

The medical model of disability is based on an assumption that it is the child that has the problem. The child is, therefore, expected to adapt to the environment and the way it is organised. This model promotes an atmosphere of **dependency**, as the opportunity for children to take part and make choices is reduced. It means that children may have separate services or activities provided for them. This segregates them from other children. An inclusive curriculum would not be consistent with this model.

Social model

The social model of disability starts from the assumption that there are barriers within each environment that can prevent children from taking part. Early assessment will help practitioners to recognise and remove these barriers. Children will then be able to access services and take part in all activities. In this model diversity is celebrated, with each child being valued for who they are. This empowers children and promotes high self-esteem. Their strengths are recognised before any disability. Inclusive practice is based on the social model of disability.

Figure 10.5 shows the thoughts of two practitioners while supervising an outdoor activity.

Meeting children's additional needs

When children have additional needs it is important to break down barriers so that all children can take part in activities. You can do this by providing additional support, by adapting the environment or by adapting the activities. It is important that you first identify the child's difficulty and what is causing a barrier to their participation.

Additional support

Support is essential for children who have learning and/or physical difficulties. It is important to know the child and what they are capable of so that you do not do something that the child could do for themselves. Support might be, for example, simplifying the teacher/tutor's instructions or perhaps using **Makaton** symbols to help children to understand. For many children it may simply be a case of helping them to concentrate and giving praise and encouragement.

> **Key terms**
>
> **Dependency** – having to rely on others and lacking independence.
>
> **Makaton** – a system where signs are used to help children with specific difficulties understand the spoken word.

Adapting the environment

The environment may provide a barrier to participation. It could just be the layout that makes movement around the room difficult, for example. For children with a visual impairment it is important to consider the lighting in the room. For children with a hearing impairment, smaller, quieter areas would reduce distractions. Children with more complex needs may need specialist rooms with soft play or sensory equipment.

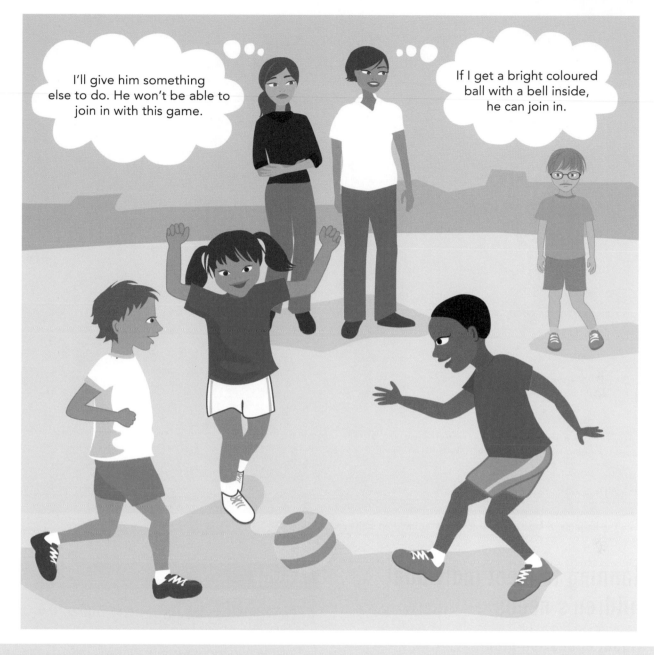

Figure 10.5 Which of these adults is reflecting the social model of disability in their thoughts about the boy who is not joining in with the activity?

Resources and activities

Activities can be adapted in various ways. Timings should be adjusted, for example, for children with concentration difficulties. Working in smaller groups would benefit a child with learning or communication difficulties. Often the resources themselves need to be adapted. Children with physical difficulties may need larger equipment that can be more easily held, such as large, soft balls or chunky paintbrushes.

What are the benefits of multi-sensory activities for children with complex needs?

Planning to meet individual children's needs

Individual education plan

An individual education plan (IEP) will be produced at each stage of support. This does not include information about all the care and education children will receive. An IEP only includes support that is 'additional' or 'different' from that provided for other children of the same age. IEPs include the specific targets (usually three or four) and the strategies that will be used to achieve these. The practitioners involved, such as the teacher/tutor, SENCO, SEN support assistant and specialists, will contribute to the planning and the review. Reviews should be carried out at least once a term. Figure 10.6 shows part of an IEP.

Activity

The example of the IEP used in Figure 10.6 shows one of the targets planned for James.

1 Write two more targets that will help James to meet his expected stage of development.

2 Suggest support strategies for each target.

3 Identify the measure of success – that is, how practitioners will know if James has met each target.

SEN STAGE: EARLY YEARS ACTION [x] EARLY YEARS PLUS [ ]			

NAME: James Cooper   **D.O.B:** 07.03.08   **DATE:** 28.09.12   **REVIEW:** 14.12.12

People involved: E. Cooper (mother), P. Kaur (SENCO), M. Taylor (teacher), L. Page (support assistant)

Child's strengths and needs: James is an active child. He enjoys outdoor play and has good coordination and balance. James finds it difficult to concentrate and express himself. James can recognise colours but cannot name them.

Targets	Strategies/support	Measure of success	Outcome
1. To be able to name primary colours	James will take part in small group and one-to-one activities each day, e.g. sorting cars or painting and collage.	James will be able to identify and name red, blue, yellow and green objects correctly on three occasions.	

Figure 10.6 Part of an IEP

The Special Educational Needs Coordinator (SENCO)

The role of the SENCO

Each early years education setting and school must identify a member of staff as the Special Educational Needs Coordinator (SENCO). Figure 10.7 outlines the SENCO's role.

Working in partnership with parents

Local authorities must have provision for Parent Partnerships, which provide information, advice and guidance about provision for children with additional needs, including practical support. These may be delivered by them or by other agencies such as charities.

Figure 10.7 The SENCO's role

The involvement of parents is important at all stages. Early years settings and schools have a duty to tell parents if they need to make provision for a child's additional needs. After all, the parents are the ones who best know the strengths and needs of their child. It is important that professionals draw on this knowledge when they review a child's needs or plan for support. When parents are partners with the setting the support given will be more effective and children will be more likely to meet the planned targets. Working closely with parents will help to prevent any difficulties arising between professionals and parents. Where disagreements do occur there must be resolution services available.

Parents often find dealing with professionals difficult. The language and ways of working are likely to be unfamiliar to them. It is important that parents are given detailed information in plain language and in a format that is easy to understand, including, where appropriate, in the parent's home language. Parents may have additional needs themselves, which must be considered, for instance, by providing information that is recorded for a parent with a visual impairment. Some parents may need the help of an interpreter or **advocate** during meetings.

Parents have a responsibility too. They must keep early years settings or schools informed of concerns about their child. They must also keep to any agreements they have with the setting regarding their own role in providing support.

Key term

Advocate – someone who speaks on behalf of another to represent their views.

Figure 10.8 shows the professionals who may be called on to provide help or specialist expertise.

Portfolio building activity   CYPW

CYP 3.7, Assessment criterion 3.7

Find out about services that are available to support children.

Select three roles from those identified and find out more about the work that these practitioners do.

How can parents be encouraged to become more involved in their child's learning and development?

Speech and language therapists

Speech and language therapists assess and put into place support programmes for children who have speech and language problems, including problems with swallowing. Therapy is usually given in blocks of around six sessions, after which parents and settings will be given advice and exercises to carry out with the children. They will then be called back after a period of time for a follow up.

Educational psychologists

Educational psychologists assess children and plan for their support when they have learning and development difficulties that affect their learning. They will visit the setting several times a year to assess children that the SENCO has concerns about. They will often speak to parents to discuss how to best work with the setting to meet the child's needs moving forward.

Visual support services

This service provides help, advice and support for children with visual difficulties and who are blind. They help children to care for spectacles.

Advocates

Advocates speak on behalf of the child or their parent(s) to represent their views. An advocate helps the child and family to understand issues and make their own decisions.

Portage workers

Portage workers provide a home-visiting service for preschool children with additional needs. They provide support for the children and their families. They may come into the setting to discuss children with additional needs.

Professionals who may be called on to offer their expertise

Behaviour support workers

Behaviour support workers provide support for children whose behaviour is affecting their learning and development. They help settings to develop strategies for managing unwanted behaviour.

Health visitors

Health visitors work in the community to provide health advice for children under 5 years and their families. They may come into the setting at regular intervals to advise staff and work with them to support families.

Hearing support services

This service provides help and advice to support children with hearing impairment to develop communication skills. They help children to care for hearing aids, cochlea implants and radio aids.

Learning support assistants

Learning support assistants work alongside a teacher to support individual children or groups of children with their learning.

Paediatricians

Paediatricians are doctors who specialise in the health and care of children and young people.

Occupational therapist

Occupational therapists work with children who have difficulty with their fine motor skills. The children will be given a block of therapy and then parents (and sometimes the setting) will be given some additional exercises for the children to work on.

Physiotherapists

Physiotherapists assess and support children who have mobility problems. Their support may include massages, therapeutic exercises and hydrotherapy. Children will often need to carry out physical exercises following therapy and depending on your role in the setting, you may be asked to support children doing these exercises.

Figure 10.8 Professionals who may provide additional help for children and their families

Additional help or specialist expertise

Earlier in this section, you read that when children progress to Early Years Action Plus or School Action Plus, or have a Statement of Special Educational Needs, it is because they need additional help or the expertise of a specialist to help them to reach planned targets. Specialists provide support for the child but to do this effectively they must work closely with the child's family and other specialists or professionals such as early years practitioners and teachers.

In some instances support will be in the form of advice, for example, from a behavioural specialist who does not work directly with the child but gives advice on strategies to use. Some specialists, such as physiotherapists, may show practitioners how to help children with exercises to use between their visits.

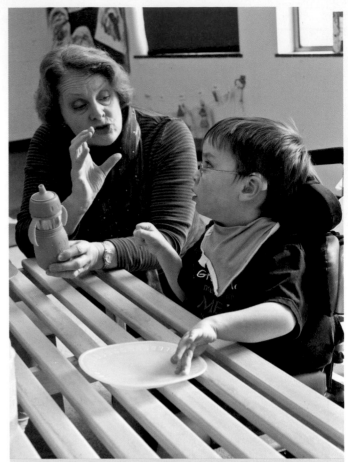

How is this adult supporting the child in this nursery?

Assessment practice 10.3   3C.P7 | 3C.P8 | 3C.P9   3C.M4 | 3C.D2

You work in a primary school supporting children in the reception class and at Key Stage 1.
You have been asked to produce information for parents on ways that the school supports children with additional needs.

Produce a presentation that gives information on:

- the support that is available for children with additional needs, referring to the framework and requirements
- how the models of disability influence practice in the school
- the role of the SENCO
- the ways in which children with additional needs will be supported
- the role of the adult in planning for children with additional needs.

Portfolio building activity   CYPW

CYP 3.1, Assessment criterion 3.4
Extend your presentation to explain how different interventions can help to provide positive outcomes for children.

Further reading and resources

Hodgman, L. (2011) *Enabling Environments in the Early Years: Making provision for high quality and challenging learning experiences in early years settings*, Salisbury: Practical Pre-School Books.

Websites
BBC Religion: www.bbc.co.uk/religion
Information about different religions

The Department for Education:
www.education.gov.uk
Current information on the EYFS, National Curriculum and SEN Code of Practice

Equality and Human Rights Commission:
www.equalityhumanrights.com
Information about protecting and enforcing human rights

Ready for work?

Sarah Adams Nursery manager

I manage an 88-place nursery setting for children aged 0 to 5 years. I have worked with children for 16 years, of which seven have been at management level.

As a setting we work towards the elimination of any form of discrimination and promote equality of opportunity throughout. We have an 'Equality of opportunity policy (valuing diversity and promoting equality)'. Our policy states: 'Our setting will ensure that our service is fully inclusive to meet the needs of all children and their family.' The policy ensures that children within the setting feel secure, safe, valued and included to encourage self-confidence and a positive approach to learning.

Staff are recruited based on their knowledge, understanding and occupational skills. Staff, learners and volunteers are expected to be positive role models for children, and display and promote tolerant and respectful behaviour, language and attitudes. Staff ensure that displays and activities show and reflect a positive image of the world in which we live.

Play and activities are planned to ensure that all children are included and supported. Resources are age- and ability-appropriate and reflect differing lifestyles in society. Our environment supports children to develop a positive outlook towards others, whom they may see as different from themselves.

Skills for practice

Practise things that make children and their families feel welcome and included.

- Learn key words in the child's first language such as greetings, 'please' and 'thank you'.

- Find out how to address parents. If their names are unfamiliar, practise how to say them so that you can pronounce them correctly when you greet the parents.

- Find out about children's interests and experiences, and use this information in your interactions with them.

Introduction

Learning to think about and question the effectiveness of your work with children is now considered an important part of being a professional. Reviewing your strengths and weaknesses and checking that your knowledge is up to date help to ensure that you give children the best start possible. This unit is about knowing how to recognise your strengths and weaknesses and how to take steps to improve your practice, especially in relation to the area of communication and language development, which in turn supports children's cognitive development, their behaviour and their emotional and social development.

Assessment: You will be assessed by an Edexcel-set assignment.

Learning aims

In this unit you will:

A understand the purpose of reflective practice in relation to work with children

B be able to reflect on own early years practice with children aged birth up to 8 years in relation to promoting children's communication and language

C understand how to develop own early years practice with children aged birth up to 8 years to promote children's communication and language through planning.

When I first started working with children, I thought this reflective practice stuff was a waste of time. Now I can see that by talking about the way we work with other team members, we can make a real difference to the way we work with children.

Anna, *room leader in a day-care setting*

Reflecting on Own Early Years Practice

11

BTEC Assessment Zone

This table shows what you must do in order to achieve a **Pass**, **Merit** or **Distinction** grade, and where you can find activities to help you.

Assessment criteria		
Pass	**Merit**	**Distinction**
Learning aim A: Understand the purpose of reflective practice in relation to work with children		
3A.P1 Explain the role of reflective practice in work with children in early years settings. **Assessment practice 11.1**	**3A.M1** Assess how reflective practice contributes to work with children in early years settings. **Assessment practice 11.1**	**3A.D1** Evaluate the impact of reflective practice in improving communication and language in children. **Assessment practice 11.1**
Learning aim B: Be able to reflect on own early years practice with children aged birth up to 8 years in relation to promoting children's communication and language		
3B.P2 I&CT English Select evidence about own practice with children aged birth up to 8 years to promote their communication and language. **Assessment practice 11.2** **3B.P3 I&CT** Explain personal factors that affect own practice in promoting children's communication and language. **Assessment practice 11.2**	**3B.M2** Compare own practice with current best practice in promoting children's communication and language development with children aged birth up to 8 years using evidence. **Assessment practice 11.2**	**3B.D2** Assess effectiveness of own practice, recommending areas for development. **Assessment practice 11.2**
Learning aim C: Understand how to develop own early years practice with children aged birth up to 8 years to promote children's communication and language through planning		
3C.P4 I&CT Maths Create appropriate plans to develop own practice with children aged birth up to 8 years to promote communication and language. **Assessment practice 11.2**	**3C.M3 Maths** Analyse the value of planning to develop own practice in promoting children's communication and language. **Assessment practice 11.2**	**3C.D3 Maths** Evaluate the contribution of continuous reflection in the development of own practice in promoting children's communication and language. **Assessment practice 11.2**

English   English Functional Skills signposting

I&CT   Information and Communication Technology skills signposting

Maths   Mathematics Functional Skills signposting

How you will be assessed

This unit will be assessed by an assignment that is set by Edexcel. It will be marked internally by your teacher/tutor and verified by an Edexcel Standards Verifier. Throughout this unit you will find assessment practice activities that will help you work towards your assessment. Completing these activities will not mean that you have achieved a particular grade, but you will have carried out useful research or preparation that will be relevant when it comes to your final assignment.

Getting started

What do you think your strengths and weaknesses are when working with children? How good are you at encouraging children's speech and language? When you have finished this unit, see whether you feel your answers to these questions are still an accurate reflection of your practice.

A Understand the purpose of reflective practice in relation to work with children

All adults working with babies and children are encouraged to think about the way they work. This is known as **reflective practice** and it is considered an essential way of improving practice. In this section we will look at how reflective practice can help you to become a more effective practitioner.

The term 'reflective practice' is therefore used to describe the process by which practitioners become aware of their limitations and gaps in their knowledge as well as their strengths and good qualities. Reflective practice should be used in all areas of your professional work with children and their families. This is shown in Figure 11.1.

What is meant by reflective practice?

The idea of reflective practice is relatively new to early years. It is a way of working that can improve practice considerably. For years it has been known that the quality of our work has a huge impact on children and their families, but finding ways of developing and maintaining this quality was not easy. Inspections, reports by line managers and ongoing staff training have all been tried. Today, it is realised that the best person to help you work effectively with children is yourself.

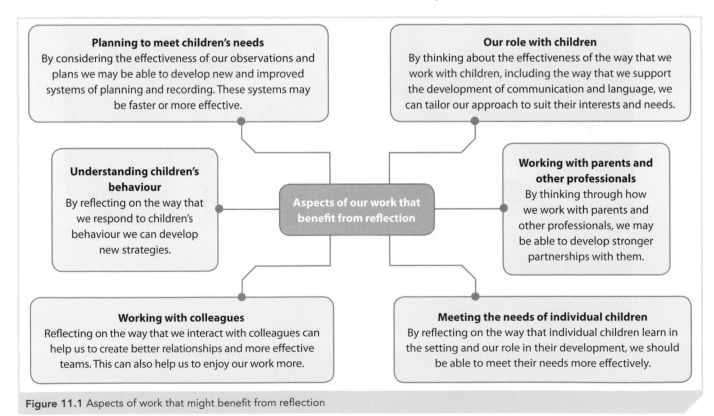

Planning to meet children's needs
By considering the effectiveness of our observations and plans we may be able to develop new and improved systems of planning and recording. These systems may be faster or more effective.

Our role with children
By thinking about the effectiveness of the way that we work with children, including the way that we support the development of communication and language, we can tailor our approach to suit their interests and needs.

Understanding children's behaviour
By reflecting on the way that we respond to children's behaviour we can develop new strategies.

Aspects of our work that benefit from reflection

Working with parents and other professionals
By thinking through how we work with parents and other professionals, we may be able to develop stronger partnerships with them.

Working with colleagues
Reflecting on the way that we interact with colleagues can help us to create better relationships and more effective teams. This can also help us to enjoy our work more.

Meeting the needs of individual children
By reflecting on the way that individual children learn in the setting and our role in their development, we should be able to meet their needs more effectively.

Figure 11.1 Aspects of work that might benefit from reflection

Link

Go to Section B in this unit to find more information about gaining feedback from parents, colleagues and children.

A continuous cycle

There is a process involved in reflective practice. It can be seen as a cycle, as it is continuous and never-ending. Figure 11.2 shows this continuous cycle. Interestingly, you may find that experienced practitioners often say that they are still learning. This is because every child is different, every family is different and there are often changes to resources, the curriculum and approaches to early education. This all feeds into your practice with children. Although this unit focuses on communication and language, reflective practice covers every aspect of your work, including your relationships with parents, colleagues and other professionals.

Figure 11.2 The continuous cycle of reflective practice

Monitoring

This is about being aware of what you are doing when you are with children. You may look at children's reactions or consider how children are using equipment or enjoying an activity. Monitoring is also about being aware of children's outcomes and progress, then relating this to your practices and those in the setting. As well as self-monitoring, you can also gain feedback from a range of sources such as parents, colleagues and children.

Evaluation

As you monitor and gain information from a wide range of sources, you need to evaluate its significance and then consider whether any aspect of your practice requires changing.

Revising own practices

As a result of ongoing evaluation, experienced practitioners will often try out new ideas, change their practices or change the routine or equipment of the setting. In some cases, you will need to change your own behaviours or style of working with children.

The importance of reflective practice

There are many reasons why reflective practice is important in the workplace. If you are a reflective practioner, not only will you improve outcomes for the children you work with, but you will also develop your own skills and career.

Early learning experiences for children

Reflection can be used to support your personal and professional development. However, the most important reason for using reflection is to improve the quality of experiences for children. We know that children who have sensitive and reflective adults with them are more likely to have better early learning experiences. These adults are likely to be more skilful at forming relationships, and at noticing and responding to children's development and so supporting their overall development.

The type and range of early learning experiences planned for children are particularly important, and these should be accompanied by good opportunities for communication and language development.

Personal and professional development

When you first begin working with children, you will face a steep learning curve. You will need to adjust to working in a new environment as well as learning how to use the skills and knowledge that you acquired in your training. Being able to be a reflective practitioner and using the process that we will look at in the later sections will help you become more confident and, of course, competent.

Reflection will also help you to keep developing, as you will start to think about what new skills and areas of knowledge you would like to develop further. You may become interested in working with children who have additional needs or you may want to learn more about working with babies, for example.

Continuous quality improvement

While the basic needs of children have not changed for centuries, society and the perception of childhood are constantly changing. In addition, new developments from research into children's learning have also influenced the curricula and expectations of work with children. There are also changes to the legislation in areas such as health and safety, employment and the rights of children. It is therefore important that settings and individual practitioners

keep abreast of developments and are ready to reflect on, change and improve their practice. This needs to be a continuous process, which is planned and organised.

Shared understanding

In settings where reflection is built into the routine of the day, a more dynamic and interesting work environment is created. Practitioners can discuss different options, approaches and ideas for working with children. This professional discussion can support a team's development, but also the individual development of team members. The impact on practices within the setting is usually very positive and a culture of open discussion and readiness to try out new ideas will emerge.

The importance of continuous reflection

Reflection is something that you should be doing all the time in order to carry on building your strengths and any ideas that have come about from your original reflections. Reflection is also important to ensure that changes in your practice are working as you had hoped.

This team is reflecting on the quality of the toys in the setting.

This is particularly important because sometimes you may make changes that work well with a particular group of children or a specific child, but you may need to revise these changes at a later stage. For example, although children's interest levels may increase when you first introduce a new activity or resource, they are likely to decrease once children have become accustomed to them. Through the process of observation, reflection and monitoring, you can create a more dynamic environment that is keenly matched to children's interests and levels of development.

Assessment practice 11.1   3A.P1 | 3A.M1 | 3A.D1

You have been asked to give a presentation to group of Turkish early years educators who are on an exchange visit. They are interested in finding out about the concept of reflective practice. To help the translator, you will also need to prepare detailed notes in advance of the presentation.

Your notes and presentation should include:

- an explanation of what is meant by the term 'reflective practice'
- why reflection is important in early years settings
- to what extent reflective practice might improve outcomes for children.

B Be able to reflect on own early years practice with children aged birth up to 8 years in relation to promoting children's communication and language

You will need to be able to use the skills of reflection in all aspects of your work with children and families. In this section, we focus on how this process might be applied specifically to promoting children's communication and language.

Link

Go to Unit 6 in Student Book 1 to find more information about promoting speech and language.

Current best practice

One starting point when reflecting on practice is to be aware of what constitutes best practice. In Student Book 1, you looked at ways to promote children's speech and language – including the importance of building positive relationships with children, the notion of playfulness and play opportunities. You will need to read this again, as well as information from other sources such as I CAN, a charity that specialises in promoting children's communication, so that you are familiar with the latest thoughts about what constitutes best practice in relation to promoting children's communication and language. You can access the website for I CAN by going to www.pearsonhotlinks.co.uk and searching for this title.

Information about promoting communication and language

In order to find out about best practice and how it can be applied to your own work and setting, you will need to find information, ideally from a range of sources. Examples are shown in Figure 11.3.

Reading articles and books

Articles and books can provide you with new information or food for thought for new activities. Magazines and professional journals can also make you aware of new developments within the sector, so it is a good idea to find the time to look through them.

Figure 11.3 Where to find information to support practice

Diagram: "Where to get the support you need to help you change your practice" connects to:
- Relevant websites
- Further training
- Consultation with your supervisor/line manager
- Consultation with your tutor/teacher

Research

Find out the titles of three magazines or journals that are published for the early years sector. Which ones does your setting subscribe to? Are any available in your local library?

Meeting other professionals

Many early years teams organise 'cluster groups', which enable practitioners from a particular area to meet up. Meeting other professionals in this way can help you to explore different ideas and reflect on your practice. Sometimes other professionals will tell you about how they have brought in a new system or piece of equipment to their setting, and their experiences can help you to explore your own ideas.

Research

Find out if there are any professional networks in your area. Contact your early years team, education department or a national organisation such as the National Childminding Association, or Early Education, a charitable organisation that supports families and the professional development of people working in early childhood education.

Attending training

Training courses can provide you with new ideas and thoughts about practice. Many settings will organise their own internal training sessions, either by closing for a day or as part of ongoing staff meetings. In addition, most early years advisory teams provide training courses, as do many national organisations such as Early Education. It is important to attend training in areas of your work that you feel strong in as well as those where you know your knowledge needs to be updated. This is because it is easy to become so comfortable with one way of working that you overlook other possibilities.

It is useful to write up your notes and thoughts following a training event. You can then look back at your notes and share them with colleagues.

Shadowing others

Sometimes you can reflect on the way in which you work, by noticing how other people handle situations, plan activities and relate to children. The term 'shadowing' is used to describe observing what others are doing in order to learn. Looking at how others work should not be about comparison, or it can become too negative. It is about reflecting on others' and your own strengths. This can be done in your own setting with experienced colleagues or those who have particular specialisms or interests. It can be helpful, after watching others, to take the time to sit with them and talk about what you have seen. This will help you understand the reasons behind their actions and also learn any tips from them.

This adult is observing a colleague playing with a child

Visiting other settings

It is also useful to watch others who are working in a similar setting in order to gain a different perspective and learn about their approaches. When visiting other settings, it is important to be respectful and polite even if you are unsure of their way of working. Interestingly, most people who visit other settings find that they come away with new thoughts or ideas.

Case study

Improving practice by visiting other settings

Joachim works at a day-care nursery but is spending the morning in a local preschool. He is particularly keen to find out more about how the preschool encourages children's communication and language development. He has been invited to the preschool as a result of making contact with the supervisor during a local network meeting. During the morning, he picks up many ideas and is interested in the different approaches that are being taken to support children who have English as an additional language. He also likes the way that the key persons spend set times with their key children. The staff are very friendly and quite open. Next week the supervisor of the preschool is due to visit his nursery.

1 Why is it important for Joachim to have an open mind during the visit?

2 How will Joachim benefit from seeing another early years setting in action?

3 How will the children in Joachim's nursery benefit from his visit to another setting?

Gathering information to reflect on your own practice

As part of the reflection process, you will need to think about what you are currently doing and how effective this is. This requires you to gather information about your own practice from many different sources, so you can get an overview. You need to do this in a systematic way, which may include keeping notes and making sure that those providing information know what you wish them to focus on. The information might include feedback from colleagues, parents and children.

Sources of information

There are plenty of different sources of information about your own practice.

Observation by others

Being observed by others, such as colleagues, teachers/tutors or inspectors may seem scary, but it can provide a valuable source of information. You may also find that your line manager carries out observations as part of the quality assurance process within your setting. Gathering information from others who have seen you in action is helpful because they may notice habits that you have acquired, such as saying 'okay' at the end of a sentence or not giving children sufficient time to respond. If you are being observed by colleagues, you may wish to talk to them about what you would like them to focus on. This might include your posture, tone or eye contact.

Feedback from colleagues

Listening to others can provide you with vital information that will help you to reflect on your practice. Feedback works best if you trust the people giving it and if they feel that they can give you an honest point of view. Listening to feedback carefully and avoiding being defensive is a skill in itself. It is easy to defend the reasons why you do things, but the key is to remember that the focus is on moving on and improving performance.

Feedback from children

You can gain feedback from children of all ages by simply noting down their reactions to what you do and by noticing what seems to engage them. Toddlers and older children can also tell you about activities that they enjoy and you can use photos to help them remember things that they have done with you.

Feedback from parents

You can ask for feedback from parents. Parents may notice how their child's speech and language has developed and which activities or ways of working seem to have been effective.

Assessment of children's outcomes

By tracking children's progress, you can consider whether your practices are effective. If there are several children that you have responsibility for who are not making the expected progress, you may need to consider whether you need to improve opportunities for speech and language within the setting.

A good way to check whether children are making progress is to carry out sound recordings, as you can listen to these each month and look for progress.

Link

Go to Unit 9: Section B to find more information about making sound recordings.

Evaluating your own practice

There are many skills you need to evaluate your own practice, but one of the most important is the ability to be objective and open-minded. If you close your mind to any information that you have gained, you will not be able to make progress. However, you also need to avoid being too self-critical and negative as this can sap your confidence. The key when evaluating your own practice is always to bear in mind that the aim of reflection is to move forward.

Factors that might affect your own practice

As part of your reflection process, you need to understand factors that might be affecting your practice. This is important, as sometimes these can lead you to be defensive about your practice, or over-critical.

Experiences

Your own experiences will affect your practice. Firstly, what you have seen on placement or in your working life will be a major influence. This is one reason why it is a good idea to visit a range of settings so that you can see different approaches. In addition, past experiences of being criticised or being given feedback may also determine your immediate reactions.

Case study

Evaluating practice

Kay has been working with toddlers for a year. She recently attended a course about working with 2-year-olds. She realised that she had not been spending sufficient time talking to the children and that she had not been monitoring their language. At the start of the training day, she was sure that she would not learn anything new and was cross that she had to get up earlier than usual to attend.

After the training day, she returned to work upset and demotivated. Her manager noticed the change in her attitude and Kay told her that she was feeling useless and was considering resigning. Her manager explained that working with children was a learning process. Together they discussed what elements of the course could be implemented immediately and they agreed to talk about Kay's progress after a week or so.

1 How might reflection help Kay improve her practice?

2 Why might Kay's new knowledge improve the quality of outcomes for the children?

3 Why is it important for Kay to be supported by her manager?

Values

Your own values and beliefs about childhood and how children should behave will affect your practice. Interestingly, this often shows in the way that you manage children's behaviour. If you are aware of your own underlying values, you may find it easier to be open-minded.

Own education

Some people's own education may influence the way that they work with children. A good example of this is play-based education. This is now the approach taken in all of the home countries' curricula. If your own education was more formal, it may be that your tendency is to intervene or try to structure play unnecessarily. Understanding how you were educated and comparing it to the current ways of working would be a good starting point.

These children are being taught formally. If you experienced this type of education, how might it affect your own practice?

Theory into practice

Look at the following questions. Use them to evaluate your current knowledge and practice in promoting children's communication and language. For each question, provide an answer and work out how you know this.

Knowledge

- Do you know how you would support a child who was learning more than one language?
- What would you do to support a child who had a stammer?
- How many Makaton signs do you know?
- What are the signs that a child has glue ear?
- At what age would you expect a child to be joining two words?
- What is the difference between expressive and receptive language?

Relationships

- How strong are your relationships with each of the children that you work with?
- Are there any children who interact less with you than others do? Why might this be?
- How do children respond to you?

- What is your tone of voice like when you talk to children (warm, clear)?
- Do you give children sufficient time to respond?
- Do you know how to acknowledge children's vocalisations?
- Do you make eye contact with children in ways that show interest and support?

Play opportunities

- What type of play opportunities do you plan to support communication and language?
- How do children engage with these opportunities?
- What levels of interaction are achieved during these activities?
- What is your average length of interaction with individual children?

Assessment

- How knowledgeable are you about usual developmental stages in speech and language?
- How do you know that children are making progress with their speech and language?

C Understand how to develop own early years practice with children aged birth up to 8 years to promote children's communication and language through planning

You have seen ways in which you might be able to consider and evaluate your practice. The next step is to change your practice. In this section we look at where to gain support and how to create a plan to support your progress.

Where to get support

It can be hard to change practice alone. Most people benefit from having input, encouragement and also further feedback. There are many ways of gaining support, as Figure 11.4 shows.

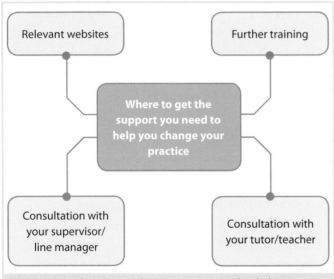

Figure 11.4 Where to get the support you need to help you change your practice

Training

You might be able to gain information that will help you to develop your practice by taking further training. You may go on a short course organised by your local early years team, college or national organisation. You may also decide to take a course of further study resulting in a qualification. This may be helpful in progressing your career or moving into another area.

Websites

Websites and social media can give you support, but you must be aware of confidentiality issues and also your setting's policy in relation to social media. This means that you may not be able to share everything that you are doing on a website. On the other hand, you may find suggestions for practice and information about what others have tried.

Teachers/tutors

While you are studying, your teacher/tutor will be a good source of support. They may observe you as you work and give you feedback. They may also help you to draw up an action plan and suggest ways of developing your practice a step at a time.

Supervisors

Your line manager or supervisor may be a good source of support. They may be very experienced and able to give you suggestions for how to put your ideas into practice. They may also be able to arrange further training for you or put you in contact with other practitioners.

How to create an action plan

When you have decided on an area of practice that needs to be developed, the next step is to create an action plan. This is important because the process of drawing up a plan can help you to focus your ideas and thoughts. It also provides a framework within which you can monitor and review your progress. Many people will draw up an action plan alongside a manager, teacher/tutor or someone they trust within the setting.

Creating an action plan

There are five simple steps to take when drawing up an action plan.

1 Decide in detail about what you wish to change or develop. Base this on your evaluation. These will become your goals.

2 Break down each of your goals into smaller tasks and think about what you will need to do complete each task. (If you have many goals and therefore many tasks, you may create an action plan for each goal.)

3 For each task, set yourself a target for when you hope to complete it.

4 Write down a date or dates when the plan will be reviewed to check on progress.

5 Provide a timescale by which all of the tasks will be completed and the goals achieved.

SMART targets

The acronym 'SMART' is often used when creating plans. The aim of SMART goals or targets is to help people focus clearly on what they want to achieve and avoid situations where goals are unrealistic. SMART stands for:

S = Specific

M = Measurable

A = Achievable

R = Realistic

T = Time bound

Specific

Try to make sure in your planning that you have thought clearly about what you need to learn, experience or develop. Phrases such as 'become better at talking to children' are too vague, but 'making eye contact and getting down to a child's level' would be better.

Measurable

Consider how you will know whether you have achieved this part of your plan. You may for example want an individual child to approach and interact with you more frequently. You could measure how often this happens now and then set a target, such as at least five times during the day. Or you may want

to support a child who uses Makaton, but not know many signs yourself. Your target might be to learn 50 signs.

Achievable

When thinking about your plan, make sure that it is possible to complete each target.

Realistic

There is always a danger of being over-enthusiastic and optimistic at the start of any project. Think about how you normally cope and check that your plan will meet your needs and suit the way in which you learn and work.

Time bound

Thinking about how long each part of the plan will take is essential. Many people need a set start and end time to help them work effectively. Working out a realistic timescale will help you remain motivated.

Deciding on priorities

Most people will find that their action plan contains many tasks and sometimes several goals. It will therefore be important to prioritise what needs doing first. Sometimes this is quite easy, because certain tasks or goals obviously come before others. For example, you may need to gain knowledge before you can plan your activity. It might be a good idea to put a goal that can be achieved quickly at the start of an action plan so you feel that you are making progress.

It may be helpful to ask your teacher/tutor or manager for support when deciding on priorities. They may have useful suggestions and help you feel that you are not alone in implementing your plan.

If it is not clear what you should do first, try to prioritise tasks or goals that will most benefit the children you are working with.

Checking progress

It will be important for you to regularly review your progress and consider which tasks have been achieved. How often you do this will depend on the complexity of your plan and its timescales.

Amending plans

When checking on progress, you may find that you need to add further tasks if you have realised that there is more to learn or more skills to acquire. If this is the case or you have met an unforeseen obstacle, you will need to amend your plan. You can do this directly on the original plan, or you can create a revised version to keep alongside the original.

Changes in practice

It is often the reactions of children and feedback from others that help us to recognise when we are improving our practice. Armed with this information, you can then review how well your plan is working and amend if necessary.

Link

Go to Section B in this unit to find more information about ways of gathering information about our practice.

Completing the plan

As we have seen, reflection should be a continuous cycle. Once you have completed your plan, you may need to look at other areas of your practice beyond communication and language, for example, a plan that looks at your skills in working with parents or colleagues.

Assessment practice 11.2

3B.P2 | 3B.P3 | 3B.M2 | 3B.D2 | 3C.P4 | 3C.M3 | 3C.D3

One of the Turkish delegates is in the UK for three months and will be spending time in the nursery where you work. She is keen to be shown how reflective practice is put into practice. She has asked if she could shadow you as you reflect on one area of practice, draw up an action plan and then review it. You have chosen to focus on communication and language.

You should do the following so that she can see the process:

- Based on information gathered from a range of sources, summarise your strengths and weaknesses in this area.

- Draw up a plan that clearly shows how you intend to improve your practice.
- Review the plan.

In addition, you will need to explain to the Turkish practitioner what the barriers are when trying to reflect on own practice, the strengths and weaknesses of your plan, and how the concept of continuous reflection could affect children's outcomes in the nursery in relation to communication and language.

Further reading and resources

Canning, N. and Reed, M. (2009) *Reflective Practice in the Early Years*, Thousand Oaks: Sage Publications.

Cortvriend, V. *et al* (2008) *Advanced Early Years Care and Education for Levels 4 and 5* (2nd ed.), Oxford: Heinemann.

Lindon, J. (2010) *Reflective Practice and Early Years Professionalism: Linking Theory and Practice*, London: Hodder Education.

Website

I CAN: www.ican.org.uk

Information services that provide help about speech, language and communication. Available for download: Stages of Speech and Language Development poster – a guide for early years practitioners

Ready for work?

Ming Lee Nursery manager

We are keen to remain an outstanding setting. As a manager, I believe that our success is partly down to the professional development that our staff undertake. Each staff member is regularly given opportunities to reflect on their practice and to draw up an action plan. Sometimes, we have a whole setting focusing on particular areas. This year we are looking at communication and language, and next year, we will be looking at outdoor play.

To help us in improving practice, each staff member is paired with a colleague. They look at each other's work, give suggestions and help each other in drawing up an action plan. We are also part of a cluster group and through this network, staff also see what other settings are doing. This works very well and recently we have been twinned with a nursery in Finland – we are aiming to learn more about how they work with children.

What is good about having a setting where everyone is involved in continuous reflection is that we are all learning. It makes for a great atmosphere and the children really benefit from the additional stimulation.

Skills for practice

Frequently asked questions:

The training course my manager wants me to go on is on a Saturday. She will pay for the course, but not for my time.

Strictly speaking, you do not need to attend if it is not in your usual work hours. Having said that, in terms of your career, you would be making the wrong decision. First of all, you will be gaining more knowledge and ideas, which will stand you in good stead when there is a promotion opportunity in your setting. Second, if you apply for a job outside your setting, you would be able to offer particular expertise or knowledge. Finally, when you attend courses, you are likely to meet other people who may be useful contacts in the future.

You might also like to think of the children that you work with. Surely gaining additional skills and knowledge will help you to be a better practitioner?

We have a child who stammers in the setting. He is my key child. Where can I find information about stammering and what I should do?

A good starting point is to visit the British Stammering Association's website. You can access this website by going to www.pearsonhotlinks.co.uk and searching for this title. You could also contact your local speech and language team, and they may have information that could help your practice. If you do this, remember that you cannot talk about the particular child in the setting unless you have parental consent. You could ask general questions, though.

Introduction

Being able to carry out effective research is an important skill for working with young children. It will help you to draw conclusions from facts rather than assumptions. Research in early years might include observations of children, questionnaires to parents or a review of the latest theories that support childcare practice. For example, it is easy to reach assumptions about a child's behaviour and the factors that influence it without any real evidence, but using observations as a method of research provides you with the first-hand evidence to be able to back up any conclusions you draw. Understanding research and how to carry it out effectively will help you appreciate the ways in which it can increase your understanding of children and their development, plan for their learning or even improve the setting you are working in.

Assessment: You will be assessed by an Edexcel-set assignment.

Learning aims

In this unit you will:

A   be able to produce a research proposal related to work with young children

B   be able to carry out a small-scale research project related to work with young children

C   be able to evaluate the research project.

Whatever childcare setting you work in, you will use research skills as part of your everyday routine. You may not realise it, but you will be gathering information, analysing it, drawing conclusions and taking action as a result. This is research. However, it is important that you do not draw conclusions without well-researched and analysed evidence as this can lead to mistakes. Therefore, an ability to understand how the research process works is essential.

Andrew George, *manager of a childcare setting*

Research Skills

BTEC
Assessment Zone

This table shows what you must do in order to achieve a **Pass**, **Merit** or **Distinction** grade, and where you can find activities to help you.

Assessment criteria		
Pass	**Merit**	**Distinction**
Learning aim A: Be able to produce a research proposal related to work with young children		
3A.P1 Explain the role of selected research relating to work with young children in early years settings. **Assessment practice 12.1**	**3A.M1** Analyse how the literature review informed and shaped the research proposal and choice of research methods. **Assessment practice 12.1** **Assessment practice 12.2**	**3A.D1** Discuss research objectives in terms of feasibility and application to practice. **Assessment practice 12.1**
3A.P2 I&CT Summarise reviewed research to inform the research proposal. **Assessment practice 12.1**		
3A.P3 I&CT Describe the objectives of the selected research proposal, giving reasons. **Assessment practice 12.2**		
3A.P4 Explain the suitability of the selected research methods for the research proposal, including related ethical issues. **Assessment practice 12.2**		
3A.P5 Create a realistic research proposal. **Assessment practice 12.2**		
Learning aim B: Be able to carry out a small-scale research project related to work with young children		
3B.P6 I&CT Maths Collect and record research findings relevant to the project objectives. **Assessment practice 12.3**	**3B.M2** Produce a coherent argument and relevant conclusions based on the research findings. **Assessment practice 12.4**	
3B.P7 English Present research findings in a relevant format. **Assessment practice 12.4**		
Learning aim C: Be able to evaluate the research project		
3C.P8 Describe how the research findings relate to the original research question. **Assessment practice 12.4**	**3C.M3** Review the chosen research methods in relation to the results obtained, any sources of bias or error and ethical considerations. **Assessment practice 12.4**	**3C.D2** Evaluate the extent to which the findings from the research undertaken can be implemented. **Assessment practice 12.4**
3C.P9 Explain the possible implications of the research findings for current practice. **Assessment practice 12.4**	**3C.M4** Recommend possible improvements to the research, referring to any relevant implications and ethical issues. **Assessment practice 12.4**	

English	English Functional Skills signposting	I&CT	Information and Communication Technology skills signposting
Maths	Mathematics Functional Skills signposting		

How you will be assessed

This unit will be assessed by an assignment that is set by Edexcel. It will be marked internally by your teacher/tutor and verified by an Edexcel Standards Verifier. Throughout the unit you will find assessment practice activities that will help you work towards your assessment. Completing these activities will not mean that you have achieved a particular grade, but you will have carried out useful research or preparation that will be relevant when it comes to your final assignment.

For your final assignment you will be required to carry out a small-scale research project and present your findings in a report. The research project will need to focus on a topic related to work with children that you have chosen in consultation with your teacher/tutor.

The assessment will test your ability to:

- understand the importance of research for work with children
- produce a valid research proposal
- plan a small-scale research project related to work with young children
- carry out a small-scale research project and present a report of the findings
- evaluate the processes involved in your research.

Getting started

How much do you know about how research is used in early years settings? Discuss the following examples of research and explain why you think they might be useful:

- observing a child who is biting other children
- asking parents about their experiences in the setting
- researching a particular medical condition that a new child attending the nursery may have.

A Be able to produce a research proposal related to work with young children

A good place to start is to think about why we carry out research when working with children.

The role of research

Research is an activity where we aim to find out information and/or gain knowledge about something. It is carried out in an organised way. Research can range from observations about how a child interacts with others in a setting to a nursery carrying out a questionnaire with parents to see how its service might be improved.

Sometimes people draw conclusions but may not have any evidence to back them up. When statements or assumptions are made about things that happen with children, research can provide the evidence to support or disprove those statements. The results of research can make people change their minds about something they may have seen or help them to decide what action to take to improve or change something, or to help a child progress.

Research within the early years field can also be used to:

- inform policy or practice
- highlight gaps in provision
- extend our knowledge and understanding
- improve outcomes for children by improving our practice
- help professionals to reflect on their work.

Research activities could cover several of these things. For example, a piece of research on how children use outdoor play areas could extend your knowledge and understanding of children's play habits and how they use outdoor play equipment. As a result it could inform policy on how outdoor areas are used in the curriculum and might also highlight gaps in terms of the facilities available for outdoor play provision. Changes that may happen as a result of these findings would lead to improving practice and, in turn, outcomes for children.

How to carry out a literature review

A literature review is a good place to start when you begin thinking about a research topic. At this point, you are likely to have several ideas.

Carrying out a literature review means looking at material that has already been written on the topics you are researching. This task should always come at the beginning of a piece of research, as it will give you an idea of the issues linked to your topic area as well as an understanding of any previous research that has been carried out. It may also give you some idea of the focus of the work and the **primary research** methods you should be using. Being able to compare your own findings with the information from the literature review will help to inform your conclusions and recommendations.

A literature review might include a range of sources such as textbooks, journals, newspapers and the Internet.

The features of secondary research

There are several sources that can be used for **secondary research**. These include textbooks and journals, the Internet, media sources such as newspapers and magazines, and government publications including statistics. The topic chosen will determine which type of secondary information is relevant. There will usually be some secondary source material, whatever your topic. However, for more current topics, the sources are likely to be in a professional journal or found on the Internet rather than in textbooks. It can take up to a year for new information to appear in textbooks.

Assessing secondary sources of information is not always easy. When looking at any secondary research, think about the way in which the information has been collected. If the research methods have not been carried out thoroughly and accurately, the results will not be **valid** or **reliable**.

Key terms

Primary research – finding things out – new information – for yourself.

Reliable – this means that your research will produce similar information to that found by someone else using the same methods with a similar sample.

Secondary research – finding things out using material produced by others.

Valid – this means that the research produces information that is well supported, justifiable and trustworthy.

Identifying a focus for research

All research projects begin with a decision on what to investigate. The area chosen for the project needs to be focused enough to enable a detailed piece of work in the timeframe allocated. The timeframe for the project and the resources available to you will determine what you might study.

You should always study something that is of interest to you – make this the starting point for choosing your area of study. It might start off as a very broad topic, such as imaginative play, or it could be something much more focused such as the value of a communal lunchtime for children's development of social skills.

If you start with a broad area, it is important to quickly focus your thinking on an area that is manageable. If your project remains too broad, the work will not be achievable.

It is useful to have a number of areas of potential interest, which you then try to narrow down to establish the area of focus that might be available to you. At this point you need to consider the availability of sources of research, as this may impact on your final decision. You also need to make sure that your final topic area offers a realistic area for research.

You will need to formulate a title for your work. Often the best titles are written as questions as they provide a focus for the work. If you do decide to use a question, try not to write one that has a 'yes' or 'no' answer. Use a sentence stem instead, such as 'To what extent does…' or 'How far does…' as this type of question requires a detailed response.

Discussions with your teacher/tutor

Your teacher/tutor will be a good source of ideas for your research project. They may be able to give you ideas or help you narrow down a broad idea to a more focused and manageable area of research.

You may also wish to discuss ideas with your placement supervisor. They may have ideas about a piece of research that would help them in the setting.

Observations of practice

Throughout your course, while on placement, you will be involved in observing children and how they react to each other and their environment. You will see similarities as well as differences in how children react to the same event, game or activity. Something you might have seen in this kind of situation could provide a stimulus for your research.

We look at the different types of observations that you could carry out on children later in this section.

During your placement experiences you will be working with early years professionals in different settings. You will see a range of approaches to early years work, depending on the philosophy of the setting (e.g. Montessori, or the Forest School approach) and the ways that the setting is organised. You may want to look at the way that these philosophies influence the practices within the setting as part of some secondary research.

Journal articles

During your course, you will have been encouraged to keep up to date with the latest thinking on early years issues. These are usually reported in journals first, rather than in textbooks, as textbooks take a while to be published. Therefore, journals could provide a source of inspiration for your area of research.

Previous research

Information you have gathered for previous assignments or even just reading around a subject might provide a stimulus for your research project. You may have read something that interested you and want to investigate further or you may have come across information outside of the work you had been doing that could provide a potential avenue for research.

Suitability of chosen focus

Once you have decided on your chosen focus, you need to ensure that your topic is suitable. This means you need to consider any ethical issues that may impact on your ability to carry out primary research. You need to make sure that you can carry out your research without causing distress to anyone who may be involved. Consider the following checklist:

- Make sure you have gained permission from your teacher/tutor and any other appropriate people such as placement supervisors if carrying out the work in a setting. They will need to check your work regularly to ensure you do not go wrong.
- Make sure you have asked the permission of the people you wish to involve in your project, or their parents or guardians if they are children. You do

not want to plan an elaborate project only to find that the people you need to be able to carry it out do not wish to be involved. Remember, you will need **informed consent**.

- Be ready to explain the purpose of your research in detail: what you are trying to find out, the research methods you want to use and how you will use the information. This will help your participants make an informed decision.
- Ensure you are clear about confidentiality and how you will maintain this. Your participants will want reassurance before agreeing to take part, particularly if your focus is a sensitive one.

The subject of ethics is looked at in more detail later in this section.

Importance of achievable aims and objectives

Aims and objectives will help you focus your work and clearly set out the boundaries of your study. Aims are broad statements that identify what the study hopes to find out. They will further clarify the title or **hypothesis** and outline the direction of study that the project will take.

Aims will usually begin with verbs, which describe what the work hopes to achieve through the different research methods that are used. Examples include:

- to find out
- to establish
- to discuss
- to explore
- to identify.

Written well, aims will set the scope of the work and help to identify the research methods that will be used.

Research methods

As well as being either primary or secondary, research can be either quantitative or qualitative.

Quantitative research

Quantitative research methods produce data that can be statistically analysed. They usually generate large quantities of information, and sample sizes (the number of people studied) are big. Questionnaires and surveys are generally considered quantitative research methods, as they aim to gather information from large numbers of people. To be able to handle the large amount of data, most researchers would design questionnaires and surveys with questions that have a choice of specified answers.

The most effective way to make sense of the information is by presenting it in a manageable format – usually a graph, chart or diagram. This allows the reader to see patterns easily and analyse the results.

Qualitative research

Qualitative research methods such as interviews or observations are designed to achieve a response that has more depth. Therefore the quality of the response is more important than the number of people who respond. These methods focus on finding out attitudes, opinions and thoughts. They allow the researcher to understand a situation in more detail.

This type of information cannot be easily analysed in a mathematical way and therefore qualitative data is not usually converted into graphs or charts. This is because a lot of the quality and meaning of responses would be lost through this process. The information is used to support arguments, and is often quoted as it has been said.

A student and parent are engaged in a two-way conversation. What type of research method is the learner likely to be using here – quantitative or qualitative?

The features of primary research

Primary research involves collecting your own original data using a primary research technique. Figure 12.1 shows examples of primary research methods.

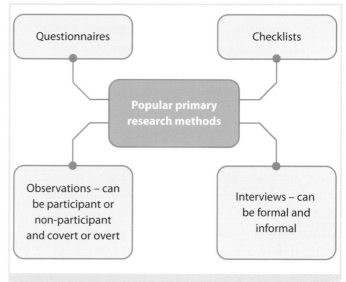

Figure 12.1 Popular primary research methods

Key terms

Hypothesis – an explanation for an observation or scientific problem made using limited evidence as a starting point for further investigation.

Informed consent – getting agreement from the person involved in the research, ensuring they fully understand what is happening and why.

Qualitative research – exploratory research that allows us to go deeper into the research issues. Common methods to collect data include interviews and observations.

Quantitative research – research that tries to quantify the problem and uses statistics to analyse results. Common methods to collect data include questionnaires and surveys.

All of the primary research methods need careful planning if they are to produce information that is valid and reliable. The primary research methods chosen will depend on the focus of the topic and what the researcher hopes to find out.

Questionnaires

A questionnaire is a list of questions, which are given to potential respondents in a written format. Questionnaires are not usually completed with a researcher present and therefore can be a cost-effective way to gather a lot of information.

Questionnaires are often used because they give breadth of information about a subject. However, they do not generally provide any depth – depth of information is best gained through interviews.

A questionnaire is a piece of quantitative research in that it can provide lots of responses relatively easily and responses can be directly compared, collated and analysed. It is a good way of asking straightforward questions of a large number of people.

However, it does take time to collate and analyse the large number of responses that are gained.

Key features of a good questionnaire

To design a good questionnaire, there are a number of stages that you will need to go through to ensure that you design it in such a way that you get the information you need. If you miss out or rush through any stage, it is likely that the finished result will not be useful or will yield unreliable or invalid results.

Figure 12.2 shows the things to think about when designing a questionnaire.

Planning the questionnaire

Before you start to design the questionnaire, consider the following.

- **The length of the questionnaire**

Long questionnaires tend to put potential respondents off and they are less likely to complete them. Keep your questionnaire as short as possible by only asking what really needs to be asked.

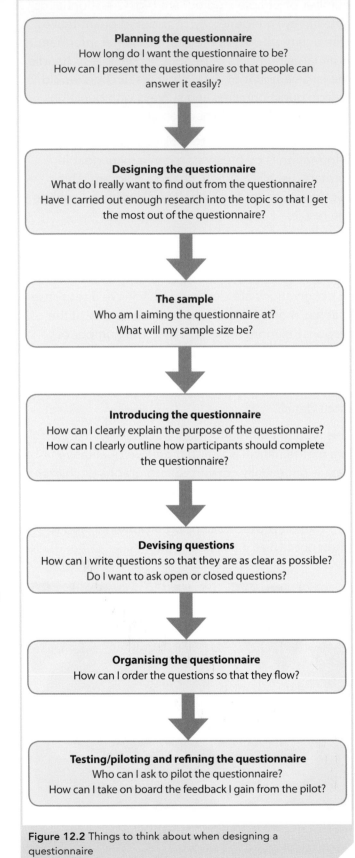

Figure 12.2 Things to think about when designing a questionnaire

• The presentation of the questionnaire

People are less likely to complete a questionnaire that looks complicated, wordy or asks for information that is non-essential or too private. When designing a questionnaire, aim for an attractive layout with plenty of space around each question, as this gives the appearance of fewer words. Position the response boxes on the right, as most people are right-handed and this makes it easier for the respondent to complete.

Designing the questionnaire

You need to have a very clear idea from the outset what you want the questionnaire to find out, as this will ensure that the information you gather will be of genuine use in your research.

In order to do this effectively, you must have researched your topic well. A good questionnaire often comes from thorough research of secondary source material such as textbooks and media articles. This research should help direct you towards what you hope to find out and will also give you something to compare your results with when you analyse them.

Sometimes the area you wish to investigate has no previously published material available. If this is the case, you will have to consider your line of enquiry even more carefully to ensure that you are clear about the purpose of your questionnaire.

Decide on your sample

To ensure your questionnaire produces valid and reliable information, it is important to consider who you will give it to, and how many people you will ask. Remember, however, that a small sample, especially a sample of less than 20, is not likely to be representative regardless of how the sample has been chosen.

Most samples will be a balance between the ideal and what is practical. The choice is likely to be affected by cost, time and resource limitations, but as long as this is recognised in the analysis of the results, this is reasonable.

Introduction to the questionnaire

A clear, concise introduction is important as this explains the purpose of the questionnaire. It should outline what the questionnaire is trying to achieve

and why, as well as how the results will be used. Confidentiality should also be mentioned, as this reassurance will encourage more people to complete the questionnaire.

The introduction should also outline how to complete the questionnaire, the deadline and how to return it. This is particularly important, as response rates to questionnaires are typically below 30 per cent, and it is therefore important to make the questionnaire as easy to return as possible.

Theory into practice

Devise an introduction for a questionnaire on childcare choices for working parents. How might you choose your sample for such a questionnaire?

Devising questions

Writing good questions for questionnaires is a challenge. Questions need to be clear to ensure that the respondents understand what is being asked. It is easy to write a question that you believe will gain information in a specific way, but those completing the questionnaire may interpret it completely differently. Therefore, it is worth spending some time considering your questions to ensure they are clear.

Open versus closed questions

Questions are usually open or closed. Open questions require more than a yes/no answer. They will prompt a wide range of responses and are, therefore, more difficult to analyse. For example:

> 1. What do you think is the most effective way of encouraging children to eat healthily?

However, the responses to open questions give a more personal insight into the respondents' thoughts.

Closed questions are more limiting in their possible responses for the respondent. They generally require a yes/no answer, or else there are a number of predetermined responses for the respondent to choose from. For example:

> 2. Did you ensure your child had five pieces of fruit or vegetables yesterday?
>
> Yes [ ]
> No [ ]

This question would be answered 'yes' or 'no'.

Closed questions are useful if you are covering facts or where it is reasonable to guess the range of possible responses. They are also used when you need to categorise age or time.

When using preselected responses, it is important that they have clear meanings. Avoid using words such as 'poor', 'adequate' or 'good', as each respondent will have a different interpretation of these words. Try a grading scale instead, for example, from 1 to 5, as this may bring a better response for analysis.

It is also important that each option is sufficiently distinct to allow the respondent to be able to make a clear choice.

For example, when classifying age groups there should not be any cross-over in the categories. Use 20 or under, 21–35, 36–50 and so on, rather than 20, 20–35, 35–50, etc. – otherwise those who are 20, 35 or 50 will not know which category to tick.

Closed questions are easy to analyse and are also easy for the respondent to complete as often they only involve ticking a box. For example:

> 3. Meat is a good source of
> a) protein [ ]
> b) vitamin D [ ]
> c) vitamin C [ ]
> d) fibre [ ]

Multiple questions

It is easy to write a question that really asks more than one question. An example would be:

> 4. How many times a week do you read with your child for more than half an hour, and what time do you usually read?

With such questions, some respondents will only answer one aspect of the question and this will reduce the reliability of your results.

If both parts of a question are important, it is better to break the question up into parts or even make it two separate questions. Breaking up a question into separate parts will ensure that all respondents are clearly directed into answering it completely.

Other things to consider

There are several other points to bear in mind when devising questions for a questionnaire. Table 12.1 will help you avoid the potential pitfalls.

Organising the questionnaire and testing the questions

Questions need to be grouped in an ordered manner so that, where appropriate, one question leads to another. Once all the questions have been drafted, they can be written on small pieces of card or sticky notes and ordered and reordered until they flow well. This is a good way of assessing the way the final questionnaire will look before typing it up.

Piloting the questionnaire

A questionnaire must be piloted by a small number of people to see if it is effective and to highlight any areas that might have been missed. As the writer, you will not always see the errors, mistakes or confusing sections because you are so close to the work. It is always better to ask objective people with a fresh eye to look at it. Ask people to comment on such things as the clarity of the instructions and layout, time for completion, any ambiguities as well as any questions they feel are irrelevant or offensive. Use the comments to adjust the original questionnaire before sending it out to the main group of respondents.

Carry out the questionnaire

The next stage is to carry out the actual questionnaire and wait for the responses to come back.

Collate and analyse the results

Questionnaires generally produce large amounts of data that need analysing. The method of analysis chosen will depend on the way the questions have been asked. Closed questions lend themselves to graphical presentation (i.e. charts or graphs), as the

Table 12.1 Potential pitfalls when writing questionnaire questions

Potential pitfall	Factors to consider
Irrelevant questions	Questions must be relevant. Questions on age, gender and occupation are often included on questionnaires but you need to consider if this information is relevant to your study. The rule is, if the question is not relevant to the study, leave it out.
Poor choice of language	Think carefully about the language you are using and who you are hoping will complete the questionnaire. Choose words that are straightforward and that people will understand. People are less likely to answer a question if it looks complicated.
Asking too much personal information	Respondents do not like giving personal information, so only ask for it if it is necessary and relevant. If personal information is needed, use a range rather than asking for exact information, as people are more likely to answer that. Questions requesting personal information are often placed at the end of the questionnaire as the respondent is more likely to have completed most of the questionnaire before they get to that section. If the respondent chooses not to complete this part, then you still have the information from the rest of the completed questionnaire.
Asking questions that make assumptions	Always avoid questions that assume something about the opinions or actions of the respondent. This also applies to knowledge and experiences.
Asking questions that require a good memory	Most adults may be reasonably expected to remember events from the preceding year with relative accuracy. However, it is not wise to ask people for information about things that happened five or ten years ago. Where detailed information from the past is needed, interviews are probably a better research method.
Asking leading questions	It is important to devise questions that do not suggest a preferred response to the respondent. This trap can be easy to fall into if you hold a particular view yourself.

data will be quantitative, whereas open questions will produce qualitative information, which is best presented in a written format.

Interviews

An interview provides more detailed information than a questionnaire. Interviews often take longer to carry out than questionnaires but they make it possible to explore issues in more depth. This is particularly useful when researching beliefs, attitudes and feelings, as these cannot be fully explored through either observations or questionnaires. Interviews draw out reasons and explanations, due to their very structured nature. Interviews also allow people to speak directly and at length in a way that questionnaires cannot.

Interviews are a responsive method of research, as it is possible to change the questions in response to the answers the interviewee gives. This means that an interviewer can get more information than might otherwise be possible.

Interviews also have better response rates than questionnaires, as questionnaires can be easily lost or forgotten. If asked directly, people are more likely to agree to answer questions. Interviews can also be recorded. This means that the researcher can replay an interview as many times as needed to collect the information accurately.

Interviews rely on effective communication between two people. For an interview to be successful, the interaction between the interviewer and the participant is very important, as this can affect the responses. Factors such as the interviewer's appearance, gender, age and even accent can affect the answers given, as the interviewee may form an opinion about them. Interviewers can also influence responses without knowing they are doing so, through normal mannerisms such as nodding or smiling. Uttering 'mmm' or even 'yes' when someone speaks can influence the relationship. You must remain non-judgemental when interviewing to get the best outcome. A good rapport may allow you to ask questions of a sensitive or more personal nature, but it is worth remembering that interviewees may sometimes respond to questions with what they feel the interviewer wants to hear rather than their true feelings or behaviour.

Interviews are generally one to one and are therefore quite time consuming. They are generally used for relatively small samples.

The nature of the data collected during interviews makes it difficult to draw overall conclusions or generalisations. Such qualitative data is not generally used to produce detailed statistics.

Types of interview

There are two main approaches to interviews as a method of research.

Formal interview

A formal interview is one in which there is a standard set of questions that are asked to each participant. The interviewer can only ask these questions, whatever the responses given, and can neither adapt the wording of the questions nor change them in any way. This is a very rigid form of interviewing, similar to a questionnaire. However, using such standardised questions allows generalisations to be made. There is also less chance for the interviewer to introduce bias, as they have to ask a specific set of questions.

The problem with being so rigid is that opportunities for developing information may be lost, as interviewers cannot follow up on answers that may be of interest.

Informal interview

In an informal interview, the interviewer has much more control and influence over the questions that are asked. Interviewers have the freedom to develop the questions as they feel appropriate. The informal interview process is similar to a discussion, rather than just being a question-and-answer session, which can make it more unpredictable.

An interviewer usually has a list of areas or issues they wish to cover during the interview. These are often called 'trigger questions'. They are also able to follow up on responses and develop the interview more fully. This type of interview has the advantage that it can produce richer information, as interviewers can probe for thoughts and develop what might appear to be off-the-cuff comments into fuller answers. It is therefore a good source of detailed qualitative data.

You can combine both formal and informal interview techniques, and this is called a semi-structured interview. This enables you to benefit from the advantages of both methods.

Case studies

A case study might be used within a research project to investigate a particular aspect of the project that is based on an individual or organisation. For example, if a research project was looking into the support the voluntary sector provides for children in a particular town, a case study of a voluntary organisation would be extremely relevant. A case study may also be used if looking at a topic where you wanted to see how something applied to a child. For example, you might research why some parents do not have their children vaccinated, and a case study of a child who was not vaccinated would be a useful research method for that topic.

A case study requires an in-depth investigation where historical evidence is taken into account. Case studies look at the impact of past and present events on the topic being studied.

Most case studies will draw on a range of research methods within them. You might start a case study with some secondary research and then use interviews, questionnaires or observations to investigate the case study further.

Observations of children

Observations of children can be used to study all aspects of development, including physical, social, emotional and intellectual. They can be used as the main method of research as part of a longitudinal study – a study that takes place over a long period of time, perhaps six months or more, to chart developments over the period. Observations may also be used as a research method to support other methods you may have used, or as one-off pieces of work.

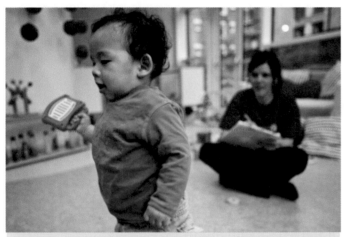

This practitioner is observing a child. What method of observation could she be using?

Participant and non-participant observations

There are two different types of observation, the main difference being whether the observer chooses to get involved with what they are observing or not.

- **Participant observation**

This is where the observer becomes part of the group they are observing. Being part of a group and observing at the same time can make recording detail difficult. The observer may also influence the outcome by being involved. However, this type of observation can result in a more reflective picture of what goes on, as the observer is part of the group.

- **Non-participant observation**

In this type of observation, the observer is an onlooker who is not involved in the action in any way. They record only what they see and have no interaction with the person or people being observed at all. The observer can record a lot of detail in this way as they can concentrate on this rather than getting involved. They can also see things that are

not immediately obvious when part of a group. The main disadvantage with this type of observation is that the observer may have an effect on what happens, as those involved know they are being watched. They may feel intimidated or self-conscious.

Overt or covert

In both participant and non-participant observations the observer can be overt or covert. Overt observation is where the observer does not hide the fact that they are observing or why they are observing. In covert observation, on the other hand, the observer does not inform those being observed that this is what they are doing or why they are doing it. This type of observation is useful when observing children who are likely to behave differently when surroundings or people change. However, in some circumstances, covert observation may raise ethical issues, as those being observed may feel they have been misinformed when they find out.

Main types of observations

There are many different types of observations that can be used in an early years setting, depending on the focus of the work – for example, an event sample, a checklist and a time sample.

Link

Go to Unit 9: Section B to find more information about methods of observation.

Limitations on observations

Observation as a method of research in childcare settings can have limitations that affect the quality of the results gained. The objectivity of observation can be affected by the actions of the observer. Other factors can also affect the situation and the child or children being observed so that they behave in a way that is out of the ordinary. It is worth being aware of some of these factors.

- **Knowing the environment**

If the environment in which the observation is taking place is familiar, those being observed will be more relaxed and feel more comfortable. This situation is likely to result in a more accurate impression than one that takes place in unfamiliar surroundings.

- **The timing of the observation**

If a child is tired they may have a lower concentration span and, therefore, an observation is likely to show non-typical behaviour. This is not the best situation in which to carry out a straightforward observation. It may be, however, that observing in this situation is done deliberately to look at how unknown or stressful situations affect behaviour.

- **Environmental factors such as the weather**

Windy or stormy weather is known to have an effect on behaviour and make children excitable. Therefore you may get observations that are outside the norm if observing in these conditions.

- **Times of the year**

There are certain times of the year when people traditionally act out of character because they are excited, such as Christmas, and this is likely to affect observation results.

- **Changes in the immediate environment**

Changes in noise levels, changes in the organisation of the immediate environment or changes in the people who are usually in an area (for example, a new practitioner) can all trigger changes in behaviour that will be reflected in any observation that is carried out.

This child is tired and irritable. How might this behaviour affect an observation?

An observation needs to be a true record that is not adversely affected by anything as this makes it easier to interpret. It also gives a fairer analysis of what is going on. However, due to the nature of observations, you should not use observations to prove cause and effect as they are not controlled as a scientific experiment would be. An observation can only provide an understanding of what is happening with a particular child at that particular time.

Checklists

A checklist is a list of skills, attributes or signs being looked for or assessed during an observation. These can be used to assess against norms or expectations. Checklists can also be used to compare skill levels across different groups, such as gender, age or developmental stage.

When may a checklist be used?

A checklist may be used to assess physical development, gross and fine motor skills, social skills, levels of ability (such as reading levels) or key health indicators (such as blood pressure and heart rate).

Advantages and disadvantages

A checklist is very quick to carry out and produces clear results, which are easily interpreted. However, to be really effective, the checklist needs to be well prepared and thought through. It is important that the observer only records what they see. There may be a risk of not getting true results if the person being observed feels under pressure to perform.

Scientific experiments

Scientific experiments might be used in the early years environment to understand causal relationships. This means looking at instances where something happens (the cause) to produce a reaction (the effect). This approach is often used in psychology to look at behaviour. The plan of the experiment will involve identifying one factor that you want to change, so that you can see the effects of that change. The factor is called the **variable**. Keeping all the other factors (variables) the same will allow you to see the impact of the change you have made. Within any experiment there is always a control group where the variables are not changed.

It is important that experiments are set up accurately and carried out with precision to get valid results. An experiment is reliable if, when repeated by another person at a later date, using the same variables, they get similar results.

Key term

Variable – an element, feature or factor in a research project that is likely to change.

Experiments could be used in a research project if you were looking at a child's cognitive development. You could use some of Jean Piaget's experiments to look at the stages of cognitive development.

Research Piaget's experiments and design your own experiment that you could use to test the stage of a child's cognitive development.

Try your experiment out and then compare your results to Piaget's theory. What conclusions can you draw?

Selecting appropriate research methods

Once you have decided on your research project title, you need to think about the research methods you might use and how you will carry these out. This can also act as a way of double-checking that your project has the potential to meet all of the assessment criteria for this unit.

To do this successfully, you should identify all the potential research methods and think about how you might apply them to your project. You should also think about how to record the results. Figure 12.3 gives you a good way to do this.

Once you have completed the table in Figure 12.3, you need to review your title and the potential research possibilities against the assessment criteria. You must be able to carry out primary research, so if the table shows that your topic only lends itself to secondary research, you need to rethink either your title or your approach.

It is better to change a project at this stage rather than spending a significant amount of time on something that has to be abandoned later. Careful planning will help ensure that your project does meet the criteria and will get you the marks you would like to achieve.

Ethical issues

Research usually involves finding out information from different people – often the information is about themselves and their decisions or thoughts. It is important that you consider the rights of the person involved in the research before you carry out any research. This means thinking about how you can ensure confidentiality, so that the people you use in your research remain anonymous. This is an important consideration.

Research method	Can it be used for this project? (Yes/No)	How can the method be used?	Are there any ethical issues I need to consider?	How can the results be recorded?
Secondary research: • books • journals • magazines • newspapers				
Interviews				
Questionnaires				
Observations				
Visits				

Figure 12.3 An example of a table to help you identify a suitable research method

Ethics is all about human behaviour – it looks at whether the way something is carried out is right or wrong. It includes considering whether behaviour is morally right as well as the way in which any actions may affect others.

When talking about ethics, we may also think about **attitudes**, beliefs and **values**. These things influence what we think is 'ethical'.

The beliefs held by an individual are based on the knowledge and information they have about the world around them. They are often personal opinions based on what that individual believes to be true.

Values influence behaviour, and guide people into choosing appropriate behaviour in different circumstances. Values can also encapsulate the beliefs and accepted standards of behaviour within a social grouping.

Ethics is an abstract concept and understanding exactly what it is can be difficult, as it is based on attitudes, values and beliefs that are hypothetical – that is, based on ideas or thoughts. Ethics are used as guidelines when making decisions. Every individual has a set of ethics. They may differ from person to person but will be broadly the same in any society and define what individuals believe is right and wrong. Ethics are based on the values individuals are brought up with and they will influence behaviours and attitudes as well as conscience.

In every aspect of research that you carry out, you will be applying ethics. Ethics also applies to the way the information that has been gathered is used. In practice this means you need to take a responsible attitude to the work being carried out and the results obtained.

Confidentiality

Confidentiality is an important issue. Any information that is collected through different primary research methods should be confidential. Often people involved in your research will be giving you personal and sensitive information about something. It is important that this information is treated with respect, which includes respect for people's cultural and life-choice differences. Remember that different people have different opinions about what is sensitive information and what they would want repeated. Therefore, the best approach is to treat any information that is given to you in any research method as confidential. Do not repeat information to anyone in a form that can be traced back to the person who gave it.

It can be very easy to forget the importance of confidentiality when chatting casually to family and friends, but you could find yourself in a difficult situation if you were overheard or if someone repeated your comments. Others will be interested in what you are doing so you should be prepared to give an overview or general findings but not to attribute comments to individuals.

Children's rights

In recent years, the importance of children's rights has been promoted. It is now recognised that the views of children should be listened to and acted on. This could influence how children are involved in research. There is a lot of debate around children's rights when it comes to being involved in research. Some people believe that children should not be part of a research activity, as they believe children cannot give informed consent. Others believe that children can be involved in research provided they are not hurt in any way as a result.

It is important that you consider the rights of the child and all related ethical issues when using children in research.

Seeking informed consent

Anyone you ask to become involved in research has a right to know how the information that is being collected about them will be used. This means that for people to consent to taking part in research they need to understand the purpose of the research and how any information they provide may be used. Formal written permission may be needed before some information can be collected, especially if the research involves gaining information from children or researching in a particular organisation or establishment.

It is also worth remembering that participants have the right to withdraw from research at any point if they feel uncomfortable about the process.

The Nuremberg Code

The Nuremberg Code is a set of principles that provide the guidelines within which experiments involving humans should be carried out. The code was developed after the Second World War, following the Nuremberg Trials where the Nazis were tried for carrying out experiments on humans in concentration camps.

The Code has 10 points, the most important of which states that anyone taking part in experiments must give informed consent, which means they must understand what is happening and any potential risks. No one should be forced into taking part in experiments.

Among other things, the Code makes it clear that a subject (in other words, a person) can choose to leave an experiment at any time if they wish. It states that an experiment should be stopped if it becomes evident that it could harm humans. The Code also makes clear that the risks should not outweigh the benefits of any experiment.

Reflect

Look at the Nuremberg Code in more detail. How might the code impact on research involving children? Can children give informed consent?

Assessment practice 12.1   3A.P1 | 3A.P2 | 3A.M1 | 3A.D1

All early years practitioners need to be able to carry out effective research. To do this they need to understand the importance of research methods in early years settings.

Prepare an article for an early years magazine on the importance of research in early years settings, using examples. Make sure you:

- explain the value of research when working with children
- summarise the potential ethical issues in research related to work with children
- assess the role of research in work with children
- evaluate the impact of research on improving outcomes for children.

■ Producing a research proposal

Once you have identified the topic you want to research, you need to produce a research proposal. First, you need to consider the title or the research question you are going to explore. It is important to think carefully about the question you use and to make sure it is not one with a 'yes' or 'no' answer. For example, use the sentence stem 'to what extent…', as this will prevent you from falling into this trap.

Once you have identified your question, and your aims and objectives, you can plan your research project in detail, and this will help you identify the methods you will use, the target group you are focusing on and the samples you will use for each research method you have decided to use. Producing a detailed action plan as outlined in this chapter will help you organise yourself within the timeframes allocated to the work.

Once you have your plan, it is essential that you monitor and review it regularly as you progress through your project and modify it as needed. You may find that findings from a piece of research will lead you to want to explore something that you had not originally planned at the start of the piece of work. You need to be flexible enough to be able to change your plan as you go along to ensure you produce the most effective piece of work.

You need to plan a small-scale research project related to young children.

1 Think about different areas you might want to research and consider the opportunities for carrying out different research methods.

2 Choose one of your ideas to develop as your research project. Describe your focus and give reasons for your choice.

3 Identify current reading or research relevant to your research and explain why you have chosen these sources.

4 Carry out the literature review and record your findings. Analyse how your literature review will inform and shape your research project.

5 Plan your research methods and explain how you will carry them out.

B Be able to carry out a small-scale research project related to work with young children

To be able to carry out a good research project, you need to combine a number of skills.

Skills required to carry out research

Figure 12.4 shows the things you will need to consider when carrying out research.

Planning your time

Planning your time effectively is as important as having a well-focused title that has the potential for good research opportunities. Even the best projects can fail as a result of poor planning and poor time management.

It is important that you plan the time you have to carry out the research project effectively. It is easy to underestimate how long research can take, particularly primary research, where you may be relying on others to return questionnaires or you may need to carry out observations over a period of time. In addition to carrying out the research, remember that it takes time to record and analyse the results.

You can design an action plan however you like, but it is important that the plan works for you.

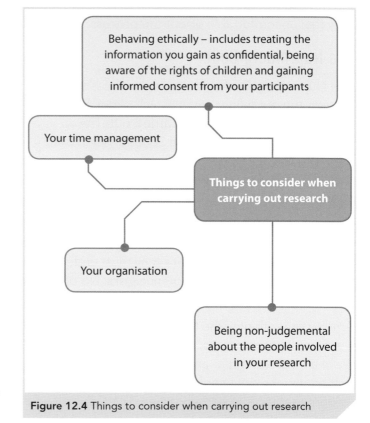

Figure 12.4 Things to consider when carrying out research

An effective plan has a number of elements. An outline for an action plan is given in Figure 12.5.

Timeframe for the research (from start to finish)	What is my overall aim?	What do I need to do?	What materials do I need?	Have I achieved my aim?	If not, what do I need to do?
12th February–12th March	To find out how the nursery could make cooked lunch more attractive.	Plan a questionnaire to find out why parents choose a particular type of lunch for their children.	Questionnaire		

Figure 12.5 An example of an action plan

Good time management is essential if you are going to carry out a valid research project effectively. Therefore, it is important that every research project is well planned and that you stick to that plan in order to meet the deadlines set.

Research projects often have long deadlines and it is a mistake to concentrate on work that is due in earlier to the detriment of the longer-term elements of the project.

Tips for effective time management are:

- start the project straight away
- develop a realistic plan, with timings, and stick to it
- work on the project at regular intervals
- always follow the plan you have set and monitor how you are doing at regular intervals
- if you fall behind, allocate some additional time to the work to catch up
- talk to your teacher/tutor regularly about the research project's progress – they will help to ensure you remain on schedule.

Organisational skills

Good organisational skills are essential if you want to produce a good piece of work within a given time frame. A research project normally takes place over a longer period of time and consists of several pieces of work, so you need to be well organised to do this effectively.

In addition, the project will produce a lot of data and you will need to do written work. Therefore, you should have an effective way to organise your notes and research findings so that you can access them easily when you need to write up the results.

It is advisable to write up the work as you go along and not leave it all until you have carried out all of your research methods. You will find that this written work takes longer than you may think.

You need to manage your time very effectively and ensure that you do keep to your plan.

Non-judgemental practice

When carrying out research, it is important that you keep an open mind and do not make judgements about the people involved in your research, particularly if they express ideas that are different from yours. This is not always easy, as you may communicate your thoughts through your body language and facial expressions as well as through the tone of your voice and the language you use. Therefore, you need to work to ensure that you appear non-judgemental in every way.

It is also important that, as a researcher, you do not introduce bias by influencing the participants through the way you ask questions or reply to responses given. It is important to remember that it is likely that participants will have different views and ideas from your own. You must appear neutral and non-judgemental if you are to gain open responses and valid information from participants.

■ Carrying out the research

When you carry out your research project, you will be implementing each of the secondary and primary research methods you have chosen to use and, from this, generating your research findings. You need to make sure you carry out each research method systematically and thoroughly to get the best results you can. Good results are important, so that you are able to draw valid conclusions.

It is important to follow your action plan during the research project. As projects are often carried out over a long period of time, it would be easy for you to put this to one side in favour of more immediate, short-term pieces of work. However, this would be a mistake – rushing such a detailed, demanding project will show in the poor quality of the end result.

You need to be strict with your time. If you are unable to carry out an activity as planned, you need to work out immediately how to get yourself back on track. You will also need to monitor your progress as you carry out your project, using the final two columns on the plan in Figure 12.5.

Think about bias or potential errors as you reflect on each research method you have carried out. Bias or errors can impact on your results and therefore the conclusions you draw from the results.

It is useful to note down any thoughts you have on the process as you go through, as this will help you when you write your reports and reflect on your evaluation.

It will also be helpful to plan regular review sessions with your teacher/tutor in which you can explain what you are doing. You should set yourself goals to achieve before each of these sessions. This will give you a target to aim for and is another way to help you keep on track.

Triangulation

Triangulation is an important concept in research. It involves the researcher using at least three methods to collect data on a topic – for example, secondary research, an interview and an observation. The aim of this is to show that there are similarities in the findings across the three research methods and so adding to the validity and reliability of the work. You need to think about this when considering how valid your data is.

■ Analysing data

Research produces a lot of information, known as **data**. This **'raw' data** is then analysed and the findings presented so that you can draw conclusions from it. Raw data may be condensed or may not be presented as part of the finished project, but it is retained for a period of time after the project is finished in case the findings are queried. Sometimes it is presented in an appendix.

Next we will look at a variety of methods by which you can analyse data. When a large amount of data has been collected, as well as displaying this in a table or diagram, you can work out key numerical values which summarise the information. These include the statistical averages of mean, mode or median, and measures of speed, such as range.

> **Key terms**
>
> **Data** – the information that is produced by your research methods. It covers facts, statistics and perceptions. Data has to be interpreted.
>
> **Raw data** – data as it is collected, before it has been organised, analysed or interpreted in any way.

Statistics

Statistics can be generated by analysing the raw data that you have collected. They allow you to consolidate, interpret and present your findings in a concise way. Presenting information in this way may allow you to make comparisons, for example, with similar information from a previous year.

Here is an example.

Your research might look at how many children have a school lunch in a small primary school. If you can see a trend in the data you have collected, or the numbers of children are similar over a period of three academic years, then the school can draw conclusions about how many staff to employ to manage the demands for lunches.

Statistics need to be produced and handled with care. If your sample size is small, the statistics that can be generated from the data may not give an accurate picture of a situation overall.

For example, if ten children take a test and two of them fail, it follows that eight out of ten have passed. The pass rate can be worked out as 80 per cent. However, if 100 children then sat the same test and two fail, 98 children will have passed. The pass rate will then be 98 per cent.

So, if a school reviews the results of these two tests and concentrates on the pass rates in order to inform future decisions about the design of the test, the future test might end up being different depending on how many children sat the test originally.

To get a more accurate picture, the research would need to take place over several tests, with a consistent number of candidates sitting each test. This would allow for an overall outcome from which conclusions that inform the writing of future tests can usefully be drawn and acted upon.

Summary statistics

It is useful to summarise your data by working out a representative value and also by giving a measure of the spread of the data.

The representative value is called an average. There are three main types of statistical average. They are the mean, mode and median.

To measure the spread of the data, the range is often used.

Averages
Mean

The mean is the one that most people refer to as 'the average'. It is the figure calculated by adding up all the values in a set and dividing the total by the number of values in the set.

Here is an example.

Five children get the following marks out of 10 in a test: 9, 6, 4, 4, 7.

To work out the mean, add together the individual marks.

So: $9 + 6 + 4 + 4 + 7 = 30$

Then, divide by the number of children.

So: $\dfrac{30}{5} = 6$

The mean average mark for the test is, therefore, 6.

Mode

The mode is the most commonly appearing value, so the mode of the test results is 4.

The mode is a useful average when you want to know the most popular value. However, not all sets of data have a mode. Also, if there are more than two modes then the mode is not a useful average.

Median

The median is the middle value when all the values are arranged in ascending order.

The test marks in ascending order are 4, 4, 6, 7, 9 The middle value is 6, so this is the median.

Here are the marks of another group of children: 1, 6, 7, 8, 8, 10

There are two middle numbers, 7 and 8, and the median is the mean of these, i.e. $\dfrac{7 + 8}{2} = 7.5$

In this set, the mark of 1 is unusual.

The median is particularly useful when there are unusual or extreme values, sometimes called outliers, as the median is not unduly influenced by them.

Spread
Range

The range of a set of numbers is the difference between the highest and the lowest values, i.e. range = highest value – lowest value.

So, for the test marks 4, 4, 6, 7, 9, range = $9 - 4 = 5$

For the test marks 1, 6, 7, 8, 8, 10, range = $10 - 1 = 9$

The marks in the first set have the smaller range so they are less variable and more consistent.

Use of percentages

Percentages can be a useful way to analyse data as they allow you to show proportions of the 'overall' picture. For example, 65 per cent of children chose an ice cream and 35 per cent of children chose an iced lolly.

Drawing conclusions

Once you have your data, you need to draw conclusions from it. You should look for patterns or facts in the data you have found. You might look for similarities or differences between different results. You may draw conclusions from one piece of research that you are able to support with findings from another. Sometimes research may show that there is no connection or obvious conclusion to be drawn.

Make sure any conclusion you draw can be backed up by evidence from your research.

Presenting data

Presenting research findings in clear and concise formats such as tables or diagrams makes the information easier to read and more accessible.

Some data is best presented in certain formats, but generally the choice of presentation is down to your preference. Make sure the method you choose presents the information in the clearest manner.

Quantitative research methods generally produce a large amount of numerical data that is usually best presented using statistical diagrams. Take care not to misrepresent the data, especially when drawing diagrams.

Tables

Tables are a useful way to present information in a neat, clear format, particularly where comparisons are being made. For example, if you wanted to study information over a number of years and look for changes and trends, you might use a table.

The information in Table 12.2 shows the results of a fictional study of the number of parents using different forms of full-time childcare on a particular housing estate over a period of time. The years are shown across the top and the types of childcare down the side.

You can draw conclusions from Table 12.2 about which types of care are growing and which are declining. You might decide to analyse in further depth whether there is any difference in the ages of the children who attend the different types of care, for example.

A table can include a lot of information in a small area. It is therefore important that tables are clearly labelled so the reader can understand what is being depicted. Units of measurement must also be clearly stated.

Statistical diagrams

Most research projects will require you to present information in a pictorial format. Statistical diagrams, often generally referred to as 'graphs', are usually in the form of a line graph, bar chart, histogram, pie chart, pictogram or scatter graph.

There are a number of points to note when presenting information diagrammatically:

- The diagram should have a clear title.
- The source of the data should be given at the bottom of the diagram.
- Axes should be clearly labelled.
- Any units of measurement should be made very clear.
- Graphs should be presented on graph paper (not lined or plain paper).
- Pie charts should be presented on plain paper (not lined or graph paper).

Table 12.2 Forms of full-time childcare used by parents on one housing estate

Type of childcare	2007	2008	2009	2010	2011
Childminding	20	22	24	25	25
Private nurseries	18	21	24	26	28
Nanny based in own home	10	10	8	7	7
Family or friends	6	6	6	5	5

Line graphs

Line graphs have horizontal and vertical axes, which must be clearly labelled. Points are then plotted on the grid.

Line graphs are particularly useful in seeing trends over time.

Figure 12.6 is a line graph illustrating Table 12.2.

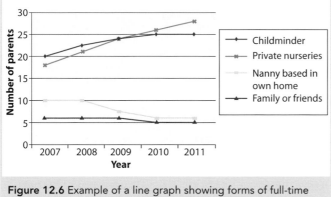

Figure 12.6 Example of a line graph showing forms of full-time childcare used by parents on one housing estate.

Bar charts

As bar charts are easy to draw and understand, they are the most common type of statistical diagram. Bar charts show information in either vertical or horizontal bars and are particularly useful for presenting data that fits descriptive categories.

Bar charts have a number of common features:

- All bars are the same width.
- Bars may be horizontal or vertical.
- The bars may be drawn next to each other or with a space between each one.
- The height (or length) of the bar indicates the frequency, that is the size of the group defined by the category label.
- The other axis shows the descriptive categories – these describe the type of data being measured.
- Bar charts are often coloured to improve the presentation.

Codes may be used to label the bars as long as a clear key or legend is included to the side of the diagram to explain what they mean. This may be useful if the labels are very long. For example, you might be measuring how often a setting carries out child-initiated activities compared to adult-initiated activities, in which case you may choose to label the axis using the labels 'C-I' and 'A-I' to save space.

Figure 12.7 is a bar chart of data taken from Table 12.2 showing the types of childcare used in 2007.

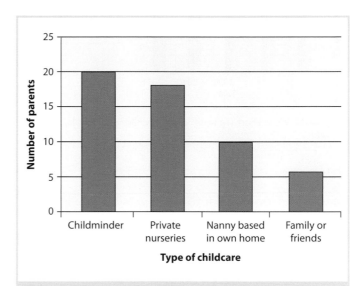

Figure 12.7 Example of a bar chart showing types of childcare used in 2007 by parents on one housing estate.

Compound bar charts are particularly useful for comparing sets of data.

Figure 12.8 is a compound bar chart to illustrate the data in Table 12.2.

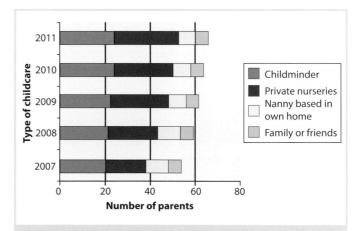

Figure 12.8 Example of a compound bar chart showing forms of childcare used by parents.

The data can also be illustrated in individual bars, as shown in Figure 12.9:

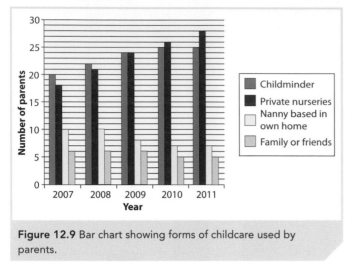

Figure 12.9 Bar chart showing forms of childcare used by parents.

Histograms

Histograms look similar to bar charts but are in fact different. Histograms have a number of common features:

- They are used for continuous data that is grouped, i.e. data that covers a band.
- They contain bars that are not always the same width – the width of the bar along the horizontal axis relates to the size of the grouped data.
- There are no gaps between the bars.
- The frequency of the class is indicated by the area of the column.

Pie charts

Pie charts are a way of presenting data according to each category's share of the total. Making one involves first converting your results into percentages. We will now look at how to do this step by step.

Imagine you have collected the data shown in Table 12.3 on how learners in three classes travel to their placements.

To work out the percentage of the different forms of travel, you need to divide the number of people who travel by a particular method by the total number of people questioned. Then, you need to multiply the answer by 100 (per cent). An example of the calculation for children travelling by car is shown below:

By car $\dfrac{24}{60}$ = 0.4

0.4 x 100 = 40%

Once you have calculated the percentage, you then need to convert this into degrees so that you can construct the pie chart.

To find how much of the pie chart should be taken up by the 40 per cent of learners who travel by car, you first need to work out how big a slice of pie 1 per cent of learners would need. This will allow you to then work out how much 40 per cent would need.

There are 360 degrees in a circle, so to work this out, carry out the following sum:

$\dfrac{360}{100}$ = 3.6 degrees

To work out the degrees required for learners travelling by car, you simply multiply the answer by 40, as follows:

40 x 3.6 = 144 degrees

This is shown in Figure 12.10.

Table 12.3 How learners travel to their placements

Form of travel	Number of people	Percentage	Degrees
Bus	15	25	90
Train	3	5	18
Walk	9	15	54
Car	24	40	144
Bike	6	10	36
Moped	3	5	18
Total	60	100	360

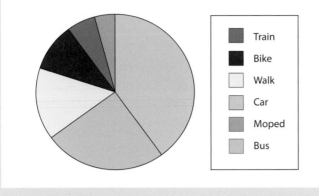

Figure 12.10 Example of a pie chart showing how learners travel to their placements.

Note that if your values are not exact, leave the numbers on your calculator during the calculation and do not round until the final stage.

You usually round up, but sometimes it may be necessary to round down to ensure that your total angle is 360 degrees.

When drawing a pie chart, remember to:

- show any calculations you do
- colour each sector to improve the presentation
- label each sector with the percentage it represents
- provide a clear key or legend so the reader knows what each sector represents
- give the pie chart a title
- present the pie chart on plain paper.

Scatter graphs

Scatter graphs are generally used where data showing two corresponding variables needs to be presented in order to see whether there is a pattern or **correlation**, such as the relationship between blood pressure and age in a group of people.

Scatter graphs may show a positive correlation, where if one variable increases, so does the other – or a negative correlation, where if one variable increases, the other decreases. Or there may be no significant correlation.

Key term

Correlation – a relationship or connection between two things.

A pattern or correlation does not always indicate that changes in one variable cause the changes in the other variable, i.e. it does not always indicate cause and effect.

When the data has been plotted on a scatter graph, it is useful to draw a 'line of best fit', which is where the main clustering of the data occurs. This line can then be used as the starting point for a hypothesis to link the two variables and make predictions of one value given the value of the other.

Figures 12.11–12.13 show scatter graphs with positive, negative and no correlation, together with a line of best fit, as appropriate.

Figure 12.11 Scatter graph with positive correlation

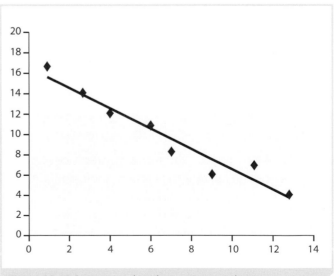

Figure 12.12 Scatter graph with negative correlation

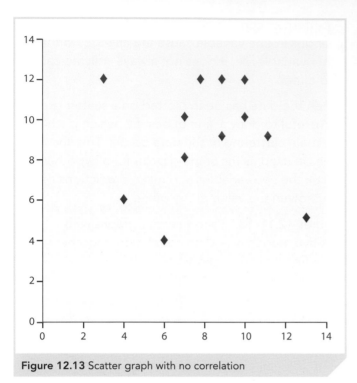

Figure 12.13 Scatter graph with no correlation

Using computers to present data

The best way to present your numerical data from methods such as questionnaires or checklists/surveys is to use a computer package such as Microsoft Excel® to present your findings. Researchers often use computer programmes to help them analyse and present their data. Computers have the advantage of being able to calculate accurately as long as the information is input correctly. Once the information is input, you can present the data in a wide range of formats at the touch of a button. This enables you to see how best to present the information with ease. You can also use the software to find the mean, mode, median or range, as well as other statistical values that may be of use.

Research

Find out more about the types of graph covered in this unit. It is useful to research their similarities and differences so that you can decide the best way to present data you have gathered. Most mathematical websites will have examples.

The conventions of report writing

Your report will need to be written in a particular way to ensure that you can access all the assessment criteria. Following is an overview of the different elements your report should contain.

Title

You should always write the title of the project at the start of the report so that the reader is clear about what you have researched.

Contents

A list of contents is important so the reader knows what is in the report and where to find it.

Abstract or summary

An abstract or summary is a brief outline of what the project is about and the general approach that you have taken to carry out the research. It is very brief and usually no longer than half a page. It is very similar to the kind of overview that you might find on the back of a novel. It should tell the reader what the work is about but not all the details – those will be in the body of the report.

Introduction

This should briefly state the aim(s) and the research hypothesis, if this is relevant. This section should include a summary of current research findings in the field of study. You may have looked at current research as part of your secondary research at the start of your project. Providing a summary of the current research will help to give some context to your own research. Some topics will have a wealth of previous research for you to draw on. However, if you have a particularly original area of research, there may not be much written about your topic.

Methodology

This section should explain the methodology used in your study. You need to outline and justify the method of study chosen, state clearly what was measured and how. You need to list any apparatus and measuring instruments used.

Key term

Debriefing – a conversation between a researcher and participant following an experiment to inform the participant about their experience and allowing them to talk about it.

There should be a brief description of the sample of participants used (indicating size, age range, location and other factors relevant to the study) and you should state and justify the sampling method used.

As we have discussed earlier in the unit, ethical issues should also be covered. This section should draw the reader's attention to the specific ethical issues raised by the study, for example, temporary mild deception where a participant may not be fully aware of the reason for the research or the risk of a participant's embarrassment on performing poorly in some measure of skill.

Finally, there needs to be a description of the procedure experienced by the participant in the order in which it happened (not the process by which you planned or designed the study). It should include reference to the initial request, a detailed description of what was done to obtain the data and reference to **debriefing**, if appropriate.

Results or findings

This should include a graphical summary of results or findings (such as a table of means, or percentages), and/or appropriate chart(s) properly labelled, as well as an analysis of the findings in relation to the aim or hypothesis.

Discussion

In this section of the report you should discuss your findings and support any conclusions you might have drawn with evidence that you have found out through your research. You might refer your reader to the appendices, where you should have presented full details of your research methods and findings.

Conclusion and recommendations

The conclusion section is where you need to draw together the findings and produce some recommendations as a result of those findings.

Appendices

This part of the report should include examples of materials used, raw data together with calculations, and a reference section, using the conventional form and giving references for all studies and authorities cited in the report.

It is not useful to put in lots of notes, but do include a bibliography of the textbooks and other sources you have used.

The appendices should be set out in an organised manner, giving details of the work carried out. Each section of the appendix should be labelled with a letter or number. In general, each section will represent a method of research. Each appendix allows you to show off the full extent of the work you have done in each research method you have used, as you may not draw on all of it for the report itself.

Referencing and writing the bibliography

There are conventions to follow for writing a bibliography. The Harvard method is commonly used (see Figure 12.14).

Below is an example of this in practice.

> Tassoni, P. (2008) *Practical EYFS Handbook*, Heinemann: Oxford.

Generally, the title of the book is written in italics or bold, or underlined to make it stand out.

The date is the published date of the edition you have used and this should be in written in brackets.

Also, note the presence of commas and full stops in the reference. This punctuation should always be used.

| Surname, initial of author | → | Date published | → | Full title | → | Where published | → | Publisher |

Figure 12.14 The Harvard method of referencing

When using a number of books, they should all be recorded in a bibliography in alphabetical order according to the author's surname.

If you refer to the books listed in the bibliography in the text of your report – for example, if you refer to the author's arguments or if you take quotes from the content – you will need to add a reference. This should be done in the main body of your report by simply writing the author's surname and the date the book was published in brackets at the end of the sentence. For example: (Tassoni 2008).

If more than one person has written a book, then the referencing is slightly different.

If a book was written by two or more authors, the bibliography should list all the authors. If a book was written by more than two authors you can write the name of the first author followed by *et al*. *Et al* means 'and the others', and this form of shorthand saves you time in writing all the names out.

Magazine articles, journal articles and chapters in edited books are referenced in a different way as well, which is not as straightforward as books authored by one person.

Research

Find out the correct way to reference books written by more than one author, chapters in edited books, journal articles and magazine articles.

Assessment practice 12.3   3B.P6

Carry out your research and present valid findings in a report based on the evidence you have collected from your primary research.

Find out how to reference articles in magazines, journals and newspapers.

It is important that you know how to reference books correctly you have used.

C Be able to evaluate the research project

Analysing the project's strengths and weaknesses

Evaluation is an important part of the research process. To evaluate your work, you need to show that you appreciate the factors that have affected the project. As you evaluate, think about each section of the research project and comment on any issues that could have affected the validity and reliability of the findings, including bias or errors.

One way to evaluate successfully is to ask yourself a series of questions that make you reflect critically on the work you have carried out. Try to work your way through the research process and evaluate every stage. This will ensure that you reflect thoroughly on the work you have done. Think about the following.

Planning

- Did you plan the project well?
- Did you produce an effective plan?
- Did you keep to the plan? How did this affect your work – positively or negatively?

Secondary research

- Did you review an effective range of secondary research in relation to the topic you chose to study?
- Were the sources up to date?
- Were the sources valid and reliable? How do you know and what difference did this make to the work?
- Did you carry out enough secondary research before you designed the primary research?
- How did the results for the secondary research help you with the primary research?

Primary research

You need to evaluate each primary research method you used. The following questions can be applied to most research methods as a way of starting the evaluative process:

- Was this an effective choice of research method for the chosen topic?
- Did you plan the method well?
- Was the sample used appropriate? How did this impact on the validity of the work?
- Did the method gain the information you hoped for? If not, why not?
- Were the results presented appropriately?
- Was there any 'misuse' of the research within the project? For example, on reflection, were any of the research methods 'designed' with a particular outcome in mind? As an example, questions may have been worded specifically to elicit particular responses.
- Were there any errors or bias evident that might have impacted on the results?
- Did you follow data protection and confidentiality conventions appropriately?
- On reflection, were there other research methods that you could have used that would have provided more effective results?
- If you were to continue with the research, what would you do next and why?

The report

Think about the following questions when writing your final report.

- How far did your findings reflect the original research question?
- Did your findings triangulate and how does this impact on the findings of the project?
- Is there anything you could have changed to improve the validity and reliability of the work?
- Did you carry out an effective discussion of your findings? Were comparisons drawn between the findings of different research methods?
- How did your findings compare to current research in the area? Did they support the current thinking? If not, why do you think that was?
- How might your research findings impact on your practice in the future?

Recommendations based on research findings

The results of research can impact on work with children in many different ways. Essentially, they enable us to have a better understanding of a child's world and help adults find ways to improve that world. They should provide understanding of how children can be provided with the most effective care and education. They can be used to:

- extend knowledge of different aspects of children's development and care
- evaluate the services provided and identify how they might be improved to meet the users' needs
- monitor the development of children against norms and identify ways to support their development
- review services provided and identify any areas where there may be gaps
- develop new ways of working.

A significant amount of research is commissioned by the government, and this is used to inform both policy and practice. It is through research that the quality of a child's care and education can be improved. In this way, research can have an immense influence on the life chances of children both now and in the future.

Assessment practice 12.4

3B.P7 | 3B.M2 | 3C.P8 | 3C.P9 | 3C.M3 | 3C.M4 | 3C.D2

Once you have completed your research project, you need to show that you can reflect on your work, evaluate it and identify ways in which it might influence your practice in the workplace.

You need to:

- review the strengths and weaknesses of your research project
- analyse the effectiveness of the research methods you have used
- explain the potential impact of your research project on work with children
- evaluate the potential implications of your research for work with children and justify your conclusions.

Further reading and resources

Green, S. (2000) *Research Methods in Health, Social and Early Years Care*, Cheltenham: Nelson Thornes.

Hucker, K. (2001) *Research Methods in Health, Care and Early Years (Professional Development)*, Oxford: Heinemann.

Website

Science Museum: www.sciencemuseum.org.uk

Ready for work?

Ben Hunt Preschool manager

All professionals in early years settings use research skills as part of their everyday work. For example, you might need to find out some information about a condition that one of your children has or you might be concerned that a child in your care is not developing at the pace you would expect. In both of these scenarios you could observe the children and compare your findings against theory.

In our preschool, members of staff use their research skills to collect information about the children they look after and make judgements about their development. They then use this information to provide activities and experiences that move children on to the next stage of their learning.

Skills for practice

- Visit an early years setting and try out a time sample. Choose a child to watch over a period of an hour. Record everything they do. What conclusions can you draw from your observations?

- Choose a topic of interest to you in the area of early years. Carry out literature research and summarise your findings into key points.

- Choose a stage of development, for example, 0 to 3 months, 9 to 12 months, 12 to 18 months or 2 to 3 years. Research the physical development you would expect to see at your chosen stage of development. Devise a checklist that you could carry out to assess the physical skills of children in your chosen age range against these expectations.

Introduction

All children have rights. It does not matter where they live or whether they are rich or poor. Their rights are enshrined in UK legislation. Knowing about children's rights will help you to understand the role of adults in protecting these rights and supporting children and their families to access health, education and social care services. You will also explore early years education, curriculum frameworks and how settings are inspected. As you gain experience in working with children you will develop an understanding of the importance of working closely with other professionals to improve outcomes for young children and their families.

Assessment: You will be assessed by a series of assignments set by your teacher/tutor.

Learning aims

In this unit you will:

A   understand the provision of health, education and social services for children and their families

B   understand the context in which early years education is provided

C   understand the role of multi-agency work for children and their families.

> Although I knew about some of the services that are available, until I started studying this unit I hadn't realised that children have a right to these in law. Young children can't stand up for their own rights so they rely on us as adults to make sure they receive the services they deserve.
>
> Chloe, *a student on an early years course*

Health, Education and Social Services for Children and Their Families

13

BTEC
Assessment Zone

This table shows what you must do in order to achieve a **Pass**, **Merit** or **Distinction** grade, and where you can find activities to help you.

Assessment criteria		
Pass	**Merit**	**Distinction**
Learning aim A: Understand the provision of health, education and social services for children and their families		
3A.P1 Explain the services and benefits children and families have a right to access, to include: • health • education • social services. **Assessment practice 13.1**	**3A.M1** Assess how services and benefits support children and families, with examples. **Assessment practice 13.1**	**3A.D1** Evaluate the extent to which services and benefits could impact on outcomes for children. **Assessment practice 13.1**
3A.P2 Explain why families may need to access named services. **Assessment practice 13.1**		
Learning aim B: Understand the context in which early years education is provided		
3B.P3 Explain the differences between settings which provide for children's early years education. **Assessment practice 13.2**	**3B.M2** Compare the advantages and disadvantages to children and families of different types of early years education. **Assessment practice 13.2**	
3B.P4 English Explain how early years education is inspected in the home country. **Assessment practice 13.2**		
Learning aim C: Understand the role of multi-agency work for children and their families		
3C.P5 Explain the role of a multi-agency approach in work with children and families. **Assessment practice 13.3**	**3C.M3** Discuss how multi-agency working contributes to meeting the needs of children and families, with examples. **Assessment practice 13.3**	**3C.D2** Evaluate the extent to which multi-agency working might impact on outcomes for children. **Assessment practice 13.3**

English   English Functional Skills signposting

How you will be assessed

This unit will be assessed by a series of internally assessed tasks set by your teacher/tutor. Throughout this unit you will find assessment practice activities that will help you work towards your assessment. Completing these activities will not mean that you have achieved a particular grade, but you will have carried out useful research or preparation that will be relevant when it comes to your final assignment.

In order for you to carry out the tasks in your assignment, it is important that you check you have met all of the Pass grading criteria. You can do this as you work your way through the assignment.

If you are hoping to gain a Merit or Distinction, you should also make sure that you present the information in your assignment in the style that is required by the relevant assessment criterion. For example, Merit criteria require you to assess, compare and discuss, and Distinction criteria require you to evaluate.

The assignment set by your teacher/tutor will consist of a number of tasks designed to meet the criteria in the table opposite. This is likely to consist of a written assignment but may also include activities such as:

- a leaflet
- a case study
- a presentation
- a guide to services.

Getting started

How many different services for children and families can you think of? Work in a small group and share your ideas. Write each idea on a separate sticky note. Then, sort the services under the following headings: health, education, social services.

A Understand the provision of health, education and social services for children and their families

Statutory services are provided by central or local government. These services may be organised in different ways but are there to meet children's education, health and welfare needs. Many of these services are accessed by the vast majority of families, for instance, nurseries, schools and health services, but there are occasions when families need additional support to help them maintain the health and well-being of their children.

Legislation that supports the rights of children and families

Everyone has rights that are set out in law. Some legislation, such as human rights laws, protects the rights of all people. Other legislation, such as the Children Act 1989, protects the particular rights of children and their families.

The United Nations Convention on the Rights of the Child (UNCRC)

In 1989 the fundamental rights of children worldwide were agreed. They were set out in an international agreement known as the United Nations Convention on the Rights of the Child (UNCRC).

The UNCRC comprises 54 Articles, and of these, 40 Articles deal specifically with the rights of the child. For example, Article 24 states that 'every child has the right to the best possible health' and Article 28 that 'every child has the right to free primary education'.

Research

You can find more information about the Articles that describe the rights of all children by visiting the UNICEF website. You can access this website by going to www.pearsonhotlinks.co.uk and searching for this title.

In 1991 the UK ratified the rights set out in the UNCRC. This means that UK law must be compatible with each right.

Legislation and frameworks

Table 13.1 summarises the key legislation and frameworks that underpin children's rights to health, education and social services.

Key terms

Common Assessment Framework (CAF) – a process to assess a child's strengths and needs and to plan for improvement.

Holistic – all the child's needs, to include physical, emotional, social and cognitive.

In need – this refers to children who are unlikely to maintain, or be given the opportunity to maintain, a reasonable standard of health or development, or whose health could be impaired without the support of local authority services. It also includes children who are disabled.

Table 13.1 Legislation and frameworks

Legislation	Aims and objectives
National Health Service Act 2006	Everyone has the right to a free and comprehensive health service. This Act defines the duties of the Secretary of State to provide for: • the improvement of physical and mental health • the prevention of ill-health, diagnosis and treatment.
National Service Framework for children, young people and maternity services 2004	Confirms the right of children to a good start in life. It identifies problems relating to health inequalities and the need to deliver individualised health care, which provides for children's **holistic** needs. It establishes the rights of children and their families to high-quality integrated services.
Children Act 1989	Relevant to England and Wales. It is based on the principle that the child's needs are paramount. It identifies the duty of the local authority to identify those children **in need** and to provide services to meet those needs. It also establishes the concept of parental responsibility.
Children Act 2004	Relevant to England and Wales. It extends the 1989 Act to bring about greater integration of services. It introduces the **Common Assessment Framework** with the aim of early identification of children's additional needs. Following its introduction, local authorities must show how they plan and deliver coordinated services. Every Child Matters outcomes were introduced in response to this Act. These are now referred to as 'Help Children Achieve More'.
Childcare Act 2006	Sets out the rights to childcare for England and Wales, including free education for children aged 3 to 5 years. Aims to improve the outcomes and reduce inequalities between children by establishing a Sure Start children's centre in every community. Includes a requirement to provide information and support for parents. Brings together the Birth to Three Matters and EYFS curriculum to form a new early years curriculum framework (EYFS) for children aged 0 to 5 years.
Education Act 1996	Confirms the rights of children to full-time education from 5 to 16 years in England and Wales. Establishes the responsibility of parents or carers to ensure that their children receive education. Incorporates the Code of Practice for Special Educational Needs (see below). It gives children with special educational needs (SEN) the right to education in mainstream schools.
Code of Practice for Special Educational Needs 2001, and the SEN Code of Practice Wales 2002	Early education settings and schools must give regard to the Code when providing for children with special educational needs. Establishes children's right to have their needs assessed quickly and for appropriate support to be put into place. The Code also outlines the rights of parents or carers to advice and information.
Children and Young Persons Act 2008	Extends the statutory framework for children who are in care in England and Wales. It protects children's rights to high-quality care and services appropriate for and adapted to their individual needs. It places a duty on local authorities to appoint an independent person to look after the interests of children in care and to provide them with support and advice.
Child Poverty Act 2010	Aims to reduce inequalities and the associated disadvantage for children and families. Part 1 of the Act relates to the whole of the UK and requires strategies to be put into place. This Act sets targets for a minimum income for families by the year 2020 to reduce poverty. The Child Poverty Strategy of each home county provides the framework for the Act.

Portfolio building activity   CYPW

CYP 3.7, Assessment criterion 2.1

The Every Child Matters (ECM) framework was introduced alongside the Children Act 2004. The five outcomes in the framework are now referred to as 'Help Children Achieve More'. All childcare services, including schools, must show how they strive towards the outcomes listed below:

- be healthy
- stay safe
- enjoy and achieve
- make a positive contribution
- achieve economic well-being.

1 Write a brief definition for each of the five positive outcomes.

2 Give examples of ways that practitioners can support children and young people to achieve each outcome.

■ Services and benefits

Local authorities have a duty to improve the well-being of children and young people. They must put into place a Children and Young People Plan (CYPP) to show how they will do this.

Health care services

Health care is provided by the National Health Service (NHS) and is the responsibility of the Department of Health. All families with young children need access to a wide range of health care services. Parents often feel that they are constantly at the doctors' surgery or baby clinic as children are prone to common infectious illnesses and minor accidents. The primary health care services available through GP surgeries, NHS Direct, baby clinics, dental practices or optometrists are universal services and meet the majority of the health needs of children and families. Some children may face acute health problems that require access to secondary health services. These are provided by hospitals, A & E units or specialist health centres, through planned or unplanned admissions. Children with chronic conditions such as asthma or diabetes, or with a disability, will require long-term specialist health services.

Health surveillance

Health and development reviews are a free entitlement for all children and their families, starting with the baby in the womb and continuing at regular intervals throughout early childhood. Reviews are carried out by health visitors, GPs or practice nurses and include:

- identifying the strengths and needs of the child and family, including factors that may put children at risk of illness or abuse
- observing and taking measurements of growth and development – where children are not following expected patterns of development, support can be put in place to promote development and lessen long-term problems

- providing information, advice and responding to concerns – this **empowers** parents to make healthy choices for their children and family
- detecting abnormalities – identifying health or developmental problems so that support or medical or surgical interventions can be offered.

Key term

Empower – to enable individuals to make choices about their own lives.

Screening

Screening tests form part of the child health surveillance programme. At birth babies are examined for abnormalities of the heart, hips and eyes, and testes (in males). Within a few days blood spot screening (heel prick) takes place, and this identifies children who may have or develop serious but rare diseases such as sickle cell disorders or cystic fibrosis. Within the first few weeks of life babies also undergo a hearing test. Before children start school they will have further hearing and vision screening tests.

Immunisation

Health professionals have a responsibility to inform parents about the benefits of immunisation. Immunisation may be accessed in different settings such as baby clinics or GP surgeries, or given by the school nurse. Vaccines are available to all babies and young children to protect them against infections that may cause serious complications or even fatality. Infectious diseases such as measles and mumps are becoming far less common, and polio has now been eradicated from the UK. When the majority of children are vaccinated, this also reduces the likelihood of the disease passing to those who are not immunised.

Research

For more information on the immunisation programme for the UK, visit the NHS website. You can access this website by going to www.pearsonhotlinks.co.uk and searching for this title.

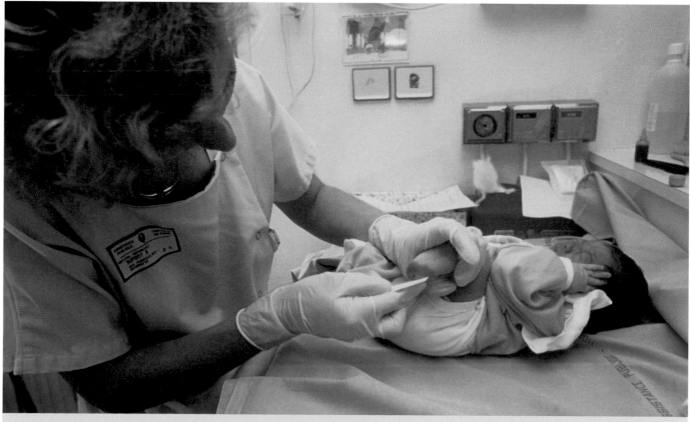

This baby is having a blood spot screening.

Children's social services

Children's social services are the responsibility of each local authority. From time to time children and their families may need additional support. This may be provided by family support workers, or by voluntary organisations such as Home Start. Children's social services provide support for the family when there are concerns about a child's welfare or when they are at increased risk of harm or abuse. Social services are also responsible for **looked-after children** or those in the process of being placed for adoption. Social workers aim to work in partnership with parents, empowering them to make the necessary changes to improve the well-being and ensure the safety of their children. However, the child's needs must come first, and in exceptional circumstances social workers have the powers to apply for a care order to remove children to a place of safety, such as foster care or a residential home.

Theory into practice

Find out more about the work of children's social workers on the government's education website by going to www.pearsonhotlinks.co.uk and searching for this title.

Key terms

Child poverty – according to the UK government, children and families are deemed to be living in poverty when their reported income is less than 60 per cent of the UK median income before housing costs have been paid.

Looked-after children – children who are in residential care, such as foster care or a residential home.

Early years education

The Department for Education has overall responsibility for children's services and education. Each local authority has a duty to ensure that there is sufficient good-quality early years provision in its area. Education does not start when a child enters school at the age of 5 years but at birth. Research shows that the learning and development that take place in these first five years are critical, as they provide a firm foundation for the child's development and attainment. This stage is referred to as the Early Years Foundation Stage (EYFS). From the age of 5, education becomes compulsory and children must attend school full time. From 5 to 7 years is referred to as Key Stage 1. Care and education are provided by a wide range of settings, and these are explored more fully in the next section. All home countries must provide for children's educational needs but the curriculum phases are different in Scotland and Northern Ireland.

Entitlement to education

There is an entitlement to free care and education for children aged 3 to 5 years, for 15 hours each week for 38 weeks of the year (10 hours per week in Wales). The aim of this entitlement is to improve social mobility for disadvantaged children. In Northern Ireland, where children start compulsory education at 4, there are entitlements to free places in early years settings during the preschool year. From 2013, 2-year-olds from disadvantaged families will also qualify for free early years places in England and Wales.

Link

Go to Section B in this unit to find more information about the types of education settings and services.

Benefits

Parents may be eligible for a range of benefits, designed to help alleviate the effects of **child poverty**. Poverty is more than just the lack of income. Poverty affects all aspects of life for the child and family by reducing access to suitable housing, leisure facilities, health care and educational opportunities. The government's Child Poverty Strategy aims to address the causes of poverty for children and families in an attempt to reduce inequalities and improve outcomes. Figure 13.1 shows the financial support that is available to families.

The way that tax credits are worked out is quite complicated and depends on income and the number of children in the family. Extra credit is also available for parents of disabled children who are

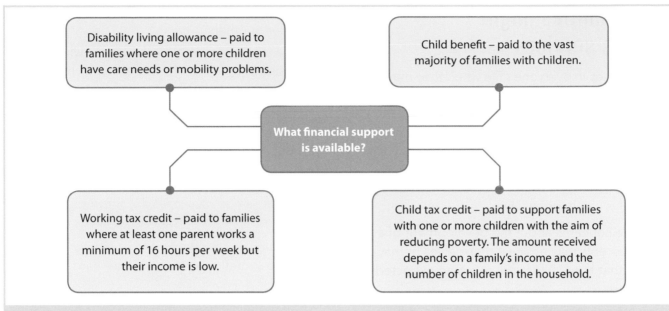

Figure 13.1 The financial support that is available to families

claiming disability living allowance or whose child is registered blind. Some families are able to claim additional credits to pay for childcare.

Information for families about education and services

There are many places where families can find information about education and services. Some of the sources of information are listed in Figure 13.2.

Research

You can find more information about the services that are available by visiting the websites for the National Association of Family Information Services and Directgov. You can access these websites by going to www.pearsonhotlinks.co.uk and searching for this title.

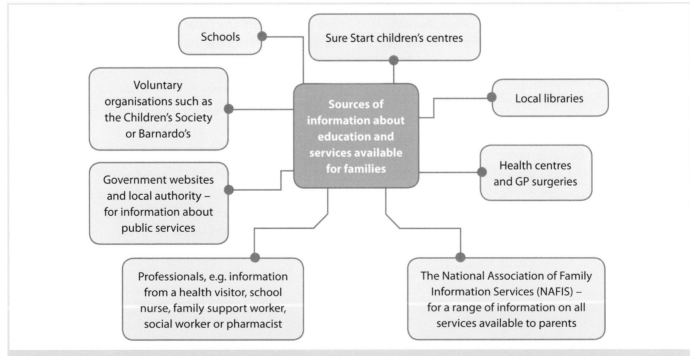

Figure 13.2 Sources of information about the education and services that are available

Why families might access services

There are times in everyone's life when they may need to access services. This is particularly true of families with young children. Sometimes families require advice so that they can resolve a problem themselves. However, there may be times when their needs are more acute or complex, and in this case support from one or more specialist services may be needed. This can happen when:

- there are concerns about the development of a child – parents may notice it themselves or may be told that their child is not reaching expected milestones
- there are concerns about the health of a child – this may be a minor or more serious illness
- a child has a special educational need or mobility problem
- a child requires emergency health care for serious illness or injury
- there is lack of knowledge – about immunisation or diet and nutrition, for instance
- a family is in debt and does not have enough money for basic needs such as food and clothing

- a child is at risk of harm or abuse – from a family member or others
- there are concerns about education – where to access education or concerns about a child's lack of progress
- a referral is made by a childcare professional
- a parent or carer is unable to provide care for a child because of their own physical or mental health problems or a disability.

Reflect

Some families are reluctant to access services. They are sometimes referred to as 'hard to reach families'.

- Discuss reasons why families may not access services with your supervisor or manager.
- Suggest three ways in which you could encourage families to access services.

Key term

Curriculum – all of the experiences and learning that are provided by a setting.

Assessment practice 13.1

3A.P1 | 3A.P2 | 3A.M1 | 3A.D1

There are three children in the Cooper family. Sam is 5 years old and attends the local primary school. Sam is doing well at school but he has cerebral palsy, which affects his mobility. Alice is 3 years old. She has just started nursery school for three mornings each week. During a recent review, concerns were raised about her speech and language development. The baby, Jack, is just 2 months old and is meeting the expected milestones for his age.

The family finds it quite a struggle to make ends meet. Mum, Claire, does not work at present but hopes to go back to working part-time when Jack

is 6 months old. Dad, Jason, works long hours as a security guard but his income is quite low.

1 Explain the services and benefits that the Cooper family has a right to access.

2 Give reasons for why the family may need to access the services and benefits you identified.

3 Suggest ways in which the services and benefits are likely to support the family, giving examples.

4 Evaluate how each service and benefit that the family may access could contribute to the outcomes for Sam, Alice and Jack.

B Understand the context in which early years education is provided

Early years education takes place in a range of settings. It may be provided by the local authority, private or voluntary organisations, or in the child's own home. Until the term after the child's fifth birthday, when full-time education becomes compulsory, it is often sessional or part time. Although there is no requirement for parents to send their child to an educational setting until they reach 5 years, many parents choose to do so as it gives their children the opportunity to socialise with children of the same age. They can also take part in a wide range of play and hands-on activities that promote their all-round development.

Types of settings

Whatever the context of early education provision and type of setting, practitioners have a responsibility to provide a challenging environment and deliver a **curriculum** appropriate for the needs and age group of individual children. Some children attend more than one setting, for instance, a nursery class and childminder. The majority of primary schools offer extended services from 8.00 a.m. until 6.00 p.m., often referred to as 'wrap-around' care. Schools may also run holiday schemes.

Table 13.2 lists a variety of educational settings open to children.

Table 13.2 Types of educational settings

Setting	Description	Type
Nursery schools and classes	Provide early education for children from 3–4 years. They may be separate from or attached to a local mainstream school or managed separately. Usually part-time. Some preschool classes may form part of an independent school and be privately funded. Others may be run by third-sector organisations such as Barnardo's.	• Local authority • Private • Voluntary
Sure Start children's centres	Provide part or full day care and education for children aged 0–5 years. Centres also provide integrated health and care services for children and families. Their main purpose is to improve the outcomes for children and their families, focusing on those that are disadvantaged.	• Local authority
Day nurseries	Provide part or full day care and education for children aged 0–5 years. Sometimes based in the workplace.	• Local authority • Private • Voluntary
Playgroups	Offer part-time, sessional care and education for children aged 2–3 years. Playgroups are run by volunteers but must be registered and run by a qualified leader. They are often located in local community halls or schools.	• Voluntary

continued

Table 13.2 (continued)

Setting	Description	Type
Childminders	Childminders provide care and education for children in their own homes. Where this is provided for children under 8 years and over 2 hours per day, childminders must be registered and accredited.	• Private
Reception classes	Classes within a mainstream school (see below) providing full-time education for children from 4 years until they begin statutory education at the age of 5.	• Local authority
Primary schools (mainstream)	Provide full-time education for children from 4–11 years. From the reception class (4–5 years) children progress to Year 1 (5–6 years) and then to Year 2 (6–7 years).	• Community Schools are entirely run by the local authority (LA). • Some schools such as Foundation and Trust schools are run by a governing body in consultation with the LA. • Voluntary aided schools are usually faith schools and are partly funded by the LA. • Voluntary controlled schools are similar but are run by the LA.
Free Schools or Academies	The nature, organisation and curriculum of Free Schools and Academies are varied. They are accountable for the outcomes of children but are not required to follow the EYFS or the National Curriculum. Some offer nursery facilities.	• Independent from local and national government but publicly funded through the Education Funding Agency (EFA). • Set up and run by community groups including charities, parents, businesses, universities or other interested educational groups.
Special schools	Some children with a learning disability or physical disability may attend a special school if this is appropriate. Special schools may be community or foundation schools, or independent.	• Local authority • Private
Independent schools	Sometimes called private schools. They provide statutory education from 5 years. Usually they have preparatory classes for children from the age of 3 years. Some private schools follow particular teaching methods or a philosophy, such as Montessori schools or Steiner Waldorf schools. Private schools must provide an appropriate curriculum but do not have to follow the EYFS or National Curriculum.	• Privately funded

The structure of early years education

In England, early years education is divided into two distinct phases, the Foundation Stage and Key Stage 1.

Early Years Foundation Stage

This ranges from 0 to 5 years. At this stage education is not compulsory. The Early Years Foundation Stage (EYFS) provides the curriculum framework.

Primary education to Key Stage 1

From the term following a child's fifth birthday, full-time education becomes compulsory. At primary school the National Curriculum provides the curriculum framework.

The Early Years Framework

The EYFS was introduced in 2008 and revised in 2012. It provides a mandatory curriculum framework for children from birth until the end of the reception year in registered early years settings. During their early years, children's learning will be supported through play and hands-on activity. Practitioners must provide a high-quality environment and design a curriculum that takes into account three characteristics of learning: active learning, creating and thinking critically, and playing and exploring.

Areas of learning

The EYFS identifies three prime areas of learning:

- personal, social and emotional development
- communication and language
- physical development.

There are also four specific subject areas: literacy, mathematics, expressive arts and design, and understanding the world.

Link

Go to Unit 2 in Student Book 1 to find more information about the importance of play for children's learning and development.

Key Stage 1 curriculum

At Key Stage 1 the curriculum becomes a little more formal. The National Curriculum (NC) forms a major part of the whole curriculum for children attending state-maintained schools. It is divided into four key stages. Key Stage 1 is the curriculum framework for children aged from 5 to 7 years. There are two underlying principles or aims of the NC, which must be adhered to:

- Children must be given opportunities to learn and achieve.
- There must be opportunities for spiritual, moral, social and cultural development.

At Key Stage 1, the National Curriculum comprises the ten **statutory** subject areas shown in Figure 13.3. Religious Education is also a statutory subject but is not part of the National Curriculum. Guidelines for teaching Citizenship, and Personal, Social and Health Education (PSHE) are also included but these aspects of the curriculum are non-statutory.

For each statutory and non-statutory subject area, there is a programme of study. Programmes of study provide the knowledge, understanding and skills that must be taught. However, they do not prescribe the ways in which subjects should be taught. Children continue to benefit from play and **experiential learning** methods that they enjoyed in the Foundation Stage.

Settings must provide indoor and outdoor learning opportunities for young children.

Did you know?

The National Curriculum is presently being reviewed by the government. It is planned to introduce the new KS1 and KS2 curriculum in September 2014. Keep abreast of the planned changes at the Department for Education website. You can access this website by going to www.pearsonhotlinks.co.uk and searching for this title.

If you work in Wales or Northern Ireland, find out about the curriculum frameworks for your own home country.

Key term

Experiential learning – taking meaning from direct experience and hands-on activities.

Figure 13.3 The Key Stage 1 statutory curriculum

In Wales, the statutory school age is 5 years, as in England, but the curriculum phases are a little different. The Flying Start programme provides guidance for the education and welfare for children aged 0 to 3 years. Children then progress to the Foundation Phase – the statutory curriculum for children aged 3 to 7 years. The foundation curriculum comprises seven areas of learning, including the requirement for Welsh language development. Children do not progress to the Welsh National Curriculum until Key Stage 2 at the age of 7 years.

In Northern Ireland, the statutory school age is 4 years. There is a preschool curriculum for settings for children aged 3 to 4 years. Children do not access the Foundation Stage curriculum until they start school at 4 years. The curriculum stages for Northern Ireland are:

- Preschool:
  - 3 to 4 years
- Foundation Stage:
  - 4 to 5 years (Primary 1)
  - 5 to 6 years (Primary 2)
- Key Stage 1:
  - 6 to 7 years (Primary 3)
  - 7 to 8 years (Primary 4).

The Foundation Stage and Key Stage 1 curricula for Northern Ireland comprise areas of learning similar to England. You can find more detail about the curriculum phases in Wales and Northern Ireland by going to the websites for the Welsh Government and Department for Education (Northern Ireland) respectively. You can access these websites by going to www.pearsonhotlinks.co.uk and searching for this title.

Assessment

Children develop at different rates so will reach the expected goals or levels relating to each area of learning at their own pace. Individuals may even achieve at different levels across the areas of learning or subjects, for instance, achieving the goals expected for their age in literacy but not in mathematics. It is therefore important that curriculum planning takes account of the stage the child has reached and not their age.

Assessment is the method by which progress and achievement are measured. Ongoing assessment, described as **formative assessment**, is an essential part of the planning cycle. How would we know what to plan for the next stage of learning without knowing what a child already knows or can do? You will probably see practitioners making notes of their observations as they interact with children. You will also see that practitioners keep samples or photographs of children's work.

Summative assessment provides information on what children know and can do at a set point in time. It is a statutory requirement and the data is sent to the local authority. During the Foundation Stage, when a child is 2 years old, practitioners carry out a progress check against the three prime areas of learning. Then, at the end of the reception year, when a child is 5 years old, practitioners complete an EYFS Profile for the child. They make judgements about each child's knowledge, understanding and abilities relating to the EYFS areas of learning.

During Key Stage 1, at the end of Year 1, children must undergo a statutory phonics test. Then, at the end of Key Stage 1, at the age of 7 years, children are formally assessed by their teacher in reading, writing, speaking and listening, mathematics and science. Their progress is measured against the expected levels of attainment for each subject. The information provided by these assessments is important in helping teachers plan for the next stage of children's learning and development.

Key terms

Formative assessment – assessment that takes place during the learning process on an ongoing basis, or 'assessment for learning'.

Summative assessment – assessment of what a child knows and can do at the end of a period of learning, or 'assessment of learning'.

The role of inspectorates

The Education Act 2005 (Section 5) sets out the legal requirements for the inspection of schools. In England, childcare and education services including schools are regulated and inspected by the Office for

Standards in Education, Children's Services and Skills (Ofsted). The type of inspection will depend on the setting, the ages of the children and the type of care being provided. The Childcare Act 2006 provides a legal framework for registration and inspection of early years care and education, and care of children and young people under 18 years.

If you work in Wales or Northern Ireland, it is important that you find out about the inspectorate for your own home country. In Wales, Estyn is the inspectorate for schools and for nurseries that are maintained or receive funding from local authorities. A separate inspectorate, the Care and Social Services Inspectorate Wales, inspects childcare services. In Northern Ireland the Education and Training Inspectorate (ETI) inspects preschool settings and schools.

Registration

Those providing care and education for young children must register. To do this, providers must show that they meet minimum requirements, for instance, that staff are suitable and have appropriate qualifications and that the environment will meet the welfare requirements of children. There are two types of registration:

- the Early Years Register – for settings providing care for children up to 5 years, such as nurseries, preschools, childminders and playgroups
- the Child Care Register – for those providing care for children from birth to 18 years.

Inspection of early years education settings

Early years education settings are inspected on a regular basis. This is done with little notice or sometimes with no notice at all. Inspections are usually completed in half a day. During the inspection of early years settings an inspector will check that the requirements of the Early Years Foundation Stage framework are being met. They will look for evidence that:

- the children are being well looked after with regard to their health, social and emotional development, and well-being
- the environment is safe and stimulating
- the setting is being well managed
- the setting is providing opportunities for high-quality learning that lead towards the EYFS goals for children aged from 0 to 5 years
- the setting is supporting children's development.

Inspection of childcare providers

Inspection of childcare providers is done with a lighter touch, with the process taking less than 2 hours. Unlike early years settings, inspections are random unless Ofsted receives a complaint about a setting. The purpose of the inspection is to check provision against the requirements of registration, for instance, that the person providing care is suitable and that the environment is safe and meets welfare requirements.

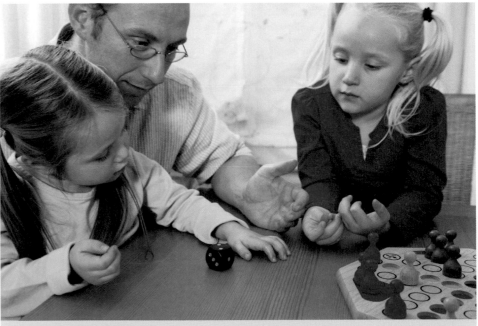

Children should be stimulated and have opportunities for development. Playing board games stimulates children's social skills.

Inspection of schools

Ofsted is responsible for ensuring that schools meet the required standards set out in the Education Act 2005. School inspections will also include inspection of early years provision where this is managed by the school. Inspections usually take place every few years, but timing varies depending on how well the school has done in previous inspections. The key aims of inspection are to:

- evaluate the effectiveness of the provision to meet the care and educational needs of children
- identify areas of provision that need to improve.

Inspectors base their evaluations on information provided by the school, by talking to parents, staff and children, and by direct observation. You may have been aware of an inspection that took place at your own school. Can you remember being asked questions about your experiences?

As well as academic progress, inspectors look at how well the school provides for children's holistic needs, including:

- how well the children are doing with the curriculum, including the National Curriculum attainment targets
- the quality of teaching and learning happening both in and out of the classroom
- whether the school is providing equality of opportunity. The school must demonstrate that it meets the needs of all children regardless of race, culture, disability or individual need
- the processes in place to safeguard children from harm
- how well the school works with parents and outside agencies to improve the well-being and outcomes of the children.

How inspection reports are used

The purpose of inspection is two-fold. First, and most important, it works to raise the standards of early years provision. Reports indicate the extent to which the standards have been met: that is, where settings are doing well in providing for children's needs, or in some instances not so well. These reports are then used as part of each setting's continuous review and development. Action plans must be put in place to develop areas of provision where improvement is needed. This could be one aspect of the setting, for instance, relating to health and safety, the quality of play provision or how well it provides for children's special educational needs. Improvements in standards will be measured at the next inspection.

Second, inspection reports can help indicate to parents which setting will best provide for their child's needs. Reports can be accessed from the setting or Ofsted by anyone with an interest in finding out how well a setting is doing. Although most parents will visit the setting or school where they intend to send their child, inspection reports provide them with additional information about the quality of care and education that their child will receive.

Produce an article for a local parenting magazine that:

- explains the difference between at least four different settings that provide early years education (to include private, voluntary and state provision)

- explains how each setting will be inspected

- identifies the main features for each of the four settings, comparing the advantages and disadvantages of each one for the child and their family.

C Understand the role of multi-agency work for children and their families

In your role as childcare practitioner you will be expected to work alongside professionals from other agencies, such as health, children's social care and education, and perhaps even the police or voluntary organisations. This is referred to as multi-agency working.

What is multi-agency working?

Multi-agency working is when professionals from different services work together in collaboration with parents to improve the outcomes for children. You may also hear the terms 'joint working' or 'partnership working' being used. Professionals who work together are not always based in the same organisation or setting but they will contribute to the assessment of children's needs, share information and work towards improving the outcomes for children. In this way, children and their families are placed firmly at the centre of any reviews, planning and delivery of services. Membership of the team will vary depending on a specific child's needs. Multi-agency working is essential when children and families need support from more than one agency, for instance, when a child in need has a disability, is at risk of harm or abuse or is looked after.

The following services may work together to support children and families:

- schools
- early years settings
- housing authorities
- benefit agencies
- health services
- advocacy services
- hearing units
- social services
- foster care
- child psychology services.

The role of multi-agency work

Multi-agency working is not a new way of working. There have been examples of agencies cooperating and working together for many years. However, until more recently this way of working has been ad hoc and service-led, rather than being led by the needs of children and their families. In 2003, following the death of Victoria Climbié, a report highlighted that failures of professionals to share information had contributed to her death. This resulted in the Children Act 2004 and the legal requirement for agencies to work more closely together in the interests of children and families.

The role of multi-agency working is to achieve a holistic approach to assessment and delivery of services, by providing:

- easier access to services for children and families
- early intervention
- better outcomes for children and families
- integrated support, enabling children to stay with their families or in their local school.

Research suggests that it is this holistic approach of multi-agency working that improves the outcomes for children. In Unit 1 you explored how each area of a child's development is interlinked, so you can understand that for support to be effective, all of the child's needs must be considered. Putting in place services to meet a child's health needs, for example, will not address their emotional and social needs.

Multi-agency working means that families only deal with one person. Families find this far less stressful than having to meet with lots of different professionals or having to travel to different settings. Children with complex needs may require as many as ten different services. Effective coordination of these services ensures that support can be put in place immediately. Delays or inappropriate or insufficient support may put children's health and well-being at risk. The delivery of the most appropriate service, delivered at the right time, improves outcomes for children and their families.

For children who are in need or at risk or have a special educational need, well-targeted support means that their needs can be provided for in their own home and/or their local school. For instance, a child with a disability may continue to attend their local mainstream school because their physiotherapist and health care worker work in partnership with the teacher and parents. Working as a team to support the needs of the whole family may reduce the risk of children being taken into care. For example, by giving parents advice and practical help, such as information on benefits or support for their own health needs, they will be more able to provide care for their own children.

Children in need

Under the Children Act 1989, Section 17, there is a duty on local authorities (LAs) to 'safeguard and promote the welfare of children within their area who are "in need"' (see the legal definition of 'in need' in Section A of this unit). LAs must provide 'a level of services appropriate to those children's needs'. The most effective way that LAs can carry out their duty is for services to work together. When concerns are raised that a child is in need, it is important to carry out an initial assessment as soon as possible. The Common Assessment Framework (CAF) is the assessment tool used for this purpose because, as its

name suggests, it is shared by all children's services. The purpose of the assessment is to identify a child's holistic needs at an early stage so that support can be put in place before the family reaches crisis point.

Children with special educational needs

The SEN Code of Practice 2001 requires that children's educational needs are assessed and that their needs should be met in a mainstream setting or school. When early years practitioners or teachers become concerned that a child is not achieving the level expected for their age, they too will use the CAF process to assess needs. Once a child's needs have been established, an Individual Learning Plan (ILP) will be agreed by the setting and any other relevant agencies.

Support for children with SEN is a staged approach. Children are identified at the first stage when professionals working together in the child's own setting are able to provide for all their needs. This stage is called Early Years Action (for children under 5 years old) or School Action (from the age of 5 years). Children who do not make progress at this stage, or have been identified as having more complex needs, will require support from services outside the school. This stage is called Early Years Action Plus or School Action Plus. The school or early years setting will lead on the assessment but information may also need to be gathered about the child from other agencies and the parents. Agencies may include, for instance, an educational psychologist or hearing support worker. Children may require a Statement of Educational Needs when additional finance and resources are needed to support more complex needs.

Link

Go to Unit 18 to find more information about working with children with additional needs.

Children at risk

When concerns are raised about a child's safety and welfare, children's social services have a duty to investigate if there is 'reasonable cause to suspect that a child is suffering or likely to suffer **significant harm**' under Section 47 of the Children Act 1989. A core assessment of the child's needs will then be carried out, drawing on information from their initial assessment and from relevant professionals.

If concerns are substantiated, a child protection conference will be held, led by a social worker and involving a number of agencies – for instance, a health worker, police officer and early years practitioner. A detailed Child Protection Plan will then be agreed, in partnership with the child's parents, that identifies the services required to ensure the safety of the child and supports them and their family.

How agencies work together

Multi-agency work can be organised in different ways. Agencies may be fully integrated or come together to work in partnership for a particular purpose. There are also times when professionals contact each other informally for advice and information. Some examples are given below, but as you explore multi-agency working in your own area you may find variations on the following models.

• Multi-agency panel

Professionals from a range of different services or agencies such as health, education and social services come together to form a 'panel' to discuss particular cases where there are problems faced by children and their families. Panel members may carry out casework and report back, or one professional may be appointed as the lead. In this model each panel member continues to be based within their own service or agency and is responsible to a manager there. Multi-agency panels may be formed when staff from one setting, for instance, a nursery, identify that a child and their family require support from other services, such as behavioural support or a housing association.

• Multi-agency team

Although team members may continue to have links to their own 'home' agency to undertake training and access resources, they will work under the leadership of one manager. This is a more permanent arrangement than a panel, with professionals being appointed or sometimes seconded to the team. They will work towards the same goal – to improve the outcome for the child and their family. An example of this model is a special school that employs early years practitioners, teachers and a school nurse, but other professionals such as hearing support workers are seconded or appointed to meet the particular needs of individual children.

• Integrated services

These are similar to multi-agency teams, but are fully integrated. Professionals work together under the same manager to deliver services to children and their families. An advantage of this model is that right from the start there is a shared philosophy, shared methods of working and well-established communication channels. A good example of this model can be seen in a Sure Start children's centre where a range of services (for instance, health services, breastfeeding and weaning support groups, parenting classes, family support workers, nursery and playgroups) are available within one building.

Support centred on the child

Whichever model of multi-agency working is in place, in order to be effective the support must be centred on the child. This process is sometimes referred to as the Team Around the Child (TAC). Also key for successful team working are the following:

- Shared aims and purpose – it is important that, when working together, professionals have agreed ways of working, a clear purpose and mutual respect and trust.
- Effective channels of communication – communication will be far more effective where services are integrated, as there will be a shared language and methods of working.

The cycle of integrated assessment and support

Agencies must work together at each stage of the process from the initial assessment until the planned outcomes are met. This means that the review, which follows a period of support by agencies, may not be the final stage in the process but may lead to further assessment and planning. Support for children and their families must, therefore, be viewed as a continuous cycle.

Assessment

An assessment of a child's needs may be initiated and led by any agency, so all adults who work in children's services must be familiar with the CAF process. The exception is when children are considered to be 'at risk', in which case a social worker from the local authority or the National Society for the Prevention of Cruelty to Children (NSPCC) will lead. Whichever agency leads, professionals from different services will work together to share information about the child and their family. When sharing information it is essential for professionals to observe confidentiality. This means that parents must always be consulted before sharing information unless there is concern that this would put the child at risk of harm or abuse.

Information should include the strengths and interests as well as the needs of the child. The situation of the family must also be considered, as this will affect support planning and the role the parents will play. For instance, a health visitor may provide information about the child's health and their home environment, a social worker on the parents' ability to provide support, a hearing support worker on the extent of a child's hearing loss or a teacher about a child's behaviour and academic achievement. Parents know their child best, so wherever possible they, and if appropriate the child, should contribute to the assessment.

Planning

Following assessment, a plan will be agreed on how the five outcomes – be healthy, stay safe, enjoy and achieve, make a positive contribution and achieve economic well-being – can best be achieved. The format of the plan will depend on the child's needs. For instance, an Individual Learning Plan (ILP) is for children with SEN, while a Child Protection Plan is for children at risk of significant harm or abuse. Each agency will share its particular area of knowledge and expertise, aiding decision making about the best way to provide support and, where necessary, solving problems. By working together in this way professionals are able to coordinate support more effectively, ensuring that there is no duplication of services or, worse, that some of the child's needs go unnoticed.

Each plan will be agreed by the professionals involved, and should include:

- a lead professional to coordinate assessment, planning and reviews and to be the first point of contact for parents and other professionals
- the short- and long-term targets for the child and family
- detail about how these can be achieved
- the timescale for support and review
- the roles and responsibilities of each agency and the parents in providing support
- resource requirements.

Support

Once the plan is in place the lead professional must continue to coordinate the support, but each agency will be accountable for delivering their part of the plan. Support may be provided directly, for instance, a learning support assistant who works alongside a child in the classroom, or indirectly, such as advice given to a teacher by a child psychologist on ways to manage a child's behaviour.

Concern has been raised about Billy's progress in the reception class. His language is delayed compared with children of the same age. He also finds concentration difficult and can often be aggressive towards other children. His teacher is aware that his father lost his job last year and the family is finding it difficult to manage. They may even have to move out of their house.

1 What would be the assessment process for Billy?

2 Who would be likely to lead the assessment?

3 Which agencies might be involved in contributing to assessment and supporting the family?

4 How might they work together and with the parents?

Even though a date will have been agreed for review, it is important that progress is constantly monitored by each professional, to ensure that support plans are appropriate and that they can continue to be delivered. They must also inform the lead professional if the child or family's circumstances change at any time. When professionals work together in one setting they may find that there is a merging of roles, so it is important that they are clear about their individual responsibilities. Although this can be a barrier to effective working, the sharing of knowledge and expertise in delivering the plan can ultimately be of benefit to the child, family and the professionals involved.

Review

A review date must be agreed as part of the plan. The lead professional will then arrange the meeting and invite professionals from each agency and the parents. They will discuss what has gone well and what support has not been effective and the reasons for this. The result of the review may be that the child has met the identified targets and that their family no longer requires support from all or some of the agencies in the team. When some or all of the targets have not been met, the support may need to continue or be adapted. In some cases the child may need additional and/or specialist agencies to be involved. An amended support plan will then be put in place and the cycle will continue.

CYP 3.7, Assessment criterion 2.2

Produce information for parents using a method of your choice, such as a leaflet or poster, on the importance of designing services around the needs of children and young people.

Produce a presentation for your peers and your teacher/tutor. Your presentation must include information on:

- the role of a multi-agency approach in work with children and their parents

- ways in which multi-agency working meets the needs of children and their families, with examples to support this information

- the extent to which multi-agency working may impact on the outcomes for children.

Further reading and resources

Barker, R. (2008) *Making Sense of Every Child Matters*, Bristol: Policy Press.

Walker, G. (2008) *Working Together for Children: A Critical Introduction to Multi-agency Working*, London: Continuum.

Working Together to Safeguard Children: A guide to inter-agency working to safeguard and promote the welfare of children (Department for Education 2010).

Websites

Department of Health: www.dh.gov.uk

Department for Education: www.education.gov.uk

Office for Standards in Education, Children's Services and Skills: www.ofsted.co.uk

Public services: www.direct.gov.uk

National Health Service: www.nhs.uk

Ready for work?

Sonia Kaney
Family support worker based in a children's centre

How long have you been working as a family support worker?

I worked as a volunteer for the first six months alongside a colleague. When I completed my childcare course three years ago I was appointed full-time.

What does your work involve?

My work is really varied. I usually go into the homes of families with young children to provide support but I also lead groups at the children's centre. For instance, the last one was about how to prepare simple, nutritious meals. During my visits some families need more practical help and others more emotional support. A few months ago I visited a mum who found it really difficult to leave the house and was nervous of meeting others. This meant that she was not turning up for her toddler's health reviews and immunisations. I went with her to the children's centre and introduced her to the health visitor and two other mums. Now that she has got to know other mums I have noticed that she is visiting the centre regularly.

What knowledge and skills do you need to be a family support worker?

It is so important that you get on with people. You need to be a good listener and non-judgemental. Most important are good observational skills and knowledge of child development. Family support workers see families regularly and are often the first to notice that there may be a problem, that a child may not be developing as expected or may be at risk of abuse.

What do you enjoy about your job?

The work can be quite tough at times and writing reports is not my favourite task! Despite this I get on really well with other professionals at the centre and learn a great deal from them. When I work alongside a family and see them beginning to take more control of their own lives it gives me a great deal of satisfaction. I really feel that I'm making a difference.

Skills for practice

Professional relationships with adults

You should consider ways to build professional relationships with adults. Use the following tips to help you.

- Ask advice from colleagues at your placement and perhaps make suggestions.
- Use role play to practise using the telephone and speaking with a professional tone in a range of scenarios.
- Greet parents and other visitors with a smile and address them appropriately.

Introduction

The food children eat affects their health and development in many ways. The nutrients provided by food influence children's physical and intellectual development. Social skills are developed at mealtimes, and food can also have an impact on behaviour.

Most children enjoy cooking, as it provides a positive social activity. Cooking involves both mathematical and scientific skills. Preparing and eating food can also develop language skills. Growing the food that children then cook or eat adds another dimension.

Snack and meal provision are common in many day-care settings and you may be required to prepare food for children. It is important that you understand how to do this safely as well as how you can make the most of these learning opportunities.

Assessment: You will be assessed by a series of assignments set by your teacher/tutor.

Learning aims

In this unit you will:

A1 understand how to provide food for children to encourage health and development

A2 understand the role of the adult in encouraging children to develop healthy eating habits

B understand the role of the adult in preparing and serving food safely.

"Whatever childcare setting you work in, you will need to know something about nutrition and food provision. Many settings involve the provision of food either as snacks or lunch and you need to be able to encourage children to eat healthily. Adults have a strong influence on what children eat, and food can also be used as a vehicle for learning.

Abigail Fleming, *a nutritionist*

Food and Mealtimes in the Early Years

14

BTEC
Assessment Zone

This table shows what you must do in order to achieve a **Pass**, **Merit** or **Distinction** grade, and where you can find activities to help you.

Assessment criteria		
Pass	**Merit**	**Distinction**
Learning aim A1: Understand how to provide food for children to encourage health and development **Learning aim A2: Understand the role of the adult in encouraging children to develop healthy eating habits**		
3A1.P1 Explain the impact of diet on children's health and development. **Assessment practice 14.1**	**3A1.M1** Analyse a child's diet in relation to current expert guidance. **Assessment practice 14.1**	**3A.D1** Evaluate the extent to which an early years setting contributes to children's health and development through the provision of food. **Assessment practice 14.3**
3A1.P2 Explain how to work with parents in early years settings to meet children's individual dietary needs. **Assessment practice 14.2**	**3A1.M2** Discuss the role of partnership working with parents in relation to children's attitudes to food. **Assessment practice 14.3**	**3A.D2** Recommend improvements to an early years setting's contribution to children's healthy eating habits. **Assessment practice 14.3**
3A2.P3 English Explain how children's attitudes to food are influenced. **Assessment practice 14.3**		
3A2.P4 Explain the role of adults in developing children's healthy eating habits. **Assessment practice 14.2**		
Learning aim B: Understand the role of the adult in preparing and serving food safely		
3B.P5 Explain responsibilities and practices for working safely in an early years setting when preparing and serving food to children. **Assessment practice 14.4**		

English   English Functional Skills signposting

How you will be assessed

This unit will be assessed by a series of internally assessed tasks set by your teacher/tutor. Throughout this unit you will find assessment practice activities that will help you work towards your assessment. Completing these activities will not mean that you have achieved a particular grade, but you will have carried out useful research or preparation that will be relevant when it comes to your final assignment.

In order for you to achieve the tasks in your assignment, it is important that you check you have met all of the Pass grading criteria. You can do this as you work your way through the assignment.

If you are hoping to gain a Merit or Distinction, you should also make sure that you present the information in your assignment in the style that is required by the relevant assessment criterion. For example, Merit criteria will require you to discuss and analyse, and Distinction criteria will require you to evaluate and make recommendations for improvements.

The assignment set by your teacher/tutor will consist of a number of tasks designed to meet the criteria in the table. This is likely to consist of a written assignment but may also include activities such as:

- case studies
- a leaflet
- an assignment.

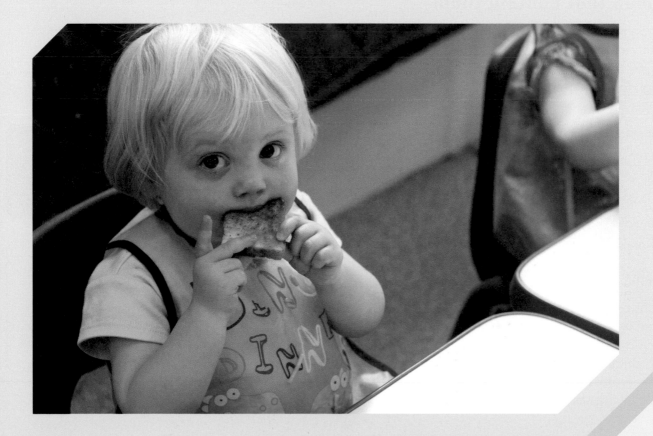

Getting started

Think about your own eating habits.

- How do you think these were formed?
- Who influences what you like and dislike?
- How have adults shaped your food choices throughout your life?

A1 Understand how to provide food for children to encourage health and development

A well-balanced diet is essential for all children for healthy growth and development. Providing food that is nutritious and also appeals to children can be challenging. This section will help you to understand the nutritional needs of children and the food that will provide the necessary nutrients to meet these needs.

Nutrients required for health and development and foods that contain them

An understanding of the nutrients required by children is essential if you are to provide them with a healthy diet. These nutrients need to be provided through food whatever the age of the child, but the amounts that are needed may vary.

There are five main dietary nutrients:

- proteins
- fats
- carbohydrates
- vitamins
- minerals.

Proteins

Proteins provide essential amino acids, which are needed for the growth and repair of our body's cells. They are particularly important for babies and young children. Proteins have to come from food and therefore are essential in the diet. Foods that contain all the essential amino acids are known as high biological value (HBV) foods. Foods that are sources of protein but do not contain all the essential amino acids are known as low biological value (LBV) foods. If two LBV foods are eaten together, one may compensate for the deficiencies in the other – beans on toast is a good example. This is known as the complementary action of proteins.

Protein has another important function, which is to act as a secondary source of energy. The body's first sources of energy are fat and carbohydrate, but if energy is not available from these sources, it will use protein to keep going.

Figure 14.1 outlines the functions and sources of protein.

Function in the body:

- for growth, repair and maintenance of body cells
- a source of energy (secondary)
- used to form enzymes, hormones and antibodies.

Protein

Sources in the diet:

- HBV proteins found in foods derived from animals, such as meat, fish, eggs, milk, cheese
- HBV proteins also found in soya
- LBV proteins found in peas, beans and lentils.

Figure 14.1 The functions and sources of protein

Fats

Of all the nutrients, fats contain the highest amount of energy: 9 kilocalories per gram. Therefore, too much fat in the diet can contribute to obesity, in both adults and children. Fat can be saturated or unsaturated. Animal fats are generally saturated and should be eaten in moderation. Vegetable and fish fats are usually unsaturated. Fat has the effect of making foods more palatable (pleasant to taste), and for this reason it is easy to eat too much of it.

Figure 14.2 outlines the functions and sources of fat.

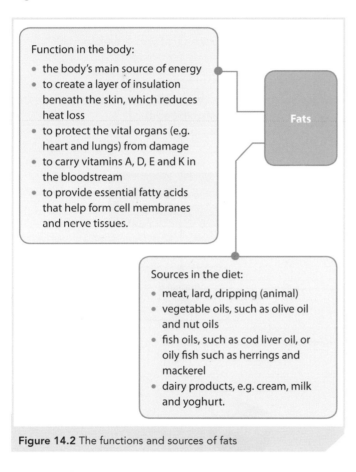

Function in the body:

- the body's main source of energy
- to create a layer of insulation beneath the skin, which reduces heat loss
- to protect the vital organs (e.g. heart and lungs) from damage
- to carry vitamins A, D, E and K in the bloodstream
- to provide essential fatty acids that help form cell membranes and nerve tissues.

Fats

Sources in the diet:

- meat, lard, dripping (animal)
- vegetable oils, such as olive oil and nut oils
- fish oils, such as cod liver oil, or oily fish such as herrings and mackerel
- dairy products, e.g. cream, milk and yoghurt.

Figure 14.2 The functions and sources of fats

Carbohydrates

As much as 50 or 60 per cent of the energy in our diet should come from foods containing carbohydrate. Carbohydrates have an energy value of 3.75 kilocalories per gram. They are divided into three sub-groups:

- Monosaccharides or simple sugars – these are the simplest kinds of carbohydrate molecule.
- Disaccharides, or sugars, such as sucrose (found in cane sugar) and lactose (found in milk).
- Polysaccharides, or complex carbohydrates, including starch (found in potatoes) and cellulose (found in lettuce).

Sugar is easily digested and therefore provides an 'instant' source of energy. Complex carbohydrates, such as starchy foods and cellulose, take longer to break down in the body and therefore provide a slow release of energy.

Some carbohydrates (in the polysaccharides group) provide what is known as dietary fibre. Fibre increases the water content in the body and helps the stools remain soft, thereby helping to prevent constipation.

Figure 14.3 outlines the functions and sources of carbohydrates.

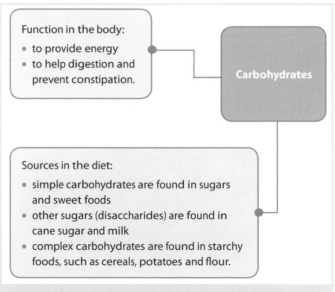

Function in the body:

- to provide energy
- to help digestion and prevent constipation.

Carbohydrates

Sources in the diet:

- simple carbohydrates are found in sugars and sweet foods
- other sugars (disaccharides) are found in cane sugar and milk
- complex carbohydrates are found in starchy foods, such as cereals, potatoes and flour.

Figure 14.3 The functions and sources of carbohydrates

Vitamins and minerals

Vitamins and minerals are also known as **micronutrients** as they are needed in small quantities in the diet. Proteins, fats and carbohydrates, on the other hand, are known as **macronutrients** as they are needed in larger quantities.

Vitamins and minerals are **organic** compounds and are essential for life even though they are only needed in small quantities. Except for a few vitamins and minerals, the body cannot **synthesise** these and, therefore, they must be included in the diet regularly. Vitamins are divided into two groups according to how they are dissolved and carried in the body, as shown in Figures 14.4 and 14.5.

Figure 14.4 Fat-soluble vitamins

Figure 14.5 Water-soluble vitamins

Green leafy vegetables, carrots and tomatoes are a good source of vitamins.

Dairy products are also a good source of vitamins.

Tables 14.1, 14.2 and 14.3 provide a description of the vitamins and minerals, together with their function in the body and main sources.

Table 14.1 Fat-soluble vitamins

Fat-soluble vitamin	Function	Sources
Vitamin A (retinol) Vitamin A comes from two sources. In animal products it is found in the form of retinol and this is the form the body uses. In vegetables, it is found in the form of beta-carotene.	• Vital for the formation of a pigment in the eye (rhodopsin, or visual purple) which helps the eye adjust to the dark • Contributes to maintenance of the skin • Used in the development of the skeleton including the skull and the vertebral column	• Rich sources: liver oils such as cod liver oil or halibut liver oil • Good sources: liver, carrots, spinach, butter, margarine • Useful sources: cheese, eggs, tomatoes, milk, salmon, herrings
Vitamin D Vitamin D is known as the 'sunshine vitamin' because the body can make vitamin D itself with the action of sunlight on the skin.	• Essential for the formation of bones and teeth • Promotes the absorption of calcium and phosphorus by the small intestine • Aids the withdrawal of calcium from the bones to maintain the correct amount of calcium in the blood	• Fatty fish such as salmon, herring and sardines • Dairy products such as butter, eggs, milk, cheese and margarine • Sunshine on the skin
Vitamin E (tocopherols) Studies have shown that a deficiency of Vitamin E in rats leads to degeneration of the muscles.	• Essential for normal **metabolism**	• Most foods contain a trace of vitamin E. Good sources include: • seed oil, particularly wheatgerm • eggs • liver.
Vitamin K (phylloquinone) Vitamin K is needed in small amounts in the body. Although many diets are deficient in Vitamin K, it is produced by bacteria in the large intestine. Half the daily requirement can be met by this.	• Important component in blood clotting	Good sources include: • liver • green leafy vegetables • milk.

Table 14.2 Water-soluble vitamins

Water-soluble vitamin	Function	Sources
Vitamin C (ascorbic acid) Vitamin C is highly unstable and easily lost in cooking and food preparation through heat and oxidation. It can be lost from fruit and vegetables as they are cut, as well as being destroyed by heat. In cooking, it leaches into the cooking liquid. Therefore, to maximise vitamin C intake, you should cut up fruit and vegetables close to the cooking time, cook in a small amount of liquid for the least amount of time possible and use the cooking liquid in gravy and sauces.	• To make the connective tissue which binds body cells together • Essential in the manufacture of blood and the cell walls of blood vessels • Aids resistance to infection – it is believed it helps fight the common cold but there is no definite evidence to prove this • Deficiency may lead to slow repair of cells after injury	Good sources include citrus fruits, blackcurrants and vegetables. Potatoes are also a good source of vitamin C for the British. Although there is not a high amount in them, they are a staple of the British diet. As so many potatoes are eaten, they make up a significant source.
Vitamin B complex • Vitamin B1 (thiamin) • Vitamin B2 (riboflavin) • Niacin • Vitamin B6 (pyridoxine) • Vitamin B9 (folic acid) • Vitamin B12 (cobalamin)	• Essential for the release of energy from proteins, fats and carbohydrates • Needed for growth and normal functioning of the nervous system • Maintains muscle tone • Formation of red blood cells • Deficiency may lead to a feeling of being run-down, tiredness, loss of appetite or retarded growth in children • In severe cases, deficiency can cause nervous diseases such as beriberi, pellagra and anaemia	Good sources include: • brown rice • offal, such as liver or kidney • milk • eggs • fruit and vegetables • flour and most breakfast cereals – it is added by law.

Table 14.3 Minerals

Mineral	Function	Sources
Iron Iron is found in the body in the form of haemoglobin in the red blood cells. Red blood cells have a lifespan of about four months, after which they are replaced.	• Formation of haemoglobin in red blood cells, which enables cells to carry oxygen around the body to other cells and tissues • Important during growth spurts – particularly necessary during childhood	• Animal sources include offal such as liver and black pudding, as well as eggs and fish. • Vegetable sources include green vegetables, cocoa, parsley and flour.
Calcium Calcium works hand in hand with phosphorus. If there is a lack of calcium in the diet, this can lead to stunted growth, badly formed teeth and rickets in children. Children require 600 mg/day.	• Necessary for the formation of the skeleton – strong bones and teeth • Necessary to help the blood to clot • Helps the normal functioning of the muscles	Good sources include: • milk and milk products such as yoghurt • tinned fish, particularly where the bones are eaten, including salmon • hard water • green vegetables • flour, as calcium is added during manufacture.
Phosphorus Phosphorus works in conjunction with calcium. It is the second most abundant mineral in the body and is found mainly in the bones.	• Contributes to the formation of strong bones and teeth • Essential component of the blood • Necessary for metabolism, to harvest energy from foods	• Phosphorus is present in most animal and vegetable foods and therefore a deficiency is unknown. • Phosphates are also added to a number of foods during manufacture.
Iodine There is between 20 and 50 mg of iodine in the body; 8 mg is found in the thyroid gland. A deficiency of iodine can lead to lack of energy and obesity. It can also lead to goitre, which is a swelling thyroid gland in the neck.	• Essential component of hormones manufactured by the thyroid gland in the neck, including thyroxine, which control the body's metabolic rate • The recommended daily intake is very small – 0.05 to 0.30 mg/day	• Good sources include seafood and seaweed . • Iodine can be found in plant foods but the amount depends on the soil in which they are grown and therefore the amount is irregular.
Zinc Zinc is a trace element that is found in most foods, particularly in association with protein.	• Essential for tissue growth • Required for enzyme reactions in the body	Good sources include: • oysters • kidney • green vegetables • wholegrain cereals.

Guidelines for providing food and drink

When babies are born, they are able to suck but not bite or chew. They are born with the sucking reflex and this means that their diet has to be a liquid one: milk. Human babies are either breastfed or bottle fed with milk that has been modified to suit young babies. Whether to breast- or bottle feed can be a difficult decision for parents – there are advantages and disadvantages to both feeding methods.

Breastfeeding

Health experts recommend that breastfeeding is best for the human baby. It is believed that breastfeeding for the first four to six months gives babies a good start in life.

Breast milk is very complex and therefore no formula can match it exactly. It contains exactly the correct balance of proteins, fats, vitamins and minerals for a baby as well as delivering the correct amount of calories. This means that breastfed babies are less likely to become overweight than bottle-fed babies. They are also less likely to suffer from dehydration or from excess mineral intake. The protein in breast milk is easily digested and more of the essential components are absorbed into the baby's body.

Another advantage of breast milk is that it helps to protect the child from infections. First feeds, before the milk fully comes in, contain colostrum, which provides the baby with antibodies. These help babies fight infection and increase their resistance to a wide range of infections, including chest and urinary tract infections. It also contains a laxative, which allows the baby to cope with small amounts of milk while its kidneys adjust to life outside the womb. Formula milk does not contain these antibodies.

Some researchers believe that breastfeeding can help bonding between the mother and baby as it creates a special kind of closeness.

Bottle feeding

Not all women are able or want to breastfeed. Some women choose to breastfeed for the first few months and then move to bottle feeding as the child grows. Every mother is different and will do what they feel is best for their baby. If a mother does not want to breastfeed or wants to stop, bottle feeding is the alternative.

If bottle feeding is chosen, formula milk must be used. A baby cannot be given cow's milk as a drink, as it has too much protein and lacks important nutrients. Cow's milk should not be given to a baby as a drink until they are 12 months old.

Modern formula milks have been developed to replicate breast milk as closely as possible. They are made from dried cow's milk that has been modified to make it more digestible for a young baby. Most formulas are based on whey or casein, and these are the main source of protein. Whey-based formulas are usually given to young babies as they replicate breast milk more closely and are easier for a young baby to digest. Casein-based formulas often contain more minerals and protein and are therefore suited to hungrier babies.

Formula milks are produced with clear instructions on how to make the feeds up to the correct proportions and consistency. It is important that these instructions are followed exactly. The formula should not be made stronger by adding more powder, as this makes the mixture too concentrated and can cause dehydration.

With bottle feeding, a mother can see exactly how much milk a baby has taken. However, it is important that a baby is not forced to finish a feed, as they may not need it all and excess calories will be converted to fat. This can lead to an increase in weight that can be difficult to shift later in childhood. However, if a baby is still hungry after a feed, an additional feed can be easily made up to satisfy that hunger whereas, if breastfeeding, it would take a couple of days for the body to adjust to the increased demand.

Some women find breastfeeding in public embarrassing, despite it being seen as more acceptable than it used to be and supported by legislation. Bottle feeding avoids this potential embarrassment and means a baby can be fed when out and about. It gives the mother more freedom in this way.

Weaning

Weaning is the process of expanding a baby's diet to include food and drink other than breast milk or infant formula.

Weaning should start from about 6 months. Although all babies develop at different paces, it is recommended that weaning should not be started with babies younger than 6 months for the following reasons.

- **Neuromuscular coordination** needs to be adequately developed and an infant of less than 6 months is unlikely to be able to maintain a suitable posture for swallowing. They are also unlikely to be able to move food from the front to the back of the mouth for swallowing.

- They are not usually willing to experiment with different flavours, textures and consistencies.

- The kidney function may not be mature enough to deal with the greater concentration of **solutes** and reduced fluid volume that is associated with weaning.

- Secretion of digestive juices in the gut is not adequately developed to cope with digestion.

- Absorption capacities of the small and large intestine are not adequately developed.

- The gastrointestinal system is more prone to food-related allergies such as **coeliac disease**.

- Children should not have too much energy-dense food too early as it may lead to obesity.

From about the end of the sixth month, babies can cope with soft foods of a slightly thicker consistency than milk, such as baby rice or baby rusks softened with milk. They can suck and swallow these feeds. Babies cannot bite and chew lumps of food until they are 5 or 6 months old.

Solid foods are introduced when milk alone is unable to meet a baby's nutritional needs. Signs that suggest a baby needs to start solids include:

- the baby still seems hungry after a good milk feed

- the baby starts to demand to be fed more often, suggesting that the milk feed is not satisfying them

- the baby starts to wake in the night for a feed after previously sleeping through.

The move from a wholly liquid diet to a solid one is a gradual process. Each stage builds on the previous one, ensuring that the baby's digestive system can cope with the changes in textures and types of food. Weaning has a number of stages.

> ## Key terms
>
> **Coeliac disease** – a digestive condition caused by gluten intolerance.
>
> **Neuromuscular coordination** – the joint operation of different muscles to produce a movement, e.g. raising your arm.
>
> **Solutes** – a substance that is dissolved in another substance.

6 to 9 months (Stage 1)

Weaning usually begins with offering some solid food after one milk feed during the day. First foods are simple unprocessed foods such as puréed vegetables or fruit, or non-wheat-based cereal such as baby rice mixed with milk. These foods are bland and are unlikely to upset the baby's digestive system. It is important not to give a wheat-based product at this stage, as wheat can upset the digestive system.

Recent guidance from health visitors on weaning includes an approach known as 'baby-led weaning'. This can be used alongside giving puréed foods or on its own. The idea is that you allow babies to choose what they eat from the outset. You offer them different foods cut to suitable sizes, and if they like a food, they choose to eat it. If they do not like a food, they will not eat it. This allows babies to enjoy the same foods as the rest of the family and develop their own tastes.

If the food is to be offered heated, make sure it is not too hot. Microwaves should not be used to heat baby food due to the hot spots that can occur. There are many ready-prepared first foods such as baby rice available. Remember to follow the instructions on the packet or jar if using commercially produced foods.

If, when starting to wean, the baby seems not to want the food, it is important not to force them to eat. Put the process on hold for a week and then try again.

Food is given in small amounts on a clean spoon or fingertip. Babies will take time to learn how to take food from a spoon and there will be spitting and mess as they learn. Often babies get frustrated when they first start solid food as they are used to the milk coming in a continuous flow, and eating is a slower process, with pauses.

Solid food should never be added to bottles as this can cause choking.

Table 14.4 summarises the foods to try and foods to avoid at Stage 1.

Table 14.4 Stage 1 of weaning: foods to try and foods to avoid	
Foods to try	Foods to avoid
<ul><li>Vegetable or fruit purées (potato, yam, spinach, apple, banana)</li><li>Thin porridge made from rice, cornmeal, sago or millet</li><li>Rusks mixed with breast or formula milk</li></ul>	<ul><li>Wheat-based foods such as bread or biscuits</li><li>Milk other than breast or formula</li><li>Eggs</li><li>Citrus fruits</li><li>Nuts</li><li>Fatty foods</li></ul>

Simple unprocessed foods such as puréed vegetables are unlikely to upset the baby's digestive system.

9 to 12 months (Stage 2)

Feeds still start with the breast or bottle milk but the amount of solid food is gradually increased. The amount given will vary according to the baby's appetite.

At this point, the number of feeds at which solids are given is gradually increased to two and then three.

Cereals should be given at one feed only, and other tastes introduced. It is probably wise not to introduce more than two or three new foods each week as this will enable you to identify whether any food seems to upset the baby.

There are lots of commercially prepared baby foods available for this stage but many parents choose to offer foods they are eating themselves. These foods need to be mashed, sieved or puréed. As the baby gets used to eating solids and chewing, the food can be prepared a little lumpier. Using foods that the rest of the family are eating is cheaper and babies also get used to eating like the rest of the family. Also, parents know what is in the food and can ensure it meets any special requirements, such as being halal or kosher.

Table 14.5 summarises the foods to try and the foods to avoid at Stage 2.

Table 14.5 Stage 2 of weaning: foods to try and foods to avoid	
Foods to try	Foods to avoid
<ul><li>Purées that include meat, poultry or fish</li><li>Pulses, including lentils</li><li>Wider range of vegetables</li><li>Well-cooked eggs</li><li>Wheat-based foods</li></ul>	<ul><li>Cow's milk as a drink</li><li>Goat's milk</li><li>Nuts</li><li>Spicy foods</li></ul>

This will mean that the baby takes less and less milk from the breast or bottle. The milk feed might now be limited to just the first and last feeds of the day. Diluted fruit juices and water should also be offered as drinks with meals.

Table 14.6 goes into more detail about what foods must not be given to children under 12 months. Note that nutritional advice can change and it is essential to check current guidelines regularly.

Table 14.6 Foods to avoid giving to children under 12 months

Food	Reason
Salt	Salt can cause problems for the kidneys and later health problems. Do not buy foods that have salt in them or add salt when cooking.
Honey	Sometimes honey can contain a bacteria that is dangerous to babies and can cause an illness called infant botulism. Honey can also cause tooth decay.
Sugar	Sugar can cause tooth decay, but also give babies a liking for sugary foods later on.
Whole or chopped nuts	These can be a choking hazard.
Raw or partially cooked eggs	Eggs are a good source of protein, but must be thoroughly cooked, as they can contain bacteria that can cause food poisoning.
Shark, marlin, swordfish	Fish is good for babies, but these fish can contain mercury and so should be avoided.
Low-fat, low-calorie foods	'Diet' low-calorie foods are not good for babies because they need foods that contain plenty of nutrients. Low-fat dairy products such as low-fat yoghurt should also be avoided.
High-fibre foods	Bran, wholemeal pasta and brown rice are good for adults but are very high in fibre and stop babies digesting other nutrients. Brown bread is fine.
Cow's milk	Cow's milk is not suitable as a main drink for babies under 12 months. Full-fat milk can be introduced after this time.

12 months plus (Stages 3 and 4)

Foods can get lumpier and may be mashed rather than puréed. Once babies can hold foods they can be given finger foods such as carrot sticks, pieces of apple or bread. Sweet biscuits should be avoided as this encourages babies to expect sweet snacks. Finger foods allow babies to practise chewing and will help them learn to feed themselves. Babies should not be left alone to chew – an adult needs to be near in case of choking.

Once the baby masters chewing, food only needs to be chopped, not puréed.

Case study

Moving on to solids

Jane is a new mother. She has a 3-month-old baby whom she has breastfed. She now wants to prepare for introducing solids and comes to you for some advice.

- What recommendations would you make in terms of introducing first solids?
- Devise a first weeks plan for 6 to 9 months and 9 to 12 months to help Jane with her menus.

Table 14.7 outlines the foods to try at Stage 3 and Stage 4.

Table 14.7 Stages 3 and 4 of weaning: foods to try

Stage		Foods to offer
Stage 3	• Introduction of lumpier foods and finger foods • Vitamin drops containing A, C and D for breastfed babies • Quantity of milk feed remains the same	• Two servings per day of foods high in carbohydrates, e.g. potatoes, yams • Two servings per day of foods high in protein, e.g. eggs, meat, fish, tofu, beans • Fruit and vegetables to be part of two or more meals per day
Stage 4	• Introduction of minced or chopped foods • Increasing quantities of food so that the baby has three main meals a day • Milk remains important (500–600 ml per day)	• Three to four servings per day of foods high in carbohydrate • Three to four servings of fruit and vegetables • Two servings of foods high in protein • Fruit and healthy snacks if baby is hungry between meals

Note: Salt, honey or sugar must not be added to or in any of the foods.

Research

More information about weaning can be found on the NHS website, under the 'Healthy Eating' tab. You can access the relevant part of the website by going to www.pearsonhotlinks.co.uk and searching for this title.

Use small plates to encourage children to eat what is in front of them – large plates of food can be off-putting.

Children aged 1–5 years

By the age of 1 year, most infants are able to feed themselves. They will also have enough teeth to be able to bite and tear food. In the second year, molar teeth also develop and the ability to grind and chew food increases.

Portion size

Portion size is important, as large plates of food can be off-putting for children. Small children have high energy requirements in relation to their size but they are not able to eat large amounts of food at any one time. Therefore, they need to eat small portions frequently, and the foods need to be full of energy or 'energy rich'.

This means their diet will contain foods that are proportionally higher in fat and lower in fibre compared to the ideal diet of an adult. This is also why children under 5 years should not be given skimmed milk as a main drink, as they need the calories provided by whole milk. Children at the age of 2 can, however, gradually move to semi-skimmed milk as a main drink if they are growing well.

Children also need more nutrients relative to their size than adults. Children often eat a smaller range of foods than adults, but the selection offered should be varied enough to provide a good mixture of nutrients in different amounts. All children should be encouraged to follow healthy eating guidelines, such as eating five portions of fruit and vegetables a day.

The amount children want to eat is often affected by their physical activity and physiological growth. This means children's appetites may fluctuate as their growth does. Parents sometimes worry if their child is small or appears to be eating very little. It is important that they do not force children to eat more or make a fuss of the amount they eat as this could have a negative effect. Remember that growth often happens in spurts, and as long as the child is healthy and is growing well overall, it is likely that all is well.

Prevention of dental decay

Tooth decay is common in children. There are a number of small changes that you can easily make to a child's diet to reduce the risk of dental decay. Figure 14.6 shows ways to reduce the risk of tooth decay.

Good dental hygiene routines are very important. Children should be encouraged to clean their teeth thoroughly at least twice a day using a toothpaste that contains fluoride. They should also go to the dentist every six months – starting this from an early age can help to prevent fear developing. Fluoride is routinely added to tap water and this can help reduce tooth decay.

This practitioner is helping children to brush their teeth.

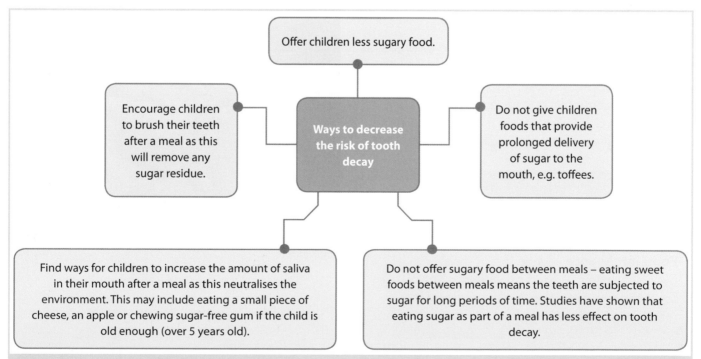

Offer children less sugary food.

Encourage children to brush their teeth after a meal as this will remove any sugar residue.

Ways to decrease the risk of tooth decay

Do not give children foods that provide prolonged delivery of sugar to the mouth, e.g. toffees.

Find ways for children to increase the amount of saliva in their mouth after a meal as this neutralises the environment. This may include eating a small piece of cheese, an apple or chewing sugar-free gum if the child is old enough (over 5 years old).

Do not offer sugary food between meals – eating sweet foods between meals means the teeth are subjected to sugar for long periods of time. Studies have shown that eating sugar as part of a meal has less effect on tooth decay.

Figure 14.6 Ways to decrease the risk of tooth decay

Working with parents to meet individual children's food needs

Meeting children's individual food needs can sometimes be challenging for parents. Parents want their children to have a healthy diet but there may be factors that influence their diet such as allergies, food intolerance or restrictions due to social, cultural or religious reasons. This may mean that parents and carers need to adapt the way that food is prepared for the family to accommodate special diets. It is important that you understand the related issues so you can provide appropriate advice and support to parents.

Providing a healthy diet

There are some foods that you need to bear in mind when preparing foods for children.

Salt

It is important that salt is not added to a baby's food. A baby's digestive system cannot cope with more salt than that which is naturally found in food. Therefore, if you are cooking food for adults or older children that will also be puréed or mashed for a baby, salt should be left out of the cooking process. Babies and young children should also not be given salty snacks such as crisps.

Sugar

Extra sugar should not be added to food or drinks, as this can lead to tooth decay. Sugar is often listed on packets as glucose, sucrose, fructose, maltose, syrup honey or concentrated fruit juice, so you will have to read labels carefully to avoid it. Try to ensure that children are given as much savoury food as possible.

> **Key terms**
>
> **Food allergy** – when the body has an abnormal reaction to a food or a component of a food.
>
> **Food intolerance** – when the body is hypersensitive to a food or a component of food; there is a reaction but the reason for this reaction is not always clear.

Allergies and intolerances

Parents may decide to exclude certain foods from their children's diet, as they believe they are linked to **food allergies** or **intolerances**. A food allergy occurs when there is a reaction to certain food, and this happens every time that food is eaten. The body is actually producing antibodies to 'fight' the food and these can be detected in a blood test.

Physical signs of an allergic reaction might include a rash, breathing difficulties, swelling of the lips or throat, or hyperactivity.

A food intolerance also produces a reaction every time a food is eaten, but antibodies are not produced. However, a food intolerance can still provoke similar reactions to a food allergy.

In children, the incidence of food-related allergies and intolerances is very low, and therefore self-diagnosis is not recommended. Removing certain foods from a child's diet without proper medical advice could lead to under-nutrition. Any parent who suggests that their child has an intolerance or allergy should be advised to seek confirmation from their doctor.

Medical advice will also determine whether a reaction to a food is the result of an allergy or an intolerance.

This nurse is administering an allergy test. Parents should seek medical advice if they suspect their child has a food allergy or intolerance.

Foods that might cause reactions

Cow's milk, wheat and eggs are linked with allergies, and therefore babies should not be given them until they are at least 6 months (except cow's milk, which should not be given as a main drink until 1 year). They should then be introduced in small quantities and one at a time so any reactions can be seen. If there is a history of allergies in the family it is possible that they may be allergic as well. Egg yolk is more digestible than egg white, so this is often given first.

Cow's milk should not be used as the main drink until 1 year because of its low iron content, but it can be used in food preparation after 6 months. Once a baby starts having cow's milk, they should be given whole milk, not semi-skimmed or skimmed. Babies need a lot of energy for their size and so energy-rich foods are important.

Goat's milk and sheep's milk can also cause allergic reactions. Goat's milk is low in folic acid, one of the most important vitamins. These milks need to be boiled and cooled before use if they are not pasteurised.

Nuts should not be given to babies or children under 5 because they could choke on them. Finely ground nuts may be given after 6 months.

Food additives are used in ready-made foods, which we tend to eat a lot of these days due to our busy lifestyles. Manufacturers use additives to make foods last longer as well as to improve the appearance and flavour of foods. Food additives can have a negative effect on young children by contributing to allergies and hyperactivity. Therefore, it is wise to try to reduce the amount of foods that contain artificial additives in a young child's diet.

Restrictions due to social, cultural or religious reasons

Many communities are made up of people from different cultures and religions, each with their own customs. Many of these customs relate to food. Most have particular foods linked to festivals or dates of religious significance. Sometimes this means that a food is forbidden, for different reasons.

Table 14.8 outlines some food restrictions linked to different cultures.

If you are working with children from cultures that have rules relating to food, it is important that you fully understand their dietary limitations and that you respect and follow them.

Table 14.8 Food restrictions relating to different cultures and religions

Religion and restrictions	Special food practices	Food preparation
Judaism • Do not eat pork. • Only eat fish with fins and scales. • Do not eat shellfish. • Do not eat foods containing meat and milk at the same meal.	• Do not prepare food on the Sabbath (Saturday). • There should be six hours between eating meat and dairy foods.	• Meat and poultry must be kosher – animals are killed in a particular way to drain the maximum amount of blood. • Separate cooking equipment must be used for meat and dairy products.

continued

Table 14.8 (continued)

Religion and restrictions	Special food practices	Food preparation
Islam • Do not eat blood. • Do not eat pork or pork-related products. • Do not consume alcohol. • Only eat with the right hand – the left is considered unclean.	• Ramadan is a period of fasting during which Muslims do not eat between sunrise and sunset – they eat light meals during the hours of darkness. • Ramadan lasts for one month and the timing varies from year to year.	• Animals must be ritually slaughtered with a blow to the head, and certain words must be spoken while this happens. • Meat slaughtered in this way is called halal.
Hinduism • Do not kill or eat any animals. • Do not eat cheese prepared in Western cultures. • Hindus are usually lacto-vegetarians. • Strict Hindus are vegan.	• Society is based on **castes**. • Hindus from upper castes cannot eat with those from lower castes.	• Ritual bathing is carried out and clean clothes are put on before food is prepared.

Key term

Caste – a system of dividing society into classes or different social groups.

Assessment practice 14.1 3A1.P1 | 3A1.M1

Produce a booklet for new parents that explains the importance of nutrition for children's health and development.

In the booklet, discuss the extent to which children's health and development can be affected by their diet. Make sure you give examples.

A2 Understand the role of the adult in encouraging children to develop healthy eating habits

Healthy eating habits are formed from the moment a child starts to eat solid food and can impact on an individual's health throughout their life. Therefore, it is important that children form healthy eating habits early on.

Helping children develop healthy eating habits

Children's food preferences begin to develop between the ages of 1 and 5. Therefore, it is important at this time to encourage children to try as many different foods as possible. This will allow them to experience different tastes and textures.

Parents and carers may not eat a variety of foods for different reasons. Some families are on low incomes and may have access to a smaller range of foods, therefore children may not have a suitably balanced diet. Others may follow particular diets from personal choice, for example, being a vegan, or for health reasons, such as having coeliac disease. In these cases, it is important that parents give children foods that they may not eat themselves to make sure they have a balanced diet.

Regular meal patterns are established in the early years and, as part of this, children's eating patterns should fit in with those of the family as this helps them develop social skills. Structured eating patterns will help children become used to eating regular meals with nutritious snacks in between. Children do need to snack in between their main meals to meet their nutritional and energy requirements. These snacks should be savoury, such as raw vegetables or cheese, rather than sweet – although fresh fruit is acceptable. Drinks should not contain sugar.

Children's diets need to be balanced. This means that they must contain all the necessary nutrients in the correct proportions. The Food Standards Agency has provided the information in Figure 14.7 as a set of guidelines for what constitutes a healthy and balanced diet.

Healthy eating guidelines should be applied with caution. A low-fat or high-fibre diet would prevent a child from obtaining the energy and nutrients they need. However, a diet that is low in salt and sugar is advisable as it develops good eating habits and prevents a child getting used to sugary foods which can lead to tooth decay.

Attitudes towards food

Rewards and treats

When food is offered as a reward for something, such as 'being good' or going through an experience that may cause anxiety, such as going to the dentist, it is often sweet food such as cakes, chocolate or sweets. Using food as a reward is tempting and may work in the short term but it may also lead to weight problems later in life. It can make a child think of sweets as 'nice' foods and other foods such as vegetables as 'not-so-nice' foods.

If you want to use food as a reward, try making fruit a reward from an early age or, better still, use outings such as trips to the park or to the beach as rewards instead.

Use the eatwell plate to help you get the balance right. It shows how much of what you eat should come from each food group.

Fruit and vegetables

Bread, rice, potatoes, pasta and other starchy foods

Meat, fish, eggs, beans and other non-dairy sources of protein

Foods and drinks high in fat and/or sugar

Milk and diary foods

Department of Health in association with the Welsh Government, the Scottish Government and the Food Standards Agency in Northern Ireland.

Figure 14.7 The eatwell plate (© Crown copyright 2011)

Association with love and nurturing

Food is often associated with love and nurturing. Many family occasions are celebrated with food, and this food is not always healthy – for example, cakes for occasions such as birthdays and Christmas, or chocolate eggs at Easter. Many parents feel that being able to provide these types of foods for their family is a sign of being a good parent.

However, it is important to separate food as an essential care-giving task from a means of showing love. Love should be demonstrated in other ways, such as hugging and through words.

Insistence on finishing food

Parents sometimes believe it is important that children finish everything on their plate. Some parents insist on children doing this before they can have a dessert or before they are allowed to get down from the table. This may be as a result of their own childhood, if their own parents insisted on the same. They see food that is left as a waste.

Generally, children will eat what they need. Insisting that they finish what is on their plate means that they learn to monitor how much they eat by external factors rather than by internal cues such as how hungry they feel and what they actually need for good health. It can lead to eating more calories than they need, and therefore to obesity. It can also make mealtimes quite stressful for children, when they should be enjoyable.

A better way may be to involve children in serving themselves and making it clear that they should only take what they can eat.

It is also important to remember that in some cultures it is seen as custom to leave a little bit of food on your plate.

Working with parents to develop healthy eating habits

There are many reasons why children choose the foods they eat, but for many children, the main influence on their diet and eating habits will be their parents and their family (see Figure 14.8).

Reflect

Think about your own diet.

- What factors influence what you eat now?
- Think back to when you were younger. Were the factors the same?
- How might you use this information when working with parents?

It can be difficult to advise parents on how to eat healthily without causing offence. You need to have a good understanding of the family situation in order to do this effectively.

For example, a family living on a low income may have a limited choice of food because of their budget. A low income not only affects what you can buy but also other issues such as what transport is available. Food is cheaper and there is a wider selection in large supermarkets, which tend to be out of town and so may be inaccessible to some families. Families on low incomes may have to shop in local shops where prices are higher and there is less choice. This will impact on a child's diet.

If the parents suffer from disabilities or medical conditions such as arthritis, the child's diet may be affected. Arthritis, for example, makes it difficult to carry out tasks that require fine motor skills such as preparing and cooking food. This may lead to the family relying on convenience foods, which often lack nutrients, for a large part of their diet.

Healthy food choices will also be affected by parents' own knowledge of food and cooking as well as their willingness to prepare a healthy diet. Their own diets may be influenced by the jobs they have. If they work long hours, they may not want to spend a lot of time preparing fresh foods when they get home and may opt for a convenience meal instead.

The foods available locally will also impact on food choice. Regional variations mean different areas have different fresh produce. For example, in areas of the country where fruit is grown, this will be readily available during the summer season. If you live near the coast, fresh fish is usually obtainable but in other areas it may not be.

If parents are able to find fresh foods that are in season, these are generally cheaper. However, preservation techniques and the improved transport system mean that many foods are available all year round.

When advising parents, it is important to do so with sensitivity. You may decide to make healthy eating information readily available for them through leaflets or websites. You may also consider holding a healthy eating information session to encourage parents to share tips on helping their children to eat healthily with each other. It is quite common for nurseries and schools to send home information on healthy lunchboxes and to have a healthy eating policy, so this would provide an avenue for offering guidance and advice to all parents.

Assessment practice 14.2   3A1.P2 | 3A2.P4

Many early years settings provide advice to parents on ensuring their children have a healthy diet.

1 Devise a leaflet that a nursery could give to parents to highlight how they can meet their child's nutritional needs.

2 Explain how the nursery encourages children to develop healthy eating habits.

Reflect

Make a list of all the food you ate yesterday. Write down why you ate the foods you did. How do they fit with Figure 14.8?

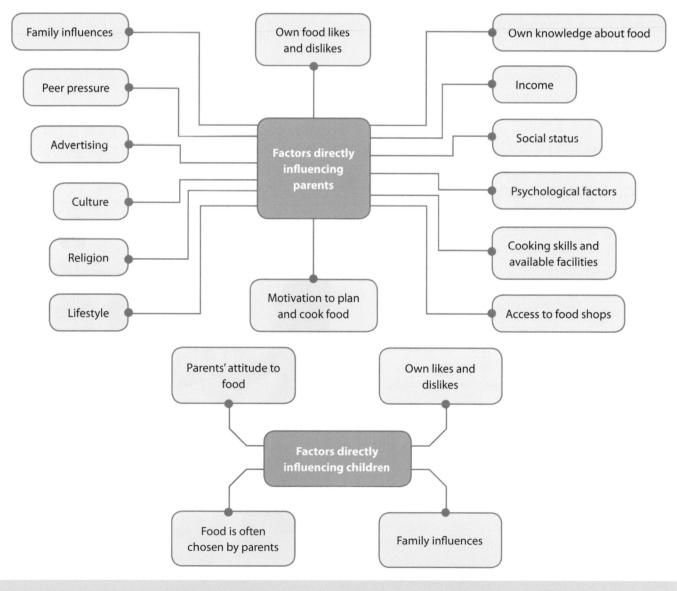

Figure 14.8 Factors influencing children's food choices

Feeding a family

Nadia is a single parent with two children aged 5 and 7. She is on a limited income and is concerned that their diets are not as healthy as they could be. Both children attend school and have school dinners.

1 What factors might affect what the children eat?
2 Nadia's 7-year-old daughter wants to take a packed lunch to school. How could Nadia ensure that she has a healthy lunch?
3 What advice would you provide Nadia with to help her provide a balanced diet for her children on a budget?

Encouraging enjoyment of food

Preparing meals can be stressful, as it takes skill and organisation to bring a meal together at the right time. However, starting children off with good eating habits will lead to a lifetime of healthy eating. This is why it is important that mealtimes are enjoyable for children, as this will help them develop a good relationship with food.

You can make mealtimes more enjoyable by making sure you have enough time to enjoy the experience. This means being able to sit down with children, eat in a relaxed manner, talk about different things and experience different foods together. A rushed meal will be a stressful one and certainly not a fun one. Adults and children should eat the same foods, and this will also ensure that you are not spending lots of time preparing different food for the children.

Talking is an important part of the mealtime experience and distractions will affect that. It is difficult to hold a conversation with others if they have one eye on the TV or are texting on their phone. You may wish to set the rule of 'no TV' at the table. Eating together gives you an opportunity to communicate with children. This not only develops their social skills but also makes them feel important, making the experience more enjoyable for them.

Encouraging independence through self-serving

Getting children involved in the meal will help them become more interested in their food. While you may not want them to decide what will be on the menu all the time (you might end up with chips at every meal), you could encourage them to make choices about how the food that has been prepared is served. You could also encourage them to serve themselves, as

this promotes independence and also helps ensure that they take the amount of food they feel they can eat.

Adults eating with children

At mealtimes adults act as role models for children. Adults and children should eat the same foods, and this will encourage children to expand their tastes. Eating with children helps to teach them social skills and good manners – these habits are likely to stay with them for the rest of their lives. Therefore, it is important that adults fully participate in the meal as well and are not distracted by texting or reading at the table, for instance. They should be fully involved in discussions as this is an opportunity to spend 'quality time' with children.

This family look like they are enjoying their meal – sit down with children and create a relaxed atmosphere.

Involving children in food preparation

Being involved with food provides children with many learning opportunities. Activities that involve food can develop physical, social, emotional, numeracy and language skills. Children can be encouraged to be part of the meal planning and then the shopping for food. The discussion and counting involved develops language and maths skills almost without children realising. It also gets them interested in food and so they are more likely to want to eat it.

Cooking

Cooking is fun and you can get them involved in cooking at an early age. Children find cooking exciting, as it gives them quick results. The fact that they can eat the results of their efforts – usually very quickly after finishing the task – adds to this enjoyment. Encouraging children to cook gives them lots of opportunities to discover things for themselves. They gain a great sense of achievement from cooking because it is so immediate.

Activity

Increase the fun aspect of cooking by encouraging children to look for 'faces' in the fruit and vegetables they are using. Raisins have faces, as do potatoes and carrots, as a result of the indentations that occur naturally on their surfaces.

1 Encourage children to look for faces as they shop for and prepare food.

2 Talk about the 'strange' names some foods have, such as 'spring onions', which could lead to bouncing around the kitchen.

3 Look for opportunities to explore unusual foods, such as purple carrots and Jerusalem artichokes.

4 What other ways can you think of to make cooking fun?

Cooking can offer many opportunities for learning. It encourages creativity, and develops self-confidence as well as self-esteem. You can talk about where our food comes from and what is healthy food and why, and what is not.

When planning to cook with children, you will need to think about safety issues, particularly when cooking with very young children. This may mean that you need to do more of the preparation if the child is too young to use a knife, for example, or to stir hot foods. Nevertheless, you can still make sure they are fully involved in the process of stirring and mixing or putting the mixture into tins.

Be ready for a mess – children are likely to be messy when preparing food but this is part of the fun. They can also be involved in the clearing up. It is important that they do this, as it is one of the least enjoyable parts of the cooking process.

If you are making something that cooks in the oven, you can use the opportunity to discuss how they think the mixture will change in terms of appearance, texture and taste as it goes through the cooking process. You will need to adjust your language to suit the age of the child but this is a good opportunity for learning. It also starts them off developing a skill they will use for the rest of their lives.

Activity

1 Find a simple recipe that you could make with children.

2 Go through each of the stages of the recipe and explain what learning opportunities there might be for children.

Growing food

Children like to be involved in growing food that they can then prepare, cook and eat. Again, growing food provides lots of opportunities for learning as it gives them the opportunity to experience the natural world and learn where food comes from.

Many nurseries and primary schools have a growing area. You do not need a traditional garden or vegetable patch to grow food. You can grow small amounts of food in tubs or window boxes, or even on a window sill.

Growing food from seed can take time and therefore it will be important to hold children's interest by looking at the progress regularly.

It may be an idea to start with a food that grows quickly, and cress is a good example. You can grow cress inside on the window sill, where children can see it change.

You might also consider buying plants from a garden centre to reduce the waiting time. Also, some plants are easier to grow if you start with a plant, and success is important in maintaining children's interest in the first instance.

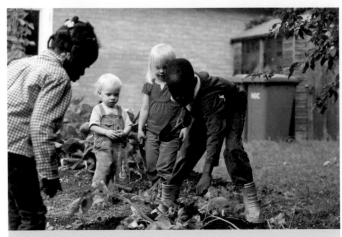

These children are enjoying being in their setting's growing area.

If you do want to grow plants from seed, consider the following points when deciding what seeds to grow with children:

- Choose plants that are easy to sow with large seeds, such as courgettes, as this will make it easier for children to handle them.
- Choose seeds that germinate quickly to keep children's attention.

- Choose plants you can grow in the same place as you sow the seeds so you do not have to transplant seedlings.
- Choose plants that will crop quickly.
- Choose plants that require minimal care other than watering and feeding.
- Choose plants that will continue to crop over a period of time.

Plants you may want to consider include courgettes, tomatoes, salad leaves and strawberries.

Assessment practice 14.3 | 3A2.P3 | 3A1.M2 | 3A.D1 | 3A.D2

Write an article for a magazine for early years professionals explaining how children's attitudes to food are influenced both at home and in the early years setting. In it:

- analyse how working in partnership with parents in early years settings can contribute to the provision of food that encourages children's health and development
- evaluate the extent to which adults in early years settings could contribute to children's health and development through the provision of food
- recommend how a setting could improve their contribution to children's healthy eating habits.

B Understand the role of the adult in cooking and serving food safely

When preparing food for children, it is important that this is carried out in a hygienic way. Unhygienic food preparation methods can lead to food poisoning. This can be severe if it happens to vulnerable groups, such as children, who may not be strong enough to cope with the illness. Therefore, it is essential that you follow good hygiene practices whether you are preparing food in a setting or in the home.

Responsibility to comply with food safety legislation

Anyone who prepares food for others has a responsibility to ensure that food is safe to eat and

will not cause food poisoning. This means that anyone preparing food must meet current food hygiene regulations. Food poisoning can make children extremely ill and, in some cases, it can be fatal. Therefore, it is essential that you are fully up to date with hygiene practices and follow them effectively. Food hygiene regulations may differ in other countries so it is important that you follow those relevant to the situation you are in.

Food Safety Act 1990

The Food Safety Act 1990 aims to protect consumers by:

- preventing illness from the consumption of food
- preventing consumers from being misled as to the nature of the food they are purchasing
- ensuring that all food produced for sale is safe to eat, of high quality and not misleadingly presented.

This Act made it illegal to sell food that has been contaminated or adulterated or is unfit for human consumption. This is why sell-by and use-by dates are used on pre-prepared or packaged food. It is also an offence to label or advertise food in a way that misleads the customer. The Act made it possible to prosecute companies and individuals who do not follow it.

Food Safety (General Food Hygiene) Regulations

These are regulations made under the Food Safety Act 1990. They apply to all types of food and food businesses but do not cover domestic preparation in the home. They do cover non-commercial activities such as charity events.

These regulations detail standards that must be followed in premises where food is being prepared. These standards state that food premises must be kept clean and in good repair. There are also regulations about design and layout, hand-washing facilities and toilets, hot and cold running water, ventilation, lighting and changing facilities.

Activity

The Food Safety Regulations state that there must be changing facilities away from the food preparation areas where staff preparing food can change from their outdoor clothes. In addition, the toilet facilities must not open on to the food preparation area. There should also be a separate hand-washing basin from the basins used for food preparation.

Why do you think these regulations exist?

The Regulations also explain the requirements for food preparation areas. There are specific requirements for rooms in which food is being prepared that include how the ceilings, floors and windows are built and what facilities are needed for cleaning utensils and equipment as well as food.

There are specific guidelines on waste disposal, as poor disposal of waste can lead to food contamination.

They also outline how different types of food should be stored to reduce the risk of contamination.

In addition, the regulations give guidelines for staff preparing and serving food. This includes ensuring that staff follow good personal hygiene rules and are trained in these. They also make clear that staff should not work if they are ill.

Safe working practices when preparing food

Children are particularly vulnerable if they suffer from food poisoning, because they are less able to cope with the symptoms than healthy adults. Preventing food poisoning is easy if you understand how bacteria multiply. If you understand this, then you can easily take steps to reduce the risk of poisoning.

How do food poisoning bacteria multiply?

To prevent the growth of harmful bacteria, you need to understand the conditions in which they grow and multiply. To grow and reproduce, bacteria require a number of conditions occurring at the same time. Figure 14.9 outlines these conditions.

Bacteria also need time to multiply; however, once the conditions in Figure 14.9 are met they multiply very fast. Bacteria multiply by a process called binary fission every 20 minutes. This means that every 20 minutes the number of bacteria doubles. Therefore, the longer the bacteria are in positive conditions for growth, the more they will reproduce.

It is therefore essential to wash your hands thoroughly before handling food and after handling raw meat. You should also ensure any cuts you may have are covered.

Reflect

Most of the food we buy in supermarkets is preserved in some way so that it lasts longer and does not suffer from decay. Food might be frozen, canned, pickled or dehydrated. How do these methods prevent food-poisoning bacteria from growing?

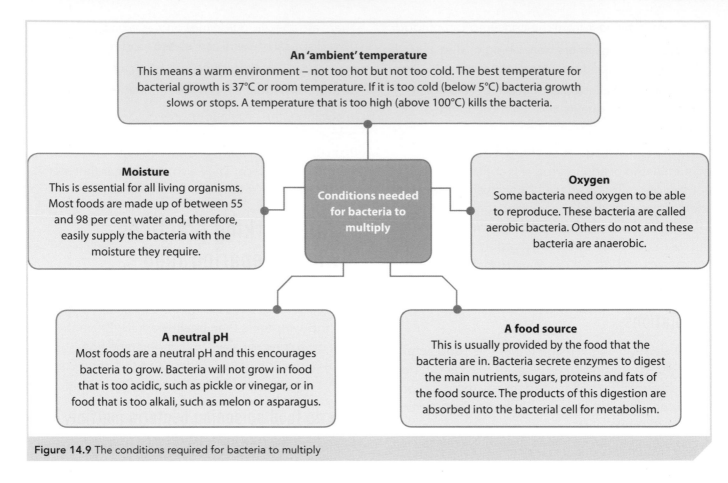

Figure 14.9 The conditions required for bacteria to multiply

Preparing food for children with allergies or intolerances

When preparing food for children who suffer from food allergies or intolerances, you have to consider other factors in addition to preventing food poisoning. Incorrect food choice or preparation can lead to illness.

- **Nut allergies** – children with nut allergies are very sensitive to any trace of nuts. Therefore, it is important that you do not prepare or serve any food with nuts in, even if it is not being served to the person with the nut allergy, as they may suffer a reaction just by being close to nuts.

- **Coeliac disease** – if a child suffers from coeliac disease they cannot eat foods containing wheat. Wheat causes damage to their small intestine, so food is not digested properly. This will result in diarrhoea and malnutrition, as nutrients from food are not absorbed. People with coeliac disease cannot eat many common foods that are typically made from wheat, such as bread, biscuits and cakes. Wheat is also found in many processed foods as a thickening agent as well as being used

to coat foods such as fishfingers. When preparing food for a coeliac, most basic food, such as meat, fruit, vegetables, cheese, potatoes and rice is suitable but other baked products need to be made with suitable flour, such as rice flour.

- **Lactose intolerance** – some children suffer from lactose intolerance. Lactose is the sugar found in milk. The body does not produce enough of the enzyme lactase which is needed to digest milk. As the milk sugar cannot be digested as it should be, it passes into the large intestine, where it causes irritation, pain and diarrhoea. Children with lactose intolerance need to avoid cow's milk. However, they can usually drink goat's or ewe's milk as these are low in lactose. Children with lactose intolerance will not necessarily have to avoid all

Research

To find out more about coeliac disease, visit the Coeliac UK website. You can access this website by going to www.pearsonhotlinks.co.uk and searching for this title.

milk and dairy products, as usually small amounts can be consumed without side effects. Cheese and yoghurt can usually be eaten as well, as they only contain a small amount of lactose and so do not cause any symptoms.

Procedures for safe food practice

The main reasons for food poisoning are bad temperature control or food being stored incorrectly. Food poisoning often happens because food is prepared too far in advance, cooled too slowly, stored incorrectly – for example, at room temperature – not reheated sufficiently or incorrectly thawed.

Food can also be contaminated with pathogenic micro-organisms or the toxic chemicals produced by micro-organisms. This is usually caused by poor food hygiene practices.

Did you know?

Some foods are naturally poisonous because they contain toxins, for example, some mushrooms, and red kidney beans (if not cooked correctly). Food can also be contaminated with toxic chemicals such as lead, copper or agricultural pesticides and herbicides. Also, chemicals such as disinfectants may contaminate food during growth, storage, preparation and/or cooking.

When food is fresh and being stored, or when it is being prepared for cooking and eating, it can be contaminated with bacteria. There are a number of simple actions that you can take to reduce the risk of food poisoning.

Personal hygiene

Personal hygiene is very simple but can also be easily forgotten when you are busy. Remember the following things.

- Wash hands thoroughly before preparing food and between handling different foods.

- All humans carry the staphylococcus bacteria on their skin and in their nose and throat. This is why you should not touch your face, hair or nose when preparing food.
- Always cover your hair or tie long hair back to keep it from falling in food – this is a physical contaminant.
- Do not cough or sneeze over food, as the droplets in the air from the sneeze or cough can transfer food-poisoning bacteria directly on to food.
- Always wash hands after using the lavatory. Salmonella is found in the human gut and therefore, bodily fluids can be a direct and indirect source of food poisoning. Salmonella can live for up to three hours on unwashed hands.
- Do not smoke when preparing food. As well as the potential for ash to drop in the food, you will constantly touch your face as you smoke the cigarette.
- If you are ill, you should not prepare food for others, as you may inadvertently contaminate food.

Food storage

Storing food correctly is important to ensure that bacteria are not given a chance to start to multiply. To prevent this happening, you should ensure that you remove the conditions in which bacteria multiply easily, as described previously. In addition:

- always choose foods that look fresh
- choose foods within their use-by dates
- use a cool bag to transport cold and frozen foods from the supermarket to home to prevent its temperature rising to one at which bacteria might start to multiply
- put frozen and chilled foods away immediately after purchase to keep them at their correct temperatures
- make sure the fridge is between 0 and 5°C and the freezer below −18°C
- store cooked and raw food separately in the fridge as raw food can contaminate cooked food
- store cooked meat above raw meat to avoid blood dripping on to cooked meat or other food that will contaminate them.

159

Food preparation

Good food preparation is essential to ensure that any bacteria are killed or that the conditions in which bacteria thrive are removed. Make sure you follow the personal hygiene guidelines. Pets should not be allowed in the kitchen, as they can carry bacteria.

When preparing food, remember the following things.

- Eat foods by the use-by dates – they are there as a guide to freshness.
- Always work in a clean area and clean the work surfaces and utensils as you go – this will reduce the risk of cross-contamination.
- Always prepare different foods in different areas – for example, fresh vegetables may have soil on them so they should be prepared away from other foods to ensure that the soil does not contaminate them.
- Use separate utensils to prepare raw and cooked foods.
- Thoroughly defrost frozen food before cooking it.
- Make sure cooked foods reach a temperature of over 63°C – they should be piping hot.
- Check meat and poultry with a food thermometer to make sure the right temperature has been reached. Juices should run clear.
- Keep hot foods hot and cold foods cold.
- Do not keep food warm for long periods of time, and particularly not between 5 and 63°C, where bacteria multiply rapidly.
- Cool foods as quickly as possible and within 1.5 hours – cover and store in the fridge or freezer.

Heating and reheating food

Heating or reheating food has the potential to cause food poisoning if not carried out thoroughly. It is essential to remember that the food should be piping hot before it is served – over 63°C. Lukewarm food is an excellent breeding ground for bacteria.

If using pre-prepared food, follow the instructions carefully.

Cleaning routines

Effective cleaning is important to reduce the risk of food poisoning. Cleaning removes dirt, food residues

and grease, all of which could attract bacteria. Cleaning may use:

- detergent – a mix of chemicals which will remove the grease, dirt and food particles but not kill germs or food poisoning bacteria
- disinfectant – this will reduce any micro-organisms to a safe level. This is either done with hot water or chemicals or a combination of both.

Cleaning should be carried out in a systematic way, working from clean to dirty surfaces. It is important that you use the correct equipment and chemicals to ensure effective cleaning. You should wear different clothes for cleaning the kitchen and toilet areas. Water should be changed frequently, as soon as it looks dirty, to ensure effective cleaning. Cloths should be disinfected after use.

Assessment practice 14.4   3B.P5

Following food hygiene guidelines is essential if you want to prepare food that is fit to eat and will not cause ill health. However, in a busy work environment, it is easy to forget these practices.

1 Prepare a poster outlining food hygiene and safety tips, which could be displayed in a food preparation area in an early years setting.

2 Produce a section for an employees' handbook that gives further information to supplement the poster.

Further reading and resources

Barasi, M. (2007) *Nutrition at a Glance*, London: Hodder Arnold.

Lean, M. (2006) *Fox and Cameron's Food Science, Nutrition and Health*, London: Hodder Arnold.

Websites
www.babycentre.co.uk

www.babyweaning.com

www.food.gov.uk

www.healthyfoodhealthyplanet.org

www.kidshealth.org

Ready for work?

Seb Bevan Deputy manager of a day nursery

The daily routine of the nursery includes snacks and lunch to ensure the children keep their energy levels up. We believe that it is important to provide healthy food at different times of the day. We always provide a cooked meal at lunchtime made from fresh ingredients. Many of our children eat their main meal with us in the middle of the day and therefore it is important that it is nutritious and healthy.

Knowledge of nutrition is essential to ensure that we plan healthy meals. It means we can be sure that the meals the children eat are contributing to a balanced diet.

Mealtimes are also important social occasions for the nursery. We always sit down together to eat. The nursery staff join the children as they can model good manners. Lunchtimes are another opportunity to develop language and social skills.

The meal offers the opportunity for children to develop confidence serving each other – they really enjoy getting involved. Eating with other children also encourages them to try new flavours or foods.

Sometimes we involve the children in preparing a part of the meal or one of the snacks we have mid-morning or mid-afternoon. We may use some of the vegetables we have grown with the children in our garden and this adds extra interest to the activity.

Anyone who works with children should take advantage of the opportunities that using food as a learning tool can bring.

Skills for practice

Caring skills
Practise doing these things to improve your skills with food.

- Develop a list of quick, healthy, nutritious snacks and main meals that you could prepare for a preschool child.
- Plan a food-based activity that will not involve cooking, which you could carry out with a 4-year-old. Try making sandwiches that you then cut into different shapes or, as a treat, cornflake cakes (children just need to stir the mixture). Watch how the children respond to the activity and listen to the language they use. Think about how you could develop their learning.
- Sit with a child during lunch. Help them to develop their fine motor skills with the cutlery.

Tips for weaning
- Go at the baby's pace – starting solid food is a change for them as they are used to a totally liquid diet. It will take time.
- Try not to rush a baby when they are eating or force them to eat more than they want. It is important to make eating a time to chat and enjoy each other's company. If food is refused, call an end to the meal.
- Try to use foods that the family is eating as soon as possible. This will help the baby learn to like a range of ordinary foods and will help avoid a fussy eater in the future.
- Fresh foods, puréed or mashed, should form the basis of a baby's diet. Use commercially prepared baby foods when in a hurry or as a convenience but not as the main component.

Introduction

In this unit you will look at how to meet the varying needs of children under 3 years, including their nutritional requirements. You will also look at the skills and qualities you need to work with children in this age range. It often takes a particular type of person to work enthusiastically and sensitively with children under 3 years. It is essential to understand child development and the specific needs of this age group. A good starting point is to revise your child development knowledge for children aged 0 to 3 that you covered in Unit 1.

Assessment: You will be assessed by a series of assignments set by your teacher/tutor.

Learning aims

In this unit you will:

A   understand how to meet the nutritional needs of children under three years

B1   understand how to meet the specific developmental needs of babies under one year

B2   understand how to meet the specific developmental needs of children from one to two years

B3   understand how to meet the specific developmental needs of children from two to three years

C   understand the skills and qualities needed to work with children under three years.

Working with children under 3 years is hard work but immensely interesting and satisfying. Their rate of development in all areas is considerable as they move from being quite vulnerable to gaining independence and confidence. The speed of their growth and development can be quite breathtaking and one of the many joys of working with this age group is to share with them the many changes that take place.

Penny Tassoni

Working With Children Under Three Years

15

Assessment Zone

This table shows what you must do in order to achieve a **Pass**, **Merit** or **Distinction** grade, and where you can find activities to help you.

Assessment criteria		
Pass	**Merit**	**Distinction**
Learning aim A: Understand how to meet the nutritional needs of children under three years		
3A.P1 I&CT Explain the nutritional needs of children from birth to three years of age. **Assessment practice 15.1**	**3A.M1** Discuss the importance of ensuring the nutritional needs of children from birth to three years are met. **Assessment practice 15.1**	**3A.D1** Evaluate how an early years setting provides for the nutritional needs of children under three years, making recommendations for improvements. **Assessment practice 15.1**
3A.P2 Describe the role of adults in early years settings in the preparation and feeding of children from birth up to two years. **Assessment practice 15.1**		
3A.P3 English I&CT Plan a menu for one day in an early years setting to meet the nutritional and energy needs of children aged two to three years. **Assessment practice 15.1**		
Learning aim B1: Understand how to meet the specific developmental needs of babies under one year **Learning aim B2: Understand how to meet the specific developmental needs of children from one to two years** **Learning aim B3: Understand how to meet the specific developmental needs of children from two to three years**		
3B1.P4 Describe how adults in early years settings respond to the individual needs of babies in care routines whilst meeting the needs of others in the group. **Assessment practice 15.2**	**3B1.M2** Analyse the ways in which adults in early years settings can meet the specific developmental needs of babies under one year old. **Assessment practice 15.2**	
3B1.P5 Explain the features of a sensory environment in an early years setting for babies under one year. **Assessment practice 15.2**		
3B2.P6 Describe how to create an environment in an early years setting for children aged from one to two years where they feel secure and supported in active exploration. **Assessment practice 15.3**	**3B2.M3** Analyse how the environment and communication aid the development and learning of children aged from one to two years using examples. **Assessment practice 15.3**	**3B.D2** Evaluate the effectiveness of creating an environment for children from birth to three years that supports and promotes different areas of development and learning. **Assessment practice 15.5**
3B2.P7 Explain the role of adults in supporting the development of communication of children from one to two years. **Assessment practice 15.3**		

continued

Assessment criteria (*continued*)

Pass	Merit	Distinction
3B3.P8 Describe accessible activities and routines which involve children aged two to three years to help promote their social, emotional and developmental needs. **Assessment practice 15.4**	**3B3.M4** Analyse how adults and accessible activities and routines contribute to the social and emotional development and positive behaviour of children from two to three years. **Assessment practice 15.4**	
3B3.P9 Explain the role of adults in promoting positive behaviour with children from two to three years. **Assessment practice 15.4**		
Learning aim C: Understand the skills and qualities needed to work with children under three years		
3C.P10 Explain the skills and qualities needed for work in early years settings with children under three years. **Assessment practice 15.5**	**3C.M5** Analyse the importance of the adult in presenting a professional and positive role model to children under three years in an early years setting. **Assessment practice 15.5**	

English English Functional Skills signposting   **I&CT** Information and Communication Technology skills signposting

How you will be assessed

This unit will be assessed by a series of internally assessed tasks set by your teacher/tutor. Throughout this unit you will find assessment practice activities that will help you work towards your assessment. Completing these activities will not mean that you have achieved a particular grade, but you will have carried out useful research or preparation that will be relevant when it comes to your final assignment.

In order for you to carry out the tasks in your assignment, it is important that you check you have met all the Pass grading criteria. You can do this as you work your way through the assignment.

If you are hoping to gain a Merit or Distinction, you should also make sure that you present the information in your assignment in the style that is required by the relevant assessment criteria. For example, Merit criteria will require you to discuss and analyse, and Distinction criteria will require you to evaluate.

The assignment set by your teacher/tutor will consist of a number of tasks designed to meet the criteria in the table. This is likely to consist of a written assignment but may also include activities such as:

- a report
- a presentation to your peers and teacher/tutor
- an assignment.

Getting started

Make a list of ways in which adults can support 2-year-olds. When you have finished this unit, see if you can add to this list.

A Understand how to meet the nutritional needs of children under 3 years

The first three years of life are characterised by significant physical growth and development. This is made possible partly by the nutrition that babies receive. In this section, you will look at the nutritional requirements of children in the first three years and how to meet them.

Nutritional requirements in the first six months

In the first six months of life, babies' nutrition is gained from milk. This will be either human breast milk or formula milk.

> **Link**
>
> Go to Unit 14: Section A1 to find more information about why bottle feeding or breastfeeding may be chosen.

Formula milk

There are different types of formula milk, and in order to meet babies' nutritional needs it is important that they are given the correct type and quantities.

Types of formula milk

The majority of formula milks are made from modified cow's milk, to which vitamins and minerals are added. The composition of a formula milk – the amounts of proteins, fats, minerals and vitamins it contains – will depend on the age of the child.

A good starting point is to understand that formula milk is available in two forms:

- ready-to-feed – a sterilised, made-up formula sold in cartons. This can be given straight to the baby at room temperature or warmed up
- powdered – this has to be made up by adding water.

Preterm babies

Wherever possible, human breast milk is given to preterm babies. Where this is not available, a formula especially for preterm babies is available. This contains more protein and fat than formula milk for full-term babies.

Newborn babies up to 6 months

Until they are 6 months old, babies should be given 'first' infant formula when they cannot be breastfed. First formula is whey-based and it is not recommended that other types of formula milk are used, unless under the guidance of a health professional. This formula is also thought to be sufficient for the first 12 months, after which babies can be given ordinary cow's milk as a drink.

Whey-based versus casein-based formula

While whey-based formula milk is recommended by health professionals, some parents choose to give their babies casein-based formula milks.

These milks are often aimed at hungrier babies and many parents believe that by giving them this type of formula milk, their baby will sleep for longer. This is disputed by health professionals.

Follow-on milks

These are formula milks that contain additional fat and protein. They are casein-based, but are not suited to the nutritional needs of babies under 6 months. Though they are suitable for babies over 6 months old, they are not considered necessary by health professionals.

Soya milk

Soya milk is made from soya beans. This type of formula milk is not recommended for babies unless advised by a doctor or health visitor. The usual reason for a baby to be given soya milk is because of an allergy. If you are working with a baby with a milk (lactose) allergy, you should never feed them any form of cow's milk, including formula.

How much formula milk should a baby have?

The amount of formula milk a baby should have depends on their weight. As a guide, use 150–200 ml per kg in 24 hours – so a newborn baby weighing 4 kg would need 600–800 ml in total per day. As young babies have small stomachs, this amount would be divided into several feeds. Most newborns feed every three hours at first, but after around six weeks they often settle into a four-hourly feeding pattern. However, it is best to feed on demand.

> **Research**
>
> Work out what type and how much formula milk a baby of 5 months weighing 7 kg would need in a day.

The advantages of breastfeeding

Health professionals, including health visitors, paediatricians and dieticians, recommend breastfeeding for babies in their first months of life. Reasons for this include:

- promoting attachment between baby and mother
- providing easily digestible milk, the composition of which adjusts according to the baby's needs and demands
- passing on antibodies from mother to baby, which strengthen the baby's immune system
- the provision of milk 'on tap' at just the right temperature.

> **Link**
>
> Go to Unit 14: Section A1 to find more information about the advantages of breastfeeding.

How to support breastfeeding mothers

It is known that breastfeeding is good for babies and so it is important that you find ways of supporting breastfeeding mothers. Some mothers will want to breastfeed their children when they are with you and others might want to express milk for a bottle that can be given later. There are several ways in which you can support breastfeeding mothers, as Figure 15.1 shows.

Finding them a comfortable space
It is important to offer breastfeeding mums a comfortable chair in a pleasant environment. You should find out whether the mother prefers to feed her baby in private but do not assume this.

Offering them drinks
Breastfeeding mothers need additional fluid.

Offering them advice
New mums can have some difficulties when breastfeeding. Having leaflets available that offer advice about breastfeeding or having the knowledge about where they can seek other information is useful.

Ways to support breastfeeding mothers

Figure 15.1 How to support breastfeeding mothers

Preparing and storing feeds

It is important that you know how to prepare and store feeds hygienically. This reduces the risk of a baby contracting food poisoning. The information below is based on guidelines that were current at the time of writing. You should regularly check information and best practice relating to all aspects of infant feeding.

Research

Find out about the latest guidelines relating to the feeding of babies by visiting the Foods Standards Agency website. You can access this website by going to www.pearsonhotlinks.co.uk and searching for this title.

Sterilisation of equipment

When babies are bottle fed with infant formula or breast milk, it is important that the bottles and equipment used are sterilised first. This includes the bottles, teats and anything else that will be in direct contact with the milk. Before sterilising, you should:

- wash hands thoroughly using soap and hot water
- wash feeding and preparation equipment thoroughly in hot soapy water, using brushes for teats and bottles
- after washing feeding equipment, rinse it thoroughly under the tap.

Commercial sterilisers

Many settings will have commercial sterilisers. You should find out how to use these in accordance with the manufacturer's instructions.

Boiling method

Another method of sterilisation is by boiling. You can sterilise feeding equipment in boiling water but you must check first that the equipment is suitable for sterilising in this way. If it is, use the following method.

1 Fill a large pan with water.
2 Place the feeding equipment in the pan, making sure there are no air bubbles inside it.
3 Cover the pan with a lid and bring to the boil.
4 Boil the water for at least 10 minutes, making sure the pan does not boil dry.
5 Keep the pan covered until the equipment is needed.
6 Wash your hands thoroughly and clean the surface you will be using, before removing the equipment.

7 If the bottles are not being used immediately, assemble them with the teat and lid in place to prevent the inside of the sterilised bottle and the inside and outside of the teat from being contaminated.

Remember never to leave hot pans and liquid unattended. Make sure the area is safe to prevent burns and scalds.

Any unfinished milk needs to be thrown away at the end of the feed.

Preparation of powdered formula feed

After all of the equipment used to feed the baby has been sterilised, use the following steps to prepare a powdered formula feed.

1 Put on a clean apron. Wash your hands thoroughly with soap and water and then dry them.
2 Boil fresh tap water in a kettle.
3 Allow the boiled water to cool to no less than 70°C. This is important because temperatures below 70°C will not kill any bacteria present in the powdered milk and so there is a danger of food poisoning.
4 Check that you are preparing the correct formula for the baby.
5 Follow the manufacturer's instructions and pour the correct amount of boiled water into the sterilised bottle. The water should always be poured into the bottle first.
6 Follow the manufacturer's instructions and add the exact amount of formula. This will be in proportion to the weight of the baby. Adding more or less powder than instructed could make the baby ill.

7 Reassemble the bottle following the manufacturer's instructions.

8 Shake the bottle well to mix the contents.

9 Cool the bottle quickly to feeding temperature by holding the bottom of the bottle under a running cold tap, or placing it in a container of cold water.

10 Check the temperature by shaking a few drops of the formula onto the inside of your wrist – it should feel lukewarm, not hot.

11 Throw away any feed that has not been used within two hours.

More information about how to sterilise feeding equipment and prepare powdered formula feed can be found on the NHS website. You can access this website by going to www.pearsonhotlinks.co.uk and searching for this title.

Storage of powdered infant formula

Tins of infant formula should be kept in a dry cupboard. Each tin should be labelled with the name of the child it belongs to.

Did you know?

The practice of making up babies' feeds in advance and storing them is no longer recommended.

Storage of ready-to-feed infant formula

Ready-to-feed formula should be kept in a dry cupboard until it is ready to be used.

Storage of human breast milk

Breast milk that has been expressed can be frozen or kept in the fridge for three days, assuming the fridge temperature is between 5°C and 10°C. It can be kept for five days if the fridge temperature is 4°C or less. It is important that breast milk is labelled with the following information:

- who the milk is for
- when the milk was expressed
- when the milk should be used by.

How to bottle feed a baby

Feeding should be a relaxing and pleasurable time for a baby. It also needs to be safe. Ideally, bottle feeds should be given by the child's **key person**, as this supports the attachment process. Interaction is a key part of feeding babies, so you should talk to them, sing and make eye contact. You must also avoid rushing. Find out from parents about whether their baby needs **winding** and if so, how they normally do this.

Key terms

Key person – a practitioner designated to take responsibility for a child's emotional well-being by having a strong attachment with them and a good relationship with their parents.

Winding – a process to help babies expel any air trapped in their digestive system during feeding.

Use the following steps for bottle feeding a baby. Warning: Do not ever leave a baby alone with a bottle.

1 Check that the feed in the bottle is the correct one for the baby you are giving it to.

2 Find somewhere comfortable where you can sit with the baby.

3 Show the baby the bottle, and gently incline the baby.

4 Put the teat on the baby's lips and wait for the baby to accept it – do not force the teat into the baby's mouth.

5 Slightly angle the bottle so that the baby is only sucking milk, not air.

6 Look at the baby all the time you are feeding them, and talk or sing.

7 Be sensitive to the baby by noticing if they turn away their head or push the bottle away when they need a rest or have had sufficient milk. Do not force the baby to keep feeding.

8 If necessary, wind the baby in the way that the parents have indicated.

9 Unused milk should be discarded if not used.

When to start weaning

The current guideline is that babies should begin this process at 6 months and that they should have a milk-only diet until this point. This is because early weaning is linked to obesity, food allergies and digestion difficulties. It is thought that babies' digestive and immune systems are not ready for solid food until 6 months. Having said this, in some cases health professionals will suggest earlier weaning if a baby is showing signs of needing additional nutrients.

Research

Many baby foods are labelled as being suitable for babies from 4 months, despite clear advice from the World Health Organization that early weaning is not desirable. Many health professionals are unhappy about this as they claim that this is misleading for parents.

- Find out about how baby foods are labelled.
- Look at the websites of baby food manufacturers to see what advice they give to parents.

Foods to offer

The Food Standards Agency suggests that weaning is a four-part process.

Link

Go to Unit 14: Section A1 to find out about the stages of weaning and what foods to offer at each stage.

Baby-led weaning

Baby-led weaning is an approach that has become popular with some parents. The idea is that babies learn to feed themselves and choose what and how to eat. Instead of the traditional staged approach, babies are encouraged to help themselves to a range of foods, usually as part of a family meal. Babies can pick up the foods that they like the look of and then explore them using their mouths.

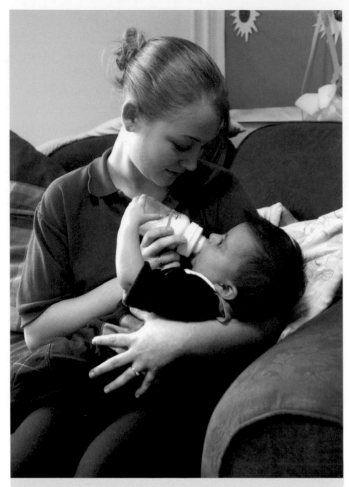

How to bottle feed a baby.

■ Weaning

Weaning is the process by which babies move from a liquid-only diet to a mixed diet of solids and liquids.

Why weaning is important

Weaning is important for many reasons. First, weaning provides babies with additional energy and iron from the added food that is introduced into their diet. These support growth and also maintain health. Babies who are not weaned at 6 months are likely to become anaemic, as the natural reserves of iron that they received in the womb from their mother will run out. Babies will also lack the energy needed to promote their physical development.

The chewing of foods also develops the muscles in the mouth that will help babies produce speech sounds. This is why it is important that once babies have begun the process of weaning, they are given foods that require them to do some chewing.

Advocates of baby-led weaning suggest that this approach prevents babies from becoming fussy eaters and also encourages them to chew early on. They also say that by missing out the spoon-feeding stage, babies have more control and independence, which is good for their emotional development. However, there are criticisms of this approach.

Criticisms

Baby-led weaning is still controversial. Critics point to an increased risk of undernourishment, as babies only take in small amounts of food at first and often spend longer playing with their food than actually eating – as baby-led weaning is not meant to include any spoon-feeding. Another criticism is that babies are more in danger of choking with this method, although advocates suggest that this is not such a problem and that usually the baby is only gagging. A final point that everyone does agree on, including those in support of baby-led weaning, is that it can be very messy.

Middle ground

While some parents will choose baby-led weaning and stick to its philosophy rigidly, many parents use a combination of the traditional staged technique along with some baby-led weaning. In practice this means that the baby will be given opportunities to play with food items, but parents will also do some spoon-feeding as well.

Meals, snacks and drinks for young children

In Unit 14, you looked at the range of nutrients that children need. Young children cannot manage with just three large meals a day – their stomachs are small and they will need snacks in between. This means that meals and snacks should be carefully planned. Below are some points to read alongside the material in Unit 14.

Energy requirements

The amount of energy a child needs depends on many factors, but particularly their amount of physical activity. It is useful when planning meals, snacks and drinks to have some idea of how many calories a child should have over a day. You can find this information in Table 15.1.

Research

Find out more about the baby-led weaning approach.

- Ask parents about what they have chosen and what they do at home.
- Find out how your placement setting approaches weaning.

Find out more about baby-led weaning by reading a leaflet that is available by going to www.pearsonhotlinks.co.uk and searching for this title.

Table 15.1 Average daily energy requirements for under-3s

Age	Energy requirements (calories)	
	Boys	Girls
1 year	765	717
2 years	1004	932
3 years	1171	1076

Source: Dietary Reference Values for Energy (2011), Scientific Advisory Committee on Nutrition.

Research

Nutritional guidelines are often being updated. This means that you should always check you are aware of the latest recommendations. A good source of information about young children's nutrition is the Caroline Walker Trust. Look out for their detailed guide to planning meals for under-3s in their booklet 'Eating well for under-5s in child care'. You can access this website by going to www.pearsonhotlinks.co.uk and searching for this title.

Fruit and vegetables

It is recommended that the under-3s should taste five different fruits or vegetables every day. You do not need to provide adult-sized portions. Fruit and vegetables can make excellent snacks, for example, carrot sticks, apple slices and orange segments.

Drinks

Water can be offered for children to quench their thirst, but whole milk is also a good drink as part of a meal or snack. Semi-skimmed milk can be offered after the age of 2 years, but only if the child is otherwise eating well. Sugary or fizzy drinks are not appropriate and may give children the taste for sweet things, even if they are sugar-free. Eating sweet things can cause dental decay.

As soon as children are able, you should help them to use an open cup rather than a beaker. This is important for their sense of independence and also for developing their physical skills.

This child will soon be ready to try an open cup.

Snacks

It is worth thinking of snacks as mini meals and being aware that they should be part of the overall calorie and nutritional intake of the child rather than being considered separately. It is also useful to get children into good habits with eating snacks, such as sitting down to eat rather than wandering around. Snacks should not be so filling that children will not be hungry for their meals.

Meals

From around 2 years, many children start to have clear preferences for and dislikes of certain foods. It is important that we make sure that mealtimes remain relaxed – we might want to encourage children to try new foods or to finish a particular food, but should avoid confrontations. Most toddlers can be tempted to try things if they are arranged into faces or pictures on the plate. Some foods can also be 'disguised' by cooking them with others or by chopping them up small.

Vitamin D

For the first time in many years, some children in the UK are now deficient in vitamin D. This deficiency can cause a bone disease known as rickets. Sunshine is the best source of vitamin D, but it is now also being suggested that more vitamin D should be included in young children's diets. Good sources of vitamin D are tuna, sardines and eggs as well as fortified breakfast cereals.

Assessment practice 15.1

3A.P1 | 3A.P2 | 3A.P3 | 3A.M1 | 3A.D1

You have been asked to write a feature by an early years magazine about how your early years setting meets the nutritional needs of children under 3 years. The editor has asked that the article covers the following.

1 The importance of meeting the nutritional needs of children and an explanation of what these are.

2 The role of adults in early years settings in the preparation and feeding of children aged 0 to 2 years.

3 Examples of daily menus that meet the nutritional guidelines for children aged 2 to 3 years.

4 An honest account of how your early years setting provides for the nutritional needs of children under 3 years, including its strengths and weaknesses as well as how the early years setting might improve its practice further.

B1 Understand how to meet the specific developmental needs of babies under 1 year

Working with babies under 1 year is very rewarding. They develop quickly, but they also have specific needs. In this section, we look at how to work sensitively with babies in this age group.

Tuning in to babies

As you saw in Student Book 1, babies need to develop attachments to the people who look after them. These will include their parents and other family members, and also their key persons. If you care for a baby, it will be important to 'tune in' to that baby. This means learning to recognise how they express their feelings and needs.

A good starting point when tuning in to a baby is to begin by talking to the baby's parents. They can tell you about their baby's reactions, preferences and little ways. Parents can also teach you to interpret their babies' cries. This is important, as although there are some similarities between babies' cries, they do differ.

As well as finding things out from parents, you also need to observe babies as you work with them, as this will soon help you to work out how they like to be held, how long they take to respond and what they like looking at or doing.

Tuning in to a baby is likely to occur more quickly when you are involved in their personal care and when you look for opportunities to hold and make eye contact with them.

Responding to distressed babies

When babies are distressed, it is very important that you find ways to comfort and reassure them.

How would you tune in to this baby?

To do this you must stay calm yourself. This is essential, as babies can tell by your tone of voice, facial expression and the way you are handling them if you are anxious or stressed.

Babies cry for a reason, and it is important once you have picked a baby up to work out why they are crying. While you are doing this, keep talking to the baby in a soothing voice and try gently rocking them or stroking their back.

Pain caused by injury or illness

Babies who are screaming may be in pain. Have a quick look to see if there are any visible signs of illness, injury or other things that might cause them discomfort.

Look at where the baby touches themself, as this may indicate the source of the pain. For instance, babies often tug at their ears when they have an ear infection.

Did you know?

Look for a rash, especially if the baby has a fever and an unusual screaming cry, as this can be a sign of meningitis.

Research

Find out more about the signs of meningitis in young babies by visiting the Meningitis Trust's website. You can access this website by going to www.pearsonhotlinks.co.uk and searching for this title.

Wind

Some babies can become very distressed shortly after a feed, as trapped wind in their stomachs causes pain. You can wind a baby by putting them over your shoulder and gently but firmly rubbing their back. Alternatively, you can sit them upright on your lap and rub their back. Apart from dissipating the pain, these actions may simply help to soothe the baby.

Tiredness

Some babies cry when they are tired. This tends to be an intermittent cry and so you may need to put the baby down to sleep, but then stay with them. Many babies respond to being rocked or stroked if they are finding it hard to fall asleep. Always check on a sleeping baby according to the procedure of the setting.

Separation anxiety

From around 7 months, babies will start to resist being separated from their parents. At first, resistance might be quite slight, but as babies develop, they will cry and become very distressed. Recognising separation anxiety is important, as it means that you will need to work on developing a stronger bond with the child. If a baby remains distressed, it is important to contact the parent.

Unexplained crying

You have looked at some of the usual reasons why babies may cry. It is also important to take unexplained crying seriously. If you cannot soothe a baby, you should always report your concerns quickly to your line manager and, if you have the authority, to the child's parents. You should also let parents know if a baby is crying more than usual even after they have calmed down.

Unexplained crying could be a sign that the child is unwell, even if no temperature is recorded. The child could be lonely and need companionship, or the crying could be an attempt to communicate. Speaking and reassuring the child can help them to understand that they do not need to worry.

Things can change rapidly with a newborn child, so any crying should never be overlooked.

Responding to individual needs in care routines

The way that you care for each baby will depend on their individual needs and also parental preferences. It is important to follow these carefully for a number of reasons.

Routines should be similar to those at home

Wherever possible, you should stick to the same sleep, feeding and nappy changing routines as those that parents use. This makes it easier for the baby to settle and feel secure. If you work closely with parents this information will be shared and when there are changes at home, these can also be implemented in the setting.

Routines must meet babies' individual needs

Care routines also need to be individualised to ensure that each baby's needs are met. It may be that one baby has a particular formula milk or another needs different skincare products. Respecting these preferences ensures that individual babies' needs are met, and also that no allergic reactions are triggered.

Avoidance of institutionalisation

Where there are a number of babies in a group who may spend long periods away from their parents, there is a danger of institutionalisation if care routines are not individualised. Institutionalisation is considered problematic as it reduces the amount of stimulation and personal attention that babies receive.

Balancing individual babies' needs with others' needs

In an ideal world, every baby would have their own key person while in group care. The reality is that babies may be cared for alongside other babies or, in the case of home-based care, with older children. Balancing the needs of the group with individual needs can be tricky.

Being organised

The key to successful group-care work is good organisation and planning. You should think ahead about what each child is likely to need in terms of feeding, play and care routines. Then you should try to prepare as much as you can, for example, getting the nappies ready for changing routines, or putting out activities and toys for older children.

Universal appeal

Where you have more than one child in your care, it is worth looking out for activities that will appeal to children of varying ages, such as blowing bubbles or moving to music. Such activities can be enjoyed by more than one child at once and older children can be watched by younger ones.

Quality time

It is important to prioritise certain times with babies, particularly those linked to care routines such as feeding and nappy changing. Again, organisation is important. If you have an older child with you, you may need to make sure that this child has something to do while you are feeding the baby or, when you are looking after babies together, you could put out a treasure basket activity for the baby who is not being fed.

How to prepare a sensory environment

Babies need plenty of stimulation. They gain this primarily from being with an adult and being held, talked to and read to. However, babies also need opportunities to use their five senses in ways that stimulate them. This means that we need to create a sensory environment for babies, both indoors and out.

Sound

There should be objects that make sounds available for babies to use, such as rattles and squeaky toys. In addition, many settings have outdoor wind chimes. It is also important to sing to babies. You can use a soundtrack for support if you are not confident at singing.

Vision

Babies are keen to look around. It is therefore helpful if there is a range of different colours, including pastels and patterns, in their environment. Babies are also fascinated by faces, so photographs are very appealing, as are mirrors for them to look into. Many settings put mirrors and different brightly coloured objects outdoors as well as inside.

Taste

A sensory environment should include the food that is offered to babies as they are being weaned and afterwards. Babies react to the taste of things and will have clear preferences. Trying out plenty of new foods can help babies become adaptable rather than fussy eaters. In addition, babies also explore using their mouths.

Babies can be stimulated by providing objects that make a sound.

Link

Go to Unit 2 in Student Book 1 to find more information about how babies explore using their mouths.

Smell

Many settings make use of sensory bags that have different smells, such as lavender bags. In some settings, the staff plant sensory gardens that contain plants such as herbs, which provide different smells.

Did you know?

When you introduce an aroma for the first time, monitor babies carefully. Some smells can trigger asthma attacks.

Texture

Babies' skin is very sensitive. They can feel texture with their feet as well as their hands. When creating a sensory environment, it is worth thinking about putting different textures on the floor as well as what things feel like when they are held.

Objects and toys to support oral exploration

All babies take items into their mouths. This is the key way in which they explore and gain sensory stimulation.

In addition to presenting natural objects for babies to choose from, we should also make sure to provide other objects and toys to allow sensory exploration. These might include household objects such as wooden spoons, hard fruit such as oranges, or different fabrics. You can give these to babies when they are sitting up or you are holding them on your lap.

Link

Go to Unit 2 in Student Book 1 to find more information about treasure basket play, in which groups of natural objects are presented for the baby to explore.

There are no right or wrong objects or toys to use for this activity, but do consider the following questions.

Safety

- Is there a risk of choking?
- Are there sharp edges?
- Are there moving parts that might trap the baby's finger?
- Could any part of the object break off if the object was sucked?

Hygiene

- Is the object clean?
- Can it be easily cleaned after the baby has finished with it?

Texture, smell and shape

- Does the object have an interesting texture?
- Does the object have an attractive smell?
- Can the baby lift the object unaided?

Assessment practice 15.2   3B1.P4 | 3B1.P5 | 3B1.M2

1 You have been asked to talk to prospective early years students about working with babies. In your talk, you should cover:
   - why it is important for adults to respond to babies' individual needs in care routines and how this might be done at the same time as meeting other babies' needs in the group.
   - the importance of sensory environments for babies under 1 year and the features of such an environment.
2 The teacher has also asked you to produce a handout that looks at the ways in which adults can meet the specific developmental needs of babies under 1 year old.

B2 Understand how to meet the specific developmental needs of children from 1 to 2 years

Children develop rapidly in this year and start turning from babies into toddlers. They begin to express themselves using words and also through movements. In this section, we look at how best to support children during this year.

Environments that support curiosity and exploration

Though a few babies stand and walk before their first birthday, most will start to do so during this year. This gives them great freedom, though even when they are still crawling they are keen to explore. It is therefore important to create environments that encourage curiosity and exploration while keeping children safe. Figure 15.2 shows the types of resources and activities that are usually provided, both indoors and out.

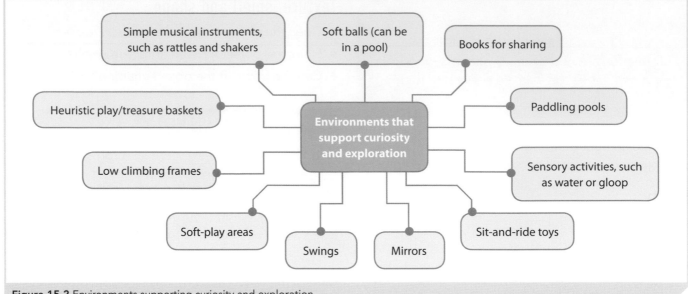

Figure 15.2 Environments supporting curiosity and exploration

The diagram shows "Environments that support curiosity and exploration" connected to:
- Simple musical instruments, such as rattles and shakers
- Soft balls (can be in a pool)
- Books for sharing
- Heuristic play/treasure baskets
- Paddling pools
- Low climbing frames
- Sensory activities, such as water or gloop
- Soft-play areas
- Swings
- Mirrors
- Sit-and-ride toys

Routines that value and respect children

Between their first and second birthdays, children will start to show signs of becoming independent. It is important, therefore, that you understand and respect their wishes wherever possible. A good starting point for this is through routine activities such as washing, feeding, nappy changing and dressing. Respecting children means being sensitive to signs that they want to do something for themselves, and to their preferences. You may, for example, ask a child whether they would like more to eat – if the child shakes their head, do not force them to eat more. Similarly, if a child is happily eating, but is doing so slowly, it is important not to rush them. Interestingly, rushing children often results in more problems and things actually taking even longer! Respecting children also means looking for ways of involving them in their care routines and, where appropriate, providing choices. You may, for example, ask children who should do the nappy change or, at mealtimes, which highchair they would like to sit in. It is important that choices are appropriate, as at this age children are not able to take long-term decisions that will impact on their health and overall well-being.

Predictability and familiarity

Routines for this age group need to feel predictable. Children like to know what is likely to happen at nappy changing time, when dressing or during meals. Predictability is often linked to adults' behaviour rather than to keeping things exactly the same each time. Children need to know that the way that the adult responds to them and acts in a situation is unchanging. This is one reason why it is good practice for just a few core people to be involved with nappy changing and washing, as after all, this is intimate care. In many settings, there are also set places where meals, naps and nappy changes take place. Along with a predictable adult, this helps the child to feel more secure.

Transitional objects

Between the ages of 1 and 2 years, children tend to have some sort of comforter, which helps them feel secure, especially in new situations or when they are not with their parents. These are known as 'transitional objects'. Children use a surprising range of objects for this purpose, although cuddly toys, blankets and scraps of fabric are especially popular. As these are important objects for children it is usual for them to be readily available and to be offered if a child becomes distressed, or at nap time.

Defiance and resistance

From around 15 months until children are around 3 years old, they start to show signs of determination and independence. This often translates into moments of defiance. This can come as quite a shock for adults, especially parents. It is important to accept that this is part of the 15-month to 3-year profile, and that things will change once children have more language and cognitive development.

Remember that toddlers are not thinking about others' feelings when they are busy pulling all the books off a shelf – they are probably just enjoying the sensation. The term 'egocentric' is often used to describe young children. This is sometimes wrongly translated as 'selfishness' when it is really only about the child's stage of development. At this stage, children are only able to focus on what they are doing and how they feel.

Supporting emotions that change quickly

One of the many interesting things about working with children between 1 to 2 years is the way their emotions can change quickly. A 15-month-old might cry because they cannot reach their beaker, but a moment later, the same child is likely to be laughing and smiling. This is normal for this age range but can take a little bit of getting used to. Emotions are liable to **fluctuate** and so tears and misery then laughter and smiles within a space of 10 minutes is pretty usual. It is important not to overreact and to stay calm when this happens and, above all, not to assume that children are being manipulative. They are simply showing typical development.

Key term

Fluctuate – to change quickly.

Using distraction to manage unwanted behaviour

Once babies are walking, a whole new world of exploration opens up to them. It is an exciting place filled with interesting objects and other children. Now that they can take things without the help of adults, they will often want to play with things that are either unsafe or not theirs. It is therefore normal for a toddler to wander over to another toddler and attempt to take whatever is in the other child's hand.

It is not uncommon for toddlers to show unwanted behaviour when they are able to walk. What would you do in this situation?

The usual strategy used to counter unwanted behaviour with this age group is distraction. Instead of focusing on what the child is attempting to do, you show the child something else that may be of interest to them. For instance, you could start singing or show them an alternative toy. Distraction has many advantages, but mainly it avoids unnecessary conflict and tears. It is also age appropriate. Trying to reprimand a child of this age or explain the error of their ways is pointless, as they do not have the language or cognitive skills to understand.

Using distraction

Cassie is a learner on placement in the toddler room. She is surprised to find how calm and happy the children are. At lunchtime, she spots that one toddler is helping himself to food from another toddler's plate. She tells the toddler to stop doing this in a firm voice. The toddler ignores her and carries on taking food. (The other toddler looks bemused but is not upset by this.) The room leader comes over and calls out the first toddler's name and smiles at him. She begins to clap her hands. All the toddlers start to join in. She starts singing a song and as she does so, she takes the toddler by his hand and steers him and his plate over to another part of the table.

1 Why did the toddler not stop when Cassie reprimanded him?

2 How was distraction used by the supervisor?

3 What were the benefits of using distraction?

Supporting communication development of children from 1 to 2 years

We know that adults need to communicate with young children in order to support their language development. As a key person you may do this in a variety of ways such as sharing books, playing simple games or just chatting and making eye contact as you are changing nappies or supporting mealtimes. Interestingly, when adults engage with children in this way, not only are they supporting their language development, but also their social and emotional development. The eye contact and interest as well as the sensitive interaction help children to gain reassurance, learn social skills and feel secure.

The years from birth to 3 are crucial in terms of children's communication and language development. From the ages of 1 to 2, children's **receptive language** will be expanding and from around 15 months, we should expect to be hearing some first words. The number of words that children produce will depend on many things, but crucially on how much adult interaction they have. The more time children spend with their key person engaging in activities, such as sharing books and playing simple games and during mealtimes, the better. When children of this age have opportunities for sustained interaction, they are more likely to understand what is happening. Increased interaction also means that these very young toddlers are more likely to feel emotionally secure.

Key term

Receptive language – language that a child can understand.

B3 Understand how to meet the specific developmental needs of children from 2 to 3 years

From 2 to 3 years, toddlers really develop. They gain in independence, confidence and also physical skills. While their language skills are developing, they are not yet able to totally express themselves, and this can lead to frustration. Working with this age group is fascinating, but also requires organisation to be able to meet their specific needs.

Assessment practice 15.3   3B2.P6 | 3B2.P7 | 3B2.M3

You have been asked by your local early years network to report on how best to create stimulating and sensory environments that encourage communication for toddlers aged 1 to 2 years.

They are particularly interested in the features and concepts that are important in environments for children aged from 1 to 2 years.

They would also like you to cover the role of adults in supporting the development of communication of children from 1 to 2 years.

Your report should conclude with an analysis of how the environment can aid communication development. This analysis should include examples.

Creating an environment that supports self-reliance

Toddlers enjoy being busy and independent. It is vital that you do not underestimate how much they are increasingly able to do for themselves. This should be reflected in the environment that you provide for them. Wherever possible, some resources should be easily accessible for them to help themselves. You also need to make sure that you give them plenty of opportunities to develop self-care skills such as dressing and feeding. When toddlers learn to do these things themselves, they will have a sense of achievement, although they will need to be allowed additional time. It is also important to judge sensitively whether a child needs help – ideally, you should ask the toddler if they need a hand.

Creating experiences for role play

From around 2 years, most toddlers start to enjoy using props that they have seen adults using. This is their first step towards role play. They often enjoy the movements and actions, but how much they are actually 'pretending' varies. Providing props that toddlers can use is important, as these often help toddlers to feel 'grown up' and also encourage vocalisation. You may find that children who are closer to 3 years old and talking well sustain role play for longer periods and may start to play with other children. Figure 15.3 shows some popular role-play props that children enjoy using.

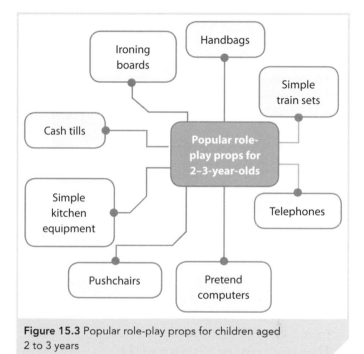

Figure 15.3 Popular role-play props for children aged 2 to 3 years

Involving children in routine activities

It is a common mistake to think that toddlers want to play all the time. While play should be a part of their daily activities, they also like helping adults – this provides additional stimulation and a change of pace. Tasks might be anything from helping to sweep the floor to putting laundry in the washing machine. This is easy to do in home-based care, but such opportunities may need to be created in group-care settings. By being involved in routine activities and tasks, toddlers gain a feeling of importance, and they also practise valuable physical skills, often involving fine motor movements. They will learn everyday vocabulary and enjoy chatting to you during the activity. When carrying out routine tasks with toddlers, it is important to be patient and expect that things will take longer than usual. Figure 15.4 shows some of the ways in which you can involve children.

Figure 15.4 Ways to involve children in activities and tasks – can you think of other activities that 2-year-olds can be involved in?

Providing manageable challenges

Two-year-olds do like to have some challenges, particularly mental and physical ones. It is therefore important to look for activities that will provide these. In addition to involving children in routine activities and tasks, you can also look at the types of toys, activities and resources that you provide. Heuristic play is a good example of this. With heuristic play, a range of objects – not toys – are put out for a toddler to explore. Toddlers can then make their own connections and challenges.

You also need to observe toddlers closely as they play and consider whether they are fully engaged – and if they are not, to think about whether the materials, activity or resources are sufficiently engaging.

Why is this a manageable challenge for this child?

Link

Go to Unit 2 in Student Book 1 to find more information about heuristic play.

Understanding impulsive behaviour

A major feature of 2-year-olds is their impulsive behaviour. This often takes people by surprise if they have not worked with this age range before. Most 2-year-olds are governed by what they see and what they feel like doing. 'I see, I want' is a good maxim to remember when working with this age group. Added to this, children of this age have developed quite fast reactions and can move quickly. This has many implications, particularly when it comes to safety. This is one reason why safety equipment must be used consistently with this age group.

The level of impulsiveness shown by this age group comes out in many ways: they may push another child down the slide if they are in the way or they may start banging a cupboard door because they like the feel of the action and the sound that it makes.

Factoring in impulsive behaviour

If you understand that children in this age group are likely to be impulsive, you can factor this in when working with them. It means that you might have equipment and toys ready for them so that they immediately have things to focus on. It also means that you might hide objects or items that you do not want them to have. You might also take certain safety measures, such as putting reins on children before you step outside for an outing.

Interestingly, as children's speech develops, they become less impulsive. This is because speech is linked to the ability to organise, plan and recognise consequences.

Research

1 Observe 2-year-olds in your setting. Can you see ways in which they are quite impulsive?

2 How does your setting manage this?

3 Now observe children aged 3 to 4 years. Can you see that most of them are less impulsive in their actions?

Guidelines for acceptable behaviour

It is important to have very realistic goals for toddler behaviour. These goals should be based on the usual patterns of child development for their age. Expecting children to behave in ways that are not linked to the usual patterns of behaviour is likely to cause conflict and frustration.

Link

Unit 7 in Student Book 1 looked at goals and expectations of behaviour. You should revisit these if you are working with this age group.

Remember that toddlers' willingness to comply will be variable, and that this is usual for the age group. This might mean that a child is fairly cooperative one moment, but then shows defiance or an impulsive behaviour later on.

It can be helpful to bear in mind the typical behaviours of this age group. Typically, children of this age:

- have no concept of sharing
- have no understanding that possessions belong to others
- are restless and active

- dislike sharing adult attention
- will snatch items from other children.

Temper tantrums

Many children under 3 will have temper tantrums. These vary in frequency and intensity from child to child. Temper tantrums are most likely to occur when a child is hungry, tired or feeling frustrated. A temper tantrum is a frenzy of uncontrolled emotion that can be triggered by a child seeing something they cannot have or being stopped from doing something. Children do not plan tantrums – they occur spontaneously.

Avoiding tantrums

Tantrums are negative experiences for everyone. Other children become anxious, adults are distracted from positive activities and the child having the tantrum also becomes very distracted. The best solution is to try to be organised so that, as far as possible, tantrums are avoided.

Tiredness

Tantrums are more likely to occur in children who are tired. A combination of tiredness and hunger increases the risk of a tantrum considerably. Making sure that children are getting around 12 hours of sleep in a 24-hour period is therefore a good starting point. This may mean moving nap times forward if a child seems particularly tired. For children who have many tantrums, it is worth finding out from parents how much sleep the child has and whether the parents need support with this.

Research

Read a booklet created for parents by the Department for Education to inform them about children's sleep. You can access this booklet by going to www.pearsonhotlinks.co.uk and searching for this title.

Hunger

Children's brains need food. Impulsive behaviours that often cause tantrums are more likely to be exacerbated when children are hungry. This means making sure that you have regular meal and snack times and that you are ready to be flexible with these if a child seems hungry.

Emotional security

Children are more likely to have tantrums when they feel insecure. A strong and effective key person system is therefore vital, and children in this age group need to spend plenty of time with their key person. Changes in the child's home life can also be a cause of tantrums. This may include the arrival of a sibling, the parents' separation or moving house. If this is the case, you will need to spend extra time with the child and you may also need to increase their nap times. This is because when children are going through changes in their lives, they are less likely to be sleeping well.

Good organisation and pace

Two-year-olds are busy people. Good organisation can prevent them becoming bored – plenty of resources and toys are needed. As toddlers will often want what another child has, a key strategy is to ensure that there are duplicates of favourite toys such as pushchairs. Playing with children gives you the opportunity to divert their attention and prevent problems from arising.

What to do if a tantrum occurs

There is a moment, just before a tantrum gets underway, when it might be possible to distract the child. Sometimes this works, other times not. If a tantrum does get underway, the best thing you can do is to reassure the other children that 'Dee is feeling a little angry now, but she will be all right' so they do not become distressed. You should then keep very calm and stay near the child. You may try to touch and comfort the child, but this is often unsuccessful and can provoke the child even more.

In some ways, it is good to see the tantrum like a storm and allow it to pass in its own time. Do not do or say anything to fuel it. Once the child has calmed down, act as if nothing particular has happened. Do not reprimand the child or talk about the tantrum. Some children may want a cuddle afterwards, while others may want to join in an activity. It can take time for some children to recover from a tantrum, so be ready to go at their pace for a while. A few minutes after the tantrum, make sure the child is given plenty of praise and attention. This helps the child to learn that positive behaviours are valued and given attention. This is particularly important if the tantrum was triggered by attention seeking.

Assessment practice 15.4 | 3B3.P8 | 3B3.P9 | 3B3.M4

You have been asked to mentor a student on placement who has not worked with children aged 2 to 3 years before. To help her, you have decided to write a guide to working effectively with children aged 2 to 3 years. Your guide should include:

- the type of accessible activities and routines that support the social and emotional needs of this age range
- the role of adults in promoting positive behaviour with children in this age range
- the effects on children's social and emotional development of having accessible activities and routines, as well as skilled adults working alongside children.

Assessment practice 15.5 | 3B.D2 | 3C.P10 | 3C.M5

You have been asked to give a presentation to a group of first-year students about the role of adults and effective environments in relation to promoting the development of children under 3 years.

Your presentation should include examples and must cover:

- the extent to which the environment created by early years settings can support and promote each of the areas of development and learning
- the skills and qualities that adults need to demonstrate in order to work with children under 3 years
- the importance of positive role modelling by adults when working with children under 3 years.

C Understand the skills and qualities needed to work with children under 3 years

There are certain skills and qualities that you need if you wish to pursue a career working with under-3s. In this section, we look at what makes a successful under-3s practitioner.

Qualities you will need

There are particular qualities that practitioners who work effectively with children under 3 seem to have. Figure 15.5 shows these qualities. If you intend to work with this age range, you might like to reflect on whether you are able to demonstrate these skills, or are willing to work on developing them.

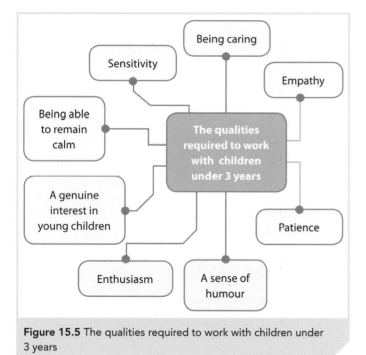

Figure 15.5 The qualities required to work with children under 3 years

Patience

While all people working with young children need to have patience, this is particularly important with this age range for a number of reasons.

First, babies and toddlers cannot be rushed. They do things in their own time and simple tasks such as dressing and getting ready to go out can be very protracted.

This age group is also fascinated by and keen to repeat certain play and activities. Toddlers will often want the same book read to them a number of times or will be keen to repeat the same movement over and over again. While this is part of their learning, it does require that adults are patient and are able to maintain their own enthusiasm.

Finally, babies and toddlers can also have rapid changes in their responses. One moment a baby may be calm and settled but five minutes later might be quite irritable.

Sense of humour and enthusiasm

Babies and toddlers can sense when adults are happy and fun to be with. Practitioners who work with babies and toddlers show that they enjoy being with them and are playful with them. Babies and toddlers also like to be with people who have a sense of humour and who show this appropriately.

Sensitivity, caring approach and empathy

There is a debate as to whether care, sensitivity and empathy can be taught or whether they come naturally. Regardless of this, these are qualities that you will need to have. Babies and toddlers need people to be very sensitive to their needs and who can respond with care and empathy. An irritable baby will need soothing and being talked to in ways that calm. Babies and toddlers are very attuned to tone of voice and facial expressions. Someone who is genuinely expressing empathy and care is likely to reassure and calm a baby or toddler. Children's speech and emotional development is linked to whether they are with people who can show sensitivity, care and empathy.

Calmness

Babies and toddlers need to feel safe with those who care for them. They can tell if a person is stressed, anxious or frustrated. This means you have to display calmness at all times, even if you are feeding a baby and at the same time a toddler wants the potty.

Genuine interest in young children

All of the qualities mentioned so far are easy to demonstrate if you have a genuine interest in young children. If you are interested in toddlers' development, you are likely to find their need to repeat play activities over and over again fascinating. If you do not have this genuine interest, you are likely to find it boring.

Children are quick to sense whether or not you have this interest, and if you do not, they are likely to demonstrate this in their responses. Parents will also pick up on this.

Skills for work with children under 3 years

As well as specific qualities, there are some skills that are essential for work with under-3s. Figure 15.6 shows some key skills that are essential for working with this age group.

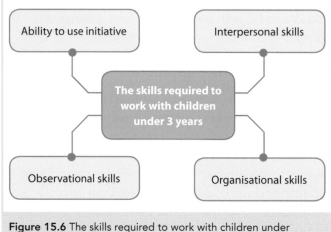

Figure 15.6 The skills required to work with children under 3 years

Interpersonal skills

It is essential that you are able to communicate with and respond to children, and also their parents or carers. Many parents will be leaving their children in someone else's care for the first time and will naturally be anxious about this. Good interpersonal skills can give parents confidence and allow you to communicate effectively with them. You also need to demonstrate good interpersonal skills with children. They will learn a lot about how to relate to other people from watching you in action.

Observational skills

Throughout this unit you have seen the importance of observational skills. Good practitioners will be closely monitoring the children they are with and, while they may not write up every observation, they will be using what they have noted to do spontaneous planning. This will be in addition to the more formal observation and planning process described in Unit 9.

Organisational skills

If you work with the under-3s, you will need excellent organisational skills. This is because they cannot wait around for food, nappy changes or play activities. Babies need to be fed on time and nappies have to be changed promptly and correctly. Toddlers who are bored and are waiting around are likely to find their own amusements, and this might not be what you had envisaged.

Initiative

The ability to take the initiative often comes gradually and will be linked to your knowledge and growing confidence. It is important, though, to be 'quick on your feet' when working with this age group, as what may be required at any point in time may change. This means that if you are someone who likes to take their time or prefers to be told what to do, you may struggle to work with this age group.

Further reading and resources

Lindon, J. (2006) *Helping Babies and Toddlers Learn: A Guide to Good Practice with Under-threes*, London: National Children's Bureau.

MacIntyre, C. (2011) *Understanding Babies and Young Children from Conception to Three: A Guide for Students, Practitioners and Parents*, London: Routledge.

Robinson, M. (2003) *From Birth to One: The Year of Opportunity*, Oxford: Oxford University Press.

Ready for work?

Caroline Jenkins   Nursery worker

I have spent most of my career so far working in the baby and toddler room. I love it here and think that anyone working with babies and toddlers is very lucky. We see the babies when they first come and get to know the parents well. As most of our babies are with us for four years, it means that whenever we go outdoors or to another room, there are always 'our' children waving and talking to us. It does take a lot of patience working in the baby and toddler room, but it is also a lot of fun. I love the way that babies and toddlers become fascinated by things that when they are older will just be taken for granted. It is also amazing to see the way that they develop and their personalities start to shine through. Some babies are clearly bold, while others seem to be great thinkers.

Some people say that working in the baby and toddler room is boring. They have never been here! We take our children outdoors several times a day and always, unless it is really pouring down, for a long walk. Babies and toddlers always find things to notice and there is always plenty to talk about as we see cats, cars going by and the odd shopper. Back indoors, it's non-stop with nappy changes, mealtimes and activities. From early on we encourage the children to do as much as they are able and visitors are often surprised when they see the babies crawling with a nappy in one hand ready to bring it to the changing room!

Skills for practice

A dummy as a transitional object

Many toddlers become attached to a dummy. This is because the current advice for preventing cot death includes the use of a dummy when a baby is put to sleep up to the age of 12 months. The dummy is meant to keep the airways open.

As a result there has been an increase in the number of dummies being brought into settings by toddlers. This can create tension because if a toddler uses a dummy, they are less likely to interact with adults and also to show the full range of facial expressions. It is therefore recommended that the use of dummies should be restricted to nap times only.

Most settings have a policy about this and will explain the reasons for this policy to parents. Ideally, an alternative transitional object such as a cuddly toy should be encouraged. This can be introduced by the parents when the child is having a good time or a cuddle so that the child associates the object with being happy and feeling secure. It will take some time for this object to be accepted and then used by the child, but it is worth persevering with it.

Introduction

Working in a home-based setting can be a rewarding experience for early years practitioners. It provides opportunities for practitioners to develop close relationships with the children in their care, through supporting their development during the pre-school years.

This chapter will focus on key areas of the role, such as working with parents and networking with other agencies, as well as looking at ways of developing play and other learning opportunities for children in home-based settings.

Assessment: You will be assessed by a series of assignments set by your teacher/tutor.

Learning aims

In this unit you will:

A   understand the value of home-based care for children and families

B   understand how to establish a safe and healthy home-based environment

C   understand how to provide play for differing ages of children in a home-based environment

D   understand how to meet the personal, social and emotional needs of children in a home-based environment

E   understand the role of parents and other agencies as partners in home-based childcare.

> By doing this unit I have increased my confidence and furthered my knowledge and understanding of how home-based practitioners work professionally to meet the needs of children and families. I hope that one day I'll be able to work with children in my own home and maybe even set up my own childminding business. Working as a childminder would enable me to carry on working even after I've started my own family.
>
> Sarah, *a student on an early years course*

Working With Children in Home-based Care

16

BTEC
Assessment Zone

This table shows what you must do in order to achieve a **Pass**, **Merit** or **Distinction** grade, and where you can find activities to help you.

Assessment criteria		
Pass	**Merit**	**Distinction**
Learning aim A: Understand the value of home-based care for children and families		
3A.P1 Explain the benefits of home-based care for children and families. **Assessment practice 16.1**	**3A.M1** Discuss the extent to which home-based care benefits children and families. **Assessment practice 16.1**	
Learning aim B: Understand how to establish a safe and healthy home-based environment		
3B.P2 Describe the role of the home-based practitioner in keeping children safe, using examples. **Assessment practice 16.2** **3B.P3** Explain how to promote healthy lifestyles in a home-based environment. **Assessment practice 16.2**	**3B.M2** Analyse how children can be kept healthy and safe in a home-based environment, using examples. **Assessment practice 16.2**	**3B.D1** Evaluate how a home-based practitioner could contribute to children's health and safety more effectively. **Assessment practice 16.2**
Learning aim C: Understand how to provide play for differing ages of children in a home-based environment		
3C.P4 Explain the role of observation in the provision of play in a home-based environment. **Assessment practice 16.3** **3C.P5** Explain, with selected examples, how to provide opportunities for play for children of mixed ages in a home-based environment. **Assessment practice 16.3**	**3C.M3** Analyse the role of the adult in providing appropriate play experiences for children of mixed age ranges in a home-based environment. **Assessment practice 16.3**	
Learning aim D: Understand how to meet the personal, social and emotional needs of children in a home-based environment		
3D.P6 Explain how to meet the emotional health needs of children in home-based childcare. **Assessment practice 16.4** **3D.P7** Explain how to support the positive behaviour of children of mixed ages in home-based childcare. **Assessment practice 16.4**	**3D.M4** Analyse how home-based practitioners contribute to meeting the personal, social and emotional needs of children of mixed ages. **Assessment practice 16.4**	**3D.D2** Evaluate approaches and techniques home-based practitioners use to support children's personal, social and emotional needs in home-based childcare. **Assessment practice 16.4**

continued

Assessment criteria (*continued*)

Pass	Merit	Distinction
Learning aim E: Understand the role of parents and other agencies as partners in home-based childcare		
3E.P8 English I&CT Explain, using examples, how home-based practitioners work with other agencies to support children and families. **Assessment practice 16.5**	**3E.M5** Analyse how the relationship between home-based carers, parents and other agencies can support children. **Assessment practice 16.5**	
3E.P9 I&CT Explain how home-based carers work in partnership with parents to support children and families. **Assessment practice 16.5**		

English English Functional Skills signposting   I&CT Information and Communication Technology skills signposting

How you will be assessed

This unit will be assessed by a series of internally assessed tasks set by your teacher/tutor. Throughout this unit you will find assessment practice activities that will help you work towards your assessment. Completing these activities will not mean that you have achieved a particular grade, but you will have carried out useful research or preparation that will be relevant when it comes to your final assignment.

In order for you to achieve the tasks in your assignment, it is important that you check you have met all of the Pass grading criteria. You can do this as you work your way through the assignment.

If you are hoping to gain a Merit or Distinction, you should also make sure that you present the information in your assignment in the style that is required by the relevant assessment criterion. For example, Merit criteria will require you to discuss and analyse, and Distinction criteria will require you to evaluate.

The assignment set by your teacher/tutor will consist of a number of tasks designed to meet the criteria in the table. This is likely to consist of a written assignment but may also include activities such as:

- an information leaflet
- case studies.

Getting started

Remember a time when you were cared for by a relative or other adult, for example, before school.

With a partner, discuss how this felt. Were there things that you liked or disliked?

A Understand the value of home-based care for children and families

This section explores the value of home-based care in providing flexible and consistent care that is able to meet the individual needs of children. The home setting promotes real-life experiences for children and supports engagement with their local community.

Consistency of care and positive relationships

Home-based childcare is unique. It provides a relaxed family environment, a home-from-home experience, and studies show that this gives children the best start. It allows parents to choose a setting that may provide similar parenting styles, beliefs and cultures to their own.

Children are able to form secure attachments to one carer. This supports their emotional development by giving them the confidence and the opportunity to try out new things.

Home-based practitioners are able to form lasting positive relationships with families, and share their children's progress with them. These effective partnerships allow you, as a carer, to share observations of the children you look after and plan for their next steps. The continuity of care you provide will support both the child and their parents.

Individual children's needs can be met, and routines and activities can be flexible and spontaneous.

Imagine that you had planned to spend the day baking with the children, then wake up to find that there has been a heavy snowfall. Home-based childcare means you can quickly adapt your plans to make full use of the learning opportunities as a result of the weather. You can use this opportunity to play outside, make footprints, show the children what happens when you bring the snow inside, make winter pictures and so on.

Being responsive to children's individual needs

Home-based practitioners are well placed to support the needs of all children. As the **key person** they will form caring relationships with, and gather a huge amount of knowledge about, the children in their care. They will be able to provide support as children enter different stages of development and provide guidance for parents, for example, with potty training.

The home-based setting is often the most suitable one in which to provide care for vulnerable children. This could be because the numbers of children are fewer and the environment, equipment and resources can be easily adapted to meet the individual needs of the child. Many home-based practitioners provide childcare and/or **respite care** for disabled children.

> ### Key terms
>
> **Key person** – a practitioner designated to take responsibility for a child's emotional well-being by having a strong attachment with them and a good relationship with their parents.
>
> **Respite care** – short-term care with the assistance of professional carers.

Flexibility to meet the needs of parents and children

Another benefit of home-based care is that children are often able to access services within their local community, such as baby clinics, local stay-and-play sessions, preschools, schools and after-school activities. This allows children to build on and maintain existing relationships while feeling part of their community.

Parents require a flexible service that meets their needs as working families. Whether they are working part- or full-time, home-based childcare can provide valuable before- and after-school care as well as overnight care to cover working shift patterns.

Home-based practitioners often have a good network of support and are able to provide holiday and sickness cover for each other in agreement with parents.

Caring for siblings together

In home-based childcare, siblings can be cared for together. This can support children and provide reassurance when settling in. Siblings can learn from each other and share experiences. This all helps support the children's emotional and social development and promotes their well-being. In addition, parents have the convenience of only having to drop off and collect from one place.

Continuity of care through to teenage years

Many home-based practitioners recount their experiences of caring for children from when they were babies right up to secondary school age. They become part of the family, and children will often go back to visit their former childminder when they return from university.

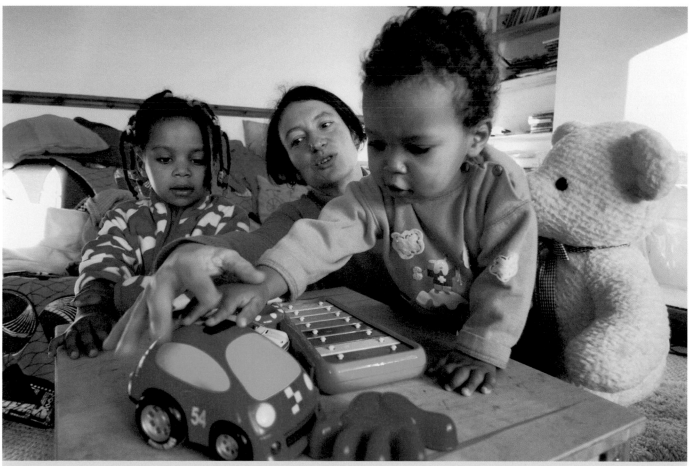

Siblings are often cared for together in home-based childcare.

193

This strong attachment, together with the reassurance and continuity it provides, supports the child's development – particularly their emotional development and well-being. Home-based practitioners are well placed to support the many **transitions** that children go through, providing a smooth passage from one environment to another. They can work with parents to prepare children for change, and recognise the impact change may have on their emotional development.

Case study

When it was time for Paul to attend nursery, his home-based practitioner spent time talking to him about the things he would do there. With permission she took photographs of the nursery and they role-played the routines that he would have to follow. She visited the nursery with Paul and his mum, and shared with them Paul's learning journal, so they could see all that Paul had achieved.

On the day that Paul started he had a book of photographs to take with him that showed where he would hang his coat, the teacher he would see and where he would have his lunch. This provided him with a visual story that enabled him to feel in control of his day.

In what way do you think the actions of the home-based practitioner helped:

- Paul?
- his mum?
- the nursery?

Key term

Transitions – the changes that happen in all children's lives, such as starting school or personal changes such as family break-up.

Real-life learning experiences

Children are able to gain real-life learning experiences in a home-based setting. These are invaluable in making sure they are equipped and resilient to cope with their life ahead. Home-based practitioners are able to support the earliest speech and language development of children, and their high-quality interactions mean children are valued and able to develop self-esteem. The routines that take place, such as dressing, putting on shoes and feeding, allow children many opportunities to practise skills.

They are surrounded by everyday experiences that not only promote the child's learning but provide real enjoyment for both the child and the carer.

Caring for children in a smaller group

Home-based childcare provides children with the opportunity of being cared for in a smaller group. Their individual needs can be clearly identified and met, and children are able to form secure attachments not only with the key person but also with the other children.

Assessment practice 16.1

3A.P1 | 3A.M1

Create a poster aimed at parents to be displayed in your local children's centre.

It should explain the benefits to children and their families of home-based childcare.

Include an evaluation of how home-based childcare contributes to meeting children's individual needs and also the needs of the child's family.

B Understand how to establish a safe and healthy home-based environment

Supporting children to keep safe and healthy is an important part of home-based childcare. This section looks at how you can promote children's independence while ensuring their safety and well-being.

Importance of identifying and managing risk

Like all practitioners, home-based child carers have a responsibility to keep children safe and healthy. Children are naturally curious and can have a limited awareness of how to stay safe. It is a legal duty for home-based practitioners to follow the regulatory requirements of their home country in relation to health and safety.

Link

Go to Unit 4 in Student Book 1 to find more information about health and safety requirements.

Research

Certain accidents and incidents must be reported by law. Research the Reporting of Injuries, Diseases and Dangerous Occurrences Regulations (RIDDOR) 1995 to find out what responsibilities you have under this Act.

They are also required to have a valid paediatric first-aid qualification, which is approved by the local authority and involves a minimum of 12 hours' training. Home-based practitioners must have a first-aid box available both within the setting and when out and about. It is also essential to seek appropriate parental permission relating to administering medicines or other treatment.

Home-based practitioners are required to follow specific policies and procedures for health and safety. These will depend on your home nation's regulatory

requirements. In England, these are the requirements of the Early Years Foundation Stage (EYFS) and in Wales, the National Minimum Standards for Regulated Childcare.

Did you know?

In order to comply with **regulations** and **legislation** relating to health and safety, home-based practitioners need to seek parental permission for a range of activities, including:

* administering medicines
* seeking emergency medical treatment
* taking children on outings
* taking photographs/videos of children
* applying sun cream.

This list is not comprehensive, and home-based practitioners have a responsibility to make sure that they refer to the regulatory requirements for their own home nation.

Key terms

Legislation – the act of making laws.

Regulations – legal requirements that have to be followed.

First-aid boxes should be up to date and complete.

Risk assessments

Risk assessments inside and outside the home-based setting will need to be carried out on a regular basis. This should also include regular outings such as the school run or one-off organised trips. A risk assessment must identify potential hazards and risks. When thinking about risk assessments, remember:

- a hazard is anything that may cause harm, such as chemicals, electricity or an open drawer
- a risk is the probability, high or low, that somebody could be harmed by these and other hazards.

For example, bleach left by the toilet is a hazard and there is a risk a child could be seriously harmed by this.

Activity

- Consider each room in your own house and the potential risks and hazards there.
- For each room, identify the particular hazard, then state what the risk to children may be. Finally, list the actions you could take to prevent harm to children. An example is below:
  - Identified hazard: Front door opens on to busy road.
  - Risk: Children may be able to leave premises.
  - Control measure: Supervision of children at all times and door locked with key accessible for emergencies.

Case study

Mary is a registered childminder. She has two teenage sons who have left their razors and shaving foam out in the bathroom over the weekend. On Monday morning Mary is welcoming three children into her setting.

1 What steps should Mary take to prevent any harm to the children?

2 What might happen if she did not?

Involving children in managing risk

When children play it is important they are allowed the opportunity to take measured risks, as this will support their learning and development. By taking these risks children will learn a range of skills, including the ability to calculate the level of risk involved in an activity and to avoid and understand the consequences of dangerous situations.

Independence and resilience

Allowing children to make decisions during their play encourages them to become independent and builds their self-esteem. This resilience supports their ability to cope with life as they reach adulthood.

Reflect

James is a nanny caring for 2-year-old twins and he has decided that they are going to make a fruit salad. How can James take a measured risk that will allow the twins to take part safely and benefit from the experience? Think about the tools he might use and the levels of supervision he needs to ensure.

Research

Visit the Health and Safety Executive website for further information on managing risk. You can access this website by going to www.pearsonhotlinks.co.uk and searching for this title.

Management of outings

It is important to risk assess both regular outings (for example, school runs) and one-off outings (such as a trip to the seaside) and seek parental permission in line with your home nation's regulatory requirements.

Inspection requirements

Remember to refer to your home nation's requirements in relation to managing risks for inspection.

The value of secure indoor and outdoor environments

Children's learning will flourish in a secure environment that allows them to experience situations in which they are able to learn to evaluate risk for themselves. Outdoor opportunities give children access to a variety of resources and a chance to improve their movement, coordination, control and use of their senses to learn about the world around them.

Home-based practitioners may care for their own children alongside the children they are minding. It is therefore important that they think carefully about how to balance the risk-taking of their own children with the need to ensure the safety of those in their care and the wishes of their parents.

The principles of safeguarding

Home-based carers have a responsibility to follow the regulatory requirements of their home nation. This would include the requirement to have a **safeguarding policy** and to follow the Local Safeguarding Children Board's **procedure**.

> ## Link
>
> Go to Unit 8 in Student Book 1 to find more information about safeguarding children.

> ## Key terms
>
> **Policy** – a written statement about what you will do.
>
> **Procedure** – an explanation of how you will do something.
>
> **Safeguarding** – the act of keeping children safe from harm.

Safe recruitment

Some home-based practitioners choose to work alongside others. They may work together as separate registered providers, or one practitioner may employ assistants or take on volunteers. In this situation the practitioner is required to seek permission from the regulatory body, who will check the proposed assistant's suitability. This will involve carrying out a Criminal Records Bureau (CRB) check. The employer must ensure that the proposed assistant is suitably qualified and understands all the relevant policies and procedures, as well as provide and carry out inductions, supervision and appraisals.

Lone workers

Working alone or in isolation is a feature of being a home-based practitioner. This can make them more vulnerable to allegations of abuse. However, there are steps that practitioners can take to protect themselves:

- Behave professionally at all times.
- Ensure all accidents and incidents are recorded accurately and factually.
- Record all injuries children arrive with at the setting.
- Ensure parents sign records, or make a note if a parent refuses to sign.
- Ensure the rest of the family are also aware of their vulnerability to allegations.
- Encourage children to be independent.

Any concerns about a child need to be recorded and stored securely. This information is confidential and should only be shared with the appropriate professionals, in line with the setting's safeguarding procedure. As lone workers, home-based practitioners do not have a manager or designated officer within the setting. Instead, there is support and guidance available through organisations such as the National Childminding Association (NCMA) or the NSPCC.

> ## Case study
>
> John and Alice are registered childminders. Their daughter Sophie has just returned from university for the Christmas holidays. One evening, a parent of a child they care for, 3-year-old Frankie, telephones to say that Frankie is very upset. He has just told her that Sophie shut his finger in a door earlier that day.
>
> 1 How should the childminders respond to this allegation?
>
> 2 What steps could John, Alice and Sophie take to prevent this happening in the future?

Impact on own family

It can be very distressing if a home-based practitioner either is accused of abuse or has to manage a child protection case within the setting. If this does happen it is important to document all conversations and records. The family may experience a range of emotions, including anger, shock and helplessness. These emotions are normal and support is available. It may be that legal advice is required, and this can be provided by the NCMA to its members or by the Citizens Advice Bureau.

Support of families

It is important to remain professional at all times. Families may be experiencing a wide range of emotions and may need to seek support from other agencies.

Promoting healthy lifestyles in a home-based setting

Practitioners working in the home are able to influence children and families to make healthy lifestyle choices. The flexibility of home-based care means that children can be actively involved in the planning and preparation of meals and hygiene practices. Home-based practitioners can also plan activities that support healthy lifestyles, such as setting up an assault course in the garden and asking the children to think about the impact of this on their body by taking their pulse at the end.

Food hygiene

Children can be seriously affected by food poisoning, so it is good practice for home-based practitioners to access guidance from the Food Standards Agency (FSA) and undertake basic food handling training. Children may have allergies, which the home-based practitioner may need to discuss with parents. Registered childminders are required to register as a food business operator with their local authority if they regularly provide snacks or meals to the children in their care.

Did you know?

The Food Standards Agency provides a free resource called 'Safer Food, Better Business' to support home-based practitioners when preparing, storing and cooking food. Download this resource from their website, which you can access by going to www.pearsonhotlinks.co.uk and searching for this title.

Home-based practitioners need to consider a range of issues relating to food and nutrition, including:

- correct fridge/freezer temperatures
- correct methods of storage; e.g. of lunches
- correct thawing, heating and cooking of food
- sterilisation of bottles and/or storage of milk
- hygiene practices
- consideration of food allergies
- support and advice on good nutrition.

In England, the School Food Trust has produced voluntary nutritional guidance for early years practitioners. Support tools include menus and recipes, self-evaluation checklists and an early years code of practice for food and drink.

The Department of Health has also issued physical activity guidelines that explain the physical activity children require from birth to adulthood. Alongside good nutrition, physical activity ensures children have the best start in life and reduces the risk of ill-health.

You can access these guidelines by going to www.pearsonhotlinks.co.uk and searching for this title.

Link

Go to Unit 14: Section B to find more information about food hygiene.

Assessment practice 16.2

3B.P2 | 3B.P3
3B.M2 | 3B.D1

Home-based practitioners often provide parents with a welcome pack explaining the service they offer, and giving them something to read before making their decision about whom to choose to care for their child.

Create two sections for the welcome pack:

1 a description for parents about how the home-based practitioner ensures children will be kept healthy and active

2 an explanation of how the children will be kept safe while also being given the opportunity to take risks.

C Understand how to provide play for differing ages of children in a home-based environment

Home-based childcare provides an environment in which children of differing ages can actively explore and learn through play. Ongoing observation and assessment ensure a range of play opportunities can be planned and children's progress can be recorded.

Recognising the play needs of children of differing ages

Children learn through play, so careful planning to ensure they have a range of opportunities is vital. Through observing the children in their care, childminders can recognise their likes and dislikes, strengths and areas for development. There are many scenarios in which children can be observed naturally. These may include:

- playing in the park
- preparing snacks and eating meals
- at parent and toddler/childminding groups.

Link

Go to Unit 2 in Student Book 1 to find more information about recognising play needs at different ages.

Recording children's progress

Recording observations does not have to be time consuming. They can be recorded by taking photos, writing on sticky notes and using video.

Using their knowledge of child development, childminders can establish the current stages of development that children in their care have reached. This knowledge then allows them to plan effectively.

The Early Years Foundation Stage requires that childminders complete a progress check when a child is between the ages of 2 and 3. This is an assessment that identifies children's progress in the prime areas of learning and development. Through both the childminder's observations and parents' feedback, the progress check is intended to highlight areas where progress is being made and agree next steps, as well as identify where progress is less than expected.

Link

Go to Unit 9 to find more information about observations.

Case study

When Anna joined Ameera's setting at 3 years, Ameera decided that she needed to get to know Anna before she started planning experiences and opportunities for her. Ameera spent time discussing Anna's development with her parents, learning more about her background and early learning experiences. She spent time observing Anna in order to understand her current stage of development and what her interests were. She noticed that Anna really enjoyed listening to a nursery rhyme CD and began to sing along . This enabled Ameera to plan for Anna's next steps in her learning and development journey. Ameera had a nursery rhyme book that she shared with Anna, and used puppets and other soft toys to sing along with them.

1 What other activities/resources could Ameera provide to support Anna's interest in rhymes?

2 How might Ameera record these observations?

Planning for children's play

In order to meet the needs of individual children it is important to provide them with a range of activities. This helps them progress while allowing opportunities for the childminder to undertake further observation and reflection. By planning experiences and activities that are challenging but achievable, you will be able to support and extend every child's learning and development.

In a home-based setting, routines are a big part of a carer's day-to-day work and, with a bit of thought, they can be incorporated into activity plans. It is important to recognise the value of learning opportunities that can be gained from everyday routines.

Table 16.1 shows some examples of routines that provide potential learning opportunities.

Children's interests change over time, so you must be flexible in your approach. You need to ensure that you make the best of any opportunities that arise during the day. For example, if on the school run a child in your care spots a ladybird, this opens up opportunities for further discussion and exploration, which could also inform future planning.

Case study

Sharon had planned a messy play session for the children in her care, aged 2, 5 and 8 years, during the school holidays. At the start of the session the 2-year-old began to get upset at the thought of putting their hands in the paint. Sharon reassured the child and offered them a paintbrush to hold instead. The child took the paintbrush and happily moved it around in the paint.

Sharon ensured the child was listened to and adapted her approach to meet the child's individual needs.

1 How and why might Sharon share this information with the child's parents?

2 How might Sharon develop the child's interest in messy play?

Key term

Positional language – using terms such as 'on top' or 'to the left'.

Table 16.1 Routines with potential learning opportunities

Activity	Potential learning
Putting away shopping	• Counting • Colour matching • Sizes • Recognition • **Positional language**
Preparing food	• Weights and measures • Understanding the world
Laying the table	• Sorting • Matching • Language and communication

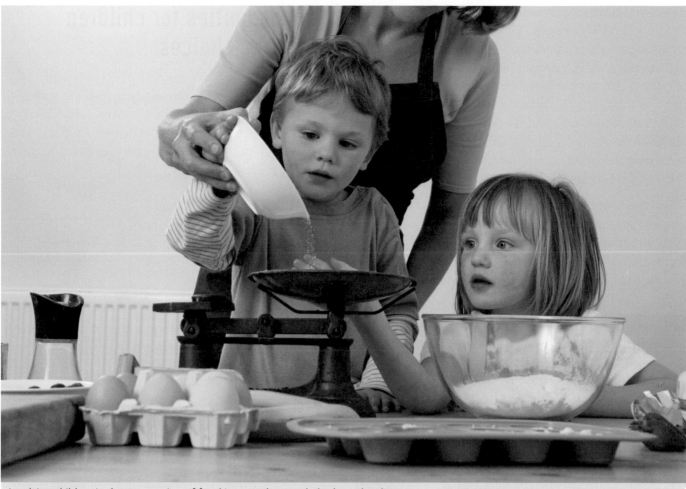
Involving children in the preparation of food is a good way to help them develop.

Home-based practitioners in England are required to follow the Early Years Foundation Stage framework for activity planning and observation. In Wales, the early years framework is called the Foundation Phase.

Different types of play for children of different ages

Home-based practitioners usually care for children of varying ages, so there will be times when they need to be encouraged to participate in different types of play. This can be achieved by good planning but also by having an adaptable and flexible approach. For example, if out on a walk, a 2-year-old might learn about their shadows on the grass, whereas a baby might enjoy waving their hands in the sun. Both children could take part in tree rubbings so this might be a good activity to engage children in.

It is important to listen to children's views and opinions and to take these into account. There may be occasions when a child does not want to participate in an activity and, in this case, alternatives need to be provided.

Balancing child-initiated and adult-led play with children of different ages

As a home-based practitioner it is important to provide a balance of child-initiated and adult-led play. Adult-led activities could include things like cooking and story-telling. They can be used to develop language and introduce concepts. The learning process is more important than the end result. For example, when baking cakes it is the learning that takes place while working through the stages that is important rather than the appearance of the finished cake.

Home-based practitioners are able to support children of different ages in smaller groups by providing resources that support the varying ages and stages of development. If we take the example of baking cakes, younger children are able to feel, smell or touch the ingredients, while older children might help to weigh and measure. Although this is predominantly adult-led, the children can be involved in making decisions, pretending to be bakers in a shop and clearing away at the end.

Often the range of ages means that older children support younger children in their play – they act as role models and encourage interactions. There are even more opportunities for these kinds of experiences during school holiday periods.

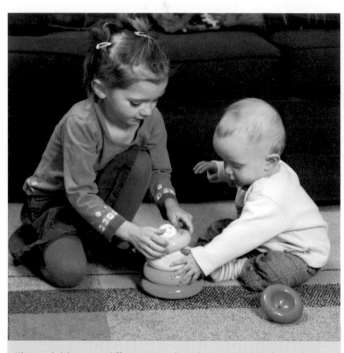

These children are different ages but they are having fun, interacting and communicating.

Child-initiated play could include role play and small-world play. You can support children to take the initiative in learning and encourage them to make their own choices in their play by ensuring that resources are accessible, appropriate and not overwhelming.

Opportunities for children to make choices

Home-based care can provide opportunities for decision making and spontaneity by making sure that activities are accessible. In fact, simple play can be supported by using everyday activities. Consider the activities in Figure 16.1, which can take place as part of a daily routine.

Figure 16.1 Activities that can take place as part of a daily routine

With a bit of thought, it is easy to see how each of these routines can support children's learning. For example, engaging children in preparing their own meals and snacks supports hand–eye coordination, measuring and weighing supports early mathematical concepts, and conversation during any activity supports the development of communication skills.

Acknowledging the value of play

Be realistic about how long everyday routines and activities take, especially with young children. Children flourish in a relaxed, unhurried atmosphere. Children can sometimes be rushed from one thing to another, but it is important to take time to praise and encourage children, asking them to share their experiences and creations.

Imagine you are caring for four children aged 9 months and 2, 5 and 9 years in the school holidays.

Plan a day that includes two physical play opportunities in a home-based setting. Consider how you will meet the individual play needs of all children and ensure that children of all ages can join in. Your plan could include the activity, resources needed, links to festivals/special events and links to the curricula. Next, consider the role of observation in helping you to identify individual children's needs. Create a spider diagram that shows why observation is important.

Reflect

Claire is a nanny caring for two children, one aged 18 months and one aged 6 years. The 6-year-old has created a model out of junk and is very proud of this. How can Claire show she values this child's work? Think about the following:

- How was the child encouraged, and were they able to make decisions?
- How can the child keep this work safe to share with parents later?
- How might Claire use this activity to inform future planning?

D Understand how to meet the personal, social and emotional needs of children in a home-based environment

Children flourish when they feel secure and valued. This learning aim focuses on the uniqueness of each child and the role of the home-based carer in providing an inclusive environment where parents and practitioners work in partnership.

Meeting the needs of individual children in a group setting

Practitioners working in home-based childcare are expected to have a knowledge and understanding of child development from birth to the teenage years. Unlike other types of childcare, where you might specialise in working with babies or 2-year-olds, in home-based childcare you would need to provide care across the ages. Therefore, it is important to have a good knowledge and understanding of children's

development beyond the early years. Home-based practitioners care for disabled children and children from a wide range of social and cultural backgrounds, and need to ensure that the unique needs of individual children are met.

This can be achieved by ensuring that all children are welcomed and valued and given equal chances. Children should be encouraged to share their story. What is it that makes them unique? Encourage parents' involvement by asking them to provide photographs and stories from home. Ensure that the resources available reflect the diversity of today's society.

Through your observations of children and knowledge of child development you will be able to identify, plan and implement enjoyable learning experiences.

Forming secure relationships with children

We all know how important first impressions are. Imagine you are a child walking into a setting for the first time. How might you feel?

First meeting

Home-based practitioners can do many things to support and develop relationships with the children they care for. The first meeting is important. This gives the parents and child a chance to meet the carer and, in the case of a registered childminder, the carer's home and family. It also gives the home-based practitioner the opportunity to find out more about the child and their family. This meeting should be fairly relaxed and a pleasurable experience, with toys available for the child to play with.

As we have already covered, some home-based practitioners like to produce a welcome pack that includes information about their service and any policies they may have. This enables parents to have something to take away and remember them by, especially if they are visiting several providers.

Other home-based practitioners provide a welcome pack for the child with some photos of themselves and their setting, and a space for the child to write about themselves, or draw a picture.

Settling in

It is important to allow time to get to know the child and to be able to support them in this transition. For children who have not been separated from their parents before, this may take time and sensitivity. As the key person, the home-based practitioner will be able to support this change by providing reassurance and allowing the child to feel safe. They may need to reassure parents that a close emotional relationship with the child will not undermine the child's feelings for them.

Settling-in visits will allow the parent to visit with the child and stay for short periods, gradually getting to the stage where the child is happy to stay in the setting on their own. This will be arranged according to the child's needs. Children should also be encouraged to bring along comfort items to make them feel secure.

The impact of new relationships

For home-based practitioners working in their own home, they may also need to prepare their own family for life caring for other children. The following ideas can help to support them in this:

- Ensuring that their own children have a safe private place for their own possessions.
- The childminder's own children will witness their parent spending time with and caring for other children in their home, and this may cause jealousy, depending on their age. It is important for the childminder to set aside time for their own children. Older children may like to take responsibility for roles within the home.
- It is also recommended as far as possible that home-based practitioners attend important events in their own child's life such as sports days or school plays.

Home-based practitioners should help children settle in to their home and build a relationship with parents.

Listening to and consulting children

Home-based practitioners have a duty to protect and promote children's rights. Rights are the basic needs that we all have to be able to live a healthy and secure life. This includes access to food and clean water, healthcare, education, play and leisure, and somewhere safe to live. Children have the right to be listened to and make their own decisions.

The United Nations Convention on the Rights of the Child (UNCRC) was drawn up in 1989 and approved in 1991. It is made up of 54 Articles that state that children under 18 have their own rights. Although the Convention itself is not legislation, its implementation has been achieved through policies and Acts such as the Children Act 2004.

Of the 54 Articles, the 7 Articles listed in Table 16.2 are most relevant to home-based practitioners.

In order to provide good-quality home-based care, all planning needs to include the thoughts and decisions of the children being cared for. By actively listening to children and involving them in decision making, we can support them to become independent learners and problem solvers.

We need to consider the age and stage of the child, and think about how we can ensure that even those children whose speech is developing are able to have a voice.

Respecting and valuing children's contributions

Children have the right to feel valued and respected. This ensures that they feel good about themselves, helps build self-esteem and enables children to feel in control. There are many ways in which you can support this in the home-based setting.

Table 16.2 Articles from the United Nations Convention on the Rights of the Child (UNCRC) relating to home-based childcare

Article number	Article aims
Article 2	Children have the right to be protected from all forms of discrimination.
Article 3	The best interests of the child must be the primary consideration in all activities and actions concerning children.
Article 7	The child shall have full opportunity to play and recreation, which should be directed to the same purposes as education – society and the public authorities shall endeavour to promote the enjoyment of this right (note this comes from the 1959 Declaration of the Rights of the Child).
Article 12	A child has the right to express his or her views freely and that view is to be given appropriate weight in accordance with the child's age or maturity.
Article 13	A child has the right to freedom of expression and exchange of information regardless of frontiers.
Article 16	Children have a right to privacy.
Article 28	A child has the right to education with a view to achieving this right progressively on the basis of equal opportunities.

Source: © (1989) United Nations. Reprinted with the permission of the United Nations.

Emma stored her resources and toys in plastic tubs with lids, stacked on a shelving unit in her conservatory. Each morning she would choose two boxes for the children, aged 6 months and 2 years, to play with. Emma noticed that the children had seemed less interested in the toys recently, and discussed this with a friend at the local stay-and-play session. Her friend suggested taking photographs of the contents of the boxes and sticking these on the outside, and moving the boxes to a height where the children could see them.

1 How will this make a difference to the children?

2 How will this support Emma in her planning and observations of children?

How can home-based practitioners support children to make decisions and have their voices heard? Here are some ideas:

- Allow choices, such as at snack time and story time.
- Ask them what clothes they might need to put on if it is raining.
- Allow children to choose where to play and offer a wide range of resources for them to choose from.
- Seek children's views on the care that is provided to them in the setting.
- Think about using different methods for children of different ages and stages of development.

The Mosaic approach

There is a large amount of research about the benefits of listening to children. One area you might wish to explore further is the Mosaic approach. This approach gives practitioners the opportunity to see the world through the children's eyes. By giving children cameras, videos and maps, you can begin to explore their world and gain a deeper understanding of their learning and the connections being made.

Find out more about the Mosaic approach. Search online, or obtain a copy of *Listening to Young Children: the Mosaic Approach* by Alison Clarke and Peter Moss (Joseph Rowntree Foundation: 2001).

Listening to children promotes their emotional development, self-esteem, self-confidence and well-being by helping them to:

- learn how to trust others
- learn how to make and maintain strong relationships
- learn how to share
- begin to understand that their views and opinions can make a difference
- learn how to empathise with others.

Meeting the emotional health needs of children

We live in a multicultural society in which different languages, religions and cultures affect our interactions and communication. Like all practitioners, home-based child carers must avoid making assumptions about the families they work with. Children look to us to reassure them that we respect and value their families and where they have come from.

First impressions are important. How does a child know they are welcomed and valued? Welcome packs for both parents and children can be helpful here.

It is important to respect different ethnic and cultural backgrounds by finding out how families wish to be addressed. The resources and activities provided must reflect the diversity in our society and any notices displayed could be in different languages.

It is useful to gather as much information about individual children as possible and remember that parents are the most important people in children's lives. Encourage children to feel proud of their individuality and share their experiences. Do not be afraid to ask or find out more about the families using the home-based setting.

Managing transition

The term 'transition' relates to the passing from one place or stage to another. What should not be underestimated is the emotional impact this can have on children. Children can experience many transitions in their early lives, such as starting preschool or moving house, as well as daily transitions as they move from one activity to another. Home-based practitioners are well placed to support children's emotional health by actively listening, working closely with parents, and preparing the child as far as possible for the transition. This preparation might be through role play, visits, use of resources such as books and giving children as much notice as possible of any change so that they feel in control.

Books are useful in helping children to prepare for transitions.

Managing behaviour

Home-based practitioners have an important role to play in supporting children to behave in an acceptable way. They work closely with parents to understand and provide continuity when managing behaviour.

Research

Refer to either Ofsted in England or CSSIW in Wales for the regulatory requirements in your home country relating to managing behaviour.

If you work as a home-based practitioner you are likely to be caring for children of different ages from varying backgrounds. All families will have their own ideas about how children should behave. It is your job to provide a safe and fair environment in which children are aware of consistent boundaries, are valued and have the opportunity to be in control of situations some of the time.

Children can be affected by many outside influences that may change the way they behave, such as the arrival of a new baby. Effective communication with the child's parents allows us to support children during these times.

Supporting and promoting positive behaviour

It is important to establish a set of ground rules that will help support positive behaviour. These rules are based on the need to keep children safe. Consider any unwritten rules already in place, for example, everyone taking their shoes off indoors. These rules can then be developed further, involving the children and parents where possible, and explaining why the rules are important. Children very quickly learn what is acceptable in different environments. Figure 16.2 shows an example of what these 'ground rules' might look like.

Consider how to promote positive behaviour, remembering the uniqueness of each child and adapting the approach to meet each individual child's age and stage of development.

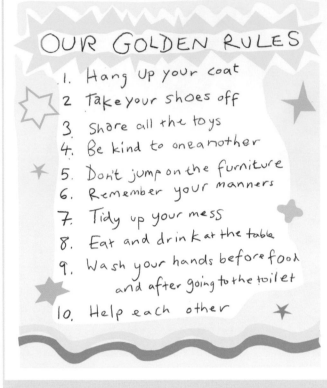

Figure 16.2 An example of rules that may be applied in a setting

Theory into practice

To help promote positive behaviour, remember the following points.

- Think about the tone and message you are sending out. Try to use positive language. For example, rather than 'don't do that' try 'let's do this'.
- Give plenty of praise.
- Use methods of distraction.
- Be consistent.
- Try to separate the behaviour from the child. Remember, you are unhappy about the behaviour, not the child.
- Be a positive role model – children learn by copying others.
- Explain to children why certain behaviour is unacceptable.
- Allow children the opportunity to make decisions and have responsibilities.

If you have children of your own, you will need to consider how you will promote positive behaviour strategies with them as well. Do you need to examine how you currently manage their behaviour?

To ensure the smooth running of your setting, your house rules and boundaries will need to apply to your own children too.

Reflect

What can you remember about how you were treated as a child by your teachers or parents? Do you think this influences how you approach behaviour management now?

The importance of inclusion

In order for all children to reach their potential they need to be fully included, respected and given meaningful opportunities to learn and develop. In order for a setting to be truly inclusive, home-based practitioners need to share with parents their policies and practices, and involve them in key decision making.

Registered home-based child carers have a personal responsibility under the Equalities Act 2010 to anticipate the individual needs of all children and families who use their service. This requires them to think about their attitudes, environment, resources and equipment they provide, and any paperwork they hand out.

Reflect

First impressions are really important. The way in which a home-based practitioner welcomes families into their home will instantly demonstrate their commitment to the children they care for.

The environment should be welcoming and accessible for children and their families, and this can be achieved by considering the layout. There should be space for children to move around, a table to sit at for mealtimes and activity times, a place for children to be calm and quiet and a garden or access to outdoor play daily. Children's artwork could be displayed on the walls, and there should be a place for children to hang their coats.

The resources provided should cover the ages and stages of development of the children being cared for. These should be stored so that children can select them for themselves. All resources should be freely available to both boys and girls.

The paperwork that is provided for families, such as a welcome pack, policies and newsletters, should be written clearly. Consideration should be given to families with a specific requirement or whose first language is not English.

Available support

Home-based childcare can be very isolating, so it is important to find out about the local support available to you. Many local authorities will provide training and resources to support inclusive practice. There are also area SENCOs (Special Educational Needs Coordinators) who can provide advice regarding children with disabilities and/or special educational needs. Children's centres will have access to specialist services, for example, speech and language support, health visitors and paediatricians. The NCMA provides factsheets and training to support members.

Theory into practice

Imagine you are asked to care for a child whose mother is visually impaired. What might you need to do to ensure that the setting is assessable? Think about the layout of the setting and any paperwork you might need to share.

Now consider a child whose first language is Polish. What might you need to do to support their language development? Where might you go for support?

Early identification of needs

Working closely with individual children allows home-based practitioners to observe their progress. They will have an understanding of children's development and be able to recognise that children develop at different rates. Through their observations they may recognise that a child needs to focus on a particular area of learning and can plan in partnership with their parents the steps that will help them to achieve this.

It is important to approach this sensitively with parents, as they may feel that their parenting skills are being judged. Think about how you would like to be approached if it was your child. If the message being delivered is particularly difficult, ensure that you:

- consider the timing – do not try to do it as the parent is rushing off to work, and instead set aside time without interruptions
- explain what you have noticed and ask if the parent has noticed this too
- remember to depersonalise things where possible and focus on what the child can do rather than what they cannot do.

Develop an awareness of other professionals and services or resources in your area that you could direct parents to, and be willing to work with other professionals to support the child's development. For instance, a speech therapist may be able to suggest activities that you can carry out in your setting.

If a parent has difficulty in recognising that their child has a need, it is important that the home-based practitioner continues to work sensitively with them and provide support. They may be able to provide information, resources and explain the benefits of working closely with them. The home-based practitioner will carry on observing and planning for that child's particular needs while the parents recognise their child's progress.

Link

Go to Unit 1 in Student Book 1 to find more information about John Bowlby and his theory.

Case study

Sarah is a registered nanny and has noticed that Jack, who is 19 months, has not yet started to walk.

1 How would you suggest that Sarah discuss this with Jack's parents?

2 What other agencies might Sarah involve?

3 How will Jack benefit from this approach?

Assessment practice 16.4   3D.P6 | 3D.P7 | 3D.M4 | 3D.D2

Attachment theory was developed by John Bowlby (1907–90), who explored the value of secure attachments to children. His research found that where mothers were available and responsive to their children's needs, this led to a sense of security for the child and a secure base from which they could explore the world. It is important for children's emotional health that they are able to form secure attachments to their caregivers.

1 Imagine yourself as a home-based practitioner.

2 Create a 'settling-in policy' that explains how you will form a secure relationship with a child. You should include:

- your procedure for gathering information about the child's likes and dislikes
- how you will support their emotional health needs and any settling-in visits
- how you might prepare the other children (including your own) for their inclusion in your setting.

Challenging discrimination and stereotypes

Children are influenced by adults at home, in the media and in their local communities. Home-based practitioners are well placed to be role models for inclusive practice. They can help children have positive attitudes towards diversity by taking the time to explain the similarities and differences of people around them. They are able to offer a wide range of resources and learning experiences that will encourage children to respect others.

Challenging discriminatory remarks that children may make is important in order to help them develop an understanding and awareness of others. An explanation that their actions are unfair should be given alongside pointing out anything that is untrue, helping the child to learn from the situation. Discriminatory behaviour should never be ignored and the victim should always be reassured to maintain their self-esteem.

We all have a role to play in challenging stereotypes and ensuring that children have access to a range of resources and materials that show both genders in different roles, such as female fire-fighters and male nurses. Children should also be able to select the toys they wish to play with by themselves and have access to cars, dolls, dressing-up props and so on, regardless of gender.

Reflect

Imagine you are a nanny caring for a boy and a girl. One day the boy decides to dress as a fairy. His father returns from work and is shocked to see his son dressed this way. What might you do and what might you say to the father?

E Understand the role of parents and other agencies as partners in home-based childcare

Parents know their children best, and their knowledge of their child is crucial to the home-based practitioner in enabling them to support and plan appropriate activities effectively. This section explores the key benefits of effective partnership, working with both parents and other professionals.

Working with parents

Many parents see home-based practitioners as experts in their field and look to them for advice and support. While this may be true, home-based practitioners must recognise that parents are experts in knowing their own children. When parents and home-based practitioners work closely together, children's outcomes are improved. There are many reasons why it is important to work closely with parents. Table 16.3 lists some of them.

Table 16.3 Benefits of working with parents

Areas where you may work with parents	Benefits
Policies and procedures	Policies and procedures are working documents that should be shared, discussed, monitored and reviewed. Parents need to be shown and to agree to the home-based practitioner's policies and procedures. Taking time to do this will mean that parents have all the required information about the service provided as well as an awareness of the regulatory requirements. They should have the opportunity to feed back about the service, which in turn informs the setting's practice.
Managing behaviour	Children benefit from clear and consistent boundaries. Sharing your house rules and policies ensures that families know what is expected. It is important to be aware of parents' own behaviour strategies, while also recognising your home nation's regulatory requirements (Ofsted/CSSIW).
Sharing information	In order to provide the best service for families you will need to establish a relationship based on trust, which allows you to share information about daily routines and events that may affect how the child is feeling or behaving. With permission it may also be useful to share information with other professionals working with the child, such as a teacher or health visitor, to support any specific needs. This ensures a consistent approach across settings.
Signposting to other agencies	Parents may look to you for advice and support that you are not able to provide. In this case it would be beneficial if you had built up an understanding and knowledge of services that could provide further support, such as links with your local children's centre.
Involving parents in children's learning and development	Children develop at different rates and while they are with you, you will observe this. You can share this with parents through your daily conversations. This allows parents to see all the stages their child passes through and gives them the chance to tell you about what they have been doing at home. For example, potty training will be most effective when parents and home-based practitioners are in agreement about the process and regularly update each other on progress.

Supporting families to access their local children's centre can provide a vital link, as children's centres are able to offer access to a wide range of services for families with children under 5 years. They are often able to signpost voluntary organisations such as Home Start, which is able to provide a volunteer to support families in their own homes, or give access to bereavement networks.

Working with other agencies

Working closely with the child's parents is important. Children are also likely to come into contact with a range of other **universal services** and/or specific services as they grow and develop. This might be the health visitor when the child is young, when specific advice may have been given about a child's dietary needs, or the reception teacher as the home-based practitioner supports parents in preparing their child to start school.

Multi-agency working allows different services to come together to support the **holistic** needs of families. All of those involved can work together to identify needs, agree where to begin, plan which service or professionals may be involved and then implement the work, ensuring that the needs of the child and the families are at the centre of it.

Links with home learning

We have previously seen how the home-based practitioner can share information about the child's progress with the parents. The use of learning journals and daily diaries gives parents the opportunity to feed back about the child's progress and developments at home. By sharing children's progress with parents and emphasising to parents the value of play, home-based practitioners are able to make links between what happens in the setting and at home.

There are also real benefits for children when parents share home learning experiences with the home-based practitioner. The practitioner is then able to extend the learning opportunities in their setting, allowing the child to make connections in a range of situations that help to reinforce positive experiences.

Case study

Aaron is 4 years old and he spent the weekend at his grandparents' house, by the sea in Southend. Aaron's grandmother took some photographs of Aaron holding a bucket with a crab inside.

When Aaron got home, his parents talked about his weekend and stuck the photograph into Aaron's diary. Aaron took the diary to Lisa, his home-based child carer, the following Monday. Lisa sat down with Aaron and the other children in her care and talked about the seaside. She remembered that

she had a collection of shells and showed these to the children. This led to a whole week of activities based around the sea, including sand and water play, ice-cream tasting and making hats to wear in the sun.

1 Why is it important to extend Aaron's weekend learning experience?

2 How might you encourage parents to share information in this way?

Professionalism

Home-based practitioners will be expected to act professionally at all times, and there will be occasions when they will be observed going about their daily routine. Consider, if you were a parent, what you would like to see for your child.

Home-based practitioners are given a large amount of information about the families they work with. This can include personal details about the family, medical needs, photographs and so on. It is important that this is not shared or discussed or posted on social networking sites.

Establishing links with other settings

Developing networks

Home-based practitioners are working alone so it is important that they network with others to share good practice. This might be other home-based practitioners, or the local preschool or nursery. Some areas may have childminding groups or networks to join. Many children's centres hold stay-and-play sessions, or opportunities specifically aimed at home-based practitioners.

Supporting transitions

Home-based practitioners will have gained a huge amount of information about the child's likes and

dislikes and will have recorded their achievements and progress. With the parents' permission it is beneficial to share the child's progress with their next setting. This will support both the child and the setting in understanding what has been learned to enable them to plan for the future.

For many children who attend the home-based setting as well as nursery or school, good communication means that planning ideas can be shared which can extend their learning. This avoids children having to repeat topics and gives them the chance to develop ideas and interests further.

Importance of boundaries when working with parents

The nature of home-based childcare means that practitioners can become very attached to the families they work with. Parents sometimes see the practitioner as a friend who can support not only their child's needs but also their entire family. This could lead to parents persistently collecting their children late, or forgetting to pay, or phoning at weekends.

It is important that home-based practitioners remain professional and clear about the service being provided. Figure 16.3 gives you some ideas about how to do this.

Figure 16.3 How practitioners can remain professional

The boxes in the figure read:

Tackle any problems as they arise. Do not leave them to get worse.

Provide parents with a welcome pack that includes information about the service and activities provided.

How to remain professional and clear about home-based childcare

Explain and share policies that affect home-based childcare with parents.

Agree the terms of your contract, and ensure all parties stick to it and review it regularly.

When working with other professionals to support the needs of families, remember to ensure that you have parental permission to share information. If you are invited to meetings, ensure you are prepared, and feel confident that your contribution to the child's well-being is equally important as that of other professionals.

Respecting different cultures and ethnicities

The regulatory body for your home nation will have specific requirements to ensure that you provide opportunities that meet the needs of all children. You will be required to show that you respect individual families' cultures and ethnicities.

Here are some ideas for ensuring this:

- Be a good role model, and think about what you say.
- Ask families to share information about their cultures with you.
- Support children to recognise their uniqueness.
- Plan activities about where children have come from, who is in their family and what they enjoy doing.

- Encourage children to recognise and respect differences.
- Challenge discrimination.

Assessment practice 16.5 3E.P8 | 3E.P9 | 3E.M5

In order to meet the unique needs of children, home-based practitioners have to work closely with parents and often other professionals.

Imagine that you have a parent coming to visit your setting.

1 Create an information sheet that explains the importance of working in partnership with parents. You should include information about how you will ensure effective regular communication at the start of the relationship and going forward.

2 Identify two professionals whom you may be required to work with.

3 Evaluate the role of the home-based practitioner when working in partnership with parents.

Further reading and resources

Websites

Early Years Foundation Stage: www.education.gov.uk

Care and Social Services Inspectorate Wales (CSSIW): www.cssiw.org.uk

Scotland, Care Inspectorate: www.scswis.com

Ireland, Department of Children and Youth Affairs: www.dcya.gov.ie

Welsh Government: www.wales.gov.uk

Food Standards Agency: www.food.gov.uk

Ofsted: www.ofsted.gov.uk

National Childminding Association: www.ncma.org.uk

Ready for work?

Vicky Jenkins Home-based practitioner

I have always worked with children, firstly caring for my younger brothers and sisters and then as a room leader in a day nursery. I had my own daughter a year ago and decided that I wanted to spend time at home with her while still having the opportunity to earn some money.

I thought I knew all about caring for children, child development, keeping them safe and healthy and how to provide lots of great activities. This was until I spoke to my neighbour Gill, who is a registered childminder. She suggested I come round for coffee and see how it works in her home.

I was really surprised at the amount of resources she had, and the age range of the children she was caring for that day. She did an amazing job of juggling three different routines. She had a baby that needed bottle feeding, a 2-year-old she was potty training and a 3-year-old who was learning to put his shoes and coat on for preschool.

It really opened my eyes to the skills and knowledge needed to work in a home-based setting. There is no one to help you – you have to be extremely organised and allow plenty of time to get anywhere.

Completing the course and having Gill to share ideas with has given me the best start in my childminding career and I am learning all the time.

Skills for practice

Practise doing the following things related to working with children in home-based environments.

- Select resources and activities that can be adapted for children at various stages of development.
- Take opportunities to discuss the children's day with parents or carers and promote the importance of working in partnership with parents.

- Plan an activity involving children in your care, assessing the potential risks in the environment. Consider the differences between a home-based environment and a group setting.

Have a look at the National Childminding Association (NCMA) website for further ideas. You can access this website by going to www.pearsonhotlinks.co.uk and searching for this title.

Introduction

When working with children, you will need to have some knowledge and understanding about what is meant by 'additional needs', and their impact on a child's development and learning. You will also need to be able to work with parents and carers alongside other professionals and agencies both within and outside the setting in order to ensure that all children are included as much as possible in all activities. As part of your role you will work with others to plan and carry out specialised learning programmes, taking into account the needs of individual children. As well as knowing about legislation and the assessment process, this includes being aware of the support organisations and networks available for children and their families.

Assessment: You will be assessed by a series of assignments set by your teacher/tutor.

Learning aims

In this unit you will:

A   understand additional needs of children

B   understand provision to support children with additional needs in early years settings

C   understand the role of adults working with children with additional needs.

> I have always wanted to work with children who have special educational needs and I learned so much on my placement. In the setting where I was working I was able to work closely with a child who had cerebral palsy and it enabled me to gain first-hand experience of the kinds of issues she faced as well as the support that is available. It was also useful to talk to colleagues about their experiences so that I was able to get a wider view.
>
> Christian, *a student on an early years course*

Working With
Children With
Additional Needs

18

Assessment Zone

This table shows what you must do in order to achieve a **Pass**, **Merit** or **Distinction**.grade, and where you can find activities to help you.

Assessment criteria		
Pass	**Merit**	**Distinction**
Learning aim A: Understand additional needs of children		
3A.P1 English Describe additional needs of children and the factors that may cause them. **Assessment practice 18.1**	**3A.M1** Analyse how the additional needs of children could impact on children and their families. **Assessment practice 18.4**	
3A.P2 Explain the effects of discrimination on children with additional needs. **Assessment practice 18.2**		
3A.P3 Explain how families may be affected by the additional needs of a child. **Assessment practice 18.4**		
Learning aim B: Understand provision to support children with additional needs in early years settings		
3B.P4 Explain how the social model of disability has influenced provision for children with additional needs. **Assessment practice 18.3**	**3B.M2** Discuss the impact of inclusive education on children with additional needs. **Assessment practice 18.3**	**3B.D1** Evaluate the extent to which effective assessment supports inclusive provision for children with additional needs. **Assessment practice 18.5**
3B.P5 I&CT Describe the process for identifying and providing support for children with additional needs. **Assessment practice 18.4**	**3B.M3** Analyse the role of assessment in providing support for children with additional needs. **Assessment practice 18.5**	
3B.P6 Explain the role of parental involvement in the assessment of children with additional needs. **Assessment practice 18.4**		
3B.P7 Explain the role of professionals who may be involved in supporting children with additional needs in an early years setting. **Assessment practice 18.4** **Assessment practice 18.5**		

continued

Assessment criteria (*continued*)		
Pass	Merit	Distinction
Learning aim C: Understand the role of adults working with children with additional needs		
3C.P8 Explain how adults can work to support children with additional needs in the development of confidence and self-esteem. **Assessment practice 18.6**	**3C.M4** Analyse the role of the adult in implementing a plan drawn up to support a child with additional needs. **Assessment practice 18.6**	**3C.D2** Evaluate collaborative and partnership working when supporting children with additional needs. **Assessment practice 18.6** **Assessment practice 18.7**
3C.P9 Explain how adults use individual education plans to support children with additional needs. **Assessment practice 18.6** **Assessment practice 18.7**		
3C.P10 Explain how to work with parents when supporting children with additional needs. **Assessment practice 18.6**		

English English Functional Skills signposting

I&CT Information and Communication Technology skills signposting

How you will be assessed

This unit will be assessed by a series of internally assessed tasks set by your teacher/tutor. Throughout this unit you will find assessment practice activities that will help you work towards your assessment. Completing these activities will not mean that you have achieved a particular grade, but you will have carried out useful research or preparation that will be relevant when it comes to your final assignment.

In order for you to achieve the tasks in your assignment, it is important that you check you have met all of the Pass grading criteria. You can do this as you work your way through the assignment.

If you are hoping to gain a Merit or Distinction, you should also make sure that you present the information in your assignment in the style that is required by the relevant assessment criterion. For example, Merit criteria will require you to discuss and analyse, and Distinction criteria will require you to assess and evaluate.

The assignment set by your teacher/tutor will consist of a number of tasks designed to meet the criteria in the table. This is likely to consist of a written assignment, including items such as:

- a report
- a response to a case study
- a written article.

Getting started

What do you understand by the term 'additional needs'? Discuss with a partner or a group and come up with your own definition.

A Understand additional needs of children

When working with children it is important for you to have a clear understanding of what is meant by the term additional needs. In the past this has also been known as **special educational needs** (SEN).

Key term

Special educational needs – used to describe children who have a learning difficulty that calls for special educational provision to be made for them – children who learn differently from most children of the same age, and who may need different or extra help from that given to others.

The Special Educational Needs Code of Practice 2001 states that:

'Children have a learning difficulty if they:

a) have a significantly greater difficulty in learning than the majority of children of the same age; or

b) have a disability which prevents or hinders them from making use of educational facilities of a kind generally provided for children of the same age in schools within the area of the local education authority; or

c) are under compulsory school age and fall within the definition at a) or b) above or would do so if special educational provision was not made for them.'

Source: © Crown copyright 2001

You will need to know how to work with colleagues, parents and outside agencies to provide additional educational support for these children. As a starting point you should look at different areas of need that children may have.

Activity

Which of the following children might cause you concern? Briefly outline the reasons why.

- A 2-year-old cries regularly and cannot be pacified.
- A 3-year-old has not yet started to speak.
- A 4-year-old does not hold a pencil correctly.
- A 6-year-old displays aggressive behaviour towards children and adults.

Areas of additional need

Additional needs are often divided into different areas, although children may have needs in more than one of these and be affected in a number of different ways. This will also affect different areas of a child's development. You will always need to approach each child differently and get to know them in order to provide the best possible support.

Physical needs

Children are defined as having additional needs if they have a disability that prevents or hinders them from making use of educational facilities of a kind generally provided for children of the same age. In other words, disability is considered an additional need only if it stops the child from participating in the day-to-day activities that are enjoyed by others. Many children who have a physical disability will be independent and able to participate without support.

Children who have disabilities will need varying levels of support and you will need to work alongside others to make individual provision for them.

Communication needs

Children who have communication needs will have difficulty in the areas of speaking and listening and the processes involved in deciphering information. They may also find it hard to understand and respond to non-verbal communication.

Communication and language are crucial to learning and development as they are linked to what we are thinking. Language lets us store information in an organised way. If children have difficulties communicating, they are at a disadvantage because they will be less able to organise what they are thinking or less able to express themselves. They may also find it harder to form relationships with others. As a result, they may become frustrated or feel isolated. Very young children in particular will not have the experience to be able to recognise the reason for their feelings and this could lead to behavioural problems. In more extreme cases, children may not speak at all.

Figure 18.1 shows some of the causes of communication difficulties and delay.

However, a child with physical needs may not necessarily have a disability. Their needs may include mobility issues such as a medical condition or they may need additional support in order to carry out routine tasks such as changing for PE or toileting. Some children may also need support to develop their **fine motor skills** so that they are able to carry out activities such as cutting or threading.

Sensory needs

Children who have sensory needs may need different levels of support from others in the class. Sensory needs may mean that the child has an impairment that is visual or auditory. In other words, they may have difficulty in seeing or hearing, and this may be temporary or permanent. For example, if a child suffers from regular colds, their hearing might be affected on a regular basis. When working with very young children, you should be aware that these kinds of sensory needs may not yet have been recognised. Look out for signs that a child is having difficulty in these areas.

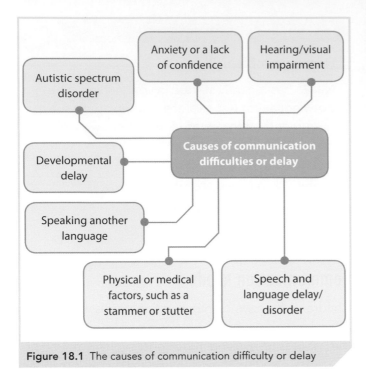

Figure 18.1 The causes of communication difficulty or delay

Learning disabilities

A learning disability will mean that a child has difficulty processing and understanding information. Children who have learning disabilities may need extra support in different areas. For example, with:

- language, memory and reasoning skills
- **sequencing** and organisational skills
- understanding and working with numbers
- problem solving
- coordination and development of physical skills.

Learning disabilities may be global or specific. In other words, they may affect all or only part of a child's learning. For example, a child who has dyslexia has a specific learning difficulty, as it may only affect this area of their learning. A child who has moderate, severe or profound learning difficulties may be affected in all areas of their learning (physical, social, emotional and intellectual).

Long-term conditions

If children are suffering from long-term or life-limiting conditions or illnesses, they will need to have additional support of some kind. It is rare for these children to be in mainstream nursery or school, but at some point in your career you are likely to work with them. These conditions may be caused by different factors and have varying effects on the child. The kinds of conditions may include cystic fibrosis, Duchene muscular dystrophy, child cancers and other conditions that may be progressive and affect children over many years.

Behavioural or emotional needs

Behaviour, emotional and social difficulty (BESD) describes children with a range of behavioural problems that may delay learning and other areas of development. This is because they may find it hard to focus on what they are doing or are disruptive to others around them. They may also be withdrawn or reluctant to join in with activities with others.

Factors that may lead to additional needs

There are a range of factors that may lead to additional needs in children.

Genetic

Children may have inherited a genetic condition or illness that means they have additional needs. These may vary in the impact they have on the child and in how they affect learning. For example, a condition such as Fragile X syndrome or muscular dystrophy may have more of an effect on a child's learning and development than a stammer or cleft palate. Some conditions may also have a genetic component but are not necessarily caused by genetic factors – these include epilepsy or cerebral palsy. There are also studies that have shown that conditions such as autistic spectrum disorder (ASD) have a genetic link, although research is still being carried out, and this condition is more often considered developmental.

Developmental disorders

Developmental disorders will occur at some stage in a child's development up to the age of 18, and are likely to prevent the child from developing normally in one or more areas. Children may suffer from a developmental condition or disorder that has not been picked up in the early years as they have not yet been required to carry out complex tasks. The most high-profile developmental disorders are ADHD (attention-deficit hyperactivity disorder) and ASD, although Down's syndrome and Tourette's syndrome are also considered to be developmental.

Environmental

Additional needs that are environmental may be caused by situations such as those occurring within the home or in domestic circumstances. Social or emotional factors may affect the child in this way. An example of this is neglect, where children are not given sufficient care and attention to thrive. Another is where children are asylum seekers and have been forced to move away from their home country. Conditions within the home such as violence, alcoholism, drugs or other social issues may affect a child's development and make it hard for them to learn.

Accidents

You may work with a child whose additional needs are the result of an accident. These needs might be physical or emotional depending on the nature and severity of the trauma, and how the child has been affected.

Assessment practice 18.1

3A.P1

Design a booklet for staff outlining the different areas of additional needs and factors that may cause them, and giving examples of how children with additional needs may need to be supported in the setting.

Emotional health and well-being needs

For children to progress in all areas of their development, it is important that they experience consistency in care, a loving and supportive home, and positive relationships with others. In cases where these basic needs are not met, children may be affected in a negative way. Children who experience a lack of interest from adults or who are subjected to domestic violence or abuse are likely to develop behavioural, emotional and social difficulties and possibly mental illness later in life.

Children's physical and emotional health are also interrelated – where a child has physical needs such as a disability or long-term medical condition, their ability to build relationships with others may be affected if they have long periods of time away from the setting, or are unable to join in easily with games and play activities with their friends. This may be even more difficult if children also have a sensory impairment or communication difficulties.

When children have a delay in their emotional health, they may also have less resilience to **transitions**. This will affect their ability to deal with difficult situations and to build friendships.

Key term

Transitions – the changes that happen in all children's lives, such as starting school or personal changes such as a family break-up.

Families might also have different views on the expectations for children's behaviour and you may notice that some parents are stricter with their children than others. While this will not necessarily have a negative impact, problems may arise if there are mixed messages between the setting and home, or if boundaries for behaviour are not consistent.

In all of these cases, children with emotional health and well-being needs will require additional positive attention from others in order to support their development.

The impact of additional needs on the child and their family

If you are working with children who have additional needs, you will need to have an awareness of how their needs affect them and those closest to them. While some children who have conditions that limit them physically may manage well, others may become frustrated or even bad-tempered. Even if this is not always apparent, it can come out in other ways, and young children in particular may not be able to express how they are feeling. As you are working with these children and get to know them, you will be able to pick up on when they are particularly affected.

As well as the condition itself, other factors may affect the child and how they cope on a day-to-day basis. Figure 18.2 outlines these factors.

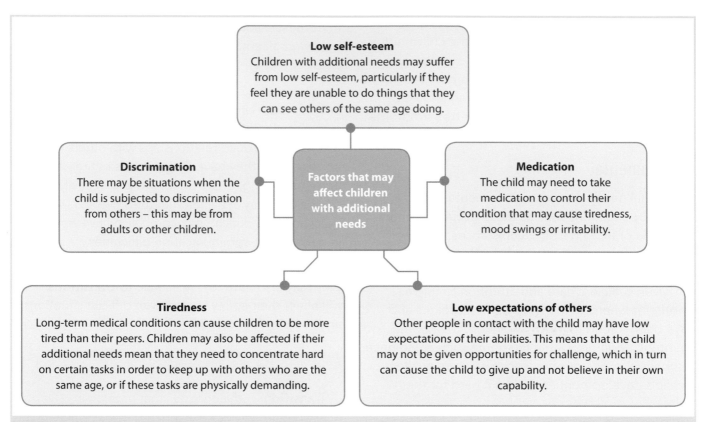

Low self-esteem
Children with additional needs may suffer from low self-esteem, particularly if they feel they are unable to do things that they can see others of the same age doing.

Discrimination
There may be situations when the child is subjected to discrimination from others – this may be from adults or other children.

Factors that may affect children with additional needs

Medication
The child may need to take medication to control their condition that may cause tiredness, mood swings or irritability.

Tiredness
Long-term medical conditions can cause children to be more tired than their peers. Children may also be affected if their additional needs mean that they need to concentrate hard on certain tasks in order to keep up with others who are the same age, or if these tasks are physically demanding.

Low expectations of others
Other people in contact with the child may have low expectations of their abilities. This means that the child may not be given opportunities for challenge, which in turn can cause the child to give up and not believe in their own capability.

Figure 18.2 Factors that may affect a child with additional needs

Assessment practice 18.2

3A.P2

Children may face discrimination in different forms.

Consider whether the following are examples of discrimination.

- How might you deal with each situation?
- How might a child with additional needs be affected in each case?

1 The parent of a child with additional needs tends to be over-protective and limits the activities that they allow the child to do.

2 A setting does not include all children in all activities.

3 A parent complains to the setting that a child with disabilities is not in the right school.

4 A setting does not train its staff on how to manage the needs of all children.

5 Another child speaking within earshot of the child with additional needs says that they cannot play because they are not like everyone else.

6 A child with global learning delay has peers who consistently leave them out of games and activities in the setting.

Depending on the needs of the child, the impact on their family will also vary. For example, if the child has always had a disability or long-term medical condition, they may have had time to come to terms with this and with the fact that they may need additional support. However, in some cases the daily pressures of caring for their child may mean that parents or carers become tired or find their needs difficult to manage. In this situation, the setting will need to work alongside parents and give support and advice or refer them to other sources of support.

Where the child's needs have been recently diagnosed, or have arisen suddenly due to an accident or environmental factor, families may need urgent support from outside agencies to enable them to cope. This could be because their needs are emotional, financial or practical.

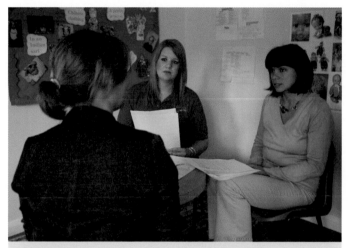

It is important to work alongside parents to offer them support and advice.

Research

Special Families is a website that provides information and advice for families of children with additional needs. You can access this website by going to www.pearsonhotlinks.co.uk and searching for this title.

What other support can you find that is available to these families? How easy is it to access the support?

B Understand provision to support children with additional needs in early years settings

Provision to support children with additional needs has changed a great deal over the last 20 years. Since the introduction of the 2001 Code of Practice in particular, children and their parents in both early years and school settings have been far more involved in the kinds of decisions that will have an impact on the provision that is provided. There have also been changes in legislation that have impacted on the provision made by schools and early years settings. This section outlines some of these changes and their impact.

Impact of models of disability on legislation and provision

In the past, there have been many unhelpful labels given to children who have additional needs. The danger of doing this is that we are more likely to focus on the child's disability or condition first, rather than looking at them as an individual. In the past, the medical model of disability has been used more frequently than the social model (see Table 18.1). The kind of language that has been used in line with the medical model has promoted the attitude that people with disabilities or additional needs must be corrected in some way to be brought in line with everybody else. This has sometimes led to unhelpful labelling of children in terms of their disabilities rather than their potential. The social model of disability values the person and celebrates diversity, and calls on society to make changes to the way in which it views those who have additional needs and disabilities. Table 18.1 outlines the medical and social models of disability.

Table 18.1 The medical and social models of disability

Medical model of disability	Social model of disability
Child is faulty	Child is valued
Diagnosis	Strengths and needs defined by self and others
Labelling	Identify barriers and develop solutions
Impairment becomes focus of attention	Outcome-based programme designed
Segregation and alternative services	Training for parents and professionals
Ordinary needs put on hold	Relationships nurtured
Re-entry if 'normal' enough OR permanent exclusion	Diversity welcomed, child is included
Society remains unchanged	Society evolves

Source: © World of Inclusion (www.worldofinclusion.com) and Richard Rieser.

Link

Go to Unit 10: Section C for more about medical and social models of disability.

Reflect

The social model of disability states that it is attitudes within society that are the barriers to inclusion, and not the person's disability. How much do you agree with this? What kinds of barriers might these be?

Assessment practice 18.3   3B.P4 | 3B.M2

Research the emergence of the social model of disability and inclusive education, and how they have changed the way in which children with additional needs are included in mainstream schools.

Legislation for children with additional needs has been affected by these changes, with the introduction of the Disability Discrimination Act 2005 to encompass schools and educational establishments and to reduce the reliance on the medical model. This has now been replaced by the Equality Act 2010, which encompasses all existing equality legislation including the Race Relations Act and the Sex Discrimination Act. In addition, all newly built schools and educational establishments must be accessible and have provision for disabled people to include ramps, handrails and disabled toilets.

Provision for people with disabilities should be made in schools and educational establishments.

Legislation and initiatives for children with additional needs

Legislation and guidelines have been changing gradually since the Education Act of 1970, which transferred the responsibility for special education from the health service to local authorities. Since this time, a key change started following the Warnock Report of 1978 in which Mary Warnock carried out a study of the needs of children with special educational needs. In her report she called for changes to specialist provision and sought the inclusion of children with additional needs in mainstream schools.

Following the Education Act of 1981, the first Special Educational Needs Code of Practice was introduced in 1996, which set out practical guidance for local authorities in providing for children with special educational needs. Finally, the Special Educational Needs and Disability Act 2001 gave a stronger right to children with special educational needs to be educated in mainstream schools, and also a right for early years providers to request support for those children who could be identified as having additional needs at an earlier age. The contribution of Parent Partnerships, and child participation in matters that involved them, were also given a high priority.

This piece of legislation is a working document for those who are working with children who have additional needs. It sets out clearly the requirements of schools and early years settings, and gives straightforward information on their roles as well as that of local authorities.

The Children Act 2004 is also a key piece of legislation, as it is closely linked to Every Child Matters (since renamed Help Children Achieve More), which set out to change children's services and to improve multi-agency working. This aims to ensure that all organisations and agencies involved with children between birth and 19 years should work together to ensure that children have the support they need to stay safe, be healthy, enjoy and achieve, make a positive contribution, and achieve economic well-being.

Aiming High for Disabled Children (AHDC) is a programme set up by the government in 2007 to transform services for children with disabilities and to make them a priority, as well as supporting their families.

Research

Find out about legislation and initiatives that are interconnected with the area of special educational needs. You may look at, for example, the Education Act 2011, the Children Act 2004 and the Help Children Achieve More government initiative.

- Why is it important to know about these?
- How much do they affect your practice on a day-to-day basis?

Identifying and providing support and the involvement of parents

Since the introduction of the Special Educational Needs Code of Practice in 2001, children in schools and early years settings have been through the same assessment process. Before this, the process did not start until the child was in school, and due to the length of the process this would often mean that support was not given for some time. Due to the importance of early diagnosis and the implementation of support at the earliest possible stage, the process needs to be started as soon as possible. Unless a child has already been given a diagnosis, for example, if they have a medical condition or a disability, nurseries are often the first places to identify developmental difficulties. Parents should also be involved from the earliest stages as they know their children the best and are their child's first educators.

You may have been asked in your setting to observe and monitor a child whom staff or parents have identified as a concern due to their progress. This may be in one or more areas of their development. If a child has been monitored and targeted by staff over time and progress is still not being made, the setting may decide to put them at the first stage of intervention. In a nursery setting, this is called Early Years Action, and in a school, School Action.

Stages of identifying and providing support

Early Years/School Action

At this stage, staff will speak to parents and discuss the child's progress. The Special Educational Needs Coordinator (SENCO) will be involved and if it is decided that the child may need additional help to make progress, they will move to the next stage. Parents will be invited to contribute any new information – in some cases this may be from health professionals or other agencies. Early Years or School Action means that the setting is putting in additional resources such as extra adult support, or additional materials or equipment, in order to help the child to progress. The strategies that are to be put in place are then recorded on an **individual education plan** (IEP) in the form of three or four targets. The IEP will be discussed with the parents and the child, and will be reviewed.

Early Years/School Action Plus

If progress is not made over time, and staff and parents still have concerns about the child, they may be moved to the next stage of intervention, which is known as Early Years or School Action Plus. At this stage, there will be involvement by outside agencies, who will give the setting advice and support in devising targets for the IEP.

Requests for a Statutory Assessment

At this stage, some children may still have made little or no progress and will be noticeably behind their peers in one or more areas of their development. The SENCO will speak to the parents and discuss making a request for a Statutory (Multidisciplinary) Assessment. This means that they will have to submit a request to the local authority for additional support for the child. The request will need to provide evidence of the steps that the setting has made to support the child, and include reports from all the professionals involved, as well as the setting and the child's parents. If the Statutory Assessment is successful, the child will be allocated a number of hours of individual provision each week and given a **Statement of Special Educational Needs**. They will need to continue to be monitored and have an IEP, with regular reviews in order to check whether the provision continues to be needed.

Link

Go to Unit 9: Section C2 to find more information about implementing an IEP.

Key terms

Individual education plan – targets and planned implementation strategies for children who have special educational needs.

Statement of Special Educational Needs – this means that the local authority will assess the child to decide whether it is necessary for them to have an additional adult to support them in school. If so, the local authority will then produce a statement that sets out what is needed for the child to access the curriculum fully.

Activity

Speak to your SENCO and find out how many children in your setting are at each stage of intervention.

Theory into practice

Looking at the Special Educational Needs Code of Practice, find out about the Statutory Assessment of children who are under compulsory school age. Does it differ in any way from that for school-age children?

▌Parental involvement

The Special Educational Needs Code of Practice 2001 emphasises the importance of involving parents at each stage of the assessment process. Parents should be informed about what is taking place and are invited to contribute by writing reports and speaking to professionals. This is because in most cases they have expert knowledge of their child and the closest relationship with them. Parents should have copies of IEPs and be involved in their reviews. In some cases, the process may alarm parents, particularly if they had not been previously aware of their child's additional needs. They will need to be given as much information as possible by early years settings and schools about the process. Health authorities and NHS trusts are also required to inform parents about additional voluntary organisations that may be able to give support or advice.

Link

Go to Unit 10: Section C to find more information about Parent Partnerships.

Assessment practice 18.4   3A.P3 | 3A.M1 | 3B.P5   3B.P6 | 3B.P7

A child has been admitted to your setting and, after a period of intervention, has needed to have a full Statutory Assessment.

- Write a report about the child, describing in detail the different stages of the assessment and the role of any professionals involved.
- You will need to include the involvement of parents at each stage of the assessment and explain why this is important.
- How might the child and family be affected if they were not aware of any issues before, and what could you put in place to support them?

Professionals involved in supporting children with additional needs

You will find that you are often required to liaise with other professionals when supporting children with additional needs. This is so that you can work together to support the child in the best possible way. Meetings may take place within or outside the setting, depending on the role of the professionals and the nature of the support.

Link

Go to Unit 10: Section C for more information about other groups of professionals that you may be required to liaise with when supporting children with additional needs.

Research

Find out more about portage by visiting the website for the National Portage Association. You can access this website by going to www.pearsonhotlinks.co.uk and searching for this title.

Assessment practice 18.5   3B.P7 | 3B.M3 | 3B.D1

Helena is 3 years old and has just started in nursery. She is an only child of very young parents and it is clear from her lack of physical and social skills that she needs some additional help.

1 Why is it important to organise some kind of assessment of Helena's needs as soon as possible?

2 What professionals might be involved in the assessment process for Helena and what would their role be?

3 How does effective assessment support inclusive practice for children with additional needs?

The role of organisations that support parents

Parent Partnership services were set up as part of the Special Educational Needs Code of Practice in 2001. They are designed to support parents who have children with additional needs and ensure that they have access to information, advice and support. This may be through the assessment process in order to gain additional support in the child's setting, but they may also refer parents to other agencies. Parent Partnership services will be made available by local authorities, which are responsible for making sure that schools and early years settings know how to access the service.

There are also a number of voluntary organisations and charities that support parents of children with additional needs. These may be specific to a particular condition, for example, the Down's Syndrome Association, which offers advice and support groups for new parents. ContinYou is an education charity that supports families of children with SEN and has links to various Parent Partnership services.

Research

Find out about Parent Partnership services in your own area. How are they publicised and made available to parents? To help you, visit the website for the National Parent Partnership Network. You can access this website by going to www.pearsonhotlinks.co.uk and searching for this title.

C Understand the role of adults working with children with additional needs

All adults working with children will need to have a good understanding of their role and how it fits in with others' roles in order to best support the children with whom they work. If you are working with or supporting children who have additional needs, you are likely to be working with a wide range of other professionals from both within and outside the setting. This section will look at how these different roles fit together and the importance of multi-agency working.

Ensuring inclusive practice

The Special Educational Needs Code of Practice 2001 was introduced in part to strengthen the right of children with additional needs to a mainstream education. However, you may find that these children still face barriers to their learning and that other people focus on what they are not, rather than what they are. It is important that you are able to support and empower children who have additional needs, in particular if they lack confidence or have a poor self-image. Barriers to learning may include the following:

- **Organisational barriers**

These may be due to school policies, lack of staff training or lack of diversity within the school curriculum. Your school or setting should have an up-to-date equal opportunities or inclusion policy that sets out its priorities for developing inclusion. It should also ensure that all staff working with children who have additional needs are fully trained and able to do so with the full support of the setting.

- **Physical barriers**

There should be no reason for a child who has a disability or special educational needs not to be able to gain access to educational facilities. If you are working with a child who has a disability or additional needs, make sure that all staff are aware that provision must allow every child to participate. This may mean that adaptations need to be made to the environment or that additional resources and equipment are purchased.

- **Barriers in the attitudes of others**

This barrier can be one of the most challenging to overcome, as it is hard to change the opinions and attitudes of others. You should always remember that the needs of the child come first and to stand up for the rights of the children you support. You may need to challenge discrimination within your setting if the views of parents or other staff are intolerant or prejudiced.

- **Barriers in their own confidence and self-image**

Some children who have additional needs are lacking in confidence or have a poor self-image. This may be for a number of reasons, including reduced opportunities, lack of support and encouragement, or simply not believing in themselves. It is important that you encourage and empower these children as much as you can when you are working with them. This includes providing an environment that celebrates diversity and provides encouragement and support to all children by identifying their strengths and needs, and working with them to help them to achieve their goals through person-centred planning. You might ask questions such as those outlined in Figure 18.3.

Activity

How would you challenge the attitudes of others if they were clearly prejudiced against children with additional needs? Carry out a role-play activity with others in your group in which you challenge the opinions or views of others showing prejudice.

Reflect

Nick Vujicic is a motivational speaker who was born without arms and legs. Visit his website, 'Life without limbs', to find out more about his inspirational story. After searching the website, think about how we can encourage children to have a similar positive attitude and self-image. You can access Nick's website by going to www.pearsonhotlinks.co.uk and searching for this title.

Planning for individual needs and reviewing progress

Planning for individual needs

When you are working with a child who has additional needs, it is important that you are clear about the stage at which they are working according to the 2001 Code of Practice.

You will need to know whether they are being monitored due to initial concerns, or whether they are on Early Years Action or Action Plus and have been given an IEP with personalised targets. IEPs are designed to give children additional provision to ensure that they are able to access the curriculum. Although lesson plans should always include differentiated activities for all, children who have an IEP will have additional targets to work on according to their needs.

Link

Go to Unit 10: Section C to see an example of an individual education plan.

Depending on whether outside agencies are involved, some of these targets may focus on their specific needs and may include speech and language, physiotherapy or behavioural targets. In addition to this, work may still need to be adapted or changed and additional resources and/or equipment used in order to facilitate children's learning. You will need to be able to monitor the child's progress at all times and intervene if necessary in order to ensure that they are able to meet the learning intention.

Figure 18.3 A person-centred approach to planning

Assessing and reviewing progress

All IEPs will need to have a review date so that the child, their parents and those working with them are able to meet and discuss the child's progress. This will mean that they will need to document whether the targets have been met or whether they are still ongoing. They will then need to set new targets together as well as a new review date.

Once a year, children who have an Assessment Statement will also have an annual review, which all professionals working with the child, as well as the child and their parents, will be invited to attend and to contribute reports to. The minutes of this meeting must then be submitted to the local authority, which will take the child's needs into consideration and decide whether they still need additional support. This is important, as children's needs will change over time, and the child may have made significant progress due to the support given.

Collaborating with other professionals

When supporting children with additional needs you will need to be able to collaborate with other professionals. This includes not only formal but also informal opportunities to talk about children's progress. You should work together in the best interests of the child and draw on one another's expertise in order to provide support. In early years settings and schools, this may start with your room leader, nursery manager or class teacher, as well as your SENCO. You may also need to work with others who are based externally. Together, you are likely to have meetings, sometimes known as multi-agency meetings or team-around-the-child meetings, in order to ensure that all of you have a joined-up approach to working with the child.

The Common Assessment Framework, or CAF, is used across all children's services in England, particularly in the early identification of additional needs in children. It is important as it encourages professionals who work with these children to work cooperatively to share information about the child.

Research

Find out a bit more about the CAF by visiting the Department for Education website and downloading the 'Common Assessment Framework for children and young people' guide for practitioners. You can access this guide by going to www.pearsonhotlinks.co.uk and searching for this title.

The Special Educational Needs Coordinator (SENCO)

The SENCO is responsible for managing and monitoring the provision for those with special educational needs within a school or early years setting.

Link

Go to Unit 10: Section C to find more information about the role of the SENCO.

▌Working in partnership with parents

The Warnock Report into special educational needs provision in 1978 stated that for children under 5 years old, there should be 'greater recognition and involvement of parents, wherever possible, as the main educators of their children during the earliest years'. It is during the early years that children learn and develop most rapidly, and it is through their parents that they will develop many of their attitudes to learning. Parents should be encouraged to communicate with the setting as much as possible, by both formal and informal means.

There are many ways in which settings can work in partnership with parents, including:

- informal events
- providing information in leaflets and newsletters
- encouraging parents to be involved in the day-to-day running of the setting
- having an open-door policy to discuss any issues
- inviting parents to contribute to IEPs and reviews.

It is important for children, and especially those who have special educational needs, that their parents are encouraged to be involved in the setting and feel able to discuss their child's needs with staff. Parents who feel excluded or are not confident enough to communicate with the setting may unwittingly start to build barriers between home and the setting.

Reflect

Your setting has a high proportion of parents who speak English as an additional language. What could the setting do in order to encourage them to liaise with staff and to become involved in the activities of the setting? What advantages will this bring?

Assessment practice 18.7   3C.P9 | 3C.D2

Write a report about how settings should work in partnership with parents to support children who have additional needs. Give examples of the kinds of formal and informal opportunities that may arise for adults in the setting to speak with parents about their children, and evaluate the impact of positive relationships between the setting and the family.

Following policies and procedures and providing for personal care

Schools and early years settings are required to have a number of different policies in place to ensure that all staff work together and follow the same procedures. As a result of this, settings are required to have a policy for children with additional needs, or a Special Educational Needs Policy. There will also be an Equal Opportunities Policy and an Inclusion Policy. You and other staff in the setting will need to ensure that you are aware of the correct procedures to follow when working with children who have additional needs. These may also include some health and safety aspects when using equipment or being asked to lift or restrain children. If you are asked to use physical restraint for any reason, you must make sure that you are following your setting's and the local authority's guidelines.

Theory into practice

How many of the following key policies have you read?

- Safeguarding/Child Protection Policy
- Health and Safety Policy
- Equal Opportunities/Inclusion Policy
- Special Educational Needs Policy
- Confidentiality Policy
- If you work in a school, the Early Years Policy

You will also need to check the setting's policy if you are asked to carry out any personal care for children, such as helping with toileting. Although all adults working with children are required to have a Criminal Records Bureau (CRB) check, you may be vulnerable if you are not aware of correct procedures and carry them out incorrectly. In most cases, adults are advised not to be alone with children at any time. However, this case may be an exception. You will also need to be sensitive to the needs of the child and allow them to carry out as much as they can independently.

Confidentiality and privacy are also important when working with children who have additional needs. You should not speak about any issues concerning a child or their family outside the setting, to ensure that their privacy is respected.

Activity

Find out about your setting's policies for managing restraint, and what to do if you need to do this.

Further reading and resources

Hodkinson, A. and Vickerman, P. (2009) *Key Issues in Special Educational Needs and Inclusion*, Thousand Oaks, Sage Publications Ltd.

Porter, L. (2002) *Educating Young Children with Special Needs*, Thousand Oaks, Sage Publications Ltd.

Wall, K. (2010) *Special Needs and the Early Years: A Practitioner's Guide*, Thousand Oaks, Sage Publications Ltd.

Special Educational Needs: Code of Practice, DfE 2001.

The Warnock Report (1978) Special Educational Needs: Report of the Committee of Enquiry into the Education of Handicapped Children and Young People, London: Her Majesty's Stationery Office.

Websites

Aiming High for Disabled Children: www.education.gov.uk

Portage: www.portage.org.uk

National Association of Special Educational Needs: www.nasen.org.uk

SEN magazine: www.senmagazine.co.uk

Many charities such as Barnardo's, SENSE, Mencap and the Hope Centre also provide support and assistance through their work and on their websites.

Ready for work?

Soriya Gupta Nursery worker

I have been working at the nursery for three years. I have worked with quite a few children who have had additional needs, from speech and language difficulties to Down's syndrome and also two autistic children. It's really important to have a good understanding of how children with additional needs are looked after in different early years settings and to have a good working knowledge of the Code of Practice. This is important, as it gives us a clear document to work from alongside our own policies and procedures.

We also need to understand the whole assessment process and be able to carry out observations so that we can feed back to colleagues and parents, and be part of a whole-team approach to managing the child's needs. I have been sent on a couple of training courses on additional needs which were run through the local authority and these have given me a really good insight into the kinds of issues to look out for and also a source of additional advice if needed.

I have also had the opportunity to work with a few other professionals, including my area SENCO, the speech and language therapists, and both occupational therapists and physiotherapists. This has been really interesting for me as I have learned a lot more about what their roles involve, and it has been great to be involved in meetings with them along with parents and really feel that I am making a difference to these children.

Skills for practice

Effective relationships with children – supporting a child with additional needs

- Get to know as much as you can about the child from parents and other staff in the setting.
- Form a relationship with the child by finding out about them and their interests.
- Make a point of saying hello and talking to them each day.
- Find out about any additional equipment or resources they may need and learn to use it too.
- Make sure you are aware of their targets and IEP.
- Work with them on different areas of the curriculum – both indoor and outdoor – and support them where needed.

Professional relationships with adults

- Show that you can work as part of a team by supporting others in your setting.
- Be organised and prepared each day when you come to the setting. If working with a child who has additional needs, you may need to bring additional resources.
- If you are working as part of a team around a particular child, remember to keep channels of communication open and be approachable.
- Keep up to date with contact details of other agencies and individuals with whom you are working to support the child.
- Develop and nurture good relationships with parents and carers, and remain approachable and easy to contact on a daily basis.

Introduction

Mathematics is a broad subject area and covers many aspects of children's learning – from sequencing, shapes and finding patterns to being able to carry out calculations, and from measuring and using money to telling the time. Children will need to have a good grounding in all these areas so they are able to progress through the different aspects of mathematics. You should be clear on the curriculum being followed, as well as the age and stage of the children with whom you are working, to develop their understanding in each area while encouraging them and stimulating their interest. You should also know about the different factors that may affect mathematical development so that you are able to put strategies in place to ensure that all children have full access to the mathematics curriculum.

Assessment: You will be assessed by a series of assignments set by your teacher/tutor.

Learning aims

In this unit you will:

A   understand the current framework used to teach mathematics to children aged from four up to eight years

B   understand children's mathematical development

C1   understand how to support children's mathematical development

C2   understand the importance of assessing children's mathematical development.

> Mathematics is an important part of our everyday lives – it has many different aspects, and a good understanding of the subject can help us in so many ways. I have found it fascinating throughout my career to work with children as they develop and explore mathematical ideas. We should encourage and inspire young children to develop their skills in mathematics through play and exploration so that they build on their natural curiosity and develop their confidence.
>
> Anna Gibbs, *mathematics advisory teacher*

Promoting Mathematical Development in Children Aged From Four up to Eight Years

19

BTEC
Assessment Zone

This table shows what you must do in order to achieve a **Pass**, **Merit** or **Distinction** grade, and where you can find activities to help you.

Assessment criteria		
Pass	**Merit**	**Distinction**
Learning aim A: Understand the current framework used to teach mathematics to children aged from 4 to 8 years		
3A.P1 Summarise the key features of the current framework used to teach mathematics to children aged from four up to eight years in the home country. **Assessment practice 19.1**	**3A.M1** Analyse the role of planning in the delivery of the mathematics framework to children across the age range from four years up to eight years. **Assessment practice 19.1**	
3A.P2 Describe, using examples, how early years settings might plan and organise their provision to deliver the current mathematics framework to children aged from four up to eight years in the home country. **Assessment practice 19.1**		
Learning aim B: Understand children's mathematical development		
3B.P3 Review how early experiences can support mathematical development. **Assessment practice 19.2**	**3B.M2** Discuss the extent to which experiences impact on the development of children's mathematical skills. **Assessment practice 19.2**	**3B.D1** Evaluate the role of consolidation in children's mathematical development. **Assessment practice 19.2**
3B.P4 Explain the importance of personal confidence in mathematical development. **Assessment practice 19.2**		
3B.P5 Describe difficulties that might arise from children not having understood earlier mathematical concepts and language when learning. **Assessment practice 19.2**		

continued

 English English Functional Skills signposting   **I&CT** Information and Communication Technology skills signposting

Maths Mathematical Functional Skills signposting

Assessment criteria (*continued*)

Pass	Merit	Distinction
Learning aim C1: Understand how to support children's mathematical development **Learning aim C2: Understand the importance of assessing children's mathematical development**		
3C1.P6 Explain how linking activities to children's own experiences supports mathematical development. **Assessment practice 19.3**	**3C1.M3** Discuss, using examples, the extent which activities could support children's mathematical development. **Assessment practice 19.3**	**3C.D2** Evaluate the extent to which adults contribute to the mathematical development of children aged from four up to eight years. **Assessment practice 19.4**
3C1.P7 English Select, with reasons, activities for children aged from four up to eight years to support development in different mathematical topic areas. **Assessment practice 19.3, 19.4**		
3C1.P8 Explain the role of the adult in supporting mathematical development in activities. **Assessment practice 19.3, 19.4**		
3C2.P9 I&CT Explain why it is important to check children's mathematical understanding. **Assessment practice 19.5**	**3C2.M4** Analyse the role of adults in assessing the mathematical development of children aged from four up to eight years. **Assessment practice 19.5**	
3C2.P10 Maths Explain the importance of recording and reporting the mathematical development of children aged from four up to eight years. **Assessment practice 19.5**		

How you will be assessed

This unit will be assessed by a series of internally assessed tasks set by your teacher/tutor. Throughout this unit you will find assessment practice activities that will help you work towards your assessment. Completing these activities will not mean that you have achieved a particular grade, but you will have carried out useful research or preparation that will be relevant when it comes to your final assignment.

In order for you to carry out the tasks in your assignment, it is important that you check you have met all of the Pass grading criteria. You can do this as you work your way through the assignment.

If you are hoping to gain a Merit or Distinction, you should also make sure that you present the information in your assignment in the style required by the relevant assessment criterion. For example, Merit criteria will require you to discuss and analyse, and Distinction criteria will require you to evaluate.

The assignment set by your teacher/tutor will consist of a number of tasks designed to meet the criteria in the table. This is likely to consist of a written assignment, but may also include:

- a case study
- an information leaflet
- a good practice guide.

What kinds of feelings do you have when you start to think about mathematics? Discuss with a partner why you think you have these feelings and where they come from. What does this tell you about how we should present mathematics to young children?

A Understand the current framework used to teach mathematics to children aged from 4 to 8 years

Learning provision for mathematics is important for children, as maths is so much part of our everyday lives. Today mathematics may be taught very differently from your own experiences in school. This is because there is now a much greater emphasis, particularly in the early primary phase, on teaching children different ways of arriving at an answer, showing them different methods of working, finding patterns in number and developing investigation skills. The aim of the mathematics curriculum is to give children a solid grounding in all aspects of numeracy on which they will be able to base their working. A key aspect of developing skills in mathematics is that children understand its purpose and can learn to apply it to real-life situations. Mathematical skills are therefore developed in the earliest stages through practical work, which introduces children to aspects of maths such as shape, pattern, counting, sorting and so on. You will need to have an awareness of the skills that children in your setting are working towards in order to support them fully and help them to access the curriculum.

Theory into practice

Have a look around your setting to see what evidence you can find of mathematics in action over the course of one day. This could be displays and information, activities or adults talking to children using mathematical language.

Frameworks and areas of mathematics

In order to support children in schools and early years settings, you should have an awareness of the current frameworks that are used to teach mathematics. These are currently undergoing change; however, in all areas of the UK, there will be a separate early years and Key Stage 1 curriculum.

In nurseries and reception classes in England, teachers will follow the Early Years Foundation Stage curriculum. From September 2012, mathematical development will be a specific area of learning and further divides the subject into numbers, shape, space and measures.

Children will explore and practise their skills in these areas through exploration, discussion, games and focused activities. For example, for numbers the expectations are for children to:

- practise and improve their skills in counting numbers
- use numbers up to 10 to do simple addition and subtraction
- find a total by counting on, and calculate how many are left from a larger number by counting back.

In England and Wales, mathematics is taught through the National Primary Framework for Mathematics as part of the National Curriculum. The age-related expectations for each area can currently be found in a document produced in 2006 by the then Department for Education and Skills called *Primary Framework for literacy and mathematics*. This lists the core learning by year group or by strand, although it is subject to change in 2014.

In Scotland, there is no requirement to follow the Primary Framework, although numeracy is divided into the following three areas:

- information handling
- number, money and measurement
- shape, position and movement.

In Northern Ireland, the curriculum was reviewed in 2007 and was phased in over the following two years. Mathematics and numeracy are now divided into the following areas in Key Stages 1 and 2:

- processes in mathematics
- number
- measures
- shape and space
- handling data.

Research

The website for the Department of Education Northern Ireland provides up-to-date information about developments in the curriculum. You can access the Department of Education's website by going to www.pearsonhotlinks.co.uk and searching for this title. Look under the 'Curriculum and Assessment' tab.

Reflect

Find out about the current framework used to teach mathematics in your country. How is the subject broken down?

The sequence in which each topic area is taught

Following on from the early years curriculum, each country has its own curriculum for the teaching of mathematics. For example, in England and Wales the current framework is the Primary Framework. This includes seven strands of learning across the entire primary phase, including the Foundation Stage. Learning objectives are then linked to the seven strands so that progression can be seen in different areas. The seven strands and corresponding areas of progression are as follows:

1 Using and applying mathematics

This area of mathematics requires children to describe what they are doing, follow a line of enquiry and present what they have found out, for example, when solving problems. By the end of Year 2 they should be able to describe sequences of numbers and make predictions about what number will come next.

2 Counting and understanding number

Children will need to learn number names and to count with confidence from an early age. They will need to start to use vocabulary such as 'more' or 'less', compare numbers, count on and back, order numbers to the nearest 10, estimate and recognise equivalents. They will also be able to find a quarter, half and three-quarters of a number, and be starting to count in 2s, 5s and 10s.

Research

The Primary Framework for mathematics provides some useful guidelines about how a child's counting and number skills should progress from the Foundation Stage to Year 3. You can access the framework by going to www.pearsonhotlinks.com and searching for this title.

3 Knowing and using number facts

Children will need to learn the relationships between numbers and will start to look out for patterns. They will look at the links between addition and subtraction, and division and multiplication. They will need to know number bonds to 10 and be able to transfer this knowledge to know and understand 20 + 80, 200 + 800 and so on.

4 Calculating

Children will need to be able to learn to calculate with confidence using the four operations of addition, subtraction, multiplication and division. They will start with very practical addition and subtraction, and move on to recorded and mental methods. They will need to know and understand place value.

5 Understanding shape

Children should have the opportunity to explore 2D and 3D shapes and to be able to describe and classify them. They will make models, shapes and patterns, and talk about their features. They will learn to recognise and use symmetry and reflections, as well as using the language of direction and movement.

6 Measuring (includes length, time, weight, capacity, area)

Children will estimate, measure, weigh and compare objects using standard and non-standard units, and use vocabulary such as 'greater', 'smaller', 'heavier' and 'lighter' to compare quantities. They will know and understand the relationships between different units of measure, for example, kilometres to metres, and grams to kilograms. They will need to learn how to read different scales and interpret these on a range of measuring instruments. They should be able to calculate the perimeter and area of regular shapes, and estimate the area of an irregular shape.

7 Handling data

Children will start by sorting familiar objects and identifying similarities and differences. They will need to learn to answer questions by collecting and recording data in different ways, such as lists and tables, and start to use block graphs, pictograms and ICT to show their results.

Research

Using your country's curriculum document, find out about the different headings and end-of-year expectations for each year group. Look at how each topic progresses through the different age groups.

If you are supporting children's numeracy development, you will need to be aware of your responsibilities under your school or setting's mathematics or numeracy policy. This will outline your school's approach to the teaching of different aspects of maths as defined by local and national guidelines. It is likely that your setting's policy will also identify exactly how numeracy is taught throughout, and how standards are monitored and assessed.

How settings might plan their provision

In the early years, mathematics will usually be taught through topic work. This means that the subject will be part of a wider study around a subject such as 'Myself' or 'Toys'.

Topics can last from between two weeks to half a term. In nurseries and reception classes, the curriculum requires that the delivery of mathematics will be mainly through practical activities and discussion. Children will carry out a range of activities that should be meaningful and in context to the topic they are exploring. This will also include bringing maths into children's routines and talking about it – for example, 'How many children are here today?' 'Do we have enough pieces of fruit for everyone?' 'Who is taller?' By hearing the language of mathematics, children will start to develop their own thinking skills.

Can you see how this practical activity is helping to deliver the mathematics curriculum to a group of reception children?

In all countries of the UK, when children move into Key Stage or Primary 1, the teaching of mathematics will be taught in different units in blocks of two- or three-week lessons so that children are able to spend some time developing their skills before moving on to the next one. For example, when working on partitioning and calculating in Year 2, the primary framework sets out what should be covered during the year and splits it into three units of two weeks. One of these will then be studied each term.

Assessment practice 19.1   3A.P1 | 3A.P2 | 3A.M1

Summarise the key features of the mathematics framework for the ages 4 to 8 years for the country you work in. Give examples of plans and describe how early years settings might organise their provision to deliver the framework. Analyse the role of planning in the delivery of mathematics for young children.

B Understand children's mathematical development

In order to understand how children learn mathematics, you will need to have some idea about mathematical theories of development. This will help you understand why maths is taught in a particular way and how different skills build on one another.

Theory of mathematical development and links to cognitive development

Link

Go to Unit 1 in Student Book 1 to find more information about cognitive development.

You should have some idea about the way in which children develop mathematical skills so that you can support them effectively. The development of mathematical skills is closely linked to children's **cognitive development**. Studies and research have taken place into the way in which mathematical development occurs, but the most influential in this area has been the work of Piaget, through **constructivist theory**.

Key terms

Cognitive development – the development of the mind and how children learn, reason and understand.

Constructivist theory – a theory that states how children learn by constructing their own knowledge through experience and that children pass through specific stages of development.

Reflect

Think about what you know about cognitive development. Before we look at the links to mathematics, what do you think these might be?

Piaget's work was mainly focused on the development of cognitive skills. Piaget believed that we learn more by building on what we know already, and that our learning will progress in this way. His theory of four cognitive stages is also closely linked to mathematical development. Piaget believed that children must pass through each stage and experience at each level in order to have a firm grounding for the next, and that they will not progress to the next until they are ready.

Piaget's four cognitive stages

1. At the sensory motor stage, (0 to 2 years), children will be developing hand–eye coordination and learning to understand object permanence. In other words, they will be starting to realise that an object is still there, even when moved or hidden. They will start to develop their concept of number, be able to link numbers to objects and will have some understanding of counting. At this stage they should be exposed to lots of opportunities to count and look at picture books with numbers so that they are able to make links between numbers and objects.

2. At the pre-operational stage (3 to 7 years), children will have an increasing ability in language and will be starting to understand symbolic thought, as well as some limited logic. This increase in language ability will mean that they are able to

carry out simple problem-solving activities but they will need to be supported by materials such as blocks, cubes, sand, water and other apparatus. These will support their development and should be used in conjunction with plenty of opportunities for questioning and discussion. However, their lack of logical thought means that they are unable to transfer what they know to different situations. For example, if they have two identical containers with the same amount of water in each and transfer the contents of one to a third, wider container, they will assume that there is less water in the third because the water level has gone down. This is known as conservation. It may also be applied to number – for example, if children are adding two piles of cubes of the same number, they will start counting from the beginning rather than counting on from the first pile. At this stage, children will only use one dimension to judge a task or situation.

3   At the concrete operational stage (8 to 11 years), there is a period of rapid cognitive growth. This is quite a dramatic period and children will now be able to consider two or three dimensions to a task. For example, they will now identify that there is the same amount of water in each container when the water is transferred because as well as seeing that the level is lower, they can see the dish is wider. At this stage there should also be plenty of hands-on and practical experiences – children will still need lots of support to make links to the abstract and be shown different representations. Their skills at ordering and grouping objects will be increasing.

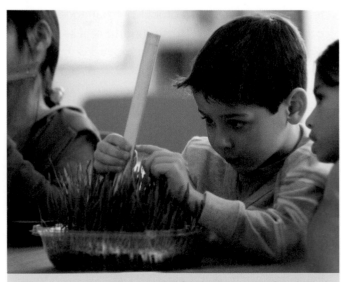

Opportunities should be provided for children to develop through hands-on and practical experiences.

4   At the formal operational stage (12 to 15 years), children will be able to think in the abstract. For example, in algebra, a child will not need to be given a word problem in order to understand a concept. Their reasoning skills will be increased and they will be able to form their own ideas.

Research

What else can you find out about theories of mathematical development? How do these theories help us to plan for children's mathematical learning?

The importance of early mathematical skills

Practical exploration is important from the earliest stages of developing mathematical skills because it enables children to have a secure grounding in different aspects of mathematics. These basic practical skills will support the development of different areas, as shown in Table 19.1.

The need for children to acquire mathematical language

When teaching young children mathematical concepts, you will need to remember the importance of language and how problems here can make a big difference to their understanding. There are different ways in which failing to understand mathematical vocabulary may come to light, including if children:

- do not understand instructions – for example, language such as 'find the difference', 'arrange in order' or 'read the table below'
- are not familiar with the vocabulary – for example, vocabulary such as 'pattern', 'in between' or 'more/less than'
- do not understand a mathematical term – for example, 'subtract', 'double' or 'match'.

We can sometimes make assumptions about what children understand, particularly in maths. If we are focusing on the concept rather than the language, some young children, or those who speak English as an additional language, may have difficulty. When

Table 19.1 Basic practical skills in early mathematical exploration

Skill	Purpose
Matching and one-to-one correspondence	One-to-one correspondence is the matching of numbers within two sets. Children will need to be able to do this in order to count effectively.
Pattern making	Pattern making is important as it enables children to identify simple repeated ideas. This is a good basis for finding patterns in numbers later on.
Sorting	Early sorting activities will help children's understanding of numbers. They should have opportunities to sort as many different materials as possible and in as many different ways as they can. This will also support the development of language – why should these items be put together? Which ones do not belong with the others? Children should also be invited to compare different objects or groups of objects, which will also help to develop language.
Counting and ordering	Children will need to become familiar with the number system, and they will do this through counting and ordering numbers and groups of numbers with the same criteria. They should also begin to count in 2s, 5s and 10s.
Recording	Children will start to record numbers, patterns and what they have found out in simple ways, through pictures and simple charts and tallies. This will lead on to later being able to express their ideas through symbols.

carrying out a new topic, or as a general activity or assessment task, teachers may introduce it by going through mathematical vocabulary to check children's understanding. Words that are used as part of a topic are likely to be displayed on the wall so that children are able to refer to them throughout the topic.

Figure 19.1 shows an example of a visual display that could be used to teach children mathematical vocabulary.

Mathematical vocabulary and language should be displayed in the learning environment. As children work on practical mathematical activities, these displays should be talked about with adults so that the children can build up their knowledge of the kind of vocabulary we use in mathematics.

It is also helpful each day to display any new vocabulary at the start of a formal lesson with children in school, particularly if you are writing a learning objective for children to refer to.

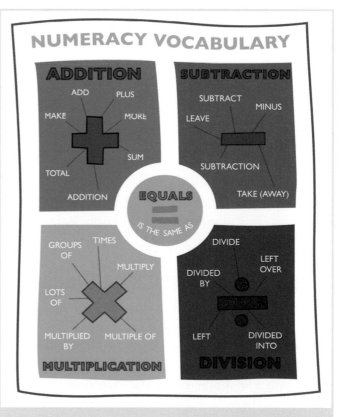

Figure 19.1 An example of a mathematics vocabulary poster

The vocabulary used

An example of the kind of vocabulary you might use by area is shown below.

Year 1: Numbers – place value and ordering

Units, ones, tens, exchange, digit, 'teens' number, the same number as, as many as, equal to, greater, greatest, more, most, larger, largest, bigger, biggest, less, least, fewer, fewest, smaller, smallest, one more, ten more, one less, ten less, compare, order, size, first, second, third etc, last, before, after, next, between, halfway between, above, below.

Source: Extract taken from the 'Mathematical Vocabulary Book', DfES 2000. © Crown copyright 2000.

It is also helpful each day to display any new vocabulary at the start of a formal lesson with children in school, particularly if you are writing a learning objective for children to refer to.

Building children's confidence

As with all other areas of learning, you will need to build children's confidence when working on mathematical ideas. From an early age, children should be presented with positive and fun methods of working with mathematical tasks in ways that engage all learners. Adults should take care to ensure that tasks are introduced in a way that stimulates children so that they do not think of mathematics as 'difficult'. Occasionally concepts may be difficult to grasp, and children will find new ideas challenging. They should be given plenty of opportunities to use games, investigations and other forms of mathematics, which will develop their skills while also encouraging them to be independent.

Difficulties that may arise in children's understanding

If children have not sufficiently understood earlier concepts, they may well experience difficulty at a later stage when they are asked to take their learning further. This may be related to different areas of mathematics – for example, adults should ensure that children understand the meaning of specific mathematical language that is relevant to the area they are working on. Adults should always think about key vocabulary and check children's understanding at each stage when working on a new area.

Where children have trouble understanding concepts, you should always give them the opportunity to talk about their understanding and any concerns that they have. Group work can be a good opportunity to do this. Children can quickly start to feel that they cannot 'do' maths and lose confidence if they find it challenging, and you will need to build up this confidence as much as possible.

Reflect

Think about how you present mathematical concepts to children and the kind of language that you use. How do you ensure that you build children's confidence and encourage them to develop their ideas?

Assessment practice 19.2 | 3B.P3 | 3B.P4 | 3B.P5 |
| 3B.M2 | 3B.D1 |

Write an account of children's early experiences, analysing their importance and showing how early concepts support mathematical development. Why is it important for children to have the opportunity to undertake these activities, and how will their confidence be developed as a result? Should children always have the opportunity to consolidate their learning? What will happen if children have not understood earlier concepts before moving ahead with their learning?

It is very important for children to have time to carry out practical activities as well as talk about and consolidate what they have learned in an environment that is not pressured. This is because some mathematical ideas are quite complex. If children carry out activities too early, before they have completed the previous stage in their learning, they will be unable to progress to the next stage. For example, if children are still at the early stages of exploring numbers and counting and combining two groups of objects, they should not progress to recording this until they have had plenty of practical opportunities to develop and become used to the language of numbers, such as more and less.

C1 Understand how to support children's mathematical development

Children will need different levels of support when they are undertaking mathematical activities. Some may be more confident and show a better understanding in different areas, but others may find all mathematical concepts difficult to grasp. Children of all abilities will also need adults to show them how mathematics is used in everyday life, and to model the correct use of mathematical vocabulary.

Linking activities to the child's experience to provide meaning

As mathematics is sometimes an abstract subject, children will need teachers and other adults to link mathematical concepts to practical activities as much as possible to make it meaningful for them. This means for the youngest children, their introduction to the subject will be mainly through play and exploration. Figure 19.2 shows the kinds of activities

that they will take part in during the early years to support mathematical development.

Can you think of an activity using raffle tickets that you could use to support children's mathematical development?

Figure 19.2 Activities that support mathematical development in the early years

Assessment practice 19.3   3C1.P6 | 3C1.P7 | 3C1.P8 | 3C1.M3

Select and describe some everyday activities for children aged 4 to 8 years that will support development in different mathematical topic areas, and discuss the extent to which they do this. Why it is important to link activities to children's own experiences when working on mathematical concepts? How can you support the children's learning in each case?

Children may also enjoy being taken on a 'maths walk' in small groups to look at numbers and shapes around the school and outdoor area or its close environment. Depending on the amount of adult support available, you may like to give them a series of questions to answer, or simply allow them to find out what they can and report back to others.

Activity

Devise and carry out a maths walk for the year group that you are currently working with. How does this engage the children? How does it support different mathematical areas and build children's confidence?

The role of the adult in supporting mathematics

When working with children on mathematical activities, you will need to act as a facilitator for their learning in a number of different ways.

Check children's understanding of the purpose of the activity

Sometimes, young children may find it hard to recall what they have been asked to do or why they are doing it. You may need to help them go over what is required. You can do this by questioning them to check their understanding or by asking them to repeat back to you what they think they need to do next. You may also need to remind them about specific teaching points – this may be because of their own individual learning needs or their ability to remain focused on a task.

Ensure they have time to process information

Very young children will need to have time to take on board a new concept or to be able to think through what they need to do.

Question children and observe their reactions

It is likely that you will use this strategy regularly with children, as they will often need to be refocused or be asked specific questions to redirect their thinking. When questioning children, you should make sure that you ask in a way that does not 'lead' them to the answer. Questions should also be open where possible, for example: 'The answer is 10. What could the question be?' Some further examples are shown in Table 19.2.

Table 19.2 Part of an example taken from the 'Mathematical Vocabulary Book', DfES 2000

Closed questions	Open questions
Count these cubes.	How could we count these cubes?
A chew costs 3p. A lolly costs 7p. What do they cost altogether?	A chew and a lolly cost 10p altogether. What could each sweet cost?
What is 6 - 4?	Tell me two numbers with a difference of 2.
Is 9 an even number?	What even numbers are between 0 and 10?
What are four 3s?	Tell me two numbers with a product of 12.

Help children to obtain and use resources

You may need to prompt children or encourage them to think about resources available to them when working on mathematical activities. These resources may include number lines, measuring instruments, games and computer software. Children may need help if they have been asked to carry out an activity with unfamiliar resources. They may not have used some items before, and younger children should always be given the opportunity to look at and explore what they will be using before starting the activity. If children have sensory support needs, you may need to speak to specialist teachers to find out what additional resources are available.

Model using mathematics in everyday activities

It is important that adults model to children how mathematics is used in everyday life, for example, when we count aloud, compare sizes or go shopping.

Explain and reinforce mathematical language, and use commentary

You should always reinforce vocabulary that you are using and also extend children's vocabulary and check their understanding of any terms used. Young children, or those who speak English as an additional language, may need you to explain mathematical terms to them. Commentary, or talking through with children what they are doing as they are doing it, enables them to become more familiar with the mathematical language they are using and also encourages them to think through the process as they are working.

Reinforce and revisit concepts

As shown through theories of mathematical development, children should always be given time to revisit different concepts and consolidate their learning regularly. When starting a new topic or idea with children, you should always spend a little time talking about what they know already. They should then always have plenty of practice using their new skill before moving on to the next thing to ensure that they have consolidated their learning.

Focus on supporting mathematical understanding

You should remember that the most important part of supporting any aspect of children's learning is to focus on what they are learning. At the end of an activity it is more important for children to have understood what they have been asked to do than to have completed the task.

Reflect

Think about the kinds of mathematical activities you carry out with children. Do you ever rush to complete a task with them rather than focusing on their understanding?

Use praise and encouragement

While children are working on mathematical activities you may need to support them through talking to them in different ways to encourage them to stay on task. You should use praise wherever possible, as it is an excellent motivator and gives children confidence. However, you will also need to ensure that children maintain ownership over their learning.

Use interactive computer programs

There are a number of interactive computer programs and websites available that encourage understanding of and reinforce mathematical concepts. Most children enjoy working with computers, and such programs can be useful for engaging them.

| Assessment practice 19.4 | 3C1.P7 | 3C1.P8 | 3C.D2 |

Write a description of three activities that you have carried out with children to support the development of mathematical skills in different topic areas. Explain your role during the activities, including whether you have used any of the strategies described. Evaluate the extent to which you consider that adults contribute to the mathematical development of children.

Working with parents to encourage enjoyment of mathematics

It is very important for schools and early years settings to work alongside parents to encourage children's enjoyment of mathematics. However, many parents may have had poor experiences while they were at school and find this hard to overcome. The

Did you know?

Many schools now use the Mathletics website to encourage children to enjoy mathematics. The website provides interactive mathematics activities for schools and it encourages children to carry out activities at home too. Take a look at the website and the service it offers. You can access the website by going to www.pearsonhotlinks.co.uk and searching for this title.

setting can help in different ways, through running information evenings, giving talks and providing guidelines or booklets for parents in how to support their child when learning mathematics. These may include ideas such as the following:

- Look for shapes and numbers in the environment. Move on to finding odd/even numbers, or numbers higher/lower than.
- Play card and board games and do puzzles with children.
- Count up small change with children after going shopping.
- Cook with children to give them experience in weighing and being able to read scales. Talk about ingredients being 'heavier/lighter than' others.
- Try not to put too much emphasis on formal 'sums', particularly with very young children. It is more important that they have plenty of practical experience of mathematics.

Parents should also be encouraged to come into the setting if possible to see maths in action and to carry out games and activities with children. In this way, they will be able to develop their own confidence as well as gain ideas. There are also plenty of excellent books for parents to support mathematical development.

Case study

Supporting children at home

Andy is a parent of twins who are in Year 2. Although both the children are at an age-equivalent level in mathematics, he would like to support them at home and has approached the school for advice, because apart from working on times tables with them he says that maths is so different from when he was at school, he is worried about 'getting it wrong'.

1 What kinds of suggestions might you be able to give Andy?
2 Why is it important to work with Andy and other parents?

C2 Understand the importance of assessing children's mathematical development

Assessment is a crucial part of the process of teaching and learning. When working with children on mathematical concepts, you will need to continually assess and review how they are progressing so that you can plan the next steps for learning.

Checking children's understanding to inform planning

As with other subjects, you will need to have a clear idea of each child's level of understanding in mathematics. This is because the planning and assessment cycle is a continuous process, and children's level of attainment will need to be clear so you can plan the next steps. Individual learners may also have their own targets or areas that they need to focus on. However, although it is important to be aware of individual needs, this does not mean that you will need to plan different activities for each individual child – it is likely that you will be working with small groups of children who may have similar or mixed abilities. Planning will need to take account of what the children have understood so far, so that activities will be meaningful for them. Planning, teaching and evaluating follow a cycle that gives structure to the teaching process. Figure 19.3 shows this cycle.

Assessing and planning for children with uneven levels of mathematical understanding

As the subject of mathematics covers a number of different areas, you should be aware that children may not acquire mathematical understanding evenly across all of these. For example, they may be able to identify and talk about 2D and 3D shapes, but find it more difficult to work on problem-solving activities. You will need to work with colleagues to ensure that assessment takes this into account and that documentation and records show details of progress in different areas.

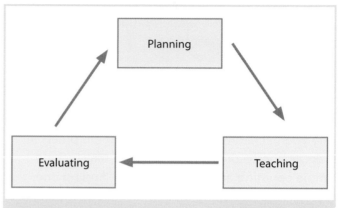

Figure 19.3 The planning, teaching and evaluating cycle

Assessing children's mathematical understanding

As in all subject areas, in order to plan for children's mathematical development, you will need to continually assess their progress and understanding in different aspects of the subject. This may be through different types of assessment, including the following.

Observation

Nurseries and early years settings will follow the guidelines of the Early Years Foundation Stage or equivalent which will require ongoing assessment to take place through observation. Key persons will need to make focused observations using a set format on specific children in all areas of learning to see how they are progressing over time. It is likely that at any one time, observations may cover more than one area of learning, for example, while observing a child who is making patterns by threading beads you may also note the development of the child's fine motor skills and interactions with another child or an adult. Levels of confidence and discussions and mathematical vocabulary used by the child should also be noted.

Older children may still be observed during mathematics lessons, although there will be fewer adults in the classroom in schools, and observation is unlikely to be as focused unless there is a specific area of difficulty. However, the observation does not need to be formal in order to gather information about a child's progress. You can note how children are working at any time and record those who are achieving well or falling below expectations.

Link

Go to Unit 9 for more information about observation and assessment.

Setting practical tasks

Adults assessing the mathematical development of very young children are likely to set them practical tasks as one-to-one activities. These may include simple counting and matching tasks, finding one more or one less using mathematical equipment, or identifying features of shapes or patterns. The adult will then record and date a sheet showing the child's achievements in different aspects of mathematics.

Questioning

Children will need to be questioned by adults during mathematical activities to assess their progress

An activity such as counting cubes could be used to assess a child's mathematical development.

and develop their learning. You should encourage children to talk about what they are doing, particularly during practical tasks, and question them in a way that encourages them to think about the task in different ways. See also examples of questioning in Table 19.2 earlier.

Activity

Think about how you use observation to assess mathematical understanding in your setting. How do you record this and share it with colleagues?

Summative assessment

Summative assessment is used at the end of a stage in order to assess the level achieved by children at a particular time. This might be, for example, at the end of the Early Years Foundation Stage, when teachers complete the Early Years Profile. As with all other areas, mathematical development will be assessed through set activities such as practical tasks.

Depending on the setting in which you are working, you may be required to record and report on mathematical development in different ways. If you have been working with a group of older children, you may feed back to the teacher verbally or through the use of a feedback sheet (see Figure 19.4 for an example). These sheets are particularly useful where there is little time for you to speak to the teacher about how the children have managed the task. It is important that there is a clear method for providing feedback so that other staff are aware of how children have managed the activity.

Assessment practice 19.5   3C2.P9 | 3C2.P10 | 3C2.M4

1 Discuss how important it is for practitioners to regularly check and assess children's mathematical understanding.

2 Why is it important for them to keep records of this and report to others?

3 Give different examples of how you might check and assess the mathematical understanding of children aged 4 to 8 years.

Teacher/TA Feedback Sheet

To be filled in by the teacher:

Teacher's name: C Scott
TA's name: G Jaynes
Class: Year 1

Brief description of activity:

> To work with children to help them understand what different coins up to 10p represent.
>
> Learning objective: To be able to identify and use coins to 10p

How session is linked to medium-term plans

> Primary Framework – money

TA's role

> To talk through with children what the coins mean so they are aware that a 2p coin is the same as two 1p coins, a 5p coin is the same as five 1p coins and so on. If the children can do this, work towards 2×2p coins making 4p. Make other totals up to 10p.

Important vocabulary

> Money, coin, pay, penny, pence, pound, price, cost, buy, sell, spend, costs more/less/the same as, how much/many, total.

Key learning points

> • For children to understand what different coins represent.
> • For children to be able to add together coins to 10p.

For use during group work/completion by TA:

Children	D	H	Feedback/assessment

D = Can do task
H = Help required to complete task

Figure 19.4 A feedback sheet showing areas to be filled in by the teacher/tutor and support staff

Further reading and resources

Boaler, J. (2010) *The Elephant in the Classroom: Helping Children Learn and Love Maths*, London: Souvenir Press Ltd.

Deboys, M. and Pitt, E. (1980) *Lines of Development in Primary Mathematics*, Belfast: Blackstaff Press Ltd.

Donaldson, M. (1986) *Children's Minds*, London: Harper Collins.

Eastaway, R. and Askew, M. (2010) *Maths for Mums and Dads*, London: Square Peg.

Ojose, B. 'Applying Piaget's theory of mathematical development to mathematics', *The Mathematics Educator*, 2008.

Sani, N. (2010) *How to Do Maths so Your Children Can Too: the Essential Parents' Guide*, London: Vermilion.

Early Years Foundation Stage document, DCSF 2008.

National Curriculum for England, DfEE 1999.

Mathematical Vocabulary Book, DfES 2000.

Primary Framework for Literacy and Mathematics, DfES 2006.

Websites

nrich: http://nrich.maths.org/public
Lots of ideas and resources to support children's mathematical development.

Mathletics: www.mathletics.co.uk
A large number of resources for teachers and exciting activities for children. Your setting will need to subscribe to access the full site.

Ready for work?

Trish Jones Nursery assistant

I am a nursery assistant at Sunshine Nursery and have been here for just over two years. At the moment I am working on my early years qualification and have decided to complete my own maths GCSE in order to do this, as I did not get a good grade when I was at school. It has been very interesting, as I have had my own issues with mathematics and I have had to develop my own confidence while working with the children. Although I found maths difficult at school, it has been really good for me to look at it again and to find out about some of the fun aspects that can be transferred to my work with the children. I am now full of enthusiasm for it and as a result have asked the setting manager if we can run an information evening for parents, which I am getting involved in. This will in turn be good for the children. It has even been good for me at home as I have been able to have more understanding of what my own teenage children are doing for their homework! My line manager says that it has been great to watch me develop my confidence in this area and I am so pleased that I have.

Skills for practice

Support learning

- Make sure that you support mathematics in different situations, for example, indoor and outdoor, and formal and informal.

- Use as many opportunities as you can to develop children's counting skills and assess their learning.

- Remember that activities such as counting songs and nursery rhymes, puzzles, measuring and talking about shapes are all forms of mathematics.

- Use ICT with children to reinforce mathematical concepts.

- Use mathematics with children in other areas of learning, for example, recording how much they score in basketball or writing numbers outside during hopscotch.

- Use other activities to consolidate mathematical concepts, for example, cooking, which uses measuring and counting.

- Look for mathematics in the environment, for example, patterns in tiles and shapes.

- Devise activities and trips for children that will encourage them to think about numbers in the environment, for example, maths walks in the local area.

Introduction

Learning to read and write is a complex process. It incorporates learning to speak and listen to others, as well as having phonemic awareness and being able to decipher text. Children also need to have the fine and large motor skills necessary for writing. You will need to look at the different pre-reading and pre-writing skills that children need, as well as looking at different theoretical approaches so that you can effectively support children through the process. Some children can find reading and writing relatively easy, while others may need considerably more support. You will need to think about how to stimulate and motivate children when they are learning to read and write and be able to recognise and act on any factors that may affect their progress.

Assessment: You will be assessed by a series of assignments set by your teacher/tutor.

Learning aims

In this unit you will:

A   understand the pre-reading and pre-writing skills that support children's literacy development

B1   understand how to support children's reading development

B2   understand how to support children's writing development

C   understand factors that might affect children's progress in literacy.

I had always thought of learning to read and write as a straightforward process, something that just happens to you as you get to school age and are ready. I have never really considered before all the different factors that need to come together in order for it to happen. I have found it fascinating to look at the different ways in which children can be supported in the development of these skills and watching as it all comes together.

Maisie, *a student on an early years course*

Promoting Literacy in Children Aged From Four up to Eight Years

20

BTEC Assessment Zone

This table shows what you must do in order to achieve a **Pass**, **Merit** or **Distinction** grade, and where you can find activities to help you.

Assessment criteria		
Pass	Merit	Distinction
Learning aim A: Understand the pre-reading and pre-writing skills that support children's literacy development		
3A.P1 Describe experiences and activities that support pre-reading and pre-writing skills. **Assessment practice 20.1**	**3A.M1** Discuss the role of pre-reading and pre-writing experiences in children's literacy development, using examples. **Assessment practice 20.1**	
3A.P2 Explain the role of a language-rich environment for children's literacy development. **Assessment practice 20.1**		
Learning aim B1: Understand how to support children's reading development **Learning aim B2: Understand how to support children's writing development**		
3B1.P3 Describe different theoretical approaches to helping children to learn to read. **Assessment practice 20.2**	**3B1.M2** Discuss the extent to which different theoretical approaches may help children to learn to read. **Assessment practice 20.2**	**3B.D1** Evaluate the extent to which adults contribute to supporting the literacy development of children aged from four up to eight years. **Assessment practice 20.2**
3B1.P4 I&CT Describe the model of learning to read as outlined within the curriculum framework that is used in the home country. **Assessment practice 20.3**	**3B1.M3** Analyse the role of adults in supporting children aged from four years up to eight years in experiences and activities provided to encourage reading. **Assessment practice 20.4**	
3B1.P5 Describe different experiences and activities used to support children aged from four years up to eight years to read. **Assessment practice 20.4**		
3B1.P6 Explain why it is important to understand the links between learning to read and learning to write. **Assessment practice 20.4**		
3B2.P7 Describe the usual sequence of writing development. **Assessment practice 20.4**	**3B2.M4** Analyse the contribution of adults in supporting the development of children's handwriting. **Assessment practice 20.4**	
3B2.P8 English Explain how different experiences and activities are used to support children aged from four years up to eight years to write. **Assessment practice 20.4**		

continued

Assessment criteria (*continued*)		
Pass	Merit	Distinction
Learning aim C: Understand factors that might affect children's progress in literacy		
3C.P9 Describe different factors that may affect children's literacy development. **Assessment practice 20.5** **3C.P10** Explain how to work with parents to support children's progress in literacy. **Assessment practice 20.5**	**3C.M5** Discuss the extent to which an early years setting works with parents to support children's literacy development. **Assessment practice 20.5**	**3C.D2** Evaluate the contribution of effective support for children's literacy development. **Assessment practice 20.5**

English	English Functional Skills signposting	I&CT	Information and Communication Technology skills signposting

How you will be assessed

This unit will be assessed by a series of internally assessed tasks set by your teacher/tutor. Throughout this unit you will find assessment practice activities that will help you work towards your assessment. Completing these activities will not mean that you have achieved a particular grade, but you will have carried out useful research or preparation that will be relevant when it comes to your final assignment.

In order for you to achieve the tasks in your assignment, it is important that you check you have met all of the Pass grading criteria. You can do this as you work your way through the assignment.

If you are hoping to gain a Merit or Distinction, you should also make sure that you present the information in your assignment in the style that is required by the relevant assessment criterion. For example, Merit criteria will require you to discuss and analyse, and Distinction criteria will require you to evaluate.

The assignment set by your teacher/tutor will consist of a number of tasks designed to meet the criteria in the table. This is likely to consist of a written assignment but may also include activities such as:

- a presentation to peers
- observations
- case studies
- a guidance document.

Getting started

What do you remember about your own experience of learning to read and write? Do you remember being read to as a child or seeing your own parents or carers reading? How were you encouraged in school and what kinds of books were you interested in? Discuss in groups how your experiences might have affected your reading and writing in later life.

A Understand the pre-reading and pre-writing skills that support children's literacy development

Although children do not start to learn to read and write as soon as they are born, they will be starting to develop many of the pre-reading and pre-writing skills that they need from the earliest stages of development. Children will be hearing and tuning into language as they learn to speak, and this in turn will lay the foundation for their literacy skills.

> **Link**
>
> Go to Unit 6 in Student Book 1 to find more information about the skills children need to learn to read and write.

The importance of speech and language

As soon as they are aware of others, babies will be starting to learn to communicate in different ways and pick up cues from those around them. They will gradually learn to tune in to speech through linking sounds with communication, and be able to hear the way in which conversations take place between one person and another.

Speech

Although a high percentage of communication is non-verbal, **speech** is the physical process through which we can instantly pass on our thoughts to others. Listening to speech enables us to hear patterns in language, such as rhyme or alliteration.

Language

Our home **language** or 'mother tongue' is the medium through which we fine-tune our thoughts and communicate them to one another. As children learn language and extend their vocabulary to include more words, they are gradually able to tell us more about their own thoughts and feelings, as well as being able to understand more about the world around them. Language may be written, spoken or signed (for example, sign language).

> **Key terms**
>
> **Language** – the medium through which we talk and communicate.
>
> **Speech** – the physical act of talking and articulating.

Speech and language are therefore crucial to the development of children's literacy skills, as they are the basis for the way in which we start to break down sounds and communicate with one another. Through speech and language, children start to make sense of the world and their own place within it. As children become more aware of the written word and start to share books with adults, they are able to extend their experiences, explore worlds outside their own and talk about new ideas. Stories, songs and nursery or action rhymes will also support the development of children's language skills by helping them to identify patterns and alliteration in preparation for learning to read.

Babies will start to learn basic communication skills from an early age.

In order to emphasise the importance of speech and language, the Early Years Foundation Stage incorporates both under one prime area of learning: communication and language. The following three aspects must be a focus during the early years: listening and attention, understanding and speaking. Literacy falls under a separate, specific area of learning and covers reading and writing skills. In Key Stage 1 (when children are in Year 1), this part of the curriculum is called literacy and is broken down into three areas:

* speaking and listening
* reading
* writing.

Engaging with books and providing a language-rich environment

Young children are naturally curious and will want to pick up books and look at them with adults. It is important to harness this curiosity and encourage them to develop this interest, through reading stories with them and making books an enjoyable experience. This will in turn motivate children to value books and enjoy reading. Both fiction and non-fiction books should be available to children, as they should be exposed to as much variety as possible. You will probably have seen a reading and/or writing area in your setting, and environmental displays and texts at children's level that encourage children to look at print in the environment. It is important that these kinds of areas are pointed out by adults and used as much as possible so that children are able to develop their literacy skills.

Figure 20.1 shows examples of how a setting can promote a language-rich environment.

Research

Look for the different places in your setting that encourage children to be aware of print or to develop their mark-making or writing skills. What kinds of messages are children encouraged to look at in the environment? How does the setting give them opportunities to try out writing for themselves?

Experiences to get children ready to learn to read

In order to be ready to learn to read, children will need to have had different experiences so that books and reading have a context. This means that they should have some understanding of where reading fits in to their world. Many young children will have been given or shown books from a very early age, which will mean that they have started to build up their pre-reading skills. Some may have been to story sessions at a local library. They may also have had plenty of experiences of rhymes, so that they begin to hear patterns in words and can start to be able to predict what comes next. They should also be read to and be given plenty of opportunities for speaking and listening.

It is important, for example, that children look at books with adults and learn how to handle them, and start to understand the way in which we hold a book, and how to turn pages. They will also start to look at the way in which we look at print from left to right and learn that print carries meaning through being read to. Often young children will be able to recite whole pieces of text from books long before being able to read, and will 'correct' adults if they get anything wrong!

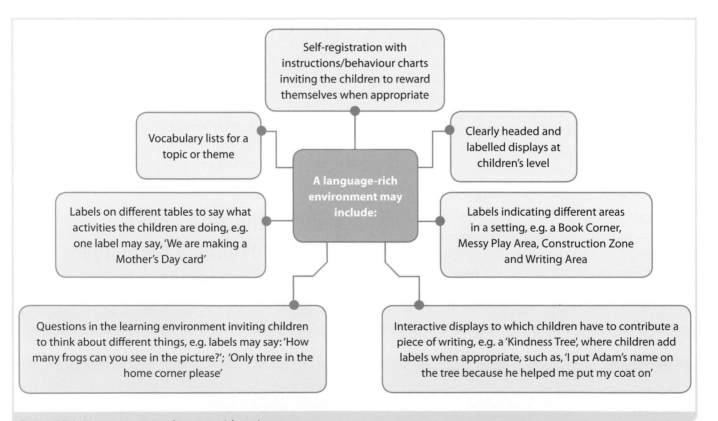

Figure 20.1 How to promote a language-rich environment

In two minutes, make a list of all the 'texts' you might read in a typical day. Using this, see if you can come up with your own definition of reading.

Importance of phonemic awareness

As well as looking at books and starting to pick up on different cues, it is important that young children begin to develop phonemic awareness as they look at and listen to words. This will take place if adults start to point at words and relate the print on the page to the sounds and words that they are saying. They should also be taught to listen for sounds within words as they begin to tune in to speech sounds, for example, through being able to hear alliteration or words starting with the same sound. In this way, children will start to understand that what they are looking at relates to what they are hearing.

3A.P1 | 3A.P2 | 3A.M1

Write a description of some of the different experiences that support the development of young children's pre-reading and pre-writing skills. Discuss the role of pre-reading and pre-writing experiences in children's literacy development, using examples.

Activities to support pre-reading and pre-writing skills

The kinds of activities that support pre-reading and pre-writing skills will be those that you will often see in nurseries and preschools, even if they do not seem to be linked to the process. These activities will, among other things, support the development of children's upper body **gross motor skills**. These kinds of activities are all-important, as they will strengthen the muscles in the upper body and arms so that the child will have more control when they start mark making and writing. **Fine motor skills** will also support children, as they will start to develop

their hand–eye coordination as well as control over their arms and hands.

Pre-reading skills

Pre-reading skills focus around speaking and listening activities, which should take place with young children on a regular basis. These will include activities such as sharing stories and action or nursery rhymes, starting to recognise letter shapes or sounds in the environment (children will often recognise the big 'M' for McDonald's or the name of a favourite shop), matching or sequencing activities, and sharing books with adults.

Pre-writing skills

During children's physical development they will start to become stronger and more skilled in both their fine and gross motor movements, all of which will support their writing skills.

Fine motor skills

Fine motor skills include those used for activities such as threading, cutting, using a knife and fork correctly, using tweezers to pick things up, using play-dough, construction or small-world toys, doing puzzles, or any activities that require fine manipulative skills. Children should also have experience in mark making using different materials and tools such as chalks, paints, brushes, crayons and pencils.

Gross motor skills

Gross motor skills include those used for activities such as throwing and catching, painting, using streamers and hoops, swimming, climbing and any other activities that require children to use upper body strength and develop their shoulder and arm control.

Fine motor skills – control of the smaller muscles, such as those in the fingers, to carry out activities such as threading, using a knife and fork, or holding a pencil.

Gross motor skills – control of the larger muscles, such as those in the arms and legs, to carry out activities such as running, or throwing or kicking a ball.

Activities requiring fine manipulative skills enable children to practise their fine motor skills.

B1 Understand how to support children's reading development

As you are working with children in an early years setting, you will need to know how to support children's reading skills and encourage them to have a love of books.

Theoretical approaches to learning to read

Different theoretical theories and approaches have emerged relating to how children learn to read, and you should have some understanding of these in order to support children effectively. However, before learning to read, it is important that children have been exposed to a language-rich environment and have been able to look at books and share them with adults regularly, as well as taking part in pre-reading

activities. This will form a solid basis for building their reading skills.

The **phonics** approach is based on the breaking down and blending of letters so that children learn to link sounds with individual letters and **phonemes**. The sound system is more complex and inconsistent in English than in other languages as there can be a number of different phonemes to represent the same sound (for example, 'f' and 'ph'). Phonics is therefore used as a method of teaching sounds as it helps us to look at the different letter patterns together, along with their sounds. There are more than 40 different phonemes in spoken English.

There are, however, different phonics methods – synthetic phonics and analytical phonics. Synthetic phonics requires the reader to learn individual

Key terms

Phonemes – the smallest units of sound in a language that help to distinguish one word from another. In the English language, for example, 'p' and 'b' are separate phonemes because they distinguish words such as 'pit' and 'bit'.

Phonics – the name of a method used to teach reading, which breaks down different letter patterns into their individual sounds.

sounds and blends in a particular order, then put them together to form words. The sounds are taught in a particular way, not to sound like the letters – for example, the sound for 't' would be taught as such and not as 'tee' or 'tuh'. The simpler and most commonly used sounds will be the first to be taught, as these are also straightforward (s, a, t, I, p and n). These can then be put together to form many simple three-letter words, which can be sounded out by children from a relatively early stage. In analytical phonics, blends are taught, rather than individual letter sounds, for example, 'sh', 'th' and 'ch', and children are encouraged to learn sets of whole words that have a similar spelling, such as 'cat', 'hat', 'mat', 'fat' and 'bat'. A disadvantage of this system is that many words in English are not written phonetically (for example, 'said', 'know' or 'was') and children will still need to learn these separately.

Another approach to phonics is the whole-language/apprenticeship approach, which has grown from Noam Chomsky's ideas about language acquisition. Chomsky theorised that we all have an innate ability to learn any language and do not learn it through imitating others. In 1967, Ken Goodman had an idea about reading that he thought was similar to Chomsky's theory. He described a system for reading by which learners have to use four different cues in order to decipher the words:

- graphophonemic – the shapes of the letters, and their corresponding sounds
- semantic – what you would expect the word to be, based on the meaning of the sentence so far
- syntactic – what word or phrase would make the most sense, based on the context and grammatical structure of the language – word order, tense and gender
- pragmatic – the function of the text.

The whole-language approach is also sometimes called the 'look and say' approach. It encourages the learner to look at and recognise whole words when learning to read, rather than breaking them down into sounds. In this way, the child will be introduced to high-frequency words such as 'said', 'because', 'they', 'were' and 'who', which do not fit into regular phonic patterns, and although the child may take longer to learn this way, they are less likely to make errors than a child who has learned synthetic phonics.

Theory into practice

Read the text below. Can you answer the questions?

'A frotterpat was losping a ticklepup. A binker wootled. The binker wisped "Frimto" to the frotterpat. The frotterpat mantereed bentistly.'

- What was the frotterpat doing?
- What wootled?
- What did the binker wisp?
- How did the frotterpat manter?

This exercise is based on Chomsky's idea that sentences can be grammatical without making sense and that we can produce new sentences without ever having heard them before. What do you think the implications of this exercise are for supporting children's reading?

Most educationalists agree that a combination of these two main approaches works best, as different children will approach reading in different ways. It is likely that in most settings, although there will be a structured environment for the teaching of reading, you will also find that children are, for example, encouraged to learn high-frequency words as well as learn to sound them out using phonics.

The current model of learning to read

You will need to be aware of the current model of learning to read in the curriculum framework in your own country and how this has an impact on the teaching of reading. At the time of writing, the curriculum is undergoing a period of change and it is possible that this will affect current models. England, for example, has been promoting the synthetic phonics approach through the Primary Literacy Framework since 2006, following trials in Scotland. However, there have been criticisms that a 'one size fits all' approach does not suit all children, and this is also being taken into consideration.

The usual sequence by which children learn to read

Even allowing for the different methods used to teach reading, the sequence by which children learn to read will follow a similar pattern. If children have had a positive experience at the earliest pre-reading stages, they will have learned that print is significant and may also have learned to recognise their own name written down, or a few basic letters and sounds. As they start to have more experience of reading, they will be more aware of the conventions of how to handle and use books, and that text reads from left to right. Children will start to be taught basic letters and sounds, which will support their reading skills and enable them to use the letters in context. There are different schemes and resources available to support the teaching of phonics, and usually these require the child to learn all the letters and sounds quite quickly so that they are able to start to use them. They will then be revised and extended to form blends and whole words, and children will start to build a visual vocabulary of these.

It is important at this stage for children to have as many different cues available to them as possible when reading, for example, pictures that tell the story, and word repetition within the text.

When listening to children read, you should ask them about the text and discuss what they are reading. This may take the form of talking about how a character might be feeling, retelling the story or discussing a point that might be ambiguous within the text. This is because decoding the writing, although important, is only part of reading. As they learn to read, children will also need to develop comprehension skills and be able to relate the text to their own experience to make sense of it.

Choosing appropriate books and activities for children

As we have already discussed, when children are in their earliest years, it is important for them to have a wide range of experiences of books and reading. They will be learning all the time from their environment and from the adults around them. Praise and encouragement are very strong motivators, and will support the child in gaining confidence. Children should also have been exposed to good adult role models so that they can see reading skills being used and the pleasure that can be derived from reading.

During the Foundation Stage, and before children start more 'formal' reading activities, there should be a range of activities available that support the development of pre-reading and reading skills. These may also include letter identification and matching activities, sound snap, small-group story time, story sequencing activities and so on.

All settings should have a wide variety of books available to children so that different interests and abilities are catered for when learning to read. At the very early stages, books should have simple storylines and vocabulary and contain some repetition. Some early pre-reading books will simply consist of pictures in a sequence so that the adult and child can discuss what is happening. Many early reading books also contain rhymes, which make it easier for children to predict words as they come up. Some children will be particularly interested in picture books and stories, while others may prefer non-fiction and information books. It is important, as you get to know children and find out about what interests them, that you are able to support them in choosing appropriate books. Many books will display a suitable age range or ability level in order to help with this. Some settings will insist on children working through a set reading scheme, but others may mix books up so that children experience a variety of different types of text.

The need for adults to be reading role models

It is important for young children to make sense of why they are learning to read and to be able to put this into context. They should have opportunities to see that adults read books for pleasure and to find out information. For this reason, they should have adult role models who read and refer to books as a matter of course. In the setting there may be limited opportunities for this, but they can still be found – for example, when referring to recipes for cooking activities, or when using books to find out information for a particular topic. Adults should draw attention to

the fact that they will need to look at a book to find things out. They may also refer to books that they are reading at home so that children can relate their own reading to adult experiences.

Adults should listen to children read as much as possible in the early stages.

How to listen to children read and give feedback

When listening to children read, it is important to ensure that children know they have your support, while at the same time developing their independence. Figure 20.2 outlines some of the ways you can do this.

As you listen to children read, you will need to support them to develop different strategies that will help them to identify unknown words and make their own guesses or substitutions. In this way, you will be promoting their independent reading.

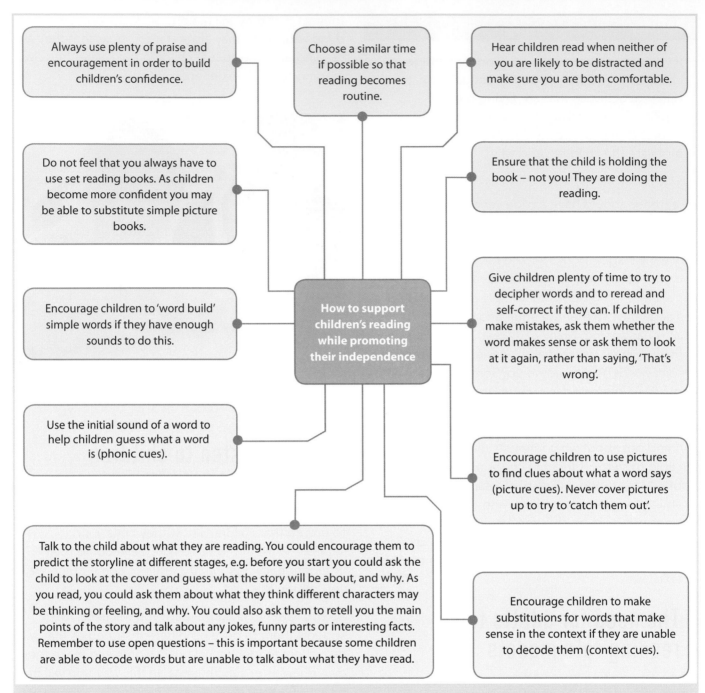

Always use plenty of praise and encouragement in order to build children's confidence.

Choose a similar time if possible so that reading becomes routine.

Hear children read when neither of you are likely to be distracted and make sure you are both comfortable.

Do not feel that you always have to use set reading books. As children become more confident you may be able to substitute simple picture books.

Ensure that the child is holding the book – not you! They are doing the reading.

How to support children's reading while promoting their independence

Encourage children to 'word build' simple words if they have enough sounds to do this.

Give children plenty of time to try to decipher words and to reread and self-correct if they can. If children make mistakes, ask them whether the word makes sense or ask them to look at it again, rather than saying, 'That's wrong'.

Use the initial sound of a word to help children guess what a word is (phonic cues).

Encourage children to use pictures to find clues about what a word says (picture cues). Never cover pictures up to try to 'catch them out'.

Talk to the child about what they are reading. You could encourage them to predict the storyline at different stages, e.g. before you start you could ask the child to look at the cover and guess what the story will be about, and why. As you read, you could ask them about what they think different characters may be thinking or feeling, and why. You could also ask them to retell you the main points of the story and talk about any jokes, funny parts or interesting facts. Remember to use open questions – this is important because some children are able to decode words but are unable to talk about what they have read.

Encourage children to make substitutions for words that make sense in the context if they are unable to decode them (context cues).

Figure 20.2 Ways to support children's reading while also promoting their independence

Having realistic expectations of children

You should always have realistic expectations of children's reading. This means that the kinds of books you are reading with them will need to be at an appropriate level for them to be able to make progress. You should not give children books that will be too challenging for them to read, or expect them to want to read everything that you present to them.

If children who are learning to read are consistently given books that are too difficult or that they do not find stimulating in some way, in terms of subject or content, it is likely that they will be less inclined to want to pick up a book. Some children will prefer to look at non-fiction texts and be less keen on story or picture books, while others may like books by a particular author. Children may be happier reading on some days than on others, and as you get to know them you may be able to identify times that are better for them.

It can be difficult, for example, to listen to them read when you have to ask them to come away from an activity that is particularly holding their interest.

Working with parents and recording progress

Your setting will almost certainly work with parents as much as possible in order to support children's progress in reading. Children should be able to take books home and should also be encouraged to use libraries with their parents. In many settings there will be a reading record or contact book to enable both home and school to write about books they have shared with the child. This record will keep parents updated with children's progress and give further suggestions or ideas for things to work on.

Most early years settings will also have a policy that encourages parents to come in and read with children. This will always be good for children as it enables them to see the setting working in partnership with the home, as well as giving them the benefit of having more adults to share books with. In larger settings there may be reading or book weeks, where children are encouraged to dress up as favourite characters. In settings with a high proportion of children from different cultures, it is important for parents to come in and work with staff, perhaps telling stories and reciting songs, or sharing experiences with children.

Figure 20.3 shows an example of a children's reading record being used both in the setting and at home.

As children become more experienced readers, they may record their own progress and start to write about what they have enjoyed reading, although adults in the setting should check these records regularly.

Date	Book	Comment
22nd April	The Red House	Great reading from Emily today. Really sounding out unknown words and making good attempts to self-correct. Try to focus at home on following the text with her finger to ensure she is able to stay focused on what she is reading. (Miss B)
23rd April	Something in the Park	Emily tried hard to follow with her finger and read the whole book but please can we have it again tomorrow as she was tired and we were not able to discuss. (Mum)
24th April	Something in the Park	Emily read well and was able to remember some of the words she has learned in her spellings (was, said). Good reading and discussion today about the story. (Miss B)
25th April	A Treat for Rosie	Emily loved this book! She enjoyed talking about Rosie's treat. She also read the book again to Nanna and Grandad. (Mum)

Figure 20.3 An example of part of a child's reading record showing comments from both teacher and parent

B2 Understand how to support children's writing development

Children in schools and early years settings will be learning to read and write at around the same time. It is important to remember that learning to read and learning to write are interrelated and that children will need to have a wide range of literacy experiences in order to support the development of each.

The link between learning to write and learning to read

Research has shown that children who read more will become better writers because they will have a wide experience of different types of text.

While reading is the way in which we find out about the world and different situations, writing is the way in which we ourselves pass on information and transfer our ideas to others in different ways. You will need to be able to encourage and motivate children who are in the earliest stages of reading and writing in order to develop their confidence.

The importance of having realistic expectations

Some children make reasonably quick progress when learning sounds and developing a reading vocabulary, but others will find this more challenging and will take longer. Learning to write is more complex as it incorporates more skills, and you will need to have realistic expectations of what children are able to achieve. Remember that every child is unique and will have strengths and experiences in different areas. For example, some children may find it very difficult to remember the spellings of their key words, or be able to put down their ideas in an organised way, while others may find forming the letters themselves more of a challenge. Learning activities may also focus on one particular area, for example, full stops and capital letters, and children will often forget other aspects of writing when concentrating on that area. It is important that as practitioners we focus on what children are able to do rather than what they are not, in order to develop their confidence, rather than expecting them to achieve in all areas at all times.

Development of handwriting skills

From the earliest stages, children will be starting to develop their handwriting skills through activities that promote hand–eye coordination and strengthen their hand muscles. They should be given plenty of opportunities to develop their fine motor skills through using different media such as brushes, pegs, tweezers, threading or mark making. They should also be developing gross motor movements in their upper body so that they have the strength needed in their shoulders to be able to write. At this stage, you could be looking out to see whether the child has developed a preference for using a particular hand and support their development of an efficient pencil grip, although children of 2 to 3 years may still be using a **palmar grip**. Chunky pencils and other writing media are available to help with this, as well as pencil grips that fit normal-sized pencils. Although a tripod grip is best, with three fingers on the pencil, there may be variations on this, and left-handed children in particular may find different grips easier.

Key term

Palmar grip – holding an object with the palm of the hand.

Older children who are at a later stage of writing development will need to learn to think about how to sit correctly when writing as well as how to hold the pencil correctly. They will need to have support with the basics of letter formation in the earliest stages of writing. In some settings, joined writing may be taught straight away. Though this may make it easier later on (by the end of Year 2, children should have clear joined handwriting), in the earliest stages it will take them slightly longer to learn.

The usual sequence by which children learn to write

When learning to write, children will usually pass through different stages as they become more skilled at forming letters and developing ideas. In the earliest stages, they may focus on forming letters and being able to talk about what they have written, and this will gradually develop into being able to word-build and write longer sentences (see Figure 20.4).

The importance of a supportive environment

For children to develop writing skills, they will need to be provided with a supportive environment. This means that they should have stimulation and resources available when their skills are developing. These may include:

- environmental print – for example, displays with captions and information, key words, clearly labelled areas within and outside the setting in all areas of the learning environment
- dictionaries and topic-based word banks
- adult role models so that children can see the purpose of writing
- a variety of clearly labelled materials and writing areas available so that children can use them to write for their own purposes.

Reflect

Look at your own setting. What kinds of examples does it provide of a supportive environment for the development of writing skills?

Motivating children to write for a purpose

During the Foundation Stage, children should be provided with opportunities to develop their pre-writing and writing skills, through activities that encourage them to strengthen and develop their muscle control. They should also be given a variety of media with which to make marks as they start to experiment with this. You should ensure that you talk to children about what the marks mean, so that they start to make links between speech and writing. These kinds of experiences may include:

- making marks in shaving foam, sand, cornflour and water and dried rice
- practising using different media such as pens, brushes and water
- using sponges or play-dough to strengthen hand muscles
- threading, sewing and using tweezers to develop fine motor control.

Children should be given opportunities to strengthen their muscle control and make marks.

As their control develops, children at this stage should be given opportunities to write for a purpose through play activities – for example, writing appointments in a diary in a role-play area that is a doctor's surgery, or keeping shopping lists. Although they may still be mark making, their writing will have a clear purpose and they will be able to tell you about it. They may also start to practise being able to write their own name.

1 In the earliest stages, children will start to form strings of letters to represent words.

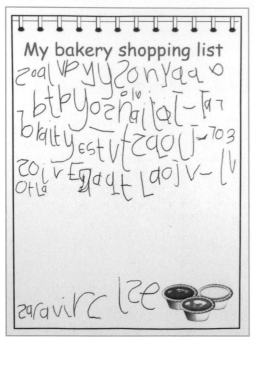

2 Children will start to be able to hear and write individual letter sounds within words – this will usually be the first and last letter of the word.

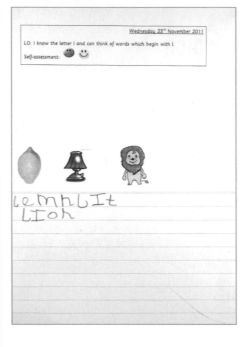

3 Children will start to be able to hear and write several sounds within a word, although letters may not all be correctly formed and spaced out.

4 Words will become spaced out and letters correctly formed with some punctuation. Children may start to use joins if they have not done so from the start.

5 As well as continuing to work on punctuation and presentation, the content of children's work will become more involved as they start to use more adventurous and descriptive language.

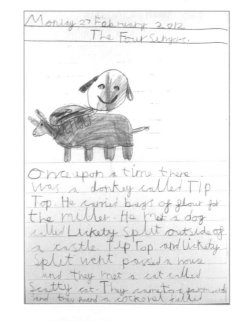

Figure 20.4 Examples of emerging writing skills

As children get older and go through Key Stage 1, they will start to work on more whole-class 'taught' and structured activities with their writing, prior to working independently. They will work on the development of identifying letters and sounds, and start to put together simple c-v-c (consonant-vowel-consonant) words such as 'cat' and 'hen'. As they start to develop, they may carry out shared and guided writing activities.

In shared writing, children work as a class or group to compose pieces of work, and discuss language, punctuation and grammar as part of the process. Teachers work through the different aspects of writing to enable children to structure and formulate their work while focusing on technical and phonic knowledge. This may be carried out two or three times a week, and the teacher will act as a scribe for children's ideas.

In guided writing, children are grouped, and have more ownership of their work. This is designed to complement shared writing and to act as a link between shared and independent work. Adults may work with children of similar ability to support the development of specific targets or objectives. During guided writing, children will also receive more directed support to help them to develop their own ideas.

Writing itself is a complex process. For this reason, many children will find it harder as they start to be aware of what they need to do, as they will need to take so many different things into account. Figure 20.5 shows the things children will need to think about when learning to write.

As children develop their independent writing, they may need varying levels of support. They will need to have a clear idea of what they have been asked to do and have support prompts available to help them, such as environmental print. As they become more confident, they will be able to concentrate more on the development of ideas.

As children start to learn to write, there are often so many things for them to remember that at times it can seem an impossible task. Depending on the age of the children with whom you are working, you should always praise and encourage them as much as possible. If they show you something they have written, take time to listen to them and let them tell you about it.

Supporting left-handed children

Children who are left-handed may need more support than their right-handed peers. You should make sure you are aware of left-handed children and give them additional attention when they are carrying out activities such as starting mark making, developing their writing skills or using scissors. When left-handed people write they may have a more 'awkward' pencil grip – so when they are starting to write and make marks, encourage them to find a grip that is comfortable, but make sure you support them. It can be difficult for them on a practical level, particularly if they are sitting next to a right-hander who is also trying to write, as they may be constantly knocking into one another. There are resources available to support left-handers such as scissors and easy-grip pens, and for older children, rulers that read from right to left.

Figure 20.5 Skills involved in writing

Did you know? ?

The lefthandedchildren.org website offers suggestions and resources for left-handed children. This is a useful resource if you have left-handed children in your setting. To access this website go to www.pearsonhotlinks.co.uk and search for this title.

Scribing for children

In the earlier stages of writing, children may sometimes practise writing through making anti-clockwise rotational marks on a page or learning that we start to write taller letters at the top. In some settings they may trace over lines or letters in order to support the development of their handwriting skills and encourage them to be accurate. There may also be times when children need adults to act as a **scribe** for them, for example, as described in shared writing activities, or for individual children when they are starting to learn to write, or if they have special educational needs that make pencil control more difficult. Some children who lack confidence in their writing like to copy beneath a line written by an adult, although this method should not be used too often as they can become reliant on it.

Key term

Scribe – an adult who writes down what a child would like to say.

Theory into practice

Is scribing used in your setting? How regularly do children write independently and how much of this kind of support are they given?

Assessment practice 20.4

| 3B1.P5 | 3B1.P6 | 3B1.M3 |
| 3B2.P7 | 3B2.P8 | 3B2.M4 |

Write a case study about a child whom you are supporting in learning to read and write. What experiences and activities have you provided in order to encourage the child to read and write, and why is it important to understand the links between the two? Providing examples of the child's writing from the earliest stages, describe the usual sequence of writing development and show how the child has passed through these. How do you see your own role in providing appropriate experiences and activities to support reading and writing?

C Understand factors that might affect children's progress in literacy

Why do some children learn to read and write more quickly than others? Although there will always be children who just seem to pick things up more quickly, there may also be particular reasons for children making slower progress than their peers.

Factors that may affect children's progress in literacy

Children's progress in literacy may be affected by a number of different factors and it is important for you to be aware of these so that you are able to put measures in place to support them. These factors may include the following.

- **Poor self-esteem**

Some children may have very poor self-esteem and think that they will not be able to read or write, or have been told that they will not be able to. If not caught early, this can be an ongoing problem.

- **Frustration**

Children may feel that they cannot read or write perfectly straight away and become frustrated as a result or give up. Some children are perfectionists and may feel unable to carry on if they are not able to do it right the first time. It is important to establish a culture in which it is not a problem to make mistakes – this is how we learn.

- **Early intervention**

If children have issues that may affect their progress, it is vital that measures are put in place as soon as possible to ensure that they can be resolved. For example, in the case of poor self-esteem, practitioners will need to find opportunities to praise children as much as they can for effort as well as achievement.

- **Speaking English as an additional language**

In some cases, children who speak English as an additional language may not make progress as rapidly as their peers, as they will have learned different sound systems. However, they should start to make progress as they learn the language, and this should happen fairly quickly.

Case study

Supporting progress with writing

Chris is in Year 2 and loves reading but finds writing challenging. He will spend a long time avoiding settling down to his task, for example, sharpening his pencil, talking to his partner or asking for spellings. When he does write, his focus of attention is very short and he is unable to maintain concentration for very long. When he is writing he spends a lot of time rubbing out what he has written because he has forgotten to use a capital letter in the correct place, or because he realises that he has spelled a word wrongly. He regularly says that he does not like writing and is not very good.

- Why might Chris's progress in literacy be affected, even though he is trying to remember what he has been taught?
- Can you think of strategies that you could put in place to support him?

Reasons for children not making expected progress

As children learn to read and write, there may be a number of reasons for them not making the expected level of progress for their age and stage of development. These include if the child has:

- conductive hearing loss
- sight problems
- specific learning difficulties.

Being in a poor language environment and having insufficient input and support from adults are also reasons why children may not make expected progress.

As you get to know children of different ages and stages, you will get to know their levels of ability and how much they are likely to progress over time. However, if a child is not making expected progress despite support from adults, this may be due to a specific health or special need, or to an environmental issue. In this case, you may need to speak to parents and refer to colleagues as well as the SENCO so that the child can be monitored more closely and targets put in place.

Factors affecting parental involvement

You are likely to find that parents are involved to a different extent in supporting their children's reading and writing skills. While some will provide maximum support for their child, there will be others who seem to be unable to support their children's progress. This may be for a number of reasons.

- **Poor literacy skills**

Parents may themselves have poor skills and feel unable to give enough support to their children.

- **Low self-esteem**

Parents may not feel that they have enough experience of reading or know enough about what to do.

- **Limited interaction**

Parents may for whatever reason not have had a great deal of interaction with people, or be limited to a small community. This in turn may affect their ability to give wider experience to their children.

- **Poor experience**

They may themselves have had a poor experience of learning to read and write. Some parents may have not been well supported in learning to read and write or may not have had a good learning environment, or may have left school very young. This will mean that in some cases there will be avoidance of or even hostility towards interactions with early years staff.

In many cases, parents in these situations will not feel confident enough to seek help. In your school or early years setting, there may need to be advice and opportunities available, ranging from leaflets and notices to meetings put on by the school or setting to guide and advise parents about how to support their children with reading and writing.

How to work with parents to support children's progress

It is important for you to be able to work with parents when children are learning to read and write, and for there to be regular contact between parents and the setting. Some parents will lack confidence or need to have some support in how to encourage their child's literacy development, and all parents will need to be kept up to date and involved with their children's progress. You can do this in a number of ways:

- Make sure all children are encouraged to take a variety of books home.
- Encourage parents to use reading record books and to write about books shared with the child.
- Ensure that parents understand the importance of other physical skills and how they relate to writing.
- Encourage children to write messages for parents.
- Provide opportunities for parents to work on handwriting skills and spellings with children.

Assessment practice 20.5   3C.P9 | 3C.P10 | 3C.M5 | 3C.D2

What are the kinds of factors that might affect children's progress in literacy?

Explain and discuss how settings might work with parents to support children's progress in literacy. You may choose to do this in the form of interviews and case studies. Evaluate the contribution of effective support to supporting children's literacy development.

Further reading and resources

Letters and Sounds (DFES-00281-2007) This is a government document produced through the Primary National Strategy, which starts in the Foundation Stage and builds up through the different stages.

Goodman, K. S. (1976) 'Reading: a Psycholinguistic Guessing Game' in H. Singer and R. B. Ruddell (eds.), *Theoretical Models and Processes of Reading*, Newark, Delaware: International Reading Association.

Rose, J. (2006) *The Independent Review of the Teaching of Early Reading* (DFES-0201-2006).

Smith, F. (1984) *Reading*, Cambridge: Cambridge University Press.

Wray, D. and Lewis, M. *From Learning to Teaching: Towards a Model of Teaching Literacy* (www.warwick.ac.uk).

Websites

National Literacy Trust: www.literacytrust.org.uk Advice, resources and case studies.

Mr Thorne Does Phonics: www.mrthorne.com Lots of very useful ideas and clips for supporting the teaching of synthetic phonics. Many of these are also available on YouTube.

The Primary National Strategy for Literacy has now been archived but is still available online: www.education.gov.uk/schools/toolsandinitiatives/nationalstrategies

Ready for work?

Wen Lui Teaching assistant

I have been working at St Mary's School for about six months, after working in their preschool for three years. I am based in the reception class but also spend two afternoons in Year 1. It has been interesting, having come from a preschool, to see how the reading and writing skills that children have developed in nursery are carried on when they are in reception and Year 1. I have always worked with the younger age group as I enjoy seeing the amount of progress that is made during the Foundation Stage.

A good understanding of how children learn to read and write is so important. As part of my foundation degree in early years, I had to research the different theories of learning to read, which has been really useful. Reading and writing is the key to much of children's learning, so we need to build on their pre-reading and writing skills so that they begin to learn to read and write.

Knowing about the different stages of learning to read and write also helps us to identify those children who are having difficulties, so that we are able to put in measures to support them as soon as possible. Although all children are different and learn at different rates, I am always amazed when things click into place and they start to make real progress.

Skills for practice

Support literacy

Practise doing the following things relating to the promotion of children's literacy.

- When you share books with children use this as an opportunity to talk and develop your relationship with them.
- Pre-reading and pre-writing skills – use opportunities to develop children's strength in their arms and body as well as fine motor skills.
- Use environmental print, label and annotate displays, and make sure that children have a rich learning environment.
- Give children time and repeat back a word correctly if they are wrong, rather than telling them it is incorrect.

- Remember that rhymes and songs also support literacy skills.
- Use props from time to time when sharing stories with children to bring books to life.
- Encourage children to write by giving them specific topics to write about.
- Create writing areas with access to a variety of things to write with and on.
- Have different word lists available for children to refer to.
- Keep up to date with observations and records.

Introduction

The Early Years Foundation Stage (EYFS) is the statutory framework for practitioners in England, which covers the curriculum, development and welfare requirements for children up to the age of 5 years. If you are working with this age group, you will need to have a firm understanding of its principles, structure and requirements, and the rationale behind each of the areas of learning. You should also know how to plan for play and activities that are both adult directed and child initiated that support children's progress towards the early learning goals at the end of the EYFS. In this way, you will be able to ensure that you meet the needs of all the children in your setting and enable them to reach their full potential.

Assessment: You will be assessed by a series of assignments set by your teacher/tutor.

Learning aims

In this unit you will:

A1 understand the structure of the Early Years Foundation Stage

A2 understand the principles of the Early Years Foundation Stage

B1 understand the safeguarding and welfare requirements within the Early Years Foundation Stage

B2 understand the education programme within the Early Years Foundation Stage

C   be able to plan play and activities that support children's progress towards Early Years Foundation Stage outcomes.

The early years are a very important time, and all children should be given the opportunity to develop their skills through play and structured activities that extend their learning and encourage them to be independent. The Early Years Foundation Stage gives practitioners the framework within which to do this. It is a wonderful age group to work with, as these young children will be discovering so much about the world and their place within it.

Anita Tempora, *nursery manager*

Implementing the Early Years Foundation Stage in England

22

BTEC
Assessment Zone

This table shows what you must do in order to achieve a **Pass**, **Merit** or **Distinction** grade, and where you can find activities to help you.

Assessment criteria		
Pass	**Merit**	**Distinction**
Learning aim A1: Understand the structure of the Early Years Foundation Stage **Learning aim A2: Understand the principles of the Early Years Foundation Stage**		
3A1.P1 Summarise the scope, legal status and structure of the Early Years Foundation Stage. **Assessment practice 22.1**	**3A1.M1** Discuss, using examples, how children may benefit from the Early Years Foundation Stage. **Assessment practice 22.2**	**3A.D1** Evaluate the potential impact of the Early Years Foundation Stage on outcomes for children. **Assessment practice 22.2**
3A1.P2 Describe how delivery of the Early Years Foundation Stage is inspected. **Assessment practice 22.1**		
3A1.P3 Explain the aims of the Early Years Foundation Stage. **Assessment practice 22.1**		
3A1.P4 Explain the requirements for the assessment of children's progress in the Early Years Foundation Stage. **Assessment practice 22.1**		
3A2.P5 English Explain the principles and themes of the Early Years Foundation Stage. **Assessment practice 22.3**	**3A2.M2** Analyse how the principles of the Early Years Foundation Stage shape practice in early years settings, using examples. **Assessment practice 22.3**	
3A2.P6 Explain, using examples from early years settings, how to apply the principles of the Early Years Foundation Stage to practice. **Assessment practice 22.3**		
Learning aim B1: Understand the safeguarding and welfare requirements within the Early Years Foundation Stage **Learning aim B2: Understand the education programme within the Early Years Foundation Stage**		
3B1.P7 Describe the scope of policies required by early years settings to meet the safeguarding and welfare requirements of the Early Years Foundation Stage. **Assessment practice 22.4**	**3B1.M3** Discuss how specific policies contribute to meeting the safeguarding and welfare requirements of the Early Years Foundation Stage. **Assessment practice 22.4**	**3B1.D2** Evaluate the extent to which the safeguarding and welfare requirements complement the education programme in the Early Years Foundation Stage. **Assessment practice 22.5**

continued

Assessment criteria (continued)

Pass	Merit	Distinction
3B2.P8 Describe the scope of each of the areas of learning in the Early Years Foundation Stage. **Assessment practice 22.5**	**3B2.M4** Discuss, using examples, ways in which areas of learning can be interrelated in play activities. **Assessment practice 22.5**	
3B2.P9 Explain how play activities may provide opportunities for several areas of learning. **Assessment practice 22.5**		
3B2.P10 Explain the reasons for balancing adult-led and child-initiated activities. **Assessment practice 22.6**		

Learning aim C: Be able to plan play and activities that support children's progress towards Early Years Foundation Stage outcomes

Pass	Merit	Distinction
3C.P11 **I&CT** Develop plans for play and activities which meet a child's needs and interests to support progress towards early learning goals, to include: • adult-led activities • child-initiated activities. **Assessment practice 22.7**	**3C.M5** Analyse the extent to which the planned play and activities provide a balance of adult-led and child-initiated activities. **Assessment practice 22.7**	**3C.D3** Evaluate the potential impact of the plans in supporting the child's progress towards early learning goals. **Assessment practice 22.7**
3C.P12 **I&CT** Explain how the planned play and activities aim to support the child's progress in areas of learning. **Assessment practice 22.7**		

English   English Functional Skills signposting   **I&CT**   Information and Communication Technology skills signposting

How you will be assessed

This unit will be assessed by a series of internally assessed tasks set by your teacher/tutor. Throughout this unit you will find assessment practice activities that will help you work towards your assessment. Completing these activities will not mean that you have achieved a particular grade, but you will have carried out useful research or preparation that will be relevant when it comes to your final assignment.

In order for you to achieve the tasks in your assignment, it is important that you check you have met all of the Pass grading criteria. You can do this as you work your way through the assignment.

If you are hoping to gain a Merit or Distinction, you should also make sure that you present the information in your assignment in the style that is required by the relevant assessment criterion. For example, Merit criteria will require you to discuss and analyse, and Distinction criteria will require you to evaluate.

The assignment set by your teacher/tutor will consist of a number of tasks designed to meet the criteria in the table. This is likely to consist of a written assignment but may also include activities such as:

• a reference document
• case studies
• a series of observations or examples from practice.

Getting started

Take a few minutes to write a brief account of what you know already about the EYFS – why it was introduced, its structure, the curriculum itself and how and when children are assessed. Share this with a partner and compare your understanding.

A1 Understand the structure of the Early Years Foundation Stage

If you are working with children in the early years and following the EYFS, you will need to know and understand in detail its structure and scope. Taking its basis from the Childcare Act of 2006, the Early Years Foundation Stage is a statutory framework, which was introduced in 2008 with the aim of improving outcomes for children in the early years and setting the standard for all early years providers.

Scope and status of the EYFS

The EYFS is made up of the curriculum, which includes the learning and development requirements, as well as specific safeguarding and welfare requirements. The EYFS has recently been reviewed and reformed, with a new EYFS coming into place in September 2012. It is important for Early Years providers to understand the legal status of the Early Years Foundation Stage as it applies to a range of settings and providers in England – those caring for children from birth to the end of the academic year in which they have their fifth birthday. The EYFS documentation defines these settings as all Ofsted-registered providers on the Early Years Register, which will include childminders, nurseries and preschools, as well as all schools in England that are attended by young children.

Activity

Before you start your work on this unit, make sure you read and are familiar with the EYFS documentation, particularly the new arrangements for 2012 if you are an existing practitioner. You should have the opportunity to take part in training sessions to ensure that your setting meets the new requirements.

Overall structure of EYFS

The EYFS is structured in such a way that it is broken down into three sections: learning and development requirements, assessment, and welfare and safeguarding requirements. These sections should be set out as follows.

Learning and development requirements

The learning and development requirements comprised three areas.

- The educational programmes and curriculum, which must cover seven areas of learning (from September 2012).
- The early learning goals, which are a summary of the knowledge and skills in each area that children should have at the end of the Foundation Stage.
- The assessment requirements, which set out how and when children's achievements must be assessed and how these should be reported.

The educational programme and curriculum

The educational programme and curriculum of the EYFS are set out within a framework of seven areas of learning. The requirements describe how settings should promote the learning and development of children in their care, so that they are 'school ready' and able to move into reception and Year 1. Figure 22.1 shows the seven areas of learning.

Each of the seven areas will be subdivided, for example, literacy will be divided into reading and writing, and mathematics into numbers and shape, space and measures.

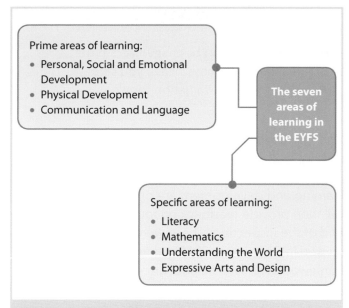

Figure 22.1 The seven areas of learning in the EYFS

The early learning goals

The early learning goals are designed to show where each child should be in each area of learning at the end of the Early Years Foundation Stage. For example, under reading, the early learning goal reads: 'Children read and understand simple sentences in stories and information books, using phonic knowledge to decode regular words and read them aloud accurately. They demonstrate understanding when talking with others about what they have read, or what has been read to them.' There are 17 early learning goals in total.

Assessment requirements

Assessment requirements may be ongoing (**formative assessment**) or structured (**summative assessment**). This means that assessment will take place throughout the Early Years Foundation Stage, but that children will also be assessed at two specific points, at between 2 and 3 years and again at the end of the final term of the year when the child reaches 5 years. This is known as the Early Years Foundation Stage Profile (EYFSP). Children aged between 2 and 3 years will only be assessed in the three prime areas.

Safeguarding and welfare requirements

Early years providers will need to take steps to ensure that all children in their care are kept safe and well. They should create settings that are welcoming and safe so that children are able to enjoy their learning.

The areas covered under safeguarding and welfare requirements include:

- safeguarding children and promoting their welfare
- promoting good health
- managing behaviour
- checking the suitability of adults who have contact with children
- checking qualifications, skills and knowledge of staff
- staff-to-child ratios
- ensuring that the facilities are safe and secure and meet health and safety requirements
- maintaining records, policies and procedures.

Theory into practice

Look at the policies and procedures in your setting for meeting the safeguarding and welfare requirements. How does the setting monitor whether each of these areas is being met?

The learning and welfare requirements are also based on four overarching principles that should influence all areas of practice in early years settings. Practitioners will need to bear all of these in mind when working with children so that they can ensure they adhere to them. These are that:

- every child is unique
- children learn to be strong and independent through positive relationships
- children should be provided with a positive environment
- children learn and develop in different ways and at different rates.

Key terms

Formative assessment – assessment that takes place during the learning process, or 'assessment for learning'.

Summative assessment – assessment of what the child knows and can do at the end of a period of learning, or 'assessment of learning'.

How settings are inspected

Providers who are registered on the Early Years or Childcare Register, whether early years or childcare providers, or childminders, will need to follow the framework of the Early Years Foundation Stage. This means that they must meet the legal requirements of the Childcare Act 2006 in order to remain registered, as well as the learning and development requirements. Early years and childcare settings will be regularly inspected (every three to four years) as part of the Ofsted framework, to look at how well they meet the requirements of the Early Years or Childcare Register and the standards of the EYFS. It is likely that the setting will be given a few days' notice of an inspection, and parents will need to be informed.

As part of the inspection process, inspectors will ask to see the setting's **self-evaluation form**. Managers should complete this form with staff on a regular basis to ensure that they are looking at the quality of provision and how well they are meeting the needs of the children and improving outcomes for them.

Key term

Self-evaluation form – a form that settings fill out on a regular basis showing how they intend to review and improve their provision.

The self-evaluation form also gives guidance on the kinds of questions that inspectors will ask providers when looking at the quality of provision in the setting. Ofsted recommend that settings complete the form thoroughly as it will give them some idea about the aspects they think are working well, and those that they are working towards improving.

Did you know?

The self-evaluation form is now available to view online on the Ofsted website. To find the form, search under 'Early Years online self-evaluation' or alternatively you can download the form by going to www.pearsonhotlinks.co.uk and searching for this title.

Theory into practice

How much have you been involved in the self-evaluation process? Have you seen your setting's self-evaluation form?

Inspectors will also carry out observations at the setting, look at paperwork, interview staff, parents and children, and assess how well children's learning and development are progressing. They will then provide feedback on four areas at the end of the inspection. These were reviewed and revised in September 2012 in line with the new EYFS framework. The final inspection report will include information on:

- outcomes for children in the EYFS
- quality and standards of the early years provision, including –
  - the role of the practitioner in supporting children's learning and development
  - the effectiveness of care practices in helping children to feel emotionally secure and develop independence
- leadership and management of the early years provision
- overall effectiveness of the early years provision in meeting the needs of the children who attend.

Each of these areas will be given a grade. At the time of writing, these grades are:

- grade 1 (outstanding)
- grade 2 (good)
- grade 3 (requires improvement)
- grade 4 (requires significant improvement or enforcement).

All inspections will be published on the Ofsted website so that the process is transparent and parents, carers or others are able to view the results.

As part of the inspection process, practitioners will also need to provide information to Ofsted, including the type of setting, the number of children and the number of hours for which childcare is provided. Inspectors will check that settings are meeting a number of requirements including those shown in Figure 22.2.

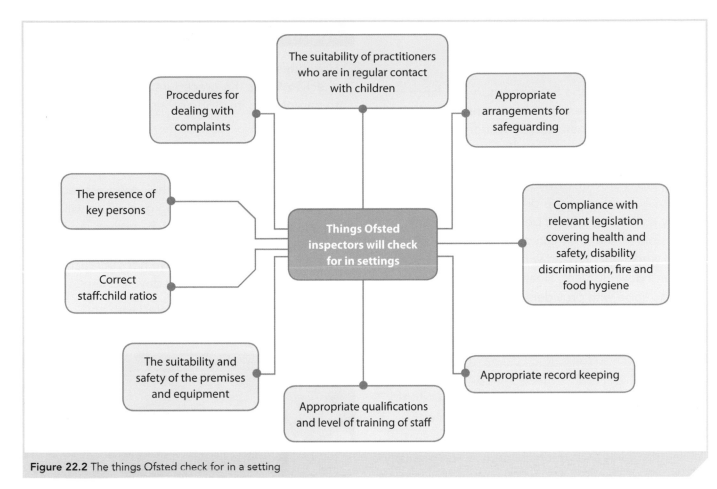

Figure 22.2 The things Ofsted check for in a setting

Theory into practice

Ofsted publishes inspection reports on their website. You can access these reports and the Ofsted website by going to www.pearsonhotlinks.co.uk and searching for this title.

Find the last report for your setting.

1 How has the report impacted on practice in the setting?

2 What development points, if any, still need to be addressed in the setting?

As they are legal requirements, the Ofsted inspection itself will assess all aspects of the setting under these headings, checking paperwork and looking at all statutory requirements. Settings can apply to have exemption from some aspects of the requirements, for example, if an individual child's family has a religious or philosophical view that is in conflict with the learning and development requirements, or if the setting is unable to meet fully the learning and development requirements due to temporary restrictions in their facilities. However, no setting may be exempted from the welfare requirements for any reason, as these requirements deal with child safety.

Activity

The Ofsted requirements are outlined in a guidance document called 'Requirements for the Childcare Register'.

In groups, download the document and choose one of the headings to focus on. You can download the document by going to www.pearsonhotlinks.co.uk and searching for this title.

1 Look at the requirements under your chosen heading. Are you aware that all of them are being carried out in your setting?

2 How could you ensure that all staff in your setting are clear about what they need to do in order to meet Ofsted requirements?

3 Present your findings to the class.

Assessment of children's development

The second part of the EYFS statutory guidance is devoted to assessment. It is important for parents, healthcare practitioners and educationalists that we regularly check children's development, particularly during their earliest years. This is because it is a time of such rapid growth, physically, emotionally and in terms of general cognitive development, that if there are any issues they should be picked up as early as possible so that they can be addressed. Parents should work hand in hand with the setting to monitor children's development. Healthcare professionals may also liaise with providers, particularly if there is an issue that adults in the setting are able to support.

Reflect

How does your setting work with parents to ensure that children are assessed and monitored throughout the Early Years Foundation Stage?

Although babies and young children will be regularly checked and monitored by healthcare professionals, issues that a baby or young child may have might not be picked up straight away, for example, any problems in hearing. It is important to look out for signs that indicate that young children may need additional support. For this reason, assessment in the early years will need to be ongoing, as well as summative.

At the 2.5-year check, children's progress in the prime areas (personal, social and emotional development, physical development, and communication and language) will be reviewed by practitioners. Parents and carers will then be given a short summary of their child's development in these areas, and will be asked to share this with other professionals, for example, health visitors or teachers if they are moving to a school-based nursery, as it will coincide with the child's health and development review. This will include observations about a child's progress as well as any concerns. If there are any areas where a child is not making expected progress, the provider should set out a plan showing how the child's future learning and development will be addressed by the setting, and showing how professionals will work together to share information. Parents will also be advised on how to support their child's learning at home.

Activity

How does your setting carry out the 2.5-year check? What is the procedure for reporting back to parents and involving other professionals if necessary?

At the end of the Early Years Foundation Stage, all children will be assessed and their progress recorded in line with the 17 early learning goals. This will be in the final term of the year in which children are 5 years old. Early years settings must state whether children have met, are exceeding or have not yet reached the expected level of learning and development.

These profiles must also be shared with and explained to parents and to the local authority.

What area(s) of learning could these children be working on?

The aims of the EYFS

As you will be working to the EYFS, you should be clear about its aims and purpose. Its overarching aim is to help all children to achieve the five outcomes under Help Children Achieve More. These outcomes are staying safe, being healthy, enjoying and achieving, making a positive contribution, and achieving economic well-being. Help Children Achieve More (originally Every Child Matters) was designed to ensure that professionals working together are able to effectively support children by working together in a multidisciplinary way. It is important that everyone working with young children is able to support each child to meet these five outcomes as far as possible.

In addition to this, the aims of the EYFS are:

- to ensure that provision is consistent across early years settings, so that each child makes good progress and is ready for school
- to provide a firm foundation for school through learning opportunities that are planned around the needs and interests of the individual child, which are regularly assessed and reviewed
- to provide equal opportunities for every child before they start school and ensure that every child is included and supported
- to ensure that all children in a setting are safe and are protected from harm
- to support partnerships between professionals, parents and early years settings.

As well as having detailed planning and assessment documentation, settings will also need to show that they are meeting the aims of the EYFS in all areas of their practice.

Terminology

The terminology used in the EYFS documentation can be confusing if you are not completely clear on the different areas. At the time of writing, new documentation is being produced that may influence the terminology applied in the EYFS. It is important that you are able to distinguish the terminology and know where to find it in the documentation so that you understand its purpose.

The statutory guidance

The statutory framework is the most important part of the documentation as it sets out the legal requirements of the EYFS and its overall structure. It is divided into:

- the learning and development requirements – these set out the different areas of learning as well as the early learning goals within each aspect
- the legal requirements relating to safeguarding and welfare.

The specific legal requirements

These are part of the statutory guidance document and outline what your setting is legally required to do under the EYFS to ensure the safety and well-being of children. They are specific to children. In other words, you will need to make sure that these are being met at all times and in different areas within each of the safeguarding and welfare requirements. For example, the specific legal requirements for outings are that a risk assessment must be carried out prior to taking the children on a trip and that they must be kept safe. As well as the safeguarding and welfare requirements, settings will also have other more general legal requirements – for example, health and safety at work, disability discrimination and so on.

The practice guidance

The practice guidance is non-statutory – that is, you do not have to follow it. However, it is useful and gives different ideas and suggestions to support practitioners in delivering the EYFS. If you look through the practice guidance, you will find that it is divided into different sections.

The first of these outlines general guidelines for implementing the EYFS, including how the different documentation is set out and general points on providing effective provision for children.

The second section provides an overview of the seven areas of learning and development and their different aspects, and is structured to show the progress that each child is expected to make within these as well as the Early Learning Goals.

The third section sets out the welfare requirements but gives more detail and information than the statutory guidance document on how providers might meet the legal requirements.

Assessment practice 22.2   3A1.M1 | 3A.D1

Discuss the benefits of the EYFS for children and evaluate its potential impact on outcomes for them.

A2 Understand the principles of the Early Years Foundation Stage

The principles of the EYFS are designed to guide the work of all early years practitioners and influence and shape practice in early years settings. They are divided into four guiding themes, each of which has a principle behind it.

Principles of the EYFS

The four guiding themes and their principles are shown in Table 22.1.

Table 22.1 The themes and principles of the EYFS

Theme	Principle behind the theme
A Unique Child	Each child is unique and begins learning at birth, and can become resilient, capable, confident and self-assured.
Positive Relationships	Children learn to be strong and independent through a base of loving and secure relationships with parents, carers and with others, including the key person in their setting.
Positive Environment	A positive environment – in which children's experiences are planned to reflect their needs, and help build their confidence, and in which there is a strong partnership between early years practitioners, parents and other professionals – is crucial if children are to fulfil their potential and learn and develop well.
Children Develop and Learn in Different Ways and at Different Rates	All areas of learning and development are important and are interconnected.

Source: © Crown copyright 2008. Adapted from the Statutory Framework for the Early Years Foundation Stage (2012).

It is important that you think about each of these principles in relation to children with whom you work at all times to ensure that you keep them at the forefront of your practice. They should also be reflected within the curriculum framework as you carry out your work with children.

Applying the principles to practice

These principles are important, as they are described in the guidance as the guiding themes that should shape practice in all early years settings. You will need to be able to show how they are being applied to your practice and you should have a clear idea about how they run through all of your setting's work with children. It would be a good idea to look regularly at the principles to ensure that you can show how they are being applied to your practice.

Unique child

You should be able to show that you are meeting the individual needs of children in different ways – through your role as children's key person, getting to know families and parents and demonstrating an understanding of the needs of the child. The curriculum framework requires you to show inclusive practice and encourage the development of children's communication and language skills so that they are able to develop their understanding and self-expression. Planning should show that the setting reflects the interests and views of individual children, for example, by taking their views into consideration.

Positive relationships

You should support children in developing positive relationships with their parents and carers as well as others. The curriculum framework requires you

to do this through planning for children's personal, social and emotional development as well as through meeting their needs on a daily basis when managing feelings and behaviour and considering the needs of others.

Do you think this child and practitioner have a positive relationship?

Positive environment

You should ensure that relationships with those outside the setting – for example, other professionals and visitors from the community – are strong and positive, and that you act as a good role model for children. The curriculum framework requires you to ensure that the learning environment – both indoor and outdoor – is rich and varied and will support each child's development through a range of learning opportunities. You will also need to show that you plan, assess and observe children in order to demonstrate that you are meeting their needs.

Children develop and learn in different ways and at different rates

You will need to be able to plan for all areas of the Foundation Stage curriculum while being mindful of the fact that they are interrelated and should reflect children's interests. You should also take into account the importance of play, which is the key way in which children learn. The curriculum framework requires you to allow children to have active learning opportunities that allow them to make their own connections and find things out for themselves.

B1 Understand the safeguarding and welfare requirements within the Early Years Foundation Stage

The safeguarding and welfare requirements form the third section of the statutory framework and focus on the safety and well-being of children. They set out in detail what settings must do to ensure that children are able to learn in a safe and welcoming environment and the range of policies they will need to have in place to do this.

The rationale behind safeguarding and welfare requirements

All children are more likely to learn and do well when they are in a healthy, safe and secure environment and are cared for by adults with whom they have a positive relationship. A number of areas are covered under the safeguarding and welfare requirements, and practitioners are required to show how they ensure that all children are cared for appropriately.

All settings will need to show that they meet the requirements and practical implications for:

- child protection, including a safeguarding policy
- suitable people, to include disclosures about staff
- staff qualifications, training support and skills
- providing a key person for each child
- staff ratios
- health and safety
- managing behaviour

- safety and suitability of premises including risk assessment
- equal opportunities
- information and record keeping.

Children's protection, including a safeguarding policy

The requirements for child protection are set out in the statutory guidance and list a number of measures that settings must have in place in order to ensure the safeguarding of children in their care.

These must include:

- **A designated safeguarding officer in the setting**
This person must be responsible for safeguarding in the setting, liaising with the local children's agencies and with the Local Safeguarding Children Board (LSCB), and providing ongoing support and training to staff, as well as attending a specific safeguarding course themselves.

- **A policy for safeguarding**
This means that all staff must be aware of the setting's policy for dealing with any safeguarding issues that arise. They will need to know how to be alert for any issues that arise in a child's life and what kinds of signs might be indicators of abuse. Policies must be in line with guidance from the LSCB and include an explanation of what will happen if there are any allegations made against members of staff. They should also include the setting's policy on the use of mobile phones and cameras.

- **Working together to safeguard children**
All settings must use this statutory guidance when addressing any safeguarding issues within the setting, and should notify agencies who have statutory responsibilities as soon as possible in this instance (local children's social care services or the police).

- **Staff training**

All staff must be trained to understand the policies and procedures of the setting and have an up-to-date knowledge of safeguarding issues.

- **Ofsted notification**

All providers must inform Ofsted if there are any allegations of serious abuse at the setting, as well as informing them of any action taken. These notifications must be made as soon as possible, but at the latest within 14 days.

Activity

Research the signs of possible abuse and neglect. How would you follow up any of these indicators in your setting? What would you do if one of these was inappropriate behaviour by another member of staff?

Suitable people

In recent years there have been several high-profile cases in which people working with children and young people have been found to be unsuitable and in some cases have harmed or abused children. Legal steps have been taken to ensure that this does not happen in the future. In order to ensure that settings meet the requirements for suitable people, they will need to:

- ensure that they have systems in place that allow them to check the suitability of all those who come into contact with children
- meet Ofsted requirements for any people living on the premises or working directly with children (childminders only)
- ensure that all staff disclose any criminal convictions that may affect their suitability to work with children through a Criminal Records Bureau (CRB) check
- record information about staff qualifications and identity/CRB checks
- inform Ofsted within 14 days if any employee is convicted or disqualified from registration
- ensure that any practitioners taking medication declare this and check that it does not impair their ability to look after children, and store any medication on the premises securely at all times.

Did you know?

Until 2002, the Criminal Records Bureau (CRB) was not in existence. It was established to reduce risks to children and vulnerable people.

Staff qualifications, training, support and skills

All those working with young children and their families must have appropriate qualifications, training and support in order to ensure that they understand their roles and responsibilities. Early years settings must provide appropriate supervision that promotes mutual support between colleagues and opportunities to discuss issues as and when they arise. This should also include regular staff appraisals and opportunities for further training if necessary.

Research

Look at the statutory guidance to find out what kind of induction training must be provided for all staff when they start at a setting.

In group settings, there must be a manager who has a full and relevant Level 3 qualification, has worked in an early years setting for at least two years and who is supported by a deputy who is able to manage the setting in their absence. At least half of all the other staff will need to have a full and relevant Level 2 qualification. In addition, at least one person with a paediatric first-aid certificate must be on the premises at all times and accompany children on any outings away from the setting. It is a further requirement that all staff in early years settings have a good command of English so that they are able to care for children effectively, keep records and understand policies and instructions.

Provision of a key person for each child, and staff ratios

All settings must provide a key person for each child so that the care meets the child's individual needs. The key person will work closely with parents and ensure that the child develops confidence and settles in well.

Link

Go to Unit 7: Section A1 in Student Book 1 to find more about the importance of attachments and the benefits of the key person system.

In addition to this, staff-to-child ratios must be appropriate to the setting and the level of qualifications held by the staff. Only those aged 17 or over may be included in staff ratios.

Table 22.2 shows the staff-to-child ratios for different settings.

Table 22.2 Staff-to-child ratios for different settings (source: Statutory Framework for the Early Years Foundation Stage, Department for Education 2012)

Provider	Age of child	Staff:child ratio	Qualifications and experience
	Under 2	1:3	• At least one member of staff to have a full and relevant L3 qualification • At least half of all other staff to have a full and relevant L2 qualification • At least half of all staff must have specified training in the care of babies • Head of under-2s room must have experience of working with under-2s
	2 years	1:4	• At least one member of staff to have a full and relevant L3 qualification • At least half of all other staff to have a full and relevant L2 qualification
Early years setting 8 a.m.–4 p.m.	3 years +	1:13	• If a member of staff has Qualified Teacher Status (QTS) or Early Years Professional Status (EYPS), there must be at least one other member of staff with a full and relevant L3 qualification
Early years setting both within and outside the hours of 8 a.m. and 4 p.m.	3 years +	1:8	• If a member of staff with QTS or EYPS is not present, there must be at least one member of staff with a full and relevant L3 qualification and at least half of all other staff must hold a full and relevant L2 qualification
Independent school	3 years +	1:30 if majority of children will reach 5 that year 1:13 in all other classes	• If there is a member of staff with QTS or EYPS, there must be at least one other member of staff with a full and relevant L3 qualification
Independent school	3 years +	1:8	• If there is no person with QTS or EYPS, at least one member of staff must hold a full and relevant L3 qualification and at least half of all other staff must have a full and relevant L2 qualification
Nursery classes in maintained schools (not reception)	3 years +	1:13	• At least one member of staff must be a schoolteacher • At least one other member of class must hold a full and relevant L3 qualification

In reception classes, there must be no more than 30 children per schoolteacher. In the case of childminders, the total number of children under the age of 8 must not be more than six.

Health of children, to include the provision of food and drink

All settings will need to ensure that they take steps to promote good health in children. This includes:

- taking appropriate action if children are ill
- taking steps to prevent the spread of any infection
- having a policy for administering medicines and gaining written permission from parents and carers for doing so
- a first-aid box accessible at all times with suitable contents for use with children and a written record of accidents, injuries and first aid given
- Ofsted and local child protection agencies must be informed of any serious accident, illness or injury to a child while in the care of the setting, as well as the action taken, within 14 days of the incident.

It is important that all staff are aware of the setting's policies and that a written record is kept of any medication that is given to a child so that this is available to parents.

Research

Find out about the statutory requirements for food and drink in early years settings. What are the obligations of providers from a staff-training point of view?

Managing behaviour

Children will need to be supported by clear and consistent behaviour management in the setting. This means that there should be a designated member of staff responsible for behaviour management, as well as a behaviour management policy that sets out how all staff will promote positive behaviour and respond to unwanted behaviour.

The statutory guidance states that no member of staff should give or threaten corporal punishment and that physical intervention should only be used

if there is a possibility of danger to another person. In some cases, settings may have a policy for the use of restraint.

Link

Go to Unit 7 in Student Book 1 to find more information about the importance of supporting children's positive behaviour and the role of the adult.

Safety and suitability of premises, environment and equipment

All early years settings must comply with requirements for keeping the environment safe for all who use it. Health and safety requirements are such that settings will need to have policies and procedures in place that ensure that the setting is kept safe and free from hazards.

Link

Go to Unit 4 in Student Book 1 to find more information about health and safety practice in early years settings.

Settings must ensure that the learning environment – both indoor and outdoor – as well as all equipment and furniture are safe for use by children and suitable for children with disabilities. Specific space requirements are given in the statutory guidance. These requirements are shown in Table 22.3.

Table 22.3 Specific space requirements

Age of child	Space requirement
Under 2 years	3.5 m² per child
2 years	2.5 m² per child
3–5 years	2.3 m² per child

The learning environment must be safe and secure and kept clean, and settings will need to have a health and safety policy that outlines procedures that will be followed when identifying, reporting and dealing with accidents, hazards and any faulty equipment. Settings must show that they have procedures in place for managing safety and have appropriate equipment such as smoke detectors, fire extinguishers and fire alarms that are regularly tested.

Other specific requirements

- In settings where there are children under 2, there will need to be a separate baby room, and in all settings there will need to be a space for children to rest or sleep.
- There should be adequate toilets and hand basins for the number of children.
- Settings will need to provide an area for any confidential meetings or discussions.
- Settings must ensure that all entering the premises are identified. Children may not leave the setting unsupervised and parents must notify the setting if other individuals are collecting children.
- The setting must have a clear risk assessment policy.
- Outings must be organised, risk assessed and should include an appropriate number of adults. Children must have written parental permission to take part in them.
- Settings must have a no-smoking policy.
- Settings must have public liability insurance.

Equal opportunities policy and challenging inappropriate attitudes

As well as having a clear policy and procedures for equal opportunities, all settings must show that they support children with special educational needs and disabilities. This should include:

- how the individual needs of all children will be met
- the name of the SENCO
- arrangements for reviewing, monitoring and evaluating practice
- how inappropriate attitudes and practices will be challenged
- how the provision will encourage children to value and respect others.

Link

Go to Unit 10 to find more information about diversity, equality and inclusion in early years practice.

Records and provision of information for parents

As in any organisation, records will need to be kept by settings and information shared with others in order for them to run smoothly. Settings will need to show how they keep the required records and how and when information is collected, stored and shared. It is important that all staff are aware of confidentiality and the requirements of the Data Protection Act 1998, which states that information must only be used for the purpose for which it was gathered.

Information about the child

Settings will need to keep basic information about the child, which they will need to gather from parents or carers before the child starts at the setting. This should include the child's full name, address and date of birth as well as the name, address and contact details of all parents or carers who have parental responsibility. These should be updated regularly in case of emergency.

Information for parents and carers

The setting will need to make certain information available to parents and carers, to include:

- staffing and the name of their child's key person
- information about the EYFS and how it is delivered in the setting, including where they can access more information
- the types of activities and experiences that are provided and how they can support their child's learning
- policies and procedures of the setting
- information about food and drink.

All of this information will need to be easily accessible to parents through different means, for example, via a website, letters, noticeboards and/or regular newsletters.

Information about the provider

As well as having a certificate of registration, the setting must keep records of the name, address and phone number of all staff working with children, as well as anyone else who will be in contact with them. They will also need to keep a register detailing when children have attended and the name of each child's key person.

Information about complaints

There must be a written procedure for dealing with any complaints as well as records kept of the outcome. All settings must investigate any written complaints within 28 days and the record of complaints must be made available to Ofsted.

As well as any direct complaints, information must be made available to parents and carers about how to contact Ofsted if they believe the setting is not meeting its obligations under the EYFS. They will also need to be given a copy of the report following an Ofsted inspection.

Changes notifiable to Ofsted

All settings will need to inform Ofsted about:

- a change of address of the premises or any changes in the premises itself that may affect the space available
- a change of the name or address of the provider, or changes in management
- any event that may affect the suitability of the provider or any person caring for children on the premises to look after children
- any proposal to change the hours of childcare
- any changes to the organisation that runs the provision, whether this is a company, charity or partnership.

Assessment practice 22.4   3B1.P7 | 3B1.M3

What policies are required in order for settings to meet the safeguarding and welfare requirements of the EYFS? Discuss how specific policies help settings meet these requirements.

B2 Understand the education programme within the Early Years Foundation Stage

The education programme for the EYFS sets out a number of requirements and you will need to understand and be aware of these in your role as an early years practitioner so that you can plan effectively.

Delivering all areas of development through planned purposeful play

The EYFS has been developed to incorporate the different areas of children's development within the seven areas of learning. These must be delivered through **purposeful play**. When planning activities under the EYFS, settings will need to ensure that play is a key part of the delivery. Play is essential for children's development for several reasons:

- It builds children's confidence.
- It encourages children to think about problems.
- It helps children relate to others.

Along with **active learning** and **creating and thinking critically**, play is also one of the characteristics of effective teaching and learning and forms the basis of child-initiated activities.

Although they are interconnected, children's overall development is usually considered in relation to different areas:

- social and emotional development – how the child relates to others and is developing emotionally, including feelings and behaviour
- physical and sensory development – how the child is developing physically, to include both fine and gross motor skills, and development of the five senses
- intellectual or cognitive, and language development – how the child is developing intellectually, or how they are learning, to include their language development.

Link

Go to Unit 2 in Student Book 1 to find more information about play in early years settings.

The rationale behind each area of learning

As can be seen from Table 22.4, the prime areas of learning relate directly to the main areas of child development. These areas are considered to be

Key terms

Active learning – the process by which children concentrate and keep on trying if they encounter difficulties, and enjoy their achievements.

Creating and thinking critically – when children have and develop their own ideas, make links between ideas, and develop strategies for doing things.

Purposeful play – through play, children investigate and experience things, and 'have a go'.

those that are particularly important in building children's capacity to learn.

The specific areas of learning, which develop the breadth of children's skills in the areas of literacy, mathematics, understanding the world and expressive arts, should be developed as children become more competent in the other three. If you are working with the youngest children, you should be focusing on these three areas, as they are the basis for successful subsequent learning.

Table 22.4 shows the relationship between the seven areas of learning and the areas of child development.

Table 22.4 The relationship between the seven areas of learning and the areas of child development

Area of child development	Area of learning and development
The prime areas of learning relate directly to the main areas of child development: • social and emotional • physical and sensory • cognitive and language.	Prime areas: • personal, social and emotional • physical • communication and language.
The specific areas of learning should be developed as children become more competent in the prime areas of learning.	Specific areas: • literacy • mathematics • understanding of the world • expressive arts and design.

By the time they reach the end of the Early Years Foundation Stage, children should be spending the same amount of time on each area of learning, so that they continue to develop their confidence in the three prime areas while also developing the others.

If children give cause for concern in any of the prime areas at any time during the Foundation Stage, they should have increased support so that they are less likely to be unprepared for the start of school. In this situation, parents would need to be informed and staff should consider whether other agencies should be involved so that the child and their family can have further support, within or outside the setting.

Link

Go to Unit 1 in Student Book 1 to find more information about how children under 5 years develop.

Scope of areas of learning and how they are interrelated

Each area of learning and development is expanded into two or three different strands, to show the scope or breadth of what children will be developing during their time in the EYFS. For example, literacy is split into reading and writing, and mathematics into numbers and shape, space and measures. As can be seen from Table 22.4, personal, social and emotional development is split into three different areas. You will need to support children in each one as they progress towards the early learning goals.

Personal, social and emotional development learning goals

The following information is taken from the Statutory Framework for the Early Years Foundation Stage 2012.

Self-confidence and self-awareness

Children are confident to try new activities, and say why they like some activities more than others. They are confident to speak in a familiar group, will talk about their ideas, and will choose the resources they need for their chosen activities. They say when they do or do not need help.

Managing feelings and behaviour

Children can talk about how they and others show feelings, can talk about their own and others' behaviour and its consequences, and know that some behaviour is unacceptable. They work as part of a group or class, and understand and follow the rules. They can adjust their behaviour to different situations, and take changes of routine in their stride.

Making relationships

Children play cooperatively, taking turns with others. They take account of one another's ideas about how to organise their activity. They can show sensitivity to others' needs and feelings, and form positive relationships with adults and other children.

Theory into practice

Look at the statutory guidance for the EYFS 2012 to see how children will be working towards these early learning goals in the area of personal, social and emotional development. What are their expected developmental goals at 2 to 3 years and 3 to 4 years in each strand?

You can access the statutory guidance by going to www.pearsonhotlinks.co.uk and searching for this title.

As you look at each of the different areas of learning, it should be clear that they are interrelated. This means that children who are learning through play will be developing in more than one area. For example, a child who is playing with play-dough with a group of children will be developing their physical (fine motor) skills as well as their communication and language skills, their personal, social and emotional development skills, and expressive arts through their imagination. They will be developing their relationships with others, playing and exploring, and learning in an active way through play. For this reason, planning for different areas of the EYFS will usually be topic-based.

Link

Go to Unit 19: Section 1 to see an example of a topic plan.

Topic-based planning has long been used as a way to introduce activities to young children, as it enables us to use ideas that are familiar to children in order to create a focus and link things together. Although it is not usually possible to cover every aspect of learning within a topic, they are a useful starting point. You will need to ensure when you are planning that you cover any areas that cannot be included as part of the topic.

Assessment practice 22.5   3B2.P8 | 3B2.P9 | 3B2.M4 | 3B1.D2

Write a report on the seven areas of learning in the EYFS and the scope of each one. How might play activities provide opportunities for several areas of learning? Discuss using examples. Evaluate the extent to which the safeguarding and welfare requirements complement the education programme in the EYFS.

Importance of observing children's development

When working with young children, you will always need to carry out observations to look at how they are progressing. These may be observations that take place away from the child, so that you can watch them interacting with other children and learning through play, or observations that you may make and note down while you are working with them. Observations allow us to look at what children enjoy when they are carrying out child-initiated activities, as well as being a measure of how their development is progressing. Parents should also be involved in the observation process – the EYFS requires settings and parents to share observations with one another.

Activity

How does your setting involve parents in observing children's development? What kinds of opportunities do parents have for sharing information with key workers and other staff?

Through carrying out observations on children, you will be able to compare their progress with the

expected achievements for their age group. The EYFS is no exception to this and observations have always been a key area of assessment. You will need to show that you use these observations to help you plan to take forward children's progress and take their learning on to the next stage.

You will need to carry out regular observations to inform your planning.

Balancing adult-led and child-initiated activities

As an early years worker, you should be aware of the importance of balancing child-initiated and adult-led activities. Much of the EYFS is based on the need for play to be part of children's learning and for adults to encourage them to develop their independence skills. However, children will also need to be guided and supported by adults as they are challenged by new concepts and ideas. As children work towards the end of the Foundation Stage, the balance of activities will gradually move more towards those that are led by adults so that children are ready for more formal learning in Year 1.

Assessment practice 22.6   3B2.P10

What are the reasons for balancing adult-led and child-initiated activities when planning in the EYFS? Use examples to back up your explanation.

C Be able to plan play and activities that support children's progress towards Early Years Foundation Stage outcomes

As an early years worker you will need to know how to plan play and activities to support children's progress towards the EYFS outcomes, while balancing those that are adult-led with those that are child-initiated.

How to plan play and activities to support children's progress

One of the key areas you will need to consider when planning is that the EYFS is based around play. Children should have opportunities to play together with little adult direction or involvement (child-initiated play), as well as having access to the kinds of activities where adults will give more direction or join in. It is also useful to look at the different ways in which settings plan, as this can be a good way of sharing ideas to get inspiration and cutting down on paperwork, too.

Your plans should show how you provide activities for each of the seven areas of learning and development and include opportunities for both child-initiated and adult-directed play. These need to reflect the needs of individual children as well as showing that they are being given opportunities to develop in each area. You will need to have long-, medium- and short-term plans to show how what you are doing fits together with what the children have done previously and will do in the future. However, you must also remember that plans should be flexible and that you will constantly need to evaluate and think about what is working or not working and what will meet the needs and interests of individual children.

Link

Go to Unit 2 in Student Book 1 to find more information about how to plan play and activities.

Long-term plans

Long-term plans are usually used in schools or large settings where practitioners need to have plans set out well in advance – smaller settings may not need to use them. They will usually give an overview of topics or themes over a long period, for example, a year, so that resources can be shared between classes. However, the length of time they cover is variable and will depend on the setting.

Theory into practice

Does your setting have long- or medium-term plans? What do they show, and where are they kept so that they can be referred to by staff and parents?

Medium-term plans

Medium-term plans will give more detail than long-term plans and are likely to last from a few weeks to half an academic term. They will set out what is going to be covered in each area of learning during each week. Some settings display them so that parents are able to look at the different areas of focus, although they should be a working document and will need to be changed and added to as they develop. Figure 22.3 shows an example of a medium-term plan.

Short-term plans

Short-term plans will be the most detailed of all and will be weekly/daily focused activity plans that reflect children's interests while building on their knowledge and skills. You will need to have a clear plan for adult-focused activities, which should indicate the learning objectives. For child-initiated activities, your setting may have a grid or provision planner to show the kinds of activities, materials and resources that will be available to children during the week.

Medium-term Planning Sheet
Week 6

Topic: Toys		Week beginning: 15/11/12	
Activities	**Learning objectives**	**Learning outcomes**	**Comments**
• Sort a collection of toys into old or new • Talk about characteristics of each set using adjectives, e.g. rusty, shiny, broken, dirty, ragged, clean	• How to decide whether an object is old or new • Describe characteristics of old and new objects	• Sort objects into old and new sets • Explain why they have grouped objects in a particular way	
• Discuss the meaning of words • Match adjectives to toys	• Collections of words linked to topics		
• Which would be the best paper for making a jigsaw (or a set of cards)? • What would the material need to be like? Strong? Rigid? • How could you find out which paper would be best? • Test ideas with papers. Say what you did.	• Suggest how to test an idea about whether a paper is suitable for a particular purpose	• Make a suggestion of what a paper for making a puzzle should be like • Suggest a way of testing the papers appropriate to the characteristic chosen	
• Make a paper sculpture			
• Why do games have rules? • What are they? • What would be fair or unfair?	• Recognise choices they can make and the differences between right and wrong • Agree and follow rules • Understand how rules help them		

Figure 22.3 An example of a medium-term plan

This may include opportunities for sand and water play, messy play, small-world play, role play, creative activities, construction and so on. However, all settings will be different and will do this in a variety of ways.

Activity

1 Ask your setting if you can look at a short-term plan to compare it with the format used in other settings.
2 How similar are the plans?
3 What ideas can you take from them?

As well as carrying out activities that tie in with your planning, you should also think about how you can bring learning into daily routines with children and be on the lookout for how you can involve them. This may be, for example, when they are having their drink and biscuit, or sitting around a table: 'Do we have enough cups or chairs? How many children are here today? Let's count!' and so on. In this way, you will be developing children's awareness of how what they are doing relates to their environment.

How settings plan for children's progress within the EYFS

Although settings will all plan in different ways, they will need to include the same key information and be clear about how children are making progress towards the early learning goals. Planning should show:

- how children's individual needs and interests are being met and are built on regular observations by staff and parents
- how the seven areas of learning are being included, as well as indoor and outdoor provision
- that there is a balance of adult-led and child-initiated activities
- how children are progressing towards the early learning goals
- how observations and assessment tie in with the process.

Meeting children's individual needs and interests

Your setting will need to show how it plans for children's individual needs. This may be the way in which it implements a programme for a child who has special educational needs, or through work that is carried out with parents to support a child or group of children who speak English as an additional language. Children's needs will change over time – for example, a child might be particularly sensitive if a family pet has just died, or if there are some issues at home due to the birth of a new sibling. All staff should be aware of these kinds of issues and in some settings a book is kept for staff to check daily so that key workers are able to note them down. When planning for children's interests, you may show this through noting down what children have said and acting on it, or developing a particular area that has caught their imagination. In some cases, whole topics can be built on children's ideas and interests.

Including the seven areas of learning

This is straightforward – planning must include the seven areas of learning and you will need to show that children have the opportunity for both indoor and outdoor play activities. If outdoor play needs to be timetabled for practical reasons, this should be shown.

Maintaining a balance of adult-led and child-initiated activities

Plans should be clear on which activities are adult-led and what kinds of activities are available for children to self-select or initiate themselves.

Progressing towards the early learning goals

When you are planning activities within the EYFS, you will need to look at clear progression, building learning on what children have previously achieved. This means that all adult-directed activities should have clear objectives. If objectives are not specific, it will be hard to measure children's progress against them. At the end of adult-directed activities, the activity plan will need to show how children have achieved. This information will then need to be transferred to the child's individual records.

Look at the following examples of learning objectives for some adult-directed activities. Are they specific? Do you think that they are achievable? If not, how could you change them so that they are?

- I can identify sounds.
- I can identify 'one more' than a number.
- I can describe what is in the feely box.
- I can play outside with the large construction blocks.
- I can find things that are taller or shorter than me.
- I can use a computer mouse.

Observations and assessment

Settings will need to show how observations and assessment of activities feed into their planning. For this reason, many practitioners will write evaluations on their daily plans or make notes while they are working with children to show how they are going to take children's learning forward over the coming days and weeks.

Record keeping

It is likely that your setting will have a file for each child, which will be the central source of information about their learning and development. The files may be paper-based or kept on the computer, as there are a number of programmes available that can be used alongside the EYFS to track children's learning. Paper files are likely to show observations and summative assessments that have been carried out with children as well as notes made by staff and parents. Records should track children's progress towards the early learning goals.

Link

Go to Unit 9: Section C to find more information about record keeping.

How to plan an adult-directed activity

Adult-directed activities may take different forms. An activity plan should show the learning intention of the activity, which should be very specific and should include the individual needs of children and what needs to be addressed. Adults must be clear on what they need to do, including vocabulary to be used and key questions to ask. In some cases, adult-directed activities may be more like a lesson, in which case an adult may talk to a larger group first and then take small groups to continue the theme, or they might just be carried out with small groups or individual children throughout the day. An activity plan should also have a space for the adult to record how children have responded to the task and whether they have met the objective, so that this information can be carried over into subsequent planning.

How to balance adult-led and child-initiated activities

Your plans will need to show how you balance adult-led and child-initiated activities, while involving all children in each and giving them all equal opportunities. In some settings, daily plans will only show adult-directed activities – there may be a few of these each day depending on staffing – while those that are child-initiated will be on a separate overarching grid for the whole week. Children should be free to self-select what they are going to do within the structure of the day – for example, if they are in the role-play area, they should be able to take resources from other areas of the room to support their play. However, all children should have access to all resources, for example, if you have a group of children that always makes for the bikes and outdoor toys, make sure that this is not preventing other children from using them. In some settings, there may be a 'wheel of activities' to prevent this from happening, so that children move to a new activity after a set amount of time. However, some practitioners do not like using this system as it interrupts the free flow of activities.

Reflect

How does your setting ensure that all children have a chance to use all resources?

Reflect

What activities have you recently carried out in your setting? How might they support more than one area of learning?

Assessment practice 22.7   3C.P11 | 3C.P12 | 3C.M5 | 3C.D3

Present two plans to support a child's progress towards early learning goals, to include:

- adult-led activities
- child-initiated activities.

Explain how each planned activity will support the child's progress in different areas of learning. Analyse the importance of balancing adult-led and child-initiated activities. Evaluate the potential impact of the plans in supporting the child's progress towards the early learning goals.

You may like to use the 'Skills for practice' observation activity at the end of this unit as a basis for your planning.

Activity

Look at the medium-term plan earlier in this section (Figure 22.3). What examples can you see of activities that will support children's progress in more than one area of learning?

What is the main area of learning that this activity is supporting?

How activities support children's progress in more than one area

Any activity that children are carrying out is likely to support their progress in more than one area of learning, as they are all interrelated. For planning purposes, however, it is more useful to focus on the main area that will be developed through the activity. For example, singing counting songs with children will mainly be supporting mathematical development, but will also be developing musical skills as well as children's phonemic awareness through rhyme. (If they are action rhymes they may also support physical development.)

Further reading and resources

Letters and Sounds (DFES-00281-2007)

This is a government-produced document produced through the Primary National Strategy, which starts in the Foundation Stage and builds up through different stages. It features valuable suggestions for progression, including focused activities.

Statutory Framework for the Early Years Foundation Stage (Department for Education 2012).

Langston, A. and Doherty, J. (2012) *The New EYFS in Practice*, London: Featherstone Education.

Moylett, H. and Stewart, N. (2012) *Understanding the Revised Early Years Foundation Stage*, London: Early Education.

Tassoni, P. (2012) *Practical EYFS Handbook*, London: Pearson.

Websites

EYFS forum: http://eyfs.info

A useful site for resources, information and support for early years practitioners.

Early Years Educator (EYE magazine): www.earlyyearseducator.co.uk

A good source of articles and information.

Nursery World magazine: www.nurseryworld.magazine.co.uk

Useful articles, information and jobs.

Ofsted: www.ofsted.gov.uk

This website has information about EYFS Ofsted requirements.

Ready for work?

Jim Collins Nursery assistant

I have recently started work in a nursery attached to a large school. I had previously worked in a small church-run nursery and it has been really interesting to find out about how the two different settings do their planning and assessment. At first I found it difficult as I had thought things would be the same, and had made quite a few assumptions about how planning, staffing and activities would take place as this is only my second job. I have had to get used to a different way of working, and have learned another way of planning, which has been good. I have also been able to bring some of my own ideas and talk about things that worked well in my previous setting.

One of the main differences has been that because the nursery is attached to the school we have different routines as part of our day, which spills over into our planning. For example, we share our outside area with the reception class, and at the moment this means that we are only able to use it on a timetabled rota. We also have to have our breaks at set times to coincide with the school day.

It has been good for me to learn about how different settings operate and I am enjoying developing my experiences. I have developed a few contacts and am trying to set up a local group for different settings to attend so that we can get together on a regular basis to look at different ways of planning and share ideas.

Skills for practice

This unit allows you to carry out many of the skills for practice through your work within the EYFS.

Although you can focus on the area of supporting learning, you may also like to ask at your setting whether you can organise the learning environment (either indoor or outdoor) to show how you can set up and maintain different areas and activities such as sand, water, role play and so on. You could also prepare resources such as making basic dough or gloop, or show how you have created a wall display using children's work and photographs. If you are working with babies, you should be able to meet many of the skills for work with babies (caring skills, preparing for play and learning, supporting play and learning, supporting literacy, and observing, assessing and planning)

through observations of your work. Look through the skills for practice in early years settings for more ideas.

Supporting learning:

- Show how you have supported children's practical learning in different areas and activities and interacted effectively with them.

Observe, assess and plan:

- Complete five observations and assessments of children aged from 2 to 4 years using the documentation/techniques employed in the setting.
- Complete five plans relevant to the appropriate curriculum framework to meet the learning/development needs of children aged from 2 to 4 years using the documentation of the setting.

Introduction

Imagine the scene: a toddler comes over to you with a plastic cup. They stand and pretend to drink from it, then they offer it to you. This is typical of imaginative play in young children. It shows that the child has reached a level of cognitive development that allows them to use symbols in their play. From this type of play most children go on to play together cooperatively and create quite complex pretend worlds. Children often play with small figures too, in what is known as small-world play.

In this unit, you will learn about the different types of imaginative play and how they support children's learning and development. It also covers how to plan for imaginative play, including how to set up and maintain the resources used. Finally, it looks at ways in which we can support children when they are engaged in imaginative play and the importance of challenging gender stereotyping.

Assessment: You will be assessed by a series of assignments set by your teacher/tutor.

Learning aims

In this unit you will:

A   understand the importance of imaginative play for children

B1   understand planning for imaginative play

B2   understand the role of the adult in imaginative play.

'Our children love role play. It is a major focus for our work and we always have a home corner and a shop as standard provision. In our setting, role play is used to cover many aspects of the curriculum, but particularly communication and language. It is surprising how much chatter comes from the role-play areas and just how imaginative young children can be. My all-time favourite was when we created a Chinese takeaway, which we started off by ordering a takeaway from a local business. It was great fun.

Debbie, *a preschool practitioner*

Supporting Children's Imaginative Play

24

BTEC
Assessment Zone

This table shows what you must do in order to achieve a **Pass**, **Merit** or **Distinction** grade, and where you can find activities to help you.

Assessment criteria		
Pass	**Merit**	**Distinction**
Learning aim A: Understand the importance of imaginative play for children		
3A.P1 Explain ways in which imaginative play supports learning. **Assessment practice 24.1**	**3A.M1** Analyse the contribution of imaginative play to children's learning and development. **Assessment practice 24.1**	**3A.D1** Evaluate how imaginative play can impact on outcomes for children. **Assessment practice 24.1**
3A.P2 **I&CT** Review the benefits of imaginative play for children's social, emotional and cultural development. **Assessment practice 24.1**		
Learning aim B1: Understand planning for imaginative play **Learning aim B2: Understand the role of the adult in imaginative play**		
3B1.P3 Explain the role of observations in supporting planning and extending children's imaginative play. **Assessment practice 24.2**	**3B1.M2** Analyse the role of the adult in planning for imaginative play. **Assessment practice 24.2**	**3B.D2** Evaluate the contribution of adults to effective imaginative play in an early years setting. **Assessment practice 24.2**
3B1.P4 **English** Explain how to provide resources in an early years setting to support: • domestic play • fantasy play • superhero play • small-world play. **Assessment practice 24.2**		
3B1.P5 Describe ways of using indoor and outdoor environments in an early years setting to support imaginative play. **Assessment practice 24.2**		
3B2.P6 Explain how adults in an early years setting can support and extend children's imaginative play. **Assessment practice 24.2**	**3B2.M3** Analyse the role of the adult as a play partner in children's imaginative play in an early years setting, using examples. **Assessment practice 24.2**	
3B2.P7 Explain why it is important for adults to challenge stereotypes in imaginative play. **Assessment practice 24.2**		

English English Functional Skills signposting	**I&CT** Information and Communication Technology skills signposting

How you will be assessed

This unit will be assessed by a series of internally assessed tasks set by your teacher/tutor. Throughout this unit you will find assessment practice activities that will help you work towards your assessment. Completing these activities will not mean that you have achieved a particular grade, but you will have carried out useful research or preparation that will be relevant when it comes to your final assignment.

In order for you to achieve the tasks in your assignment, it is important that you check you have met all of the Pass grading criteria. You can do this as you work your way through the assignment.

If you are hoping to gain a Merit or Distinction, you should also make sure that you present the information in your assignment in the style that is required by the relevant assessment criterion. For example, Merit criteria will require you to discuss and analyse, and Distinction criteria will require you to evaluate.

The assignment set by your teacher/tutor will consist of a number of tasks designed to meet the criteria in the table. This is likely to consist of a written assignment but may also include activities such as:

- a presentation for parents
- case studies and observations
- guides and information packs.

Have you ever seen a toddler talking intently on a toy phone? Or two 4-year-olds sitting pretending to have dinner? In these moments children are in their own worlds and are enjoying their play. By the end of this unit, you should know why children enjoy this type of play and how it helps their development.

A Understand the importance of imaginative play for children

Imaginative play has not always been recognised as important in children's learning and development, and in the past was often seen as 'just play'. Today its importance is recognised and provision is made for it in early years settings. In this section, we consider why imaginative play is so important for children.

Definition of imaginative play

There are many definitions of imaginative play, but the idea of suspending belief in reality and moving into a pretend world is often talked about in this context. At 18 months, most children begin to take objects and pretend to do something with them. At first the actions are quite simple and are based on what the child has directly seen or experienced, but later children develop the ability to imagine things that they have not directly encountered. By 4 years old, children are often creating quite complex imaginary scenes and are able to fully immerse themselves in them. Interestingly, if you ask children about what they are doing, they will often tell you that they are pretending, before quickly slipping back into character or into their imaginary world. This makes imaginative play a **symbolic action** as well as a creative one.

Key term

Symbolic action – a gesture that is representative of a real action.

Features of different types of imaginative play

There are different types of imaginative play that you may observe children engaging in. It is useful to understand the features of each type so that you can provide for it.

Domestic play

This is often provided by settings in the form of a home corner, as children are pretending to be in a home. They pretend to prepare meals, iron or care for a baby. Much domestic play is based on children's own observations of adults and their own experiences of domestic life. It is often a feature of young children's imaginative play, but remains popular with older children. Interestingly, children will often use domestic play in role-play areas that were designed for fantasy play. For instance, you may see two children in a space rocket making a cup of tea.

Fantasy play

Children engaged in fantasy play are basing their play on situations that they have not encountered personally, but have some knowledge of. This knowledge may come from stories, hearing about others' experiences or seeing photographs. They may, for example, pretend to be in a hospital or working in a shop. This type of play requires that children are imagining a situation rather than recreating something that they have experienced.

Superhero play

As the term implies, this type of play is about children pretending to be 'heroes' and is often influenced by television, cartoons and small-world figures such as Action Man. This type of play is often very exciting for children and usually involves plenty of noise and movement. It is often associated with boys, but many girls will also enjoy this type of play. Superhero play often poses a dilemma for settings as many children will 'arm' themselves with a pretend gun and may pretend to kill or hurt the 'baddies'. Some settings have clear policies about restricting how children engage in this type of play, whereas others take a more relaxed point of view. It is interesting that this type of play can also divide parents too.

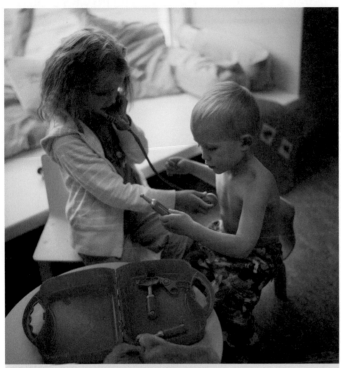

What type of imaginative play are these two children taking part in?

Research

Find out more about superhero play.

1 Talk to staff in your setting and find out about the setting's policy on superhero play.

2 Talk to parents of children and see whether they allow toy guns at home.

Small-world play

In small-world play, children play with small figures and objects such as farm animals, play people and cars. Children move these around and build stories around them. Many children will make noises for different objects or pretend to talk for the different figures. Most of the play happens on the floor or at low tables. Figure 24.1 shows the many different types of small-world toys that children may use.

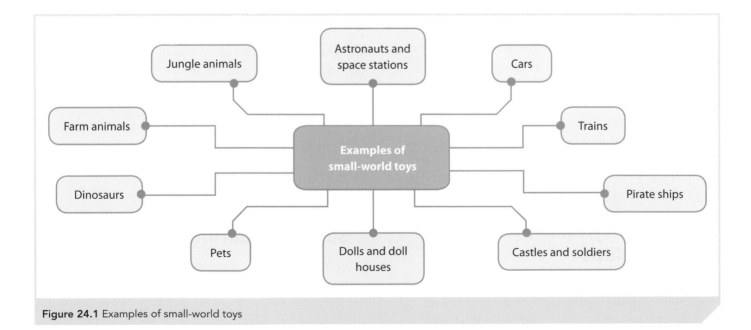

Farm animals · Jungle animals · Astronauts and space stations · Cars · Trains · Dinosaurs · Pets · Dolls and doll houses · Castles and soldiers · Pirate ships

Examples of small-world toys

Figure 24.1 Examples of small-world toys

Benefits of imaginative play for development

Imaginative play seems to play a major part in children's emotional and social development. This is one reason why it is often used therapeutically with children who have experienced a trauma. We will now look at some of the specific benefits of imaginative play.

Self-expression

While children are pretending, they are free of restrictions and can express whatever they wish. This kind of play is usually a child-initiated activity and, while it may be supported by adults, children can take on whatever role they wish. They may want to act out being a baby, or being angry or strong. This freedom allows for great self-expression.

Exploring feelings and empathy

As children's role play develops, they increasingly try to 'be' different people. They may take on the role of a tired mother, angry older brother or naughty child. Playing out these roles helps children to explore new feelings in a safe way. They know that they can stop 'being' this role at any time. By playing out different roles, children also get a glimpse of what it is like to be someone else. This in turn can help children develop empathy.

Exercising choice

Young children spend significant amounts of their time being told what to do or having limitations placed on their activity. In role play, children can choose to be whomever they want or act in any way that they wish. In small-world play, children are in control of the figures, cars and animals. They can decide who goes where and what happens to them. Having this choice, even in a pretend world, is liberating for children.

Cooperation, negotiation and resolving conflicts

From around 3 years, most children start to engage in some imaginative play alongside others. Two or three children may play together in the home corner or with small-world toys. As imaginative play is exciting and pleasurable, there is a real incentive for children to find ways of cooperating and thus learning the skills of negotiation and conflict resolution. This is interesting to listen to, particularly as children become older. Usually their imaginative play becomes more complex and so the need for organisation becomes greater. It is not uncommon for children to begin their play by deciding who should do what and what will happen during the action.

Theory into practice

Observe a group of children engaged in role play or small-world play.

Listen to their conversation and consider whether they are showing the skills associated with cooperation.

Importance of imaginative play in supporting creativity

Imaginative play is part of creativity, as it is an expression of the child's imagination and will eventually become the curriculum subject known as drama. By pretending, children are learning another way of expressing themselves and their experiences. Through imaginative play, children also learn to think creatively, by for example taking their own initiative or problem solving as they work out how to use resources in their play.

Interestingly, children often use imaginative play as a starting point for other creative activities. They may, for example, decide that their play people need a shelter and so make something using junk modelling. From around 5 years old, children may also pretend to be dancers or actors and extend this to put on a show.

How imaginative play supports learning

Imaginative play can help children's cognitive and language development. The extent to which this happens can depend on the richness of the props and the ways in which adults plan and support children's play.

Extending thinking and problem solving

In imaginative play, children incorporate experiences or information into their play. This helps them to extend their thinking and so is a good way of supporting their cognitive development. Through play, children can explore problem solving in a practical way. An example of this is the way that many children, when they are outdoors, will start gathering items to make a den or look for items that they can pretend to cook with.

Exploring mathematical concepts

Children will often put into practice the mathematical concepts that they have. They may, for example, count out 'biscuits' for the baby or set a timer to act as the parking meter. Some settings will also help children to explore mathematical concepts further by ensuring that mathematical equipment such as scales, tape measures and real money are provided as props. A pretend carpet shop might be set up, or a Chinese takeaway.

By playing shops, this child is learning to count and to recognise the value of coins and notes.

Using technology

As technology is increasingly being used in today's world, so this is reflected in children's imaginative play. Some small-world toys have technology built into them, for example, programmable robots and dinosaurs. Within role play, equipment such as toy cash registers and microwaves are also built with lifelike sounds that help children to use these technologies. In some settings, children have access

to walkie-talkies, which they can incorporate into their play. While not everyone is a fan of such gadgets, children using them do gain knowledge of technology.

Exploring and selecting materials

As with other types of child-initiated play, children are able to access and choose materials freely. What is interesting to note is the way that children are good improvisers and will often choose things from all over the setting to improve their play. This means that if children need play food, for example, they are likely to go to the dough table or over to the sand tray. Wherever possible, it is good practice to take a relaxed view of this, because through exploring and selecting materials, children are learning about their properties and are also being creative.

Developing language and literacy

Imaginative play is a great incentive for children to talk and communicate; especially when they are engaged in role play. This is one of the reasons why most early years settings will make provision for imaginative play. It is also why many settings will use role play as a way of developing children's vocabulary by setting out a new role-play experience such as 'at the garden centre' and then starting off the play by joining in. This allows children to hear new vocabulary and expressions in context.

Settings also find that children will often enjoy writing or mark making during role play. This is usually encouraged as part of the play, and so a child who is pretending to be a traffic warden may be given a clipboard and a pen so that they can write out and give 'tickets' to other children.

Supporting imaginative play to value ideas and interests

As you will see later in this unit, adults have an important role in supporting imaginative play. Key to this is the interest and value they place on it. By providing resources, being interested in what children do and giving children sufficient time, adults give children a clear message that this type of play is important. This can help children to explore more intricate and complex ideas and concepts through their play. Imaginative play also provides opportunities for children to explore their own ideas and interests freely as there is no right or wrong way to play. This helps children try out new roles and props and be adventurous, for example, by taking on the role of a superhero or a villain.

Bridging the gap between home and the early years setting

Children who have a home culture that is very different to the culture within the setting are likely to find an outlet in imaginative play. Using different types of imaginative play, they will probably play out their experiences in each of the cultures and try to make sense of the differences. For example, children whose family members take off their shoes before entering the home might remove their shoes, but later on, after seeing other children not doing this, might change their own play. Imaginative play can also help children to understand the differences between families, as they may play alongside others who do things differently. It is helpful for settings to make sure that children have props for domestic play that reflect all of the children's home cultures. This allows children to reflect and build on their own home experiences, and also broadens their knowledge of other children's experiences.

B1 Understand planning for imaginative play

It is important that adults support imaginative play by providing opportunities for it to occur. In this section, we look at practical ways in which you can plan and set up a range of opportunities.

The role of observation in planning for imaginative play

Adults have a key role to play in observing children during imaginative play. Observations will help you understand children's interests, and also help you plan further opportunities for them. This can in turn help to extend children's learning and enjoyment.

Young children often have favourite types of imaginative play that they return to repeatedly over a period of time. It can be useful to know what

particular children and groups of children enjoy doing, so you can make sure that this is provided for in the setting. Parents may help you with this, as often children engage in imaginative play at home too.

As part of observing children's play, think about the following questions.

How popular is this area?

Some areas of role play or types of small-world play go through phases of popularity with children. If this is the case, you might think about increasing the provision for them. For instance, if the home corner is very popular, you might create another 'home' in another part of the setting. This is because many imaginative play activities have a critical mass in terms of how many children can share the same story.

What is the story?

Most imaginative play develops a storyline. For instance, children may start saying that they are building the strongest train track because a dinosaur is going to come down and break it up. It is worth listening to the children and working out what the story is because this can help you develop it further by, for example, putting out new resources.

Who plays together?

From around 3 years old, children start to develop friendship and play preferences. It is worth looking at who seems to enjoy imaginative play together. This can help with planning if, for example, the setting has times when groups come together.

Setting up resources for imaginative play

Most settings have at least one designated area that is always a role-play area. This is likely to include a home corner, sometimes a shop and an area for dressing up. In addition, it is good practice for settings to have a role-play area outdoors, and this should also be well resourced.

Setting up for role play

A good starting point is to base the setting upon what you know children enjoy doing, what you have observed and any additional planning you have carried out. You can also talk to children about what equipment they would like to have out. Many settings are well resourced and this means that selections need to be made about what to put out in a session. If everything is put out at once, this can lead to a very messy and unrewarding play area for children. Do not be afraid of selecting particular resources and putting others away, but allowing children to access them if they want to.

It is good practice to give children the opportunity to engage in mark-making activities so, wherever possible, you should incorporate writing materials such as a shopping list into the kitchen or a price list into the shop.

Setting up a home corner

Domestic play is always a favourite with children and it is helpful if this area is attractive and well resourced.

This gives the children some play prompts. Within the home corner, you can sometimes give different focuses, such as 'kitchen' or 'bedroom'. This is very useful as a way of extending children's play and vocabulary.

Remember the following tips:

- Make sure the home corner area is clean.
- Take out any inappropriate toys or props that have found their way in from previous sessions.
- Try to make the area as realistic as possible – for instance, put things in the cupboards and drawers, lay the table or dress the baby.

How could this home corner be made more realistic for these children?

Dressing-up clothes

In some settings these are on a rail, while in others, they may be in a basket. Remember the following tips:

- Sort through the props, checking that they are clean and complete.
- Remove any items that are not looking attractive or need repair.
- Lay out outfits and props such as bags, belts and shoes attractively – perhaps on hangers or on tables.

Setting up small-world play

It can be helpful to put out some small-world play items for children. This gives them a starting point if they need it. A good tip is to combine sensory materials with small-world play. For example, you may put cars or diggers in a builder's tray that has gravel in the bottom of it or put farm animals in a tray of turf.

Maintaining areas

If children are enjoying their play and are very focused, try not to interfere as this may spoil their flow and concentration. This may mean that you need to do some discreet tidying-up of objects that have been discarded during children's play. You may also need to be ready to set things up again, once a child or group of children have changed their focus. This is important because, during a session, other children may want to engage in small-world play or role play and are more likely to do this if the area looks attractive. It is also important to keep observing children so that you can add resources to facilitate their play further.

Fantasy play

Fantasy play covers many scenarios, many of which the children will invent for themselves. This type of play is also often inspired by stories, books and visits. It is helpful if the props that are provided are 'real-life' ones as this will often make it easier for children to extend their play. Interestingly, children are quite resourceful and so, while it is useful to have some authentic props, they do not need every single detail to be accurate. For example, children will be happy putting their 'cupcakes' into a cardboard box that acts as the 'oven'.

Table 24.1 gives a few examples of the types of fantasy play that children may take part in, along with the types of resources that might be needed.

Superhero play

As superhero play can become quite boisterous, it is important to consider this when thinking about what resources you will provide for children. Some settings have clear policies about superhero play, especially with regard to whether or not children can have or make toy guns. It is therefore important to make sure that any resources you use are in line with the setting's approach to superhero play. In general terms, it can be useful to provide potential superheroes with some form of identification – this might mean a cape, badge or belt. As superheroes are likely to need some form of communication device, a toy phone can also come in handy. Interestingly, many settings will prevent superhero play from becoming destructive or very aggressive by providing resources that prompt superheroes to be kind and thoughtful. They may, for example, have a 'mission board' on which calls for help can be written, for example, 'a cat has gone missing' or 'someone needs help with their shopping'. Appropriate props are then provided so that these rescue missions can be enacted.

Table 24.1 Types of fantasy play and resources

Type of fantasy play	Resources required
Hairdressers'	Aprons, curlers, combs, brushes, mirrors, empty bottles for pretend shampoo, toy scissors, magazines for the waiting room
Shoe shop	Shoe boxes, measuring tape, selection of shoes, cash register, money, stools for sitting on
Hospital	Charts on clipboards, beds, stethoscope, uniform, bandages, crutches, pushchair to act as a wheelchair
Birthday party	Plates, birthday cake (made of dough with sticks for candles), pass the parcel, wrapped presents, birthday cards
Petrol station	Pumps (cardboard boxes with a tube or hosepipe sticking out), car wash (sponges, soapy water in buckets), cash register, sign

Using books and stories as a stimulus

Books and stories are often great starting points for children's imaginative play, especially for developing fantasy play. A story or images in a book can act as starting points for the creation of new role-play areas. For instance, following the story of Goldilocks and the Three Bears, a role-play area might be set up that recreates the three bears' house, along with three beds, three chairs and three bowls and spoons. Children may then recreate the story that they have heard and use the actual words in the story. Using books and stories for imaginative play is usually more successful with children who have good levels of language development and so you may find that you see this on placement with children aged 3 years plus.

Many children will also need an adult to support their play, even when they are familiar with the story. They may need the adult to join in or to help them create the space and props.

Using space and the outdoor environment

It is very interesting to observe children as they engage in imaginative play. In this way, we can often work out how best to provide the right type of space for their play.

Small-world play

Some small-world play requires that children are able to spread out, often on the floor. This is particularly true when children are engaged with train sets, cars and also play animals. To provide for this type of play, you should make sure that the floor area is comfortable – this might mean a rug on carpet, or soft grass or matting if outdoors. It is also important to provide a space that is out of the way of other children to avoid elaborate plans or play being trampled on. Children often like to have objects they will require during the play close to hand.

Some types of small-world play, such as playing with dolls' houses, pirate ships and castles, benefit from a low surface in addition to some floor space. A low table, bench or even a chair can work well for

this. In some settings, children enjoy putting items up on shelves or windowsills and then moving the characters around them on the floor.

Theory into practice

Observe children who are engaged in small-world play.

- Where are they playing, and what do they need for their play?
- Are there any difficulties with the location of their play?

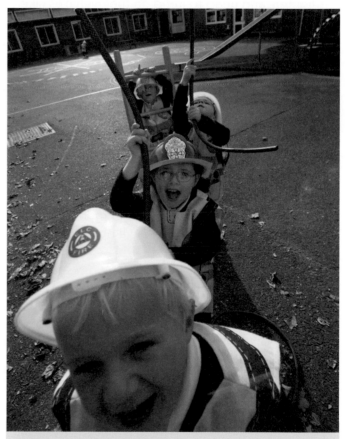

Children need enough space to move around during their play – set up play outdoors.

Role play requiring confined spaces

When children are pretending to be indoors they often like small spaces to play in. This means that if they are in the outdoor area, but are playing shop, they might choose an area next to a fence and may move objects to enclose this space. It is also interesting that when children are pretending to be indoors, they like a roof over them and for the space to be quite cramped. This means that you may need to provide more than one area of this nature if there are several children who want to role play. It also means that when organising play outdoors, you will need to create some cosy corners for children in the same way that you might indoors.

Role play requiring large amounts of space

Some types of pretend play require plenty of room to move around in. This is often because movement is an integral part of their play. A good example of this would be children who are pretending to be fire-fighters and need to jump on their vehicles (likely to be some form of wheeled toy) to get to the fire quickly. Without the possibility of this movement, much of the enjoyment and purpose of their play would be lost.

While some settings do have plenty of indoor space, this is usually quite rare, so this is one reason why it is important to provide role-play opportunities outdoors. Sometimes, this type of play may not work alongside the other play activities that are offered in the setting, so it is important to observe carefully what is happening in the play area and, if necessary, gently guide the children to a more suitable place where they can carry on playing, but in harmony with the others.

B2 Understand the role of the adult in imaginative play

While many children will happily play without adults being involved, we also know that imaginative play can be enriched by us providing resources, ideas and joining in at times. In this section, we look at the role of the adult in supporting and developing children's imaginative play.

Observing children engaged in imaginative play

One of the key ways in which we can support children's imaginative play is to observe them as they are playing. This can be done either discreetly, from the sidelines, or as we are joining in with them. Through this observation we can gain information that will help us to provide further opportunities for them. For example, we may put out additional resources connecting their play to stories and other games, or take them on visits. For instance, if a child seems very interested in playing shop, we might give them more 'stock' or plan a visit to a small shop to extend the play.

Communication and language

Observing play will also help us to assess children's development in areas such as communication and language. As most children talk while they are engaged in imaginative play, you might consider recording their speech or at least listening to it. You may, for example, notice that a child rarely talks to other children despite being very engaged with the play. This may be because they do not have sufficient language to express themselves and so you may need to look for additional activities or ways of encouraging the child to talk.

Social and emotional development

We may also spot how children's social skills are developing, as imaginative play usually brings children together. From observing children, we may assess the stage of their social development and play. We may also notice children who are consistently submissive to others and so need to develop a little more confidence. Imaginative play is also an expression of children's emotional states, and so we may look out for children who are showing feelings of anger. This could mean that we need to look for additional activities to help them express themselves.

Child protection and imaginative play

Some children who have been subjected to abuse may replay it through their play. It is important to look out for this and consider what might have influenced their play. If you see children who are playing out scenes that seem unusual or inappropriate given their age, you should pass on this information to the person in your setting with responsibility for safeguarding. Look out for unusual sexual knowledge or very detailed enactments of violence.

Link

Go to Unit 8 in Student Book 1 for more information on child protection.

Assessing effectiveness of provision

By watching children, especially the complexity of their play and how engaged they are in their play, we can use this as a tool to reflect on our provision for imaginative play. It may be that the resources, layout or props need refreshing or changing, or that we need to be more involved in their play.

Asking focused, open-ended questions

It is quite a skill to know when and how to ask questions of children as they are engaged in imaginative play. You could try talking to children about what they are doing when they are taking a break or want you to help them in some way. The key is to be genuinely interested in what children are doing and to ask questions about what is happening and why. By asking children about their play, you can learn about what is of interest to them and use this to plan further play experiences. This can help children to think about what they are doing. Sensitive questioning also helps children extend their thinking and problem-solving abilities, for example, asking them what might happen next. Sensitive questioning may also develop children's vocabulary, as you recast and expand children's explanations and thoughts.

Case study

Owen saw that a group of children were playing intensely in a den that they had made earlier in the day. It was nearly snack time and Owen asked the group if they would like to have a snack in the den. They were very keen, but he reminded them that they would still need to wash their hands. He went with them indoors and while they were washing their hands, he asked them about their play. They were happy to talk to him and when they were back inside the den, they showed him what they were doing.

He asked them what the rules of their game were. The children thought about this for a while, and then started to articulate their very complex rules.

1 How did Owen talk to the children without interrupting the flow of their play?

2 How did this approach help the children to feel that their play was valued?

3 How did their conversation help the children to articulate their play?

Supporting and extending thinking and learning by becoming a role-play partner

From an early age, children love sensitive play partners. We may pretend to be on the telephone with an 18-month-old child, or to be enjoying a cup of tea that they have handed to us. Joining in with children's role play can help them gain skills and is a good way of supporting their development. It does require sensitivity and skill, as children must still have ownership of their play and the play has to remain enjoyable.

Joining children in role play is often used in settings when a new role-play area has been created. In this way, children are able to hear the vocabulary and expressions as well as observe any skills or actions that are usually associated with this scenario. An adult may, for example, play the part of a vet and ask a child who has brought in a pet (cuddly toy) to the surgery whether the pet has been off its food and whether it has been vaccinated. The adult may then 'examine' the pet using a stethoscope before suggesting that it may need some medicine. By seeing the adult in role, the children can later use the same script and know what to do.

In the same way, an adult who is playing the part of an assistant in a shoe shop might ask a 'customer' about what kind of shoes they are looking for. This would provide an opportunity to naturally introduce words associated with shoes such as 'lace-ups' or 'boots'.

Why is it a good idea for us to join children in role play?

Theory into practice

Find out how your setting introduces new role-play themes to children.

How to explore and extend ideas using drawing, writing and ICT

Imaginative play can be used as a wonderful starting point for children to explore and develop other ideas and skills. Children, for example, who are pretending to be a superhero, may be prompted by an adult to create a map that helps them find their way to a rescue. This would involve drawing or using a computer and so would help the child gain further skills. The following are three examples of how easy it is to help children to develop their interest and skills in drawing, mark making/writing and Information and Communication Technology (ICT).

- Role-play area: hospital
  - Children might go online with an adult and print out medical charts.
  - Children may draw pictures or make cards and then make 'get well' cards for patients.

- Superhero play
  - Children might draw maps to help them 'fly' to where they need to go.
  - Children may write out the story of what happens.
  - Children could draw and paint props to support the play.

- Small-world play: trains
  - Children might make tickets.
  - Children may write signs of stations or notices to the driver.
  - Children could look at different types of trains on the Internet.

The importance of challenging gender stereotyping

From around 3 years, most children start to explore gender as a concept – what it means to be a little boy or a little girl. This starts to show in their imaginative play as they may start to restrict themselves to certain roles. They may also make comments to other children about what they can and cannot do. While the exploration of gender concept is usual, it is important that you do not encourage and support the narrowing of gender roles that have traditionally existed in our society. Early attitudes and understanding about what men and women can and cannot do can sometimes become restrictive and may later subconsciously affect a child's choices. It is therefore important to find ways to challenge gender stereotyping.

You can do this in a variety of ways.

Using photographs and images

Photographs and images are very powerful for young children. Look out for photographs of men doing tasks that have traditionally been associated with women, such as cooking, looking after children and nursing. In the same way, look out for images of women in jobs such as fire-fighting, plumbing or decorating.

Using resources

Look at the resources that are put out and consider whether they contribute to gender bias. While many girls love wearing princess-type dresses, consider whether these should be available all the time. It is also worth looking out for 'real' props as these are often more interesting than toys and are more likely to appeal to both boys and girls. Think also about the colour of toys and resources, as some colours such as pink, purple and blue send out a message to children about who the toys are for. This can be limiting.

Visitors and outings

Any real-life experience, as we have already seen, can enrich role play. If children are engaged by what they have seen or who they have met, this can help them to expand their concept of gender.

Joining in play

We can join in role play, as we saw earlier. Wherever possible, try to make sure that you engage in role play that is not traditionally associated with your gender.

Challenging comments

It is important to challenge children's comments or actions if they seem to be discriminatory. This needs to be done very sensitively, because children are often expressing views that they have either heard or have based on their experience to date – so, if in their household, they only see a women ironing, they may come to the conclusion that boys 'aren't allowed' to iron. Explaining that this is not necessarily the case is important.

Helping parents understand the value of imaginative play

Most parents will recognise that their child enjoys imaginative play, but not all will be aware of the many benefits that this type of play offers. It can be helpful to show parents that it is valuable, through the ways that we observe and talk about it. In some settings,

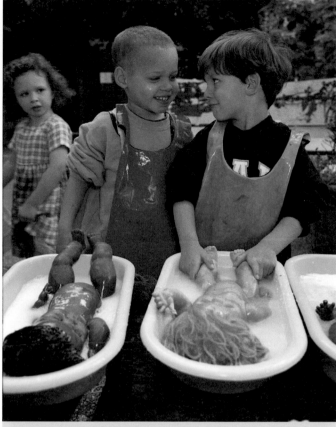

Can you see here how gender stereotypes are being challenged?

posters are put up by the home corner that indicate the benefits that children gain from this type of play, so that when parents collect their children or visit on open days, they can find out more. This approach works well, but parents may also like a more personal approach and will need to know how imaginative play is supporting their child's development. They may also be interested in understanding how imaginative play is likely to change as their child develops. Many settings will do this with parents by sharing observations with them, in particular **learning journeys** and photographs or film clips.

Key term

Learning journey – a way of assessing and planning for children's development using a narrative approach that can easily be shared and constructed with parents and children.

Learning journeys

Many settings use learning journeys as a way of sharing information with parents. Learning journeys usually comprise an observation that includes a photograph, and practitioners explore with parents what the next steps for the child might be at home or in the setting. As children are likely to engage in this type of play at home, it can be a good idea to find out how the child usually plays and incorporate this into the planning for the child. While sharing the child's learning journey, you can also talk to the parents about what the child is gaining and how you may help the child develop further.

Photographs and film clips

Most parents love watching their children in action. Using photographs and film clips, you can talk to the parents about the child's imagination, speech and social development. It can also be useful to refer back to previous photographs and film clips so that parents can see the development that has taken place.

Link

Go to Unit 9 for more information on the different types of observation methods.

Assessment practice 24.2

3B1.P3 | 3B1.P4 | 3B1.P5 | 3B1.M2 | 3B2.P6 | 3B2.P7 | 3B2.M3 | 3B.D2

An international early years group is interested in sharing perspectives on children's play. You have been asked to write an article that explains how imaginative play is valued and supported by early years practitioners. Your article should include comments about:

- the importance of observing and planning for children's imaginative play

- how play may be resourced and provided for indoors and outdoors to support the different types of role play
- the role of the adult as a play partner in imaginative play
- how adults can support and extend play
- challenging gender stereotyping in role play.

Further reading and resources

Cummings, A. and Featherstone, S. (2009) *Role Play in the Early Years*, London: A&C Black Publishers Ltd.

Duffy, B. (2006) *Supporting Creativity and Imagination in the Early Years* (2nd ed.), Maidenhead: Open University Press.

Featherstone, S. (2001) *The Little Book of Role Play*, London: Featherstone Education, Bloomsbury Publishing plc.

Harries, J. (2009) *Role Play (Play in the EYFS)*, London: Step Forward Publishing Ltd.

Ready for work?

Justin Gerrard   Teaching assistant

In the reception class we use imaginative play as a tool, primarily for children's language and literacy development. Within the room, we have a role-play area that is always a home and then, in addition, we usually set up two other areas. For the next couple of weeks, we have a shoe shop and a train! Outdoors, we have limited space, but we have a small playhouse that the children transform into anything from a spaceship to a café. We base the areas both on children's interests and the topic or book that we are reading. We think that this strikes a balance, as this way there is plenty of child-initiated play going on, but we are also creating opportunities to develop language and to support the topic.

I think that getting the role-play area up and running is absolutely key, as it is one of the most popular play activities that we have here. Children never seem to tire of pretending, and so often we can use this as a starting point for other areas of the curriculum. When the children turned the playhouse into a café, we made menus with them, took them out to the local café and also talked about healthy eating. We also worked with the children on a price list and it helped the children talk about and recognise coins. It is important, though, that these areas are maintained and set up nicely. I have been in other settings where role play is less of a priority and it shows in terms of the quality of interaction and the time that children spend there.

Skills for practice

Support outdoor play and learning

Setting up a carwash

This is a great activity for outdoors. Children love anything to do with water and so with a little preparation, this can be a great activity.

- Start by finding out whether any children are allergic to washing-up liquid, as a little bit of this in lots of water is needed.
- Look out for buckets, sponges and aprons.
- Find a space where children can bring their bikes or other wheeled toys.
- Create a sign and put out a table and a cash register.
- Get into character and ask if any children want to have their bikes washed.
- Tell them the price and ask if they would like a 'full valet service with polish' or the 'basic'.
- Explain that one service is cheaper than the other and give the prices.
- Let any child who wants to come and 'work' with you join in.
- When you feel that the role play is established, step back, but continue to supervise discreetly.

Introduction

During the past 50 years, the number of children who play out in the street or unsupervised in parks has reduced significantly. Outdoors used to be the main area for play, and older children would look after babies and young children. Today, it is rare to find children playing outside unsupervised. There are many reasons for this, but it is now recognised that we need to give children more opportunities to be outdoors as part of early years provision. While health and exercise are important, there are other reasons too, including children's psychological well-being. This is why there is such a focus in early years curricula on ensuring that all children spend time outdoors every day. This unit looks at the importance of children spending time outdoors and ways in which this might be done. It also looks at the role of the adult in promoting the development of children outdoors.

Assessment: You will be assessed by a series of assignments set by your teacher/tutor.

Learning aims

In this unit you will:

A   understand the importance of the outdoors to development and learning

B1   understand the features of effective outdoor provision

B2   understand the role of the adult in promoting development outdoors.

> We have just had a focus on outdoor play in the nursery. We observed children as they were playing, spoke to them about what they would like to do and use during play, and have now transformed our outdoor area. It has been working brilliantly and the children are getting so much from it. We have all noticed the way that children seem to be more engaged in their play and talk to each other, and there is this wonderful buzz about the place. Parents have also noticed a difference and we are planning to work with a group of parents to set up a children's garden project.
>
> Steve, *a nursery practitioner*

Promoting Children's Development Outdoors

28

Assessment Zone

This table shows what you must do in order to achieve a **Pass**, **Merit** or **Distinction** grade, and where you can find activities to help you.

Assessment criteria		
Pass	**Merit**	**Distinction**
Learning aim A: Understand the importance of the outdoors to development and learning		
3A.P1 English I&CT Explain the benefits of outdoor play to children's learning and development. **Assessment practice 28.1** **3A.P2** Describe how approaches to outdoor learning and play are applied in practice. **Assessment practice 28.1** **3A.P3** Explain the relationship between indoor and outdoor environments in promoting children's learning and development. **Assessment practice 28.1**	**3A.M1** Analyse how outdoor provision supports the needs of children in an early years setting. **Assessment practice 28.1**	**3A.D1** Evaluate the extent to which outdoor learning environments in early years settings could impact on outcomes for children. **Assessment practice 28.1**
Learning aim B1: Understand the features of effective outdoor provision **Learning aim B2: Understand the role of the adult in promoting development outdoors**		
3B1.P4 Describe the physical features of effective early years outdoor provision. **Assessment practice 28.2** **3B1.P5** Explain the importance of flexible resources in outdoor provision in an early years setting. **Assessment practice 28.2** **3B1.P6** Research resources for outdoor provision in an early years setting that will encourage children's creativity and imagination. **Assessment practice 28.2**	**3B1.M2** Analyse how effective outdoor provision can contribute to children's development and learning. **Assessment practice 28.2**	**3B.D2** Evaluate the extent to which adults in early years settings contribute to children's learning and development outdoors. **Assessment practice 28.3**

continued

Assessment criteria (continued)

Pass	Merit	Distinction
3B2.P7 Explain why it is important for adults in an early years setting to have positive attitudes to outdoor learning. **Assessment practice 28.3**	**3B2.M3** Discuss, using examples, how adults can best promote the development of children of different ages outdoors. **Assessment practice 28.3**	
3B2.P8 Explain how to support child-initiated experiences outdoors in an early years setting. **Assessment practice 28.3**		
3B2.P9 Describe how the weather and seasons can be used to support learning and development outdoors in an early years setting. **Assessment practice 28.3**		

English | English Functional Skills signposting

I&CT | Information and Communication Technology skills signposting

How you will be assessed

This unit will be assessed by a series of internally assessed tasks set by your teacher/tutor. Throughout this unit you will find assessment practice activities that will help you work towards your assessment. Completing these activities will not mean that you have achieved a particular grade, but you will have carried out useful research or preparation that will be relevant when it comes to your final assignment.

In order for you to carry out the tasks in your assignment, it is important that you check you have met all of the Pass grading criteria. You can do this as you work your way through the assignment.

If you are hoping to gain a Merit or Distinction, you should also make sure that you present the information in your assignment in the style that is required by the relevant assessment criterion. For example, Merit criteria will require you to discuss and analyse, and Distinction criteria will require you to evaluate.

The assignment set by your teacher/tutor will consist of a number of tasks designed to meet the criteria in the table. This is likely to consist of a written assignment but may also include activities such as:

- case studies
- a presentation
- training materials.

Getting started

Do you remember playing outside as a child? Being outdoors is now considered essential to support children's overall development. Make a list of the skills you think children gain by playing outdoors. By the end of this unit, see if you can add to your list.

A Understand the importance of the outdoors to development and learning

Outdoor learning is now a major part of the curricula in the UK. In this section, we look at how it supports children's development and learning.

The positive impact on well-being

It is now recognised that young children can become stressed and also depressed. We also know that being outdoors and taking part in physical exercise can reduce anxiety and thus help stress and depression, and promote resilience. This is because chemicals called endorphins that affect the brain are released by the pituitary gland. In addition, children also benefit from opportunities to engage in child-initiated play, which is known to support children's self-esteem and perseverance.

Link

Go to Unit 2 in Student Book 1 to find more information about child-initiated play.

Encouraging healthy lifestyles

Years ago, it was normal to see children playing outdoors. Today, for a variety of reasons, including fears over safety, digital entertainment and less available time, fewer children spend time outdoors. This is of great concern, as by spending time outdoors, children gain positive attitudes towards walking, running and enjoying nature. By taking exercise without realising it, they are also learning how to deal with stress. Spending time outdoors is therefore good for children's all-round health.

Positive attitudes towards being outdoors gained in childhood can also influence our attitudes towards walking and taking exercise later in life. The UK has an increasingly overweight population, so this is currently extremely relevant.

Supporting physical development

Encouraging children to enjoy the outdoors is an ideal way to support development, especially in spaces such as woodlands, fields and beaches. Such places have in-built natural challenges, such as uneven surfaces and slopes. These require children to balance and to develop stamina. Even in outdoor spaces specifically designed for children they can gain physical skills, as they may use wheeled toys, run and climb. Any vigorous activity will build stamina and strengthen bones. Figure 28.1 shows how development can be supported by outdoor activity.

Benefits of outdoor play on social and emotional development

As well as it helping to prevent stress and anxiety, children are more likely to concentrate during child-initiated play outdoors. There are other skills that children can gain by being outdoors too. They will have opportunities to play with other children and so develop their negotiation and cooperation skills. Children also benefit psychologically from the ability to be noisy and make large movements, and this is one reason why many adults, when thinking about their childhood, use the word 'freedom'.

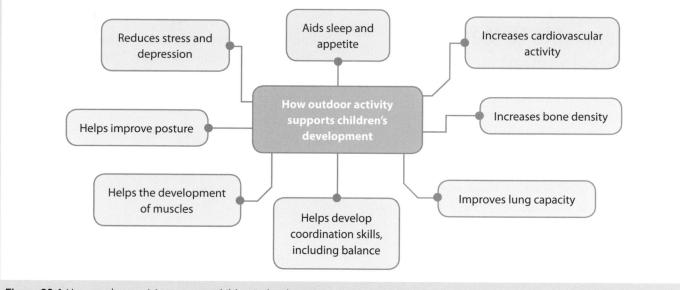

Figure 28.1 How outdoor activity supports children's development

Link

Go to Unit 3 in Student Book 1 to find more information about promoting children's physical development.

Opportunities for cognitive development

Children benefit from stimulating environments. By visiting a range of places such as parks, beaches and woodlands, as well as playing in outdoor spaces, they are more likely to learn new concepts and also develop new vocabulary. When children are outdoors, they also have the opportunity to notice things that are new or of interest, and this allows them to find out more about the natural world or scientific concepts. Interestingly, many of these learning opportunities are likely to be spontaneous, such as a child noticing a snail on the climbing frame or a gutter leaking because it is raining hard.

As you will see later in this unit, it is important that adults look for and plan opportunities to support children's learning and development. They may, for example, encourage children to design a mural or make decisions about what should be planted in a gardening area.

Offering experiences through activity or movement

Being outdoors can give children plenty of first-hand opportunities such as watering plants or washing windows. In some settings that use a **Forest School approach**, children may also (under supervision) experience some real-world activities such as fire lighting and cooking on an open fire. Such experiences are not only exciting for children, but also memorable, and so support their learning. Being outdoors in a stimulating environment seems to give children more chance of 'learning by doing' and is one reason why outdoor play is considered so important.

Key term

Forest School approach – where settings are spending time outdoors, usually in woodlands, and carry out activities typically used in Scandinavian countries.

The value of different environments to learning and development

There was a time when many adults, including parents, associated children being outdoors with play, and being indoors with work and learning. Since the introduction of the early years curricula in the UK, this thinking has been challenged. The term 'outdoor classroom' is widely used, which suggests that learning and development take place outdoors as well. To support this change in thinking, activities and resources are now used outdoors that allow children to develop skills and knowledge in all parts of the curriculum. There are now mark-making tables and role-play opportunities outdoors, for example, and not just equipment to promote physical development.

Complementing and extending indoor provision

The current trend in early years is to make sure that the outdoor provision looks at all aspects of the curricula. Thus, children may be engaged in playing

hopscotch and rolling dice or drawing pictures of items that they have gathered during a walk. There are also some activities that can start indoors and then continue to be developed outdoors. Table 28.1 shows examples of these.

Importance of free access to outdoor provision

The ideal in early years is to allow children to move from inside to outside and vice versa. This allows them to follow their play ideas without needing

Table 28.1 Activities that can start indoors and finish outdoors

Activity	Tasks	Link to the curricula
Making kites	Making them indoors and then taking them out to fly	• Understanding of concepts such as flight • Problem solving • Design
Sending balloon messages	Messages are written indoors, but are attached to balloons and let go of outdoors	• Early literacy and mark making • Cooperation • Concepts such as flight and distance
Story telling	Stories such as Jack and the Beanstalk are told indoors, but children can then role play them outdoors	• Communication and language • Negotiation • Turn taking • Imagination
Water and sand play	Children can play with water and sand indoors, but then do so again on a larger scale outdoors	• Volume and capacity • Exploring concepts such as density by observing which items float or sink

to ask permission or have a break. This concept is sometimes called 'free flow'. An example of this might be where two 3-year-olds begin indoors and pretend to go shopping. They get dressed and then go outdoors where they use the wheeled toys to 'drive to the shops'. Then they realise that they have not written a shopping list and one of them suggests that they should go indoors to write one. In this example, children can go from one place to another in support of their child-initiated play. The advantage of this style of access is that children's play becomes more meaningful and incorporates many different skills. It is also likely to be of a longer duration and so helps children to concentrate and persevere.

Approaches to outdoor play and learning in curricula

It is important to understand how the outdoors is included in the curriculum framework in the country where you are working. In the EYFS, for example, there is a welfare requirement that children are given opportunities to play outdoors every day, even when it is not dry and sunny. In the Welsh Foundation Phase, it is also clear that play and learning should take place both in and out of doors.

Research

Read the early years curriculum framework for the country in which you wish to work.

Find out what the expectations are for outdoor play and learning.

Other approaches to outdoor play and learning

During this course, you have already looked at the approaches of Froebel, Steiner and Montessori. Each of these pioneers felt that the outdoors was significant in children's learning and development. While Froebel and Steiner stressed the importance of children learning about nature and also being imaginative, Montessori set up a garden for children so that they could plant seeds and watch plants grow as part of their 'practical life' skills.

In the UK, the Forest School approach has also become popular, influenced by Forest Schools in

Denmark and Sweden. The idea is that children spend time in woodlands, learning about nature and gaining practical skills such as making fires and shelters, as well as story telling. Forest Schools are very popular with both children and their parents, and they seem to help children to gain in confidence and enjoy physical activity. As many settings do not have access to woodlands, dedicated centres have been set up (some by the Forestry Commission) to allow regular visits from settings.

Link

Go to Unit 2 in Student Book 1 to find more information about how different philosophies approach the provision of play opportunities.

Research

Find out more about Forest Schools in your area.

If possible, visit a Forest School or talk to staff in your setting to find out about Forest School training.

You can also read more by visiting a page dedicated to Forest Schools on the Directgov website. You can access this page by going to www.pearsonhotlinks.co.uk and searching for this title.

Assessment practice 28.1   3A.P1 | 3A.P2 | 3A.P3 | 3A.M1 | 3A.D1

You have been asked to write a policy for your setting about outdoor play and learning. As part of the policy process, you have to outline the benefits of outdoor play and learning to children. This needs to be sufficiently detailed so that new staff can understand the rationale behind the policy. Your policy should provide:

- information about the benefits to children's development, learning and well-being
- information on why children should have good access to the outdoors and how this is applied in practice
- ways in which the indoor and outdoor environment can be used together to promote children's learning and development.

B1 Understand the features of effective outdoor provision

The idea of having children play in and out of doors is quite simple, but in reality there are a lot of practical challenges that need to be overcome. This section looks at the features of effective outdoor provision and how these features can help overcome some of the challenges while supporting children's development.

Integrated indoor–outdoor early years provision

Wherever possible, early years settings are encouraged to find ways of enabling free-flow play, allowing children to go outdoors whenever they wish. To facilitate this, many settings have installed patio-type doors or have even moved their location. The latter is particularly true of reception classes in some schools that have been moved to be closer to outdoor areas. Some settings have also created smaller, fenced-off areas within the outdoor space to allow children to come and go without an adult always needing to be outdoors.

Integrated provision does throw up some practical issues that most early years settings have to work through. This includes whether or not an adult always has to go outside with the children, how to prevent the indoor space becoming cold and how to monitor where the children are in case of evacuation.

Theory into practice

Find out how children access the outdoor space in your setting. If your placement has patio doors or easy access, find out the following:

- Does an adult always have to be outside with the children?
- How do they monitor which children are indoors and which are outdoors?
- How do they manage the coats and shoes?
- How do they keep the indoor space warm?

Providing shade and shelter

It is important that outdoor provision has both shade and shelter if it is to be used in all weathers.

Shade

There should be some shaded areas for children, particularly in the summer months when it is important to keep children out of the sun because of the risk of dehydration and skin cancer. Figure 28.2 shows the many approaches that settings can use to create shade.

Shelter

As well as shade, you also need to think about some shelter for children. Many of the ideas for creating shade will also create some shelter, but in addition, some settings will also install tents and teepees – this can be a good activity in itself.

Different surfaces and levels

To support children's learning, it is helpful to provide as many different surfaces and levels as possible. A range of surfaces may include gravel, bark chippings, tarmac, soil and grass. A variety of surfaces gives children, especially babies, the opportunity to feel and experience different textures. It is also helpful for children to experience different levels. This helps develop their gross motor movement and balance skills. Toddlers particularly like climbing and standing on low structures or running down slopes. A variety of levels also makes an outdoor environment look more visually interesting. The following can be used by settings to enable children to experience different levels:

- steps
- ramps
- climbing frames
- raised beds or grassy areas
- treehouses
- low walls
- logs
- grassy mounds
- car tyres.

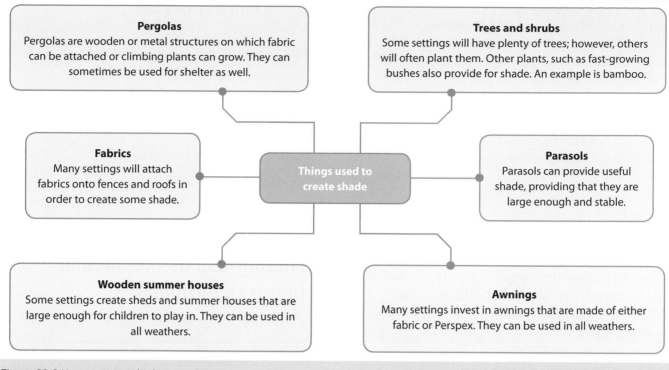

Pergolas
Pergolas are wooden or metal structures on which fabric can be attached or climbing plants can grow. They can sometimes be used for shelter as well.

Trees and shrubs
Some settings will have plenty of trees; however, others will often plant them. Other plants, such as fast-growing bushes also provide for shade. An example is bamboo.

Fabrics
Many settings will attach fabrics onto fences and roofs in order to create some shade.

Things used to create shade

Parasols
Parasols can provide useful shade, providing that they are large enough and stable.

Wooden summer houses
Some settings create sheds and summer houses that are large enough for children to play in. They can be used in all weathers.

Awnings
Many settings invest in awnings that are made of either fabric or Perspex. They can be used in all weathers.

Figure 28.2 How to create shade in outdoor areas

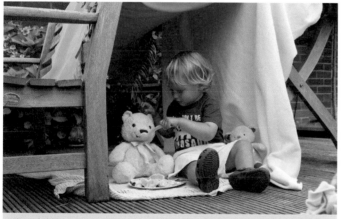

This child is being shaded by fabric that has been used to make a den.

Activity

With the permission of your placement supervisor, take a photograph of the outdoor environment when there are not any children in it. With other learners on your course, compare photographs and look to see how different early years settings manage:

- shade and shelter
- surfaces
- levels.

Independent access to resources

It is good practice for children to be able to access resources independently. This is important, as children may wish to add to their play or have clear play preferences, and by being able to freely access materials they gain independence. In many early years settings, storage both indoors and out is a big issue. If storage is poor and difficult to access, there is a likelihood that fewer resources will be put out or that there is insufficient variation in what is put out. It is important for children to be involved in the setting up and putting away of resources. Settings have different approaches to this challenge, as we will now see.

Use of sheds

Ideally, these need to have double doors for easy access, a ramp for accessing wheeled toys and a range of shelves. Sheds can also double up as play areas and for shade if they are carefully arranged.

Storage boxes and bins

Plastic storage boxes and bins are often used for smaller items that are not valuable.

They can be left outdoors and children can access them easily. Different-coloured boxes are useful as they can help children to remember what might be inside, for example, a red box contains balls, while a blue box contains items for water play.

Car ports

Some settings store wheeled toys in specific covered areas similar to car ports, and encourage children to 'park' the toys they have been using. This keeps the wheeled toys from becoming wet, although this approach will not prevent rust.

Tarpaulin sheets

Some settings will use tarpaulin sheets to cover materials and resources. This can be effective, although if it has rained, care has to be taken when removing them.

Appropriate clothing and protection

The current trend is that all children should have outdoor access all year round, not just on fine, sunny days. This means that settings have to create outdoor environments that will allow children to be outside in all weathers, hence the need for different surfaces and the provision of shelter. In addition, settings will need to make sure that children are wearing suitable clothes. In some settings, outdoor clothing is provided and settings will often buy all-in-one suits, wellingtons and rain capes as well as gloves, socks and hats. In other settings, parents are expected to provide these items for the children. However, it is quite common for settings also to keep some spare clothing just in case a child comes unprepared. Here are some simple lists of outdoor clothing that should be available for different weather types.

Clothing for sunny weather

- Long-sleeved T-shirts
- Sunglasses
- Sunhats

Note: Although not an item of clothing, sunscreen should be applied according to parents' wishes.

Clothing for rainy weather

- Wellingtons
- Rain capes/all-in-ones/waterproofs
- Umbrellas

Clothing for cold weather

- Warm socks
- Wellingtons or outdoor shoes
- Hats, gloves and scarves
- Fleeces or additional layers
- Coats/anoraks/padded all-in-ones

Making use of the special features outdoors

The main features of the outdoors that provide children with different learning experiences are the available space and the changing weather. It is important that these features are well utilised when creating outdoor environments. Many settings do this in the following ways.

Exploring the weather

Many settings will provide specific activities and resources that will help children to explore the weather. There may be thermometers, windmills and kites, as well as heat-sensitive strips. In addition, settings may also use naturally occurring opportunities such as drawing children's attention to a layer of ice in a gutter or the way in which the ground has become hard and dry.

Using the available space

Additional space should mean that children can engage in noisier and potentially bigger activities. Many settings will put up sound walls or will have large digging areas and places where children can run or use sit-and-ride toys.

Flexible and versatile provision

Some of the best outdoor spaces for children are very flexible and versatile. This means that every time the children go outdoors, they can potentially find new things to do or new ways of playing.

Open-ended resources

One way in which settings can provide flexible and versatile provision is to give children open-ended resources that they can use in a variety of ways. Car tyres are a good example of this. Children can use them as stepping stones, as seats and also as part of obstacle courses. They can also be lined and used as planters or as makeshift containers for sand and gravel. Figure 28.3 shows other popular resources that are used in settings.

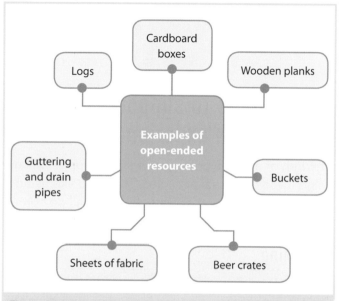

Figure 28.3 Examples of open-ended resources

Buckets are a good open-ended resource. What other activities could you use buckets for?

Supporting inclusion

As well as providing open-ended resources, settings also need to be aware of how they will support inclusion and enable all children, regardless of age, disability, medical condition or gender, access to the outdoors. This requires settings to be thoughtful when carrying out any large-scale building work such as putting in doors, ramps and fixed apparatus, to meet the needs of children with mobility needs or visual impairments, for example. Once in position, this apparatus cannot easily be changed. When steps are built or a new level added, there should always be a ramp fitted. It is also important to understand that over time there may be a range of children with different needs. Creating a large, open area may suit a child in a wheelchair, but it could be too open for a child with emotional and behavioural needs who would benefit from a cosier area. This is a good argument for not having too many static resources such as climbing frames that cannot be moved or adjusted to suit different children's needs.

As well as thinking about the physical needs of children, it is also important that the outdoor space is appealing to all children. Close observation of the activities that children are choosing or avoiding is important here.

Resources for different types of play

In most early years settings, the outdoor provision is characterised by a number of resources that will support children's play and development. The aim in most early years curricula is to ensure that children can cover each of the areas of learning both indoors and outdoors, so for example most early years settings will have areas for mark making outdoors.

Natural materials

There is a wide range of materials that can be provided outdoors for children to explore. Each material provides children with a different tactile experience and a range of possibilities that can be incorporated into children's play. In addition, as most children love 'mixing', it is usual to find children bringing together different materials in a bucket or in the digging area. Most settings will provide natural materials in a variety of ways, for example, in water and sand trays, buckets, builders' trays, inside tyres, and also directly on the ground, such as soil, bark chippings, leaves, gravel, stones and straw.

Materials for construction and den play

Children love building things outdoors. This could be anything from a hideout or den using fabrics, tarpaulin, cardboard boxes, bamboo sticks and metal frames or rods, through to using wooden or plastic blocks and beer crates to create a ship.

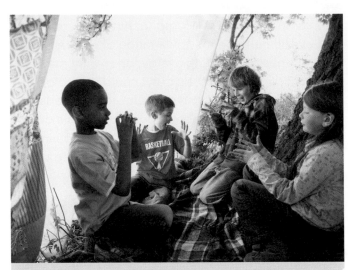

What have this group of children used to create their den?

Encouraging creative and imaginative play

The outdoors can provide opportunities for children to paint, make marks and be creative. It can also be a place where children can engage in extended role play by, for example, using a wheeled toy or bike to 'go to the shops' before going to a playhouse or den to 'unload the shopping'. Some settings will also create areas such as petrol stations, shops and garden centres to develop children's role play outdoors. Other common ways that early years settings can provide for children's creative and imaginative play are by:

- creating mark-making boards
- painting walls
- making tents
- providing role-play props, such as bags, spoons and items from the home
- providing real objects for children to explore, such as crates, tubing and brushes
- providing sand and water trays
- providing opportunities to dig and explore mud, leaves and gravel.

Resources for experiencing the natural world

Young children are often fascinated by nature. Resources to encourage this include magnifying sheets, bug boxes, wormeries and equipment for growing things such as plant pots, trowels and watering cans.

Theory into practice

Make a list of ways in which your setting supports the following types of play:

- creative and imaginative
- exploration of the natural world
- construction.

Resources to support real-world experiences

Children of all ages enjoy feeling grown-up and like being involved in real activities. They also like using real tools and resources. Many settings will do some or all of the following with children to support this.

Gardening

Children love digging and planting. Ideally, children need to experience using real tools or ones that are still effective but have been designed for smaller hands.

Hanging out the washing

This has been a traditional activity that children have been involved in for hundreds of years. Children can pass you pegs, hand up washing and even peg up smaller items for themselves.

Sweeping and clearing

Most outdoor spaces will need sweeping and clearing at times. It may be that leaves have blown in or the odd weed is appearing. Involving children in these tasks and using tools such as yard brushes can be very popular.

Washing

Most early years settings will encourage children to wash windows, wheeled toys and other items. Buckets, sponges and soapy water are the main resources for this activity.

You have been asked to look at the resources and overall provision required for a stimulating outdoor environment in a nursery that has children from 0 to 5 years and an after-school club taking children up to 8 years. Your brief is to prepare a presentation that looks at the types of resources that will support children's learning and development and features that support excellent outdoor provision. Your presentation must include:

- the importance of provision to children's overall development and learning
- the physical features of effective outdoor provision
- the importance of flexible resources and examples of resources that will support children's creativity and imagination.

B2 Understand the role of the adult in promoting development outdoors

Most children love being outdoors, so it is essential that adults working with them enjoy being outside too and that they understand how to support children's learning and development.

Having a positive attitude

If adults find being outside a chore, it shows in the way that they are not always properly dressed for the occasion and how they look for reasons to bring children back inside. This is a shame, because children pick up on the way that adults feel by noticing their facial expressions, movements and tone of voice. A positive attitude gives children permission to play and explore, but an adult who is not keen on being outdoors often prevents children from settling down to play. One of the reasons why adults often do not have a positive attitude is that they become bored. This is strange, because there are plenty of things that adults could be doing that will be interesting and helpful. When the adult is busy, children will either want to see what they are doing and join in or will go off happily and start playing themselves. Below is a list of things that adults could be doing outdoors, alongside, of course, supervising and encouraging children's play:

- weeding
- sweeping
- clearing leaves and debris

- planting
- observing children's development, friendships and interests
- supporting children's play
- organising activities for children
- observing nature and drawing interested children's attention to it.

This adult is joining in with a child's play. Make sure you show a positive attitude about playing outdoors.

The need for risk assessment

Safety is often cited as a reason why children cannot play outdoors in challenging and interesting ways. Risk assessments either support this view or are used to reduce the risks to acceptable levels. As part of your work with children, you will need to be aware of the risks of being outdoors, but you should also use common sense and look for ways of counteracting them. Table 28.2 shows the dangers commonly associated with activities outdoors, but also shows how they can be managed. This principle should be reflected in risk assessments.

Behavioural boundaries

Children will need to know what they can and cannot do when outdoors, so adults are required to set some boundaries. These will depend on the age/stage of the children and the outdoor areas. Boundaries should always be set in relation to keeping children safe and this should be based on risk assessments carried out both before and during an activity. As we have seen, it is important that children's learning and development are not hampered by over-zealous adults worried about safety.

Some of the usual boundaries set when children are outdoors are as follows – note how easy it is to understand the rationale behind them:

- Climbing equipment should only be used as intended by the manufacturer.
- Numbers should be limited and turn taking is required for equipment such as slides, climbing frames and wheeled toys.
- Children should go to the adult when they are called.
- When playing outside in public areas, children should remain in sight of an adult and should return promptly when called.
- Certain activities should only be done in dedicated areas to avoid accidents, such as the use of wheeled toys or throwing or kicking objects.

Table 28.2 Dangers associated with being outdoors

Danger	How to manage the risk
Children becoming lost or taken by strangers	<ul><li>Fencing</li><li>Supervision by adults</li><li>High-visibility jackets to be worn by staff and children</li><li>Mobile phone in case of an emergency</li></ul>
Traffic	<ul><li>Supervision by adults</li><li>High-visibility jackets to be worn by staff and children</li></ul>
Stings and bites	<ul><li>First-aid kit available</li><li>Children instructed not to approach dogs or other animals</li><li>Supervision by adults</li><li>Mobile phone in case of an emergency</li></ul>
Falls and accidents	<ul><li>First-aid kit</li><li>Supervision of staff</li><li>Visual risk assessment at the time</li><li>Mobile phone in case of an emergency</li></ul>
Weather	<ul><li>Protective clothing provided</li><li>Sunscreen applied when required</li><li>Adults aware of shelter and shade</li></ul>

Supporting child-initiated experiences

Child-initiated play is important as a way of promoting children's imagination, concentration and self-reliance. Many adults find it easiest to provide this type of play outdoors because there is more space, resources are often used differently and there is more of a sense of freedom. The following are some ways in which adults can support child-initiated play.

Allowing materials to be mixed

Many children want to use a range of materials to construct their own world. They may want to put some sand in a bucket with some water before adding a few stones. This might then become their 'magic soup'. It is important that we do not stop children from mixing materials unless there is a health and safety issue or some other pressing reason.

Not over-supervising children

When children are over-supervised, they tend not to play as well as when they feel that they are 'free'. This means keeping an eye on children, but not patrolling them. By standing back a little, we effectively give children permission to explore their own world.

Providing interesting and varied materials

Earlier we saw that children need flexible and versatile resources. These will help with child-initiated play as children can use them in a variety of ways and they can symbolise different things every time children play with them – for example, a bucket might be a saucepan, a magic pool or an oven.

Enabling freedom to explore

It is very difficult to give definite guidance about how the outdoor space should be organised, as some settings have relatively small amounts of space and many constraints, while others have whole fields! Ideally, there need to be spaces where children can play slightly away from the gaze of adults. This is why children tend to like huddling in bushes or on steps in doorways. Children also need space to use wheeled toys and it is good to provide a 'reason' for using them, for example, a space where there is a petrol station and shops alongside a path for the wheeled toy. This allows children to develop a story or rationale.

You can see that this setting has enough space outdoors to allow children to play with wheeled toys.

Using natural features

One of the wonderful things about the outdoors is the way that there are plenty of spontaneous learning opportunities to share with children. It is important that we take opportunities to explore what children have noticed or are interested in and draw their attention to things such as buds on trees or the shapes of clouds. With babies and very young children, we may simply talk about what they see and where possible allow them to touch and experience sensations. This might mean encouraging a toddler to splash in a puddle or putting up a mirror that catches the light for babies.

With older children, we can use the weather and seasons as starting points for further exploration. Table 28.3 shows some more examples.

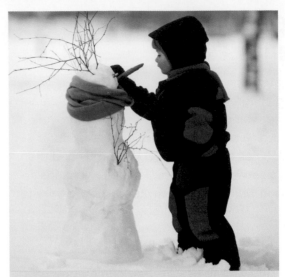

This child has been allowed to explore outdoors and make a snowman. What other play opportunities could children be given on a snowy day?

Table 28.3 Learning about the weather and seasons outdoors

Starting point	How the weather/seasons can be explored
Ice	<ul><li>How ice has formed</li><li>How long it takes to melt</li><li>How it floats on top of water</li></ul>
Snow	<ul><li>Different types of snowflake</li><li>Ways in which snow sometimes settles, but other times hits the ground and melts</li><li>Making snowmen</li></ul>
Rainbows	<ul><li>How rainbows form when there is rain and sunshine at the same time</li><li>Stories with rainbows</li><li>Count the colours in the rainbows</li></ul>
Birds and nests	<ul><li>Different types of birds</li><li>Birds that arrive in spring but are not there in winter</li><li>Nests that birds make</li><li>Putting out bird feeders and making bird food</li></ul>
Clouds	<ul><li>Different types of clouds</li><li>Noting which clouds may indicate rain</li></ul>
Mini-beasts	<ul><li>Wondering what a creature is doing, such as a spider spinning a web, and why</li><li>Learning respect for living things</li><li>Observing how they move</li></ul>
Seasons	<ul><li>Changes to temperature</li><li>Effects on animal and plant life</li><li>Change in amount of light available</li></ul>

Enabling children to return to projects

It is good practice to find ways of allowing children sufficient time and opportunities so that they can follow their interests and their play until they feel they want to stop. This may sometimes pose practical challenges, as it may be time for a session to end – especially when settings are sharing space with other settings. However, it may be possible to take photographs of what the children have been doing (such as building a den) so that we can later help them pick up where they left off.

There are huge benefits for children when we can find ways of enabling them to return to projects. First, it helps children develop patience and perseverance. It also helps them to explore concepts on a deeper level and gain more skills. These days many toys and resources provide instant gratification and do not require children's imagination and input, so it is particularly important that we prioritise giving children sufficient time to develop their projects, with opportunities for thought and making changes.

Involving children in decisions

It is good practice to involve children in decisions that will affect them. This can also be applied to outdoor provision. Many settings, when redesigning or setting up an outdoor space, ask children for their ideas and views. When this is done, the results are usually very positive, as children often know best what they would like to do and use.

We can also involve children on a day-to-day basis by asking them what they would like to do, encouraging them to access resources independently and following their interests. Children are also able to plan for their future activities as well. Younger children may need prompts such as photographs to help them do this.

Using parks and public spaces

Not all settings have a large outdoor area, and using parks and public spaces such as woods, beaches and fields is an ideal way to provide children with more outdoor experiences. As this type of resource counts

as an outing it is important that the following things are undertaken:

- risk assessments that look at security issues, health and safety and transport
- gaining parental consent for the outing.

In addition, you will need to follow the guidance or legal requirements set out in your country's early years framework or inspectorate document.

In order to get the best of any provision, it is important to visit the space that you want to use with the children and consider how it might be used. This is in addition to the practical considerations and risk assessments. It may be that a particular space such as a park will be ideal for building a den, using wheeled toys or flying kites. Other spaces, for example, woodlands or beaches, might be better for helping children learn about the natural world.

It is worth taking small groups of children first and also observing how they seem to use the space. This can then help you to see the possibilities and build on children's interests. In this way, you are also involving children in decision making.

The importance of observation for assessment

All of our work in early years should be underpinned by observing children, and using this to reflect on our own practice and as a basis for planning activities and resources. There are two areas in which observation is particularly required.

Inclusion

It is essential that we notice whether children are benefiting from and able to access different learning opportunities outdoors. It may be that groups of children are dominating some spaces or resources, or that the types of resources available do not appeal to particular children or groups. In some cases, we may need to re-evaluate our provision to ensure that it can meet a child's particular need, for example, a child with visual impairment or a child with mobility needs. As part of this work, it would also be sensible to involve parents and those who are directly involved in supporting the child, such as physiotherapists.

Challenge

For children to have ongoing learning and development experiences outdoors, they do need to find sufficient challenge and stimulation. What might be suitable and interesting for a child at 2 years may no longer hold any appeal at 4. Observing what children play with, how long they spend with it and how interested they seem can be helpful in this respect. It is also worth looking at what children are attempting to do, which often, for reasons of safety, has to be stopped. This can tell us what level of challenge they really need, given the chance. From this, we can then look for ways of creating it safely.

Link

Go to Unit 9 for more information about observations.

Case study

Providing challenge

Lara is working in a day nursery. Many of the children have been there since they were babies and she suspects that some of the older ones have become bored. She makes a note of everything that the 4-year-olds try to do, but are often stopped from doing. She focuses on their actions and after a couple of weeks, she picks out some common themes including climbing, throwing and using slopes. She talks to her manager and suggests that it might be worth looking for activities and resources that will help the children develop these themes. Over the next few weeks, part of the outdoor area is modified. A low wall is created so that children can walk along it and an area is created where children can throw safely. Lara dubs this area the 'range'. The ramp that was out of bounds for the children has been altered so that it is now safe for children to ride down on wheeled toys. The effect on the children is amazing. All the staff note that the older children seem to be playing more purposefully.

1 How did Lara approach the issue of challenge in her setting?

2 How might children benefit if there is sufficient challenge?

3 Explain the importance of observing children and then making changes to the outdoor environment.

Assessment practice 28.3   3B2.P7 | 3B2.P8 | 3B2.P9 | 3B2.M3 | 3B.D2

You have been asked to write an article about the role of the adult in supporting children's development through outdoor play and learning for a newsletter that is aimed at local practitioners. As there have been several articles about outdoor play, you will need to make some interesting points about the role of the adult.

Your article should give examples of practice and include ideas around how to use the weather and seasons, the importance of positive adult attitudes and how to support child-initiated play.

You should also provide an overview that evaluates the extent to which adults contribute to children's learning and development through outdoor play.

Further reading and resources

Bilton, H. (2010) *Outdoor Learning in the Early Years: Management and Innovation*, London: Routledge.

Featherstone, S. and Ingham, K. (2001) *The Little Book of Outdoor Play*, London: Featherstone Education Ltd.

Garrick, R. (2009) *Playing Outdoors in the Early Years* (2nd ed.), London: Continuum.

Knight, S. (2011) *Risk and Adventure in Early Years Outdoor Play: Learning from Forest Schools*, Thousand Oaks: Sage Publications Ltd.

Ready for work?

Gerard Morris Preschool assistant

I have always been a fan of outdoor play, but recently I have attended Forest School training. I am a complete convert and we are lucky that there is a small area of woodland not far away. We have approached the owner and he has given us permission to use it on a temporary basis with the children. Our first step was to carry out a thorough risk assessment that included how we would work with children to keep them from wandering off and also how to manage the journey there on foot. As everyone in my setting was keen to do this, there were no real obstacles that we could not overcome. We bought some high-visibility vests for the children and also a super buggy for toddlers to sit in! We also involved the parents and we arranged a weekly rota so that there would be some additional support. Interestingly, this has been one activity that has really appealed to some of our dads. When we get to the site, we generally try and light a small fire. The children often make some newspaper twists in the setting and then we look for sticks. It is a little like a treasure hunt and children get very excited when they find sticks that are not wet. It is these practical details that children seem to pick up quickly and already many of our 3-year-olds can tell you what a fire does and does not need to stay alight. There is something special about sitting around a fire and having a story outdoors. We have a special circle of logs that the children sit on. They know that at 'fire time' they must stay seated. We even go out when it is wet and the children love hearing the rain on the leaves and standing in the rain and catching drops on their hands! I would recommend that anyone interested in early years should visit a Forest School.

Skills for practice

Support outdoor play and learning

What should you do if your setting's outdoor area is more suited to older children?

- Babies love swings and this can be a good resource for outdoors.
- Try to install a swing that is quite high up to prevent other children from getting knocked over.
- You could also think about a circle of natural logs that would allow babies to pull themselves up to standing position and look out on the other children.
- It is important for babies to be taken out in pushchairs for walks. Remember to stop and talk about what the babies are noticing.

Glossary

A

Active learning – the process by which children concentrate and keep on trying if they encounter difficulties, and enjoy their achievements.

Advocate – someone who speaks on behalf of another to represent their views.

Attitudes – the views or opinions of an individual about an issue or topic. These views may be positive or negative.

C

Caste – a system of dividing society into classes or different social groups.

Child poverty – according to the UK government, children and families are deemed to be living in poverty when their reported income is less than 60 per cent of the UK median income before housing costs have been paid.

Coeliac disease – a digestive condition caused by gluten intolerance.

Cognitive development – the development of the mind and how children learn, reason and understand.

Common Assessment Framework (CAF) – a process to assess a child's strengths and needs and to plan for improvement.

Constructivist theory – a theory that states how children learn by constructing their own knowledge through experience and that children pass through specific stages of development.

Correlation – a relationship or connection between two things.

Creating and thinking critically – when children have and develop their own ideas, make links between ideas, and develop strategies for doing things.

Curriculum – all of the experiences and learning that are provided by a setting.

D

Data – the information that is produced by your research methods. It covers facts, statistics and perceptions. Data has to be interpreted.

Debriefing – a conversation between a researcher and participant following an experiment to inform the participant about their experience and allowing them to talk about it.

Dependency – having to rely on others and lacking independence.

E

Empower – to enable individuals to make choices about their own lives.

Ethics – the values and principles that govern the way a society operates.

Experiential learning – taking meaning from direct experience and hands-on activities.

F

Fine motor skills – control of the smaller muscles, such as those in the fingers, to carry out activities such as threading, using a knife and fork, or holding a pencil.

Fluctuate – to change quickly.

Food allergy – when the body has an abnormal reaction to a food or a component of a food.

Food intolerance – when the body is hypersensitive to a food or a component of food; there is a reaction but the reason for this reaction is not always clear.

Forest School approach – where settings are spending time outdoors, usually in woodlands, and carry out activities typically used in Scandinavian countries.

Formative assessment – assessment that takes place during the learning process on an ongoing basis, or 'assessment for learning'.

G

Gross motor skills – control of the larger muscles, such as those in the arms and legs, to carry out activities such as running, or throwing or kicking a ball.

H

Holistic – all the child's needs, to include physical, emotional, social and cognitive.

Hypothesis – an explanation for an observation or scientific problem made using limited evidence as a starting point for further investigation.

I

Individual education plan – targets and planned implementation strategies for children who have special educational needs.

Informed consent – getting agreement from the person involved in the research, ensuring they fully understand what is happening and why.

In need – this refers to children who are unlikely to maintain, or be given the opportunity to maintain, a reasonable standard of health or development, or whose health could be impaired without the support of local authority services. It also includes children who are disabled.

K

Key person – a practitioner designated to take responsibility for a child's emotional well-being by having a strong attachment with them and a good relationship with their parents.

L

Labelling – a label or description (often negative) given to an individual or group because of a characteristic. It is often the result of prejudice.

Language – the medium through which we talk and communicate.

Learning journey – a way of assessing and planning for children's development using a narrative approach that can easily be shared and constructed with parents and children.

Legislation – the act of making laws.

Looked-after children – children who are in residential care, such as foster care or a residential home.

M

Macronutrients – a type of food required in large amounts in the diet.

Makaton – a system where signs are used to help children with specific difficulties understand the spoken word.

Metabolism – the term used to describe the chemical processes that take place within the body to maintain life.

Micronutrients – a type of food required in small amounts in the diet.

N

Need-to-know policy – a way of making sure that personal information is only provided to those people who genuinely 'need to know'.

Neuromuscular coordination – the joint operation of different muscles to produce a movement, e.g. raising your arm.

Non-contemporaneous – in the context of observing children, this refers to events that are recorded or reported after they have occurred.

O

Organic – relating to or derived from living matter.

P

Palmar grip – holding an object with the palm of the hand.

Participant bias – where an observer is subconsciously recording information in a subjective way.

Phonemes – the smallest units of sound in a language that help to distinguish one word from another. In the English language, for example, 'p' and 'b' are separate phonemes because they distinguish words such as 'pit' and 'bit'.

Phonics – the name of a method used to teach reading, which breaks down different letter patterns into their individual sounds.

Policy – a written statement about what you will do.

Positional language – using terms such as 'on top' or 'to the left'.

Primary research – finding things out – new information – for yourself.

Procedure – an explanation of how you will do something.

Purposeful play – through play, children investigate and experience things, and 'have a go'.

Q

Qualitative research – exploratory research that allows us to go deeper into the research issues. Common methods to collect data include interviews and observations.

Quantitative research – research that tries to quantify the problem and uses statistics to analyse results. Common methods to collect data include questionnaires and surveys.

R

Raw data – data as it is collected, before it has been organised, analysed or interpreted in any way.

Receptive language – language that a child can understand.

Reflective practice – thinking about the way one works in order to make changes, build on strengths and stay up to date with developments.

Regulations – legal requirements that have to be followed.

Reliable – this means that your research will produce similar information to that found by someone else using the same methods with a similar sample.

Respite care – short-term care with the assistance of professional carers.

S

Safeguarding – the act of keeping children safe from harm.

Scribe – an adult who writes down what a child would like to say.

Secondary research – finding things out using material produced by others.

Self-evaluation form – a form that settings fill out on a regular basis showing how they intend to review and improve their provision.

Sequencing – being able to put events or pictures into the correct order.

Significant harm – this is defined in the Children Act 1989 as 'ill treatment or impairment of health or development'.

Sociogram – a recording method whereby children indicate their friendship preferences.

Solutes – a substance that is dissolved in another substance.

Special educational needs – used to describe children who have a learning difficulty that calls for special educational provision to be made for them – children who learn differently from most children of the same age, and who may need different or extra help from that given to others.

Speech – the physical act of talking and articulating.

Statement of Special Educational Needs – this means that the local authority will assess the child to decide whether it is necessary for them to have an additional adult to support them in school. If so, the local authority will then produce a statement that sets out what is needed for the child to access the curriculum fully.

Statutory – set down and regulated by law.

Summative assessment – assessment of what a child knows and can do at the end of a period of learning, or 'assessment of learning'.

Symbolic action – a gesture that is representative of a real action.

Synthesis – the combination of separate elements or substances to form a whole.

T

Tokenism – giving the appearance of an inclusive environment.

Transitions – the changes that happen in all children's lives, such as starting school or personal changes such as family break-up.

U

Universal service – a typical service such as the doctor's surgery, school, brownies or scouts.

V

Valid – this means that the research produces information that is well supported, justifiable and trustworthy.

Values – the principles or personal rules or standards that allow people to make decisions and choose between alternatives.

Variable – an element, feature or factor in a research project that is likely to change.

W

Whistle blowing – an employee who raises concerns about the wrongdoing of another person or group of people in the workplace.

Winding – a process to help babies expel any air trapped in their digestive system during feeding.

Index

Index